Lecture Notes in Computer Science

Edited by G. Goos, J. Hartmanis, and J. van Leeuwen

Springer
Berlin
Heidelberg
New York
Barcelona
Hong Kong
London
Milan
Paris
Tokyo

Ed F. Deprettere   Jürgen Teich
Stamatis Vassiliadis (Eds.)

Embedded Processor
Design Challenges

Systems, Architectures, Modeling,
and Simulation – SAMOS

Springer

Series Editors

Gerhard Goos, Karlsruhe University, Germany
Juris Hartmanis, Cornell University, NY, USA
Jan van Leeuwen, Utrecht University, The Netherlands

Volume Editors

Ed. F. Deprettere
Leiden University, Leiden Institute of Advanced Computer Science (LIACS)
Niels Bohr Weg 1, 2333 CA Leiden, The Netherlands
E-mail: edd@liacs.nl

Jürgen Teich
University of Paderborn, Computer Engineering Laboratory (DATE)
Department of Electrical Engineering and Information Technology
Warburger Str. 100, 33100 Paderborn, Germany
E-mail: teich@date.upb.de

Stamatis Vassiliadis
Delft University of Technology, Computer Engineering Laboratory
Electrical Engineering Department, ITS
Mekelweg 4, 2628 CD Delft, The Netherlands
E-mail: S. Vassiliadis@et.tudelft.nl

Cataloging-in-Publication Data applied for

Die Deutsche Bibliothek - CIP-Einheitsaufnahme

Embedded processor design challenges : systems, architectures, modeling,
and simulation - SAMOS / Ed F. Deprettere ... (ed.). - Berlin ; Heidelberg ;
New York ; Barcelona ; Hong Kong ; London ; Milan ; Paris ; Tokyo :
Springer, 2002
    (Lecture notes in computer science ; Vol. 2268)
    ISBN 3-540-43322-8

CR Subject Classification (1998): C.3, B.2, C.1, C.4, B.8, D.2, D.3, D.4

ISSN 0302-9743
ISBN 3-540-43322-8 Springer-Verlag Berlin Heidelberg New York

Springer-Verlag Berlin Heidelberg New York
a member of BertelsmannSpringer Science+Business Media GmbH

http://www.springer.de

© Springer-Verlag Berlin Heidelberg 2002
Printed in Germany

Typesetting: Camera-ready by author, data conversion by Olgun Computergrafik
Printed on acid-free paper   SPIN 10846084   06/3142   5 4 3 2 1 0

Preface

This textbook is intended to give an introduction to and an overview of state-of-the-art techniques in the design of complex embedded systems.

The book title is **SAMOS** for two major reasons. First, it tries to focus on the actual distinct, yet important problem fields of **S**ystem-Level design of embedded systems, including mapping techniques and synthesis, **A**rchitectural design, **Mo**deling issues such as specification languages, formal models, and finally **S**imulation.

The second reason is that the volume includes a number of papers presented at a workshop with the same name on the Island of Samos, Greece, in July 2001.

In order to receive international attention, a number of reputed researchers were invited to this workshop to present their current work. Participation was by invitation only. For the volume presented here, a number of additional papers where selected based on a call for papers. All contributions were refereed. This volume presents a selection of 18 of the refereed papers, including 2 invited papers.

The textbook is organized according to four topics: The first is **A) System-Level Design and Simulation**. In this section, we present a collection of papers that give an overview of the challenging goal to design and explore alternatives of embedded system implementations at the system-level. One paper gives an overview of models and tools used in system-level design. The other papers present new models to describe applications, provide models for refinement and design space exploration, and for tradeoff analysis between cost and flexibility of an implementation.

Section **B) Compiler and Mapping Technology** presents new techniques to exploit parallelism in future embedded systems, i.e., by mapping computation intensive applications to hardware. The papers presented include new theoretical results for scheduling loop-like programs with subprogram structure, for partitioning programs with affine data dependences, and for mapping and simulating programs as a network of Kahn-processes.

Topic **C) Embedded Processors and Architectures** is related to novel processor and architecture principles for future embedded systems. One paper gives an overview of architectures for multimedia applications and presents future trends in this direction. Two papers deal with the possibility of hardware reconfiguration as a means to adapt the processor to a certain application or domain: One gives an overview of current development in microcoded reconfigurable processors, the other deals with architecture adaptions in order to obtain energy efficient wireless image computations. A final paper is dedicated to caches.

Finally, Topic **D) Applications** presents some interesting applications of embedded computing systems including the design of a run-time reconfigurable Web-camera.

October 2001   E.F. Deprettere, J. Teich, and S. Vassiliadis

Organization

The workshop SAMOS 2001 took place from July 16–18, 2001 at the Research and Teaching Institute of East Aegean (INEAG) in Agios Konstantinos on the Island of Samos, Greece.

Organizing Committee

Ed F. Deprettere   (Leiden University, The Netherlands)
Bob Hertzberger   (University of Amsterdam, The Netherlands)
Stamatis Vassiliadis   (Delft University of Technology, The Netherlands)

Program Committee

Sorin Dan Cotofana   (Delft University of Technology, The Netherlands)
Andy Pimentel   (University of Amsterdam, The Netherlands)
Patrice Quinton   (Irisa, France)
Jürgen Teich   (University of Paderborn, Germany)
Diederik Verkest   (IMEC, Belgium)

Sponsoring Institutions

The workshop has been financially supported by the Technology Foundation STW and PROGRESS, the program for research on embedded systems and software. PROGRESS is an initiative of the Dutch organization for scientific research (NWO), the Ministry of Economic Affairs, and the STW.

The workshop has been dedicated to the memory of Jean-Pierre Veen.

Table of Contents

D) Applications

Consistency Analysis of
Reconfigurable Dataflow Specifications[*]

Bishnupriya Bhattacharya[1] and Shuvra S. Bhattacharyya[2]

[1] Cadence Design Systems
San Jose CA 95134
bpriya@cadence.com

[2] Department of Electrical and Computer Engineering, and
Institute for Advanced Computer Studies,
University of Maryland, College Park MD 20742, USA
ssb@eng.umd.edu

Abstract. Parameterized dataflow is a meta-modeling approach for incorporating dynamic reconfiguration capabilities into broad classes of dataflow-based design frameworks for digital signal processing (DSP). Through a novel formalization of dataflow parameterization, and a disciplined approach to specifying parameter reconfiguration, the parameterized dataflow framework provides for automated synthesis of robust and efficient embedded software. Central to these synthesis objectives is the formulation and analysis of *consistency* in parameterized dataflow specifications. Consistency analysis of reconfigurable specifications is particularly challenging due to their inherently dynamic behavior. This paper presents a novel framework, based on a concept of *local synchrony*, for managing consistency when synthesizing implementations from dynamically-reconfigurable, parameterized dataflow graphs.

1. Motivation and Related Work

Dataflow is an established computational model for simulation and synthesis of software for digital signal processing (DSP) applications. The modern trend toward highly dynamic and reconfigurable DSP system behavior, however, poses an important challenge for dataflow-based DSP modeling techniques, which have traditionally been well-suited primarily for applications with significantly static, high-level structure. *Parameterized dataflow* [1] is a promising new meta-modeling approach that addresses this challenge by systematically incorporating dynamic reconfiguration capabilities into broad classes of dataflow-based design frameworks for digital signal processing (DSP).

Through a novel formalization of dataflow parameterization, and a disciplined approach to specifying parameter reconfiguration, the parameterized dataflow framework provides for automated synthesis of robust and efficient embedded software.

* This research was sponsored by the U. S. National Science Foundation under Grant #9734275.

E.F. Deprettere et al. (Eds.): SAMOS 2001, LNCS 2268, pp. 1–17, 2002.

Central to these synthesis objectives is the formulation and analysis of consistency in parameterized dataflow specifications. Consistency analysis of reconfigurable specifications is particularly challenging due to their inherently dynamic behavior. This paper presents a novel framework, based on a concept of *local synchrony*, for managing consistency when synthesizing implementations from dynamically-reconfigurable, parameterized dataflow graphs. Specifically, we examine consistency issues in the context of dataflow graphs that are based on the *parameterized synchronous dataflow* [1] (PSDF) model of computation (MoC), which is the MoC that results when the parameterized dataflow meta-modeling approach is integrated with the well-known synchronous dataflow MoC. We focus on PSDF in this paper for clarity and uniformity; however, the consistency analysis techniques described in this paper can be adapted to the integration of parameterized dataflow with any dataflow MoC that has a well-defined concept of a graph *iteration* (e.g., to the *parameterized cyclo-static dataflow* model that is described in [2]).

The organization of this paper is as follows. In the remainder of this section, we review a variety of dataflow modeling approaches for DSP. In Section 2, we present an application example to motivate the PSDF MoC, and in Section 3, we review the fundamental semantics of PSDF. In Sections 4 through 7 we develop and illustrate consistency analysis formulations for PSDF specifications, and relate these formulations precisely to constraints for robust execution of dynamically-reconfigurable applications that are modeled in PSDF. In Section 8, we summarize, and mention promising directions for further study.

A restricted version of dataflow, termed *synchronous dataflow* (*SDF*) [12], that offers strong compile-time predictability properties, but has limited expressive power, has been studied extensively in the DSP context. The key restriction in SDF is that the number of data values (*tokens*) produced and consumed by each actor (dataflow graph node) is fixed and known at compile time. Many extensions to SDF have been proposed to increase its expressive power, while maintaining its compile-time predictability properties as much as possible. The primary benefits offered by SDF are static scheduling, and optimization opportunities, leading to a high degree of compile-time predictability. Although an important class of useful DSP applications can be modeled efficiently in SDF, its expressive power is limited to static applications. Thus, many extensions to the SDF model have been proposed, where the objective is to accommodate a broader range of applications, while maintaining a significant part of the compile-time predictability of SDF.

Cyclo-static dataflow (CSDF) and scalable synchronous dataflow (SSDF) are the two most popular extensions of SDF in use today. In CSDF, token production and consumption can vary between actor invocations as long as the variation forms a certain type of periodic pattern [4]. Each time an actor is fired, a different piece of code called a *phase* is executed. For example, consider a *distributor* actor, which routes data received from a single input to each of two outputs in alternation. In SDF, this actor consumes two tokens and produces one token on each of its two outputs. In CSDF, by contrast, the actor consumes one token on its input, and produces tokens according to the periodic pattern 1, 0, 1, 0, ... (one token produced on the first invocation, none on the second, and so on) on one output edge, and according to the complementary periodic pattern 0, 1, 0, 1, ... on the other output edge. A general CSDF graph can be compiled as a cyclic pattern of pure SDF graphs, and static periodic schedules can be constructed in this manner. CSDF offers several benefits over SDF including increased flexibility in compactly and efficiently representing interaction between actors, decreased buffer memory requirements for some applications, and increased opportunities for behavioral optimizations such as constant propagation and dead code elimination [3, 4].

In SSDF, each actor has the capacity to process any integer multiple of the basic SDF token production (consumption) quantities at an output (input) port, leading to reduced inter-actor context-switching, and hence improved performance in synthesized implementations [16].

In the boolean dataflow (BDF) model, the number of tokens produced or consumed on an edge is either fixed, or is a two-valued function of a control token present on a control terminal of the same actor [6]. Scheduling analysis of a BDF graph can lead to the construction of a *complete cycle*, which is a sequence of actor executions that returns the graph to its original state. Scheduling techniques for BDF graphs attempt to derive *quasi-static schedules* (schedules that are derived using compile time analysis that significantly reduces the amount of run-time scheduling involved) in which each conditional actor invocation is annotated with the run-time condition under which the invocation should occur.

Synchronous piggybacked dataflow (SPDF) is a recently-proposed extension of SDF that provides support for global states in a disciplined fashion. This development of SPDF addresses the problem of updating local parameters ("local states") of a block with global parameters ("global states") based on synchronous state update (SU) requests. SPDF accommodates this by constructing a global table for global parameters, and piggybacking a pointer to a global table entry (tuple of parameter name, and parameter values) on each data sample. A special piggybacking block (PB) is introduced that models the coupling of data samples and the global table pointers. When an SU request is delivered to an actor it will first update its local parameter with a new value of the global parameter before processing its data samples. SPDF utilizes an efficient code synthesis technique with compile-time analysis, such that the PB's function can be simulated without piggybacking (an expensive copy operation), which allows memory efficient code synthesis.

The VSDF [13] and multirate hierarchical timing pair (MHTP) [7] models are dataflow modeling techniques that are geared towards efficient hardware implementation.

Parameterized dataflow modeling differs from dataflow modeling techniques such as SDF, CSDF, SSDF, BDF, SPDF, VSDF, and MHTP in that it is a *meta-modeling* technique: parameterized dataflow can be applied to any underlying "base" dataflow model that has a well-defined notion of a graph iteration (invocation). The dataflow parameterization and parameter value reconfiguration concepts that underlie parameterized dataflow can be incorporated into any dataflow model that satisfies this requirement to significantly increase its expressive power. For example, a minimal periodic schedule is a suitable and natural notion of an iteration in SDF, SSDF, CSDF, and SPDF. Similarly, in BDF, a complete cycle, when it is exists, can be used to specify a graph iteration.

Furthermore, in contrast to previous work on dataflow modeling, the parameterized dataflow approach achieves increased expressive power entirely through its comprehensive support for parameter definition and parameter value reconfiguration. Actor parameters have been used for years in block diagram DSP design environments. Conventionally, these parameters are assigned static values that remain unchanged throughout execution. The parameterized dataflow approach takes this as a starting point, and develops a comprehensive framework for dynamically reconfiguring the behavior of dataflow actors, edges, graphs, and subsystems by run-time modification of parameter values. SPDF also allows actor parameters to be reconfigured dynamically. However, SPDF is restricted to reconfiguring only those parameters of an actor that do not affect its dataflow behavior (token production/consumption). Parameterized dataflow does not impose this restriction, which greatly enhances the utility of the modeling approach, but significantly complicates scheduling and dataflow consistency analysis. A key consideration in our detailed development of the PSDF MoC (recall that PSDF is the integration of the parameterized dataflow meta-modeling approach with the synchronous dataflow MoC) is addressing these complications in a robust manner, as we will explain in Sections 4 and 7. Such thorough support for parameterization, as well as the associated management of application dynamics in terms of run-time reconfiguration, is not available in any of the previously-developed dataflow modeling techniques.

In recent years, several modeling techniques have been proposed that enhance expressive power by providing precise semantics for integrating dataflow graphs with finite state machine (FSM) models. These include El Greco [5], which provides facilities for "control models" to dynamically configure specification parameters; *charts (pronounced "starcharts") with heterochronous dataflow as the concurrency model [9]; the FunState intermediate representation [17]; the DF* framework developed at K. U. Leuven [8]; and the control flow provisions in bounded dynamic dataflow [14]. In contrast, parameterized dataflow does not require any departure from the dataflow framework. This is advantageous for users of DSP design tools who are already accustomed to working purely in the dataflow domain, and for whom integration with FSMs may presently be an experimental concept. With a longer term view, due to the meta-modeling nature of parameterized dataflow, it appears promising to incorporate our parameterization/reconfiguration techniques into the dataflow components of existing FSM/dataflow hybrids. This is a useful direction for further investigation.

The parameterized dataflow modeling approach was introduced in [1], which provides an overview of its modeling semantics, and quasi-static scheduling of parameterized dataflow specifications was explored in [2]. This paper focuses on consistency analysis of parameterized dataflow specifications, and develops techniques that can be integrated with scheduling to provide robust operation of synthesized implementations.

2. Application Example

To motivate the PSDF model, Fig. 1(a) shows a speech compression application, which is modeled by a PSDF subsystem *Compress*. A speech instance of length L is transmitted from the sender side to the receiver side using as few bits as possible, applying *analysis-synthesis* techniques [10]. In the init graph, the *genHdr* actor generates a stream of header packets, where each header contains information about a particular speech instance, including its length L. The *setSpch* actor reads a header packet and accordingly configures L, which is modeled as a parameter of the *Compress* subsystem. The *s1* and *s2* actors are "black boxes" responsible for generating samples of this speech instance. In the body graph, actor *s2* generates the speech sample, zero-padding it to a length R. The *An* (*Analyze*) actor accepts small speech segments of size N, and performs linear prediction, producing M auto-regressive (AR) coefficients and the residual error signal of length N at its output. The model order (*ord*) and input length (*len*) parameters of the *An* actor are configured with the subsystem parameters M and N, respectively. The AR coefficients and the residual signal are quantized, encoded (by actors *q1*, *q2*), and transmitted to the receiver side, where these are first dequantized (by actors *d1*, *d2*) and then each segment is reconstructed in the *Sn* (*Synthesize*) actor through AR modeling using the M AR coefficients and the residual signal of length N as excitation. Finally, the *Pl* (*Play*) actor plays the entire reconstructed speech instance.

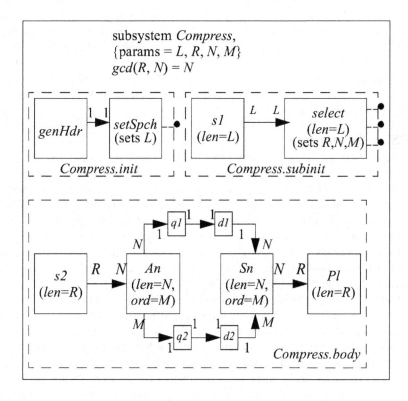

Fig. 1. A PSDF specification of a speech compression application.

The size of each speech segment (N), and the AR model order (M) are important design parameters for producing a good AR model, which is necessary for achieving high compression ratios. The values of N and M, along with the zero-padded speech sample length R are modeled as subsystem parameters of *Compress* that are configured in the subinit graph. The *select* actor in the subinit graph reads the original speech instance, and examines it to determine N and M, using any of the existing techniques, e.g., the Burg segment size selection algorithm, and the AIC order selection criterion [10]. The zero-padded speech length R is computed such that it is the smallest integer greater than L that is exactly divided by the segment size, N. From these relationships, it is useful to convey to the scheduler the assertion that $gcd(R, N) = N$.

Note that for clarity, the above PSDF model does not specify all the details of the application. Our purpose here is to provide an overview of the modeling process, using mixed-grain DSP actors, such that PSDF-specific aspects of the model are emphasized — especially those parameters that are relevant from the scheduler's perspective. All actor parameters that do not affect dataflow behavior have been omitted from the specification. For example, the quantizers and dequantizers will have actor parameters controlling their *quantization* levels and *threshold*s. The *select* actor could determine two such sets — one for the residual and one for the coefficients.

An SDF or CSDF representation of this application will have hard numbers (e.g., 150 instead of N) for the dataflow in Fig. 1(a), corresponding to a particular speech sample. Thus, for processing separate speech samples, the design needs to be modified and the static schedule re-computed. SPDF can accommodate those parameter reconfigurations that do not affect an actor's dataflow properties (e.g., the *threshold* parameter of the *quantizer* actors), but not reconfiguration of the *len* parameter of the *Analyze* actor (An), since *len* affects the dataflow of An. Thus, again separate designs are necessary to process separate speech samples.

3. PSDF Semantics

In the PSDF model, a DSP application will typically be represented as a *PSDF subsystem* Φ that is made up of three *PSDF graphs* — the *init* graph Φ_i, the *subinit* graph Φ_s, and the *body* graph Φ_b. A *set of parameters* is provided to control the behavior of the subsystem. In most cases, the subsystem parameters will be directly derived from the parameters of the application algorithm. For example, in a block adaptive filtering system, the step size and the block size emerge as natural subsystem parameters. Intuitively, in a subsystem, the body graph is used to model its dataflow behavior, while the init and subinit graphs are responsible for configuring subsystem parameter values, thus controlling the body graph behavior.

A PSDF graph is a dataflow graph composed of PSDF actors and PSDF edges. A PSDF actor A is characterized by a set of parameters ($params(A)$), which can control both the functional behavior as well as the dataflow behavior (numbers of tokens consumed and produced) at its input and output *ports*. Each parameter p is either assigned a value from an associated set, called $domain(p)$, or is left unspecified (denoted by the symbol $\perp$). These statically-unspecified parameters are assigned values at run-time that can change dynamically, thus dynamically modifying the actor behavior.

$domain(A)$ defines the set of valid parameter value combinations for A. A configuration that does not assign the value $\bot$ to any parameter is called a *complete configuration*, and the set of all possible complete, valid configurations of $params(A)$ is represented as $\overline{domain}(A)$. Similarly, the sets of valid and complete configurations of a PSDF graph G are denoted $domain(G)$ and $\overline{domain}(G)$, respectively.

Like a PSDF actor, a *PSDF edge* e also has an associated parameterization ($params(e)$), and a set of complete and valid configurations ($\overline{domain}(e)$). The delay characteristics on an edge (e.g., the number of units of delay, initial token values, and re-initialization period) can in general depend on its parameter configuration. In particular, the *delay function* $\delta_e : \overline{domain}(e) \rightarrow \aleph$ associated with edge e gives the delay on e that results from any valid parameter setting.

Now suppose that we have a PSDF graph G, and a complete configuration $C \in \overline{domain}(G)$. Then for a PSDF actor A in G, we represent the instance of A associated with C by $config_{A,C}$, and similarly, for a PSDF edge e, we define $config_{e,C}$ to be the instance of e associated with the complete configuration C. The instance of G associated with C is a pure SDF graph, which we denote by $instance_G(C)$. If the $instance_G(C)$ is sample-rate consistent, then it is possible to compute the corresponding *parameterized repetitions vector* $\mathbf{q}_{G,C}$, which gives the number of times that each actor should be invoked in each iteration of a minimal periodic schedule for $instance_G(C)$.

The *port consumption function* associated with A, denoted $\kappa_A : (in(A) \times \overline{domain}(A)) \rightarrow Z^+$, gives the number of tokens consumed from a specified input port on each invocation of actor A, corresponding to a valid, complete configuration of A. The *port production function* $\varphi_A : (out(A) \times \overline{domain}(A)) \rightarrow Z^+$ associated with A is defined in a similar fashion.

To facilitate bounded memory implementation, the designer must provide a *maximum token transfer function* associated with each PSDF actor A, denoted $\tau_A \in Z^+$, that specifies an upper bound on the number of tokens transferred (produced or consumed) at each port of actor A (per invocation). In contrast to the use of similar bounds in *bounded dynamic dataflow* [14], maximum token transfer bounds are employed in PSDF to *guarantee* bounded memory operation. Similarly, a *maximum delay value*, denoted $\mu_e \in \aleph$, must be specified for a PSDF edge e, which provides an upper bound on the number of delay tokens that can reside at any time on e. The maximum token transfer and delay values are necessary to ensure bounded memory executions of consistent PSDF specifications.

A PSDF subsystem Φ can be embedded within a "parent" PSDF graph abstracted as a *hierarchical PSDF actor H*, and we say that $H = subsystem(\Phi)$. In such a scenario, Φ can participate in dataflow communication with parent graph actors at its *interface ports*. The init graph Φ_i does not participate in this dataflow; the subinit graph Φ_s may only accept dataflow inputs; while the body graph Φ_b both accepts dataflow inputs and produces dataflow outputs. The PSDF operational semantics [1] specify that Φ_i is invoked once at the beginning of each (minimal periodic) invocation of the hierarchical parent graph in which Φ is embedded; Φ_s is invoked at the beginning of each invocation of Φ; and Φ_b is invoked after each invocation of Φ_s.

Consistency issues in PSDF are based on disciplined dynamic scheduling principles that allow every PSDF graph to assume the configuration of an SDF graph on each graph invocation. This ensures that a schedule for a PSDF graph can be constructed as a dynamically reconfigurable SDF schedule. Such scheduling leads to a set of *local synchrony* constraints for PSDF graphs and PSDF subsystems that need to be satisfied for consistent specifications. This paper is concerned with the detailed development of local synchrony concepts for PSDF system analysis, simulation, and synthesis.

A detailed discussion of PSDF modeling semantics can be found in [1], which also shows that the hierarchical, parameterized representation of PSDF supports increased design modularity (e.g., by naturally consolidating distinct actors, in some cases, into different configurations of the same actor), and thus, leads to increased design reuse in block diagram DSP design environments.

4. Local Synchrony Consistency in PSDF

Consistency in PSDF specifications requires that certain dataflow properties remain fixed across certain types of parameter reconfigurations. This is captured by the following concepts of configuration projections and function invariance.

Definition 1:   Given a configuration C of a non-empty parameter set P, and a non-empty subset of parameters $P' \subseteq P$, the *projection of C onto P'*, denoted $C|P'$, is defined by

$$C|P' = \{(p, C(p))|(p \in P')\}. \tag{1}$$

Thus, the projection is obtained by "discarding" from C all values associated with parameters outside of P'.

Definition 2:   Given a parameter set P, a function $f : \overline{domain(P)} \rightarrow R$ into some range set R; and a subset $P' \subseteq P$, we say that f *is invariant over* P' if for every pair $C_1, C_2 \in \overline{domain(P)}$, we have

$$((C_1|(P - P')) = (C_2|(P - P'))) \Rightarrow (f(C_1) = f(C_2)). \tag{2}$$

In other words, f is invariant over P' if the value of f is entirely a function of the parameters outside of P'. Intuitively, the function f does not depend on any member of P', it only depends on the members of $(P - P')$.

The motivation of consistency issues in PSDF stems from the principle of *local SDF scheduling* of PSDF graphs, which is the concept of being able to view every PSDF graph as an SDF graph on each invocation of the graph, after it has been suitably configured. Local SDF scheduling is highly desirable, as it allows a compiler to schedule any PSDF graph (and the subsystems inside it) as a dynamically reconfigurable SDF schedule, thus leveraging the rich library of scheduling and analysis techniques available in SDF. Relevant issues in local SDF scheduling can be classified into three distinct categories — issues that are related to the underlying SDF model, those that relate to bounded memory execution, and issues that arise as a direct consequence of the hierarchical parameterized representation of PSDF. SDF consistency issues such as sample rate mismatch and deadlock detection appear in the first category, while the third category requires that every subsystem embedded in the graph as a hierarchical actor behave as an SDF actor throughout one invocation of the graph (which may encompass several invocations of the embedded subsystems). Since, in general, a subsystem communicates with its parent graph through its interface ports, the above requirement translates to the necessity of some fixed patterns in the interface dataflow behavior of the subsystem. Since consistency in PSDF implies being able to perform local SDF scheduling, it is referred to as *local synchrony consistency* (or simply local synchrony), and applies to both PSDF graphs and PSDF specifications (subsystems).

More specifically, a PSDF graph G is locally synchronous if for every $p \in domain(G)$, the instantiated SDF graph $instance_G(p)$ has the following properties: it is sample rate consistent ($q_{G,p}$ exists); it is deadlock free; the maximum token transfer bound is satisfied for every port of every actor; the maximum delay value bound is satisfied for every edge; and every child subsystem is locally synchronous.

Formally, this translates to the following *local synchrony* conditions, which must hold for all $p \in \overline{domain(G)}$ in order for the PSDF graph G to be locally synchronous.
- The instantiated SDF graph $instance_G(p)$ has a valid schedule.
- For each actor $v \in V$, and for each input port $\phi \in in(v)$, we have $\kappa_v(\phi, config_{v,p}) \le \tau_v(\phi)$.
- Similarly, for each actor $v \in V$, and for each output port $\phi \in out(v)$, we have $\varphi_v(\phi, config_{v,p}) \le \tau_v(\phi)$.
- For each edge $e \in E$, we have $\delta_e(config_{e,p}) \le \mu_e$.
- For each hierarchical actor H in G, $subsystem(H)$ is locally synchronous.

If these conditions are all satisfied for every $p \in domain(G)$, then we say that G is *inherently locally synchronous* (or simply *locally synchronous*). If no $p \in domain(G)$ satisfies all of these conditions simultaneously, then G is *inherently locally non-synchronous* (or simply *locally non-synchronous*). If G is neither inherently locally synchronous, nor inherently locally non-synchronous, then G is *partially locally synchronous*. Thus, G is partially locally synchronous if there exists a configuration $p_1 \in domain(G)$ for which all of the local synchrony conditions are satisfied, and there also exists a configuration $p_2 \in \overline{domain(G)}$ for which at least one of the conditions is not satisfied. We sometimes separately refer to the different local synchrony conditions as *dataflow consistency* (the existence of a valid schedule), *bounded memory consistency* (the maximum bounds are satisfied for each actor port and each edge), and *subsystem consistency* (each subsystem is locally synchronous) of the PSDF graph G.

Intuitively, a PSDF specification Φ is locally synchronous if its interface dataflow behavior (token production and consumption at interface ports) is determined entirely by the init graph of the specification. As indicated above, local synchrony of a specification is necessary in order to enable local SDF scheduling when the specification is embedded in a graph and communicates with actors in this parent graph through dataflow edges. Four conditions must be satisfied for a specification to be locally synchronous.

First, the init graph must produce exactly one token on each output port on each invocation. This is because each output port is bound to a parameter setting (of the body graph or subinit graph). An alternative is to allow multiple tokens to be produced on an init graph output port, and assign those values one by one to the dependent parameter on successive invocations of Φ. But this leads to two problems. First, we would have to line up the number of tokens produced with the number of invocations of Φ, thus giving rise to sample rate consistency issues across graph boundaries, which needlessly complicates the semantics. Second, it violates the principle that parameters set in the init graph maintain constant values throughout one invocation of the parent graph of Φ, which in turn violates the requirements for local SDF scheduling. The interface dataflow of the hierarchical actor representing Φ is allowed to depend on parameters set in the init graph. For the parent graph of Φ to be configured as an SDF graph on every invocation, each such embedded hierarchical actor must behave as an SDF actor, for which the parameters set in the init graph must remain constant throughout an invocation of the parent graph.

Similarly the subinit graph must also produce exactly one token on each output port. Parameters set in the subinit graph can change from one invocation of Φ to the next, which is ensured by a single token production at a subinit graph output port on every invocation of the subinit graph. Recall that a single invocation of the subinit graph is followed by exactly one invocation of the body graph. Thus, a token produced on a subinit graph output port is immediately utilized in the corresponding invocation of the body graph. Any excess tokens are redundant (or viewed another way, ambiguous) and will accumulate at the port.

Third, the number of tokens consumed by the subinit graph from each input port must not be a function of the subinit graph parameters that are bound to dataflow inputs of Φ. Finally, the number of tokens produced or consumed at each specification interface port of the body graph must be a function of the body graph parameters that are controlled by the init graph. The third and fourth conditions ensure that a hierarchically nested PSDF specification behaves like an SDF actor throughout any single invocation of the parent graph in which it is embedded, which is necessary for local SDF scheduling.

In mathematical terms, the first condition (called the *init condition* for local synchrony of Φ) is the requirement that

- A. The init graph Φ_i is locally synchronous; and

- B. for each $p \in \overline{domain(\Phi_i)}$, and each interface output port ϕ of Φ_i,

$$q_{\Phi_i, p}(actor(\phi)) = \varphi_{actor(\phi)}(\phi, config_{actor(\phi), p}) = 1. \tag{3}$$

The init condition dictates that the init graph must be (inherently) locally synchronous and must produce exactly one token at each interface output port on each invocation. Similarly, the second and third conditions are the requirements that

- C. the subinit graph Φ_s is locally synchronous;

- D. for each $p \in \overline{domain(\Phi_s)}$, and each interface output port ϕ of Φ_s,

$$q_{\Phi_s, p}(actor(\phi)) = \varphi_{actor(\phi)}(\phi, config_{actor(\phi), p}) = 1 ; \text{ and} \tag{4}$$

- E. for each interface input port ϕ of Φ_s, the product

$$q_{\Phi_s, p}(actor(\phi)) \kappa_{actor(\phi)}(\phi, config_{actor(\phi), p})$$

is invariant over those parameters $p \in params(\Phi_s)$ that are bound to dataflow inputs of Φ.

We refer to Condition D above as the *subinit output condition*, and to Condition E as the *subinit input condition* for local synchrony of Φ. Thus, the subinit graph must be locally synchronous; Φ_s must produce exactly one token at each of its interface output ports on each invocation; and the number of tokens consumed from an input port of Φ_s (during an invocation of Φ) must be a function only of the parameters that are controlled by the init graph or by hierarchically-higher-level graphs.

Finally, the fourth condition for local synchrony of the PSDF specification Φ requires that
- F. the body graph Φ_b is locally synchronous;
- G. for each interface input port ϕ of Φ_b, the product

$$q_{\Phi_b, p}(actor(\phi))\kappa_{actor(\phi)}(\phi, config_{actor(\phi), p}) \tag{5}$$

is invariant over those parameters $p \in params(\Phi_s)$ that are configured in the subinit graph Φ_s; and
- H. similarly, for each interface output port ϕ of Φ_b, the product

$$q_{\Phi_b, p}(actor(\phi))\varphi_{actor(\phi)}(\phi, config_{actor(\phi), p}) \tag{6}$$

is also invariant over those parameters $p \in params(\Phi_s)$ that are configured in the subinit graph Φ_s.

Conditions (F), (G) and (H) are collectively termed the *body condition* for local synchrony of Φ. In other words, the body graph must be locally synchronous, and the total number of tokens transferred at any port of Φ_b throughout a given invocation of Φ must depend only on those parameters of Φ_b that are controlled by Φ_i or higher-level graphs.

We sometimes loosely refer to the subinit input condition and the body condition as the local synchrony conditions, and we collectively refer to the requirements of the init condition and the subinit output condition as *unit transfer consistency*.

If Conditions (A) through (H) all hold, then we say that the PSDF specification Φ is *inherently locally synchronous* (or simply *locally synchronous*). If either of the graphs Φ_i, Φ_s, and Φ_b is locally non-synchronous, no $p \in domain(\Phi_i)$ satisfies (3), or no $p \in domain(\Phi_s)$ satisfies (D), then Φ is *inherently locally non-synchronous* (or simply *locally non-synchronous*). If Φ is neither inherently locally synchronous, nor inherently locally non-synchronous, then Φ is *partially locally-synchronous*. Note that if either of the invariance conditions G or H does not hold, then that does not necessarily lead to local non-synchrony of Φ, as the system may satisfy partial local synchrony, which may acceptable if input data sequences that lead to inconsistent parameter reconfigurations do not arise in practice or are very rare.

5. Local Synchrony Examples

As discussed in Section 4, PSDF subsystems can be classified as *inherently locally synchronous*, *inherently locally non-synchronous*, or *partially locally synchronous*. An illustration of these distinctions is given in Fig. 2. Part (a) shows the body graph of a PSDF specification Φ with one interface input port, and one interface output port. Note that each of the PSDF graphs shown in the figure has two edges and three nodes. The interface edges (connecting actors in the body graph or subinit graph of a subsystem to parent graph actors) do not contribute to the graph topology in the child (body or subinit) graph. In Fig. 2(a), the body graph parameters p_1 and p_2 are configured in the associated init and subinit graph, respectively. As shown in the figure, the *topology matrix* of Φ_b is a function of the body graph parameters p_1 and p_2. The topology matrix of an SDF graph is a matrix whose rows are indexed by the graph edges, whose columns are indexed by the graph actors, and whose entries give the numbers of tokens produced by actors onto incident output edges, and the negatives of the numbers of tokens consumed by actors from incident input edges (full details on the topology matrix formulation can be found in [12]). Our illustration in Figure 2 extends this concept of the topology matrix to PSDF graphs.

From the repetitions vector $\mathbf{q}$ of Φ_b, the token consumption at the interface input port of the body graph is obtained as $2\mathbf{q}(A) = 2p_1$. Similarly, the token production at the interface output port of Φ_b is $\mathbf{q}(C) = 1$. Thus, the interface dataflow of Φ_b is independent of the body graph parameter p_2 that is not configured in Φ_i (i.e., whose value is not updated by the init graph). Hence, the body condition for local synchrony of Φ is satisfied, and if the other local synchrony requirements are also satisfied, then Φ qualifies as an inherently locally synchronous specification.

Fig. 2(b) shows a slightly modified dataflow pattern for Φ_b, such that the token consumption at the interface input port of Φ_b is obtained as $2p_2$, and thus, depends on the parameter p_2, which is configured in the subinit graph. Consequently, Φ is not inherently locally synchronous, rather, it exhibits partial local synchrony with respect

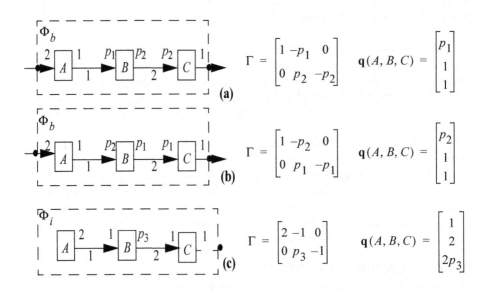

Fig. 2. The symbolic topology matrices and repetitions vectors of three PSDF graphs, used to demonstrate inherent local synchrony, partial local synchrony, and inherent local non-synchrony, respectively. Each dataflow edge is labelled with a positive integer.

to the body condition. If p_2 consistently takes on one particular value at run-time, then a local synchrony error is not encountered. However, if p_2 takes on different values at run-time, then a local synchrony violation is detected, and execution is terminated.

Fig. 2(c) shows the init graph of a specification Φ, which configures a (body or subinit graph) parameter at the interface output port of actor C. From the repetitions vector $\mathbf{x}$ of Φ_i, the number of tokens produced at this interface output port is obtained as $\mathbf{x}(C) = 2p_3$, where p_3 is a parameter of the init graph. Suppose that in this specification, $domain(p_3) = \{1, 2, ..., 10\}$. Then whatever value p_3 takes on at run-time, it is clear that Φ_i will produce more than one token at its interface output port on each invocation. Hence, no $C \in \overline{domain(\Phi_i)}$ satisfies the init condition for local synchrony of Φ, and thus, Φ is classified as an inherently locally non-synchronous specification.

6. Binary Consistency and Decidable Dataflow

Before further discussion of analysis and verification issues for PSDF, we first discuss some pre-requisite consistency notions, adapted from [3], for general DSP dataflow specifications.

In general DSP dataflow specifications, the term consistency refers to two essential requirements — the absence of deadlock and unbounded data accumulation. An *inherently consistent* dataflow specification is one that can be implemented without any chance of buffer underflow (deadlock) or unbounded data accumulation (regardless of the input sequences that are applied to the system). If there exist one or more sets of input sequences for which deadlock and unbounded buffering are avoided, and there also exist one or more sets for which deadlock or unbounded buffering results, a specification is termed *partially consistent*. A dataflow specification that is neither consistent nor partially consistent is called *inherently inconsistent* (or simply *inconsistent*). More elaborate forms of consistency based on a probabilistic interpretation of token flow are explored in [11].

A dataflow model of computation is a *decidable* dataflow model if it can be determined in finite time whether or not an arbitrary specification in the model is consistent, and it is a *binary-consistency* model if every specification in the model is either inherently consistent or inherently inconsistent. In other words, a model is a binary-consistency model if it contains no partially consistent specifications. All of the decidable dataflow models that are used in practice today — including SDF, CSDF, and SSDF — are binary-consistency models.

Binary consistency is convenient from a verification point of view since consistency becomes an inherent property of a specification: whether or not deadlock or unbounded data accumulation arises is not dependent on the input sequences that are applied. Of course, such convenience comes at the expense of restricted applicability. A binary-consistency model cannot be used to specify all applications.

7. Robust Execution of PSDF Specifications

In PSDF, consistency considerations go beyond deadlock and buffer overflow. In particular, the concept of consistency in PSDF includes local synchrony issues. As we have seen in Section 4, local synchrony consistency is, in general, dependent on the input sequences that are applied to the given system. Thus, it is clear that PSDF cannot be classified as a binary-consistency model. Furthermore, consistency verification for PSDF is not a decidable problem. In general, if a PSDF system completes successfully for a certain input sequence, the system may be inherently consistent, or it may be partially consistent. Similarly, if a PSDF system encounters a local synchrony violation for certain input sequences, the system may be inconsistent or partially consistent.

Since all local synchrony conditions have precise mathematical formulations and at the same time can be checked at well-defined points during run-time operation, the PSDF model accommodates, but does not rely on, rigorous, compile-time verification. There exists a well-defined concept of "well-behaved" operation of a PSDF specification, and the boundary between well-behaved and ill-behaved operation is also clearly defined, and can be detected immediately at run-time in a systematic fashion (by checking local synchrony constraints). More specifically, our development of parameterized dataflow provides a consistency framework and operational semantics that leads to precise and general run-time (or simulation time) consistency verification. In particular, an inconsistent system (a specification together with an input set) in PSDF (or any parameterized dataflow augmentation of one of the existing binary consistency models) will eventually be detected as being inconsistent, which is an improvement in the level of predictability over other models that go beyond binary consistency, such as BDF, DDF, BDDF, and CDDF [18]. In these alternative "dynamic" models, there is no clear-cut semantic criterion on which the run-time environment terminates for an ill-behaved system — termination may be triggered when the buffers on an edge are full, but this is an implementation-dependent criterion. Conversely, in PSDF, when the run-time environment forces termination of an ill-behaved system, it is based on a precisely-defined semantic criterion that the system cannot continue to execute in a locally synchronous manner.

In addition, implementation of the PSDF operational semantics can be streamlined by careful compile-time analysis. Indeed, the PSDF model provides a promising framework for productive compile time analysis that warrants further investigation. As one example of such streamlining, an efficient quasi-static scheduling algorithm for PSDF specifications is developed in [2]. The consistency analysis techniques developed in this paper are complementary to such scheduling techniques. In the general quasi-static scheduling framework of parameterized dataflow, it is possible to perform symbolic computation, and obtain a symbolic repetitions vector of a PSDF graph, similar to what is done in BDF and CDDF. Then depending on how much the compiler knows about the properties of the specification through user assertions, some amount of analysis can be performed on local synchrony consistency. As implied by the operational semantics — which strictly enforces local synchrony — consistency issues that cannot be resolved at compile time must be addressed with run-time verification.

Due to the flexible dynamic reconfiguration capabilities of PSDF, the general problem of statically-verifying (verifying at compile-time) PSDF specifications is clearly non-trivial, and deriving effective, compile-time verification techniques appears to be a promising area for further research. In particular, the issue of compile-time local synchrony verification of a PSDF subsystem calls for more investigation, as it arises as an exclusively PSDF-specific consideration that is inherent in the parameterized hierarchical structure that PSDF proposes. On the other hand, dataflow consistency issues (sample rate consistency and the presence of sufficient delays) are a by-product of the underlying SDF model, and have been explored before in a dynamic context in models such as BDF, CDDF, and BDDF. Compile-time local synchrony verification can take two general forms— determining whether or not a PSDF specification is inherently locally synchronous (in which case run-time local synchrony checks can be eliminated completely), and determining whether or not a specification is inherently locally non-synchronous (in which case the system is unambiguously defective).

Bounded memory execution of consistent applications is a necessary requirement for practical implementations. Given a PSDF specification that is inherently or partially locally synchronous, there always exists a constant bound such that over any admissible execution (execution that does not result in a run-time local synchrony violation), the buffer memory requirement is within the bound. This bound does not depend on the input sequences, and is ensured by bounding the maximum token transfer at an actor port, and the maximum delay accumulation on an edge. BDDF also incorporates the concept of upper bounding the maximum token transfer rate at a dynamic port. However, unlike PSDF, even with these bounds, BDDF does not guarantee bounded memory execution, since it does not possess the concept of a local region of well-behaved operation. In PSDF, inherent and partial local synchrony both ensure bounded memory requirements throughout execution of the associated PSDF system as a sequence of consistent SDF executions. The bound on the token transfer at each actor port ensures that every invocation of a PSDF graph executes in bounded memory, while the bound on the maximum delay tokens on every edge rules out unbounded token accumulation on an edge across invocations of a PSDF graph. A suitable bound on the buffer memory requirements for a PSDF graph $G = (V, E)$ can be expressed as

$$\max_{p \in \, \mathsf{v}(G)} \left(\sum_{\theta \in \, OUT(G)} [(\mathbf{q}_{G,p}(actor(\theta))\varphi_{actor(\theta)}(\theta, config_{actor(\theta), p}))] \right. \\ \left. + \sum_{e \in G} \delta_e(config_{e, p}) \right), \quad (7)$$

where $OUT(G)$ is the set of actor output ports in G, and

$$\mathsf{v}(G) = \{p \in domain(G) \, | \, \mathbf{q}_{G,p} \text{ exists}\}$$

is simply the set of complete configurations for which G has a valid schedule. From the definition of the maximum token transfer and maximum delay quantities (τ and μ), the quantity in (7) can easily be shown to be less than or equal to the following bound.

$$\sum_{e \in G} \mu_e + \max_{p \in \, \mathsf{v}(G)} \left(\sum_{\theta \in \, OUT(G)} [(\mathbf{q}_{G,p}(actor(\theta))\tau_{actor(\theta)}(\theta))] \right). \quad (8)$$

The token production and consumption quantities are bounded (by the maximum token transfer function), and the delay on an edge is also bounded (by the maximum delay value), as shown in (8). Since the token transfer at each actor port is bounded, there is only a finite number of possible different values that the repetitions vector can take on. Hence the maxima in (7) and (8) exist. Computing much tighter bounds may in general be possible, and this appears to be a useful new direction for future work that warrants further investigation.

8. Summary

This paper has developed the concept of local synchrony, and an associated framework for robust execution of reconfigurable dataflow specifications that are based on parameterized dataflow semantics. We have implemented a software tool that accepts a PSDF specification, and generates either a quasi-static or fully-dynamic schedule for it, as appropriate, and in this tool, we have integrated run-time checking of the local synchrony formulations presented here.

Promising directions for future work include modeling and consistency analysis of conditionals (if-then-else constructs) within the PSDF framework; synthesis of streamlined code that implements run-time local synchrony verification; and the development of efficient compile-time algorithms for determining whether or not a PSDF specification is inherently locally synchronous, partially locally synchronous, or inherently defective (locally non-synchronous).

References

1. B. Bhattacharya and S. S. Bhattacharyya. Parameterized dataflow modeling of DSP systems. In *Proceedings of the International Conference on Acoustics, Speech, and Signal Processing*, pages 1948-1951, June 2000.
2. B. Bhattacharya and S. S. Bhattacharyya. Quasi-static scheduling of reconfigurable dataflow graphs for DSP systems. In *Proceedings of the International Workshop on Rapid System Prototyping*, pages 84-89, June 2000.
3. S. S. Bhattacharyya, R. Leupers, and P. Marwedel. Software synthesis and code generation for DSP. *IEEE Transactions on Circuits and Systems -- II: Analog and Digital Signal Processing*, 47(9):849-875, September 2000.
4. G. Bilsen, M. Engels, R. Lauwereins, and J. A. Peperstraete. Cyclo-static dataflow. *IEEE Transactions on Signal Processing*, 44(2):397-408, February 1996.
5. J. T. Buck, and R. Vaidyanathan, "Heterogeneous Modeling and Simulation of Embedded Systems in El Greco," *Proceedings of the International Workshop on Hardware/Software Codesign*, May 2000.
6. J. T. Buck and E. A. Lee. Scheduling dynamic dataflow graphs using the token flow model. In *Proceedings of the International Conference on Acoustics, Speech, and Signal Processing*, April 1993.
7. N. Chandrachoodan, S. S. Bhattacharyya, and K. J. R. Liu. An efficient timing model for hardware implementation of multirate dataflow graphs. In *Proceedings of the International Conference on Acoustics, Speech, and Signal Processing*, Salt Lake City, Utah, May 2001.
8. N. Cossement, R. Lauwereins, and F. Catthoor. DF*: An extension of synchronous dataflow with data dependency and non-determinism. In *Proceedings of the Forum on Design Languages*, September 2000.
9. A. Girault, B. Lee, and E. A. Lee. Hierarchical finite state machines with multiple concurrency models. *IEEE Transactions on Computer-Aided Design of Integrated Circuits and Systems*, 18(6):742-760, June 1999.

10. S. Haykin, *Adaptive Filter Theory*, 3rd edition, Prentice Hall Information and System Sciences Series, 1996.
11. E.A. Lee, "Consistency in Dataflow Graphs," *IEEE Transactions on Parallel and Distributed Systems*, 2(2), April 1991.
12. E. A. Lee and D. G. Messerschmitt. Synchronous dataflow. *Proceedings of the IEEE*, 75(9):1235-1245, September 1987.
13. A. Kerihuel, R. McConnell, and S. Rajopadhye. VSDF: Synchronous data flow for VLSI. Technical Report 843, *Institut de Recherche en Informatique et Systèmes Aléatoires (IRISA)*, 1994.
14. M. Pankert, O. Mauss, S. Ritz, and H. Meyr, "Dynamic Data Flow and Control Flow in High Level DSP Code Synthesis," *Proceedings of the International Conference on Acoustics, Speech, and Signal Processing*, April 1994.
15. C. Park, J. Chung, and S. Ha. Efficient dataflow representation of MPEG-1 audio (layer iii) decoder algorithm with controlled global states. In *Proceedings of the IEEE Workshop on Signal Processing Systems*, 1999.
16. S. Ritz, M. Pankert, and H. Meyr, "Optimum vectorization of scalable synchronous dataflow graphs," *Proceedings of the International Conference on Application-Specific Array Processors*, October 1993.
17. L. Thiele, K. Strehl, D. Ziegenbein, R. Ernst, and J. Teich, "FunState—an internal representation for codesign," *Proceedings of the International Conference on Computer-Aided Design*, November 1999.
18. P. Wauters, M. Engels, R. Lauwereins, and J. A. Peperstraete. Cyclo-dynamic dataflow. In *EUROMICRO Workshop on Parallel and Distributed Processing*, January 1996.

A Methodology
to Design Programmable Embedded Systems
The Y-Chart Approach

Bart Kienhuis[1], Ed F. Deprettere[1], Pieter van der Wolf[2], and Kees Vissers[3,4]

[1] Leiden Institute of Advanced Computer Science, Leiden, The Netherlands
[2] Philips Research, Eindhoven, The Netherlands
[3] TriMedia Technologies, Inc., Milpitas, USA
[4] University of California at Berkeley, USA

Abstract. Embedded systems architectures are increasingly becoming *programmable*, which means that an architecture can execute a set of applications instead of only one. This makes these systems cost-effective, as the same resources can be reused for another application by reprogramming the system. To design these programmable architectures, we present in this article a number of concepts of which one is the Y-chart approach. These concepts allow designers to perform a systematic exploration of the design space of architectures. Since this design space may be huge, it is narrowed down in a number of steps. The concepts presented in this article provide a methodology in which architectures can be obtained that satisfies a set of constraints while establishing enough flexibility to support a given set of applications.

Key words: Y-chart approach, Architecture Template, Stack of Y-charts, Design Space Exploration, Abstraction Pyramid, Embedded Systems

1 Introduction

The increasing digitalization of information in text, speech, video, audio and graphics has resulted in a whole new variety of digital signal processing (DSP) applications like compression and decompression, encryption, and all kinds of quality improvements. A prerequisite for making these applications available to the consumer market is the complete embedding of the systems onto a single chip that is realized in a cost effective way into silicon. This leads to a demand for embedded systems architectures that are increasingly *programmable* i.e., architectures that can execute a set of applications instead of only one specific application. By reprogramming the architecture, they can execute other applications with the same resources, which makes these programmable systems cost-effective.

An example of a programmable embedded system is given in Figure 1. It is a high-performance digital signal processing system that should eventually find its way into high-end TV-sets or set-top boxes [1]. The architecture consists of one

E.F. Deprettere et al. (Eds.): SAMOS 2001, LNCS 2268, pp. 18–37, 2002.

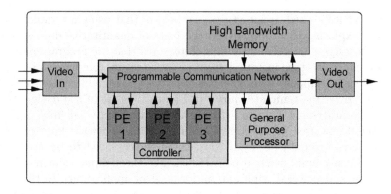

Fig. 1. High-performance digital signal processing system.

or more programmable processors (both CPUs and DSPs), some programmable
interconnect, a number of dedicated hardware accelerators (also called processing
elements) and memory, all on a single chip.

The system could be designed by specifying the architecture at a very detailed
level using hardware description languages like VHDL, or Verilog, an approach
called the *golden point design* [2]. A consequence of this approach is that designers work with very detailed descriptions of architectures. The level of detail
involved limits the design space of the architectures that designers can explore,
which gives them little freedom to make trade-offs between programmability,
utilization of resources, and silicon area. Because designers cannot make these
trade-offs, designs end up underutilizing their resources and silicon area and are
thus unnecessarily expensive, or worse, they cannot satisfy the imposed design
objectives.

Hardware/software codesign [3] is another approach to design the architecture. This design methodology uses a *refinement* approach in which one application description is refined in a number of steps into an architecture. This
refinement approach has proven to be very effective for implementing a single
algorithm into hardware. The approach is, however, less effective for a set of
applications although a first attempt has been addressed in [4]. In general, the
refinement approach lacks the ability to deal effectively with making trade-offs
in favor of the set of applications.

Yet another design methodology is to assume that the architecture shown
in Figure 1, does not represent a single instance, but rather a parameterized
description of an architecture; it is an *architecture template*[1]. The architecture
template establishes how the various elements should communicate and what the
overall structure should look like. The number of processing elements to use, the
kind of functionally the processing elements provide etc. is still open. Only by
selecting values for all the parameters is a particular architecture instance created. Based on results obtained in general purpose processor design (GPP) [5],

---

[1] Some speak about a *platform*. We use the term architecture template

in particular RISC based architectures, we believe that using a template architecture and exploring this template on the basis of quantitative data is a good approach to design embedded system architectures that are programmable.

Designing architecture instances from an architecture template imposes new design challenges. Suppose a designer needs to design an architecture for a high-end TV set, given the template shown in Figure 1. Some of the design choices are: what the processing elements (PEs) should look like, what kind of control strategy should be used in the controller of the PEs, and what kind of general purpose processor should be used. Also, these choices need to be made while a number of constraints need to be satisfied, like throughput, silicon cost, silicon efficiency, and power dissipation, all for a set of applications. In this article we will present a design methodology, which is based on the Y-chart approach, which can help designers to explore the design space of the architecture template in a systematic way, to design programmable embedded systems that are programmable and satisfy the design constraints.

The Y-chart approach presented in this article is in itself not new. It has been introduced for the first time in [6]. However, this article is the first time that we present the full methodology for designing programmable embedded systems. In this article, we will present a number of *concepts* that are part of the design methodology. The concepts include, for example, the Y-chart approach, but also design space exploration, stacks of y-charts, mapping, and the abstraction pyramid.

This article is organized as follows. We start by introducing the Y-chart approach in section 2. In Section 3, we explain how to perform design space exploration using the Y-chart. In Section 4, we explain at which level of abstraction a Y-chart needs to be constructed, leading to a particular design methodology in which the design space is stepwise reduced. Mapping applications onto architecture instances is central to the Y-chart but in general very difficult. In Section 5, we propose the basic idea that can help to make the mapping process more manageable at different levels of abstraction. In Section 6, we put the Y-chart approach in context of the design of both general purpose and application-specific processors. In Section 7, we conclude this article.

2 The Evaluation of Alternative Architectures

The problem designers face when working with an architectural template is the many architectural choices involved. In the context of the architecture template, on what basis should designers decide that one architectural choice is better than another? We somehow have to provide designers with a basis on which they can compare architectural choices in an objective way.

The ranking of architectural alternatives should be based on evaluation of performance models of architecture instances. A performance model expresses how performance metrics like utilization and throughput relate to design parameters of the architecture instance. The evaluation of performance models results in performance numbers that provide designers with *quantitative data*. This data

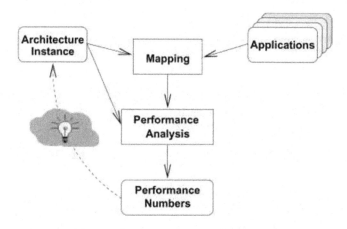

Fig. 2. The Y-chart approach.

serves as the basis on which a particular architectural choice is preferred above another architectural choice in an objective and fair manner.

We propose a general scheme with which to obtain the quantitative data, as shown in Figure 2. This scheme, which we refer to as the *Y-chart*, provides an outline for an environment in which designers can exercise architectural design and was presented for the first time in [6]. In this environment, the performance of architectures is analyzed for a given set of applications. This performance analysis provides the quantitative data that designers use to make decisions and to motivate particular choices. One should not confuse the Y-chart presented here with Gajski and Kuhn's Y-chart [7], which presents the three views and levels of abstraction in circuit design [2]. We used the term "Y-chart" for the scheme shown in Figure 2 for the first time in [8]. A similar design approach was described independently of this work in [9].

We described the Y-chart approach concept as

Concept 1. *The* Y-chart Approach *is a methodology to provide designers with quantitative data obtained by analyzing the performance of architectures for a given set of applications.*

The Y-chart approach involves the following. Designers describe a particular architecture instance (*Architecture Instance* box) and use performance analysis (*Performance Analysis* box) to construct a performance model of this architecture instance. This performance model is evaluated for the mapped set of applications (*Mapping* box and stack of *Applications* boxes). This yields performance numbers (*Performance Numbers* box) that designers interpret so that

---

[2] In Gajski and Kuhn's Y-chart, each axis represents a view of a model: *behavioral*, *structural*, or *physical* view. Moving down an axis represents moving down in level of abstraction, from the *architectural* level to the *logical* level to, finally, the *geometrical* level.

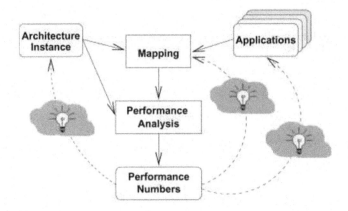

Fig. 3. The Y-chart with lightbulbs indicating the three areas that influence performance of programmable architectures.

they can propose improvements, i.e., other parameter values, resulting in another architecture instance (this interpretation process is indicated in Figure 2 by the lightbulb). This procedure can be repeated in an iterative way until a satisfactory architecture for the complete set of applications is found. The fact that the performance numbers are given not merely for one application, but for the whole set of applications is pivotal to obtaining architecture instances that are able to execute a set of applications and obey set-wide design objectives.

It is important to notice that the Y-chart approach clearly identifies three core issues that play a role in finding feasible programmable architectures, i.e., architecture, mapping, and applications. Be it individually or combined, all three issues have a profound influence on the performance of a design. Besides designing a better architecture, a better performance can also be achieved for a programmable architecture by changing the way the applications are described, or the way a mapping is performed. These processes can also be represented by means of lightbulbs and instead of pointing an arrow with a lightbulb only to the architecture, we also point arrows with lightbulbs back to the applications and the mapping, as shown in Figure 3. Nevertheless, the emphasis is on the process represented by the arrow pointing back to the architecture instance box.

Finally, we remark that the Y-chart approach leads to highly *tuned* architectures. By changing the set of applications, an architecture can be made very general or the opposite, very specific. Hence, it is the set of applications that determines the level of flexibility required by the architecture.

3   Design Space Exploration Using the Y-Chart Approach

The Y-chart approach provides a scheme allowing designers to compare architectural instances based on quantitative data. Using an architecture template [8,10], we can produce a set of architecture instances: we systematically select for all parameters p in the parameter set P of the architecture template AT distinct

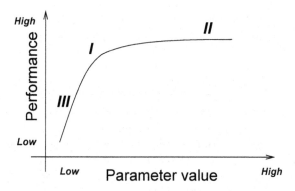

Fig. 4. The relationship between a measured performance in the architecture and a range of parameter values. Point I indicates the best trade-off between a particular performance and parameter values. Point II shows a marginal increase of the performance at a large cost and point III shows a deterioration of the performance.

values within the allowed range of values of each parameter. Consequently, we obtain a (large) finite set $\mathcal{I}$ of points I.

$$\mathcal{I} = \{I_0, I_1, ..., I_n\} \tag{1}$$

Each point I leads to an architecture instance. Using the Y-chart, we map on each and every architecture instance the whole set of applications and measure the performance using particular performance metrics, a process we repeat until we have evaluated all architecture instances resulting from the set $\mathcal{I}$. Because the design space of the architecture template AT is defined by the set of parameters of AT, in the process described above we explore the design space D of AT.

Concept 2. *The* exploration *of the design space D of the architecture template AT is the systematic selection of a value for all parameters $P_j \in D$ such that a finite set of points $\mathcal{I} = \{I_0, I_1, ... I_n\}$ is obtained. Each point I leads to an architecture instance for which performance numbers are obtained using the Y-chart approach.*

When we plot the obtained parameter numbers for each architecture instance versus the set of systematically changed parameter values, we obtain graphs such as shown in Figure 4. Designers can use these graphs to balance architectural choices to find a feasible design.

Some remarks are in order in relation to Figure 4. Whereas the figure shows only one parameter, the architecture template contains many parameters. Finding the right trade-off is a multi-dimensional problem. The more parameters involved, the more difficult it will be. Note also that the curve shown in the graph is smooth. In general, designers cannot assume that curves are smooth because the interaction between architecture and applications can be very capricious. Finally, the curve in the figure shows a continuous line, whereas the performance numbers are found only for distinct parameter values. Simple curve fitting might give the wrong impression.

4   Levels of Abstraction

We have not said anything yet about the abstraction level at which a Y-chart should be constructed. If, however, we observe the Y-chart, it is the performance analysis that determines at what level the Y-chart should be constructed. Within performance analysis, there are interesting trade-offs to be made.

Performance analysis always involves three issues: a *modeling effort*, an *evaluation effort* and the *accuracy* of the obtained results [11,12]. Performance analysis can take place at different levels of detail, depending on the trade-offs that are made between these three issues. Very accurate performance numbers can be achieved, but at the expense of a lot of detailed modeling and long evaluation times. On the other hand, performance numbers can be achieved in a short time with modest effort for modeling but at the expense of loss of accuracy. We place the important relations between these three issues in perspective in a concept that we call the *Abstraction Pyramid*.

Concept 3. *The* Abstraction Pyramid *puts the trade-off present in performance modeling between modeling effort, evaluation effort, and accuracy in perspective of system level design.*

4.1   The Abstraction Pyramid

The abstraction pyramid (see Figure 5) describes the modeling of architectures at different levels of abstraction in relation to the three issues in performance modeling. At the top of the pyramid is a designer's initial rough idea (shown as a lightbulb) for an architecture in the form of a 'paper architecture'. The designer wants to realize this architecture in silicon. The bottom of the pyramid represents all possible feasible realizations; it thus represents the complete design space of the designer's paper architecture. A discussion of the three main elements of the abstraction pyramid follows including two additional elements: the opportunity to change models and the different abstraction levels that can be found in system level design.

Cost of Modeling. Moving down in the pyramid from top to bottom, a designer defines an increasing expenditure of detail of an architecture using some modeling formalism. This process proceeds at the cost of an increasing amount of effort, as indicated on the *cost of modeling* axis at the right-hand side of the pyramid. As architectures are described in more detail, the number of architectural choices (i.e. the number of parameters in the architecture template) increases, expanding the basis of the pyramid. Each new architectural choice, albeit at a lower level of detail, thus further broadens the design space of the architecture.

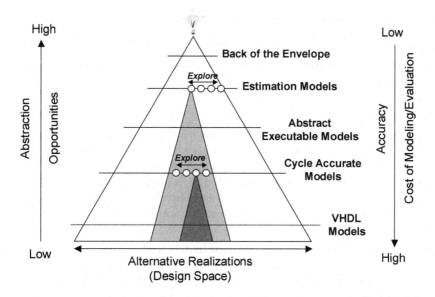

Fig. 5. The abstraction pyramid represents the trade-off between modeling effort, evaluation speed, and accuracy, the three elements involved in a performance analysis.

Opportunity to Change. As the designer moves down and includes more detail using a modeling formalism, the architecture becomes increasingly more specific. Simply because more design choices have been made, it becomes more costly to redo these design choices if another architecture is to be considered. Hence the opportunity to explore other architectures diminishes. This is indicated on the *opportunities* axis at the left-hand side of the pyramid.

Level of Detail. Lines intersecting the abstraction pyramid horizontally at different heights represent different abstraction levels found in system level design. The small circles on such line represent architecture instances modeled at that abstraction level. At the highest level of abstraction, architectures are modeled using *back-of-the-envelope models*. Models become more detailed as the abstraction pyramid is descended. The *back-of-the-envelope models* is followed by *estimation models, abstract executable models, cycle-accurate models*, and, finally, by *synthesizable VHDL models*. This represents the lowest level at which designers can model architectures.

We use the term *back-of-the-envelope model* for simple mathematical relationships describing performance metrics of an architecture instance under simple assumptions related to utilization and data rates (e.g. [5]). Estimation models are more elaborated and sophisticated mathematical relationships to describe performance metrics (e.g. [12]). Neither model describes the correct functional behavior or timing. The term *abstract executable model* describes the correct functional behavior of applications and architectures, without describing the behavior related to time (e.g. [13]). The term *cycle-accurate model* describes the correct functional behavior and timing of an architecture instance in which a cycle is a multiple (including a multiple of one), of a clock cycle (e.g. [14,15]). Finally, the term *synthesizable VHDL model* describes an architecture instance in such detail, in both behavior and timing, that the model can be realized in silicon.

Accuracy. In the abstraction pyramid, accuracy is represented by the gray triangles. Because the accuracy of cycle-accurate models is higher than the accuracy of estimation models, the base of the triangle belonging to the cycle-accurate models is smaller than the base of the triangle belonging to the estimation models. Thus the broader the base, the less specific the statement a designer can make in general about the final realization of an architecture.

Cost of Evaluation. Techniques to evaluate architectures to obtain performance numbers range from back-of-the-envelope models where analytical equations are solved symbolically, using, for example, *Mathematica* or *Matlab*, up to the point of simulating the behavior in synthesizable VHDL models accurately with respect to clock cycles. In *simulation*, the processes that would happen inside a real architecture instance are imitated. Solving equations only takes a few seconds, whereas simulating detailed VHDL models may take hours if not days. The axis at the right-hand side represents both cost of modeling and *cost of evaluation*.

4.2   Exploration

The abstraction pyramid shows the trade-offs in performance analysis. When exploring the design space of an architecture template, designers should make different trade-offs at different times. Higher up in the pyramid they can explore a larger part of the design space in a given time. Although it is less accurate, it helps them to narrow down the design space. Moving down in the pyramid, the design space that they can consider becomes smaller. The designer can explore with increased accuracy only at the expense of taking longer to construct, evaluate, and change models of architecture instances.

The process of exploration and narrowing down on the design space is illustrated in the abstraction pyramid by the circles. These circles are drawn at the level of estimation models and at the level of cycle-accurate models. Each circle represents the evaluation of a particular architecture instance. An exploration at a particular abstraction level is thus represented as a set of circles on a particular horizontal line in the abstraction pyramid.

4.3   Stacks of Y-Chart Environments

Due to the level-dependent trade-off between modeling, evaluation, and accuracy, designers should use different models at different levels of abstraction when exploring the design space of architectures. The Y-chart approach used at these

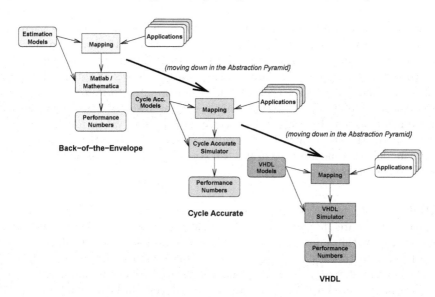

Fig. 6. A stack of Y-chart environments, with a different model at each level of abstraction.

different levels is, however, invariant: it still consists of the same elements, as shown in Figure 2. This leads to the following concept of a *Y-chart environment*:

Concept 4. *A* Y-chart Environment *is a realization of the Y-chart approach for a specific design project at a particular level of abstraction.*

The different levels represented in the abstraction pyramid thus indicate that more than one Y-chart environment is needed in a design process for architectures. Therefore, different Y-chart environments are needed at different levels of abstraction, forming a stack as illustrated in Figure 6. This figure shows three possible Y-chart environments: one at the level of *back of the envelope* models, one at the level of *cycle accurate* models, and on at the level of *VHDL* models.

In the abstraction pyramid, more than these three levels of abstraction are given. Nevertheless, we will resort to just three levels from the abstraction pyramid in Figure 5

Back-of-the-Envelope. Early in the design, designers make use of back-of-the-envelope models and estimation models, to model architecture instances. This allows them to construct many architecture instances very quickly. Designers typically employ generic tools like *Matlab* or *Mathematica* to evaluate the performance of these models by solving analytic equations. These tools can compute complex equations (symbolically) within a few seconds. The resulting performance numbers typically represent rough estimates for throughput, latency, and utilization. The tools evaluate the performance metrics either numerically or symbolically.

Cycle-Accurate. As the design space for the architecture template narrows, designers use abstract-executable models and cycle-accurate models to describe architecture instances. At this level of abstraction, designers can compare the performances of moderately different architectures. Models at this level require architecture simulators that typically run from minutes to hours to carry out a simulation. These simulators most likely employ discrete-event mechanisms. The performance numbers at this level typically represent values for throughput, latency, and utilization rates for individual elements of architecture instances. As the models become more accurate, the accuracy of the performance numbers also becomes higher.

VHDL. Finally, as the design space narrows down further, a designer wants to be able to compare the performance of slightly different architecture instances accurately to within a few percent. The designer uses detailed VHDL models to describe architecture instances, taking significant amounts of time and resources. Designers can carry out the simulations using standard VHDL simulators. Simulation time required for these architecture instances can be as much as several days. The obtained performance numbers are accurate enough that a designer can compare differences in the performance of architecture instances to within a few percent.

4.4 Design Trajectory

The abstraction pyramid presents trade-offs between modeling, evaluation, and accuracy that result in a stack of Y-chart environments being used. This stack leads to a *design trajectory* in which designers can model architectures and applications at various levels of detail. The Y-chart approach and the stack of Y-chart environments thus structure the design process of programmable embedded architectures.

Concept 5. *A* Stack of Y-charts *describes a design trajectory in which different Y-chart environments are realized at different levels of abstraction, each taking a different trade-off position in the Abstraction Pyramid, which leads to a stepwise refinement of the design space of programmable embedded architectures.*

Within this design trajectory, designers perform design space exploration at each level and narrow down the design space containing feasible designs. This approach differs from the golden point design, which is the design methodology currently used in the design of complex programmable architectures. Here a design, the golden point, is modeled directly at low level, i.e., VHDL.

In Figure 7(a), we show the golden point design. Here the golden point is modeled directly at a low level in the pyramid. Because hardly any exploration and validation of ideas took place, except for paper exercises and spreadsheets, it is first of all very much the question whether the selected point results in a feasible design. Secondly, due to the low level of detail already involved, it becomes very difficult to explore other parts of the design space, thus leading to

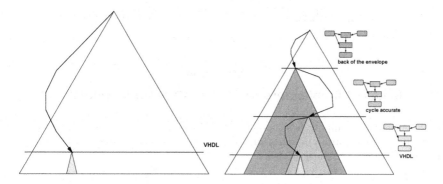

Fig. 7. (a), the golden point design approach. (b), the design approach in which designers use Y-chart environments.

sub optimal design. Thirdly, it is very likely that designers will be confronted with unpleasant surprises at late stages in the design process. This can lead to costly rework and slipping time schedules. In Figure 7(b), the design approach is shown in which designers use Y-charts at different levels of abstraction. This approach, we believe, leads to better-engineered architectures and moreover reduces risk. Each time more resources are committed to the design of an architecture, more knowledge is available to assess if a feasible design can be accomplished within its given set of constraints.

5 Mapping

Mapping pertains to conditioning a programmable architecture instance such that it executes a particular application. It leads to a program that causes the execution of one application on the programmable architecture. Mapping involves, for example, assigning application functions to processing elements that can execute these functions. It also involves mapping the communication that takes place in applications onto communication structures.

Mapping is a difficult problem, but it is essential to the Y-chart approach. To be able to do mapping, at various levels of abstraction, and to develop a mapping strategy concurrently with the development of the architecture, we now discuss the basic concept we use to make mapping as simple as possible. This mapping concept is also depicted in Figure 8.

Concept 6. *In mapping, in context of the Y-chart, we say that a natural fit exists if the model of computation used to specify applications matches the model of architecture used to specify architectures and that the data types used in both models are similar.*

To explain the matching of the model of computation with the model of architecture, we first explain what we means by these terms. Then we look at the data types found in both applications and architectures and come back to the notion of the natural fit.

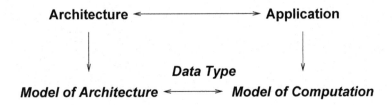

Fig. 8. A smooth mapping from an application to an architecture only takes place if the model of computation matches with the model of architecture and when the same data types are used in both models.

Model of Computation. Applications are specified using some kind of formalism that has an underlying model of computation. We define a model of computation, inspired by [16], as a formal representation of the operational semantics of networks of functional blocks describing computations.

So, the operational semantics of a model of computation governs how the functional blocks interact with one another realizing computations. Many different models of computation already exist that have specific properties. Different models have proven to be very effective in describing applications in various application domains [17]. Some examples of well-known models of computation are: *Dataflow Models*, *Process Models*, *Finite State Machine Models*, and *Imperative Models*.

Model of Architecture. In analogy with a model of computation, we define the concept of model of architecture as a formal representation of the operational semantics of networks of functional blocks describing architectures.

In this case, the functional blocks describe the behavior of architectural resources like CPUs, busses, and memory and the operational semantics of a model of architecture governs how these resources interact with one another. Although models of architecture are less mature then models of computation, one can identify characteristics like whether control is centralized or distributed, or whether there is an emphasis on control flow or data flow.

Data Types. In both applications and architectures, data that is exchanged is organized in a particular way and has particular properties. A *data type* describes these properties. Examples of simple data types are integers, floats, or reals. More complex data types are streams of integers or matrices.

To realize a smooth mapping, the types used in the applications should match with the types used in the architecture. If architectures support only streams of integers, the applications should also use only streams of integers. Suppose an application uses only matrices whereas an architecture instance on which we want to map uses only streams of scalars. Because the types do not match, we can already say that we first have to express the matrices in terms of streams of scalars. A stream of scalars, however, has very different properties from a matrix (e.g. a matrix is randomly accessible), having a profound influence on how the application executes on the architecture. Consequently, to obtain a smooth mapping of applications onto architectures, the data types in both the applications and the architectures should be the same or at least the architecture should support a more fine-grained data types then the application data types.

5.1   Natural Fit

Given an application that is described using a model of computation and an architecture instance that is described using a model of architecture, when we say the application fits *naturally* onto the architecture instance, we mean that:

1. The architecture instance provides at least primitives similar to those used in the application. In other words, the grain-size of functions and processing elements should be the same. For example, a FIR filter functions used in the application should also be found for example as a FIR processing element in the architecture instance.
2. The operational semantics of the architecture instance at least matches the operational semantics of the application. For example, if functions in the applications behave in a data-driven manner then the processing elements should also operate in a data-driven manner.
3. The data types used in applications should match the data types available on the architecture instance. For example, when an application uses only streams of samples then the architecture instance should at least provide supports for such streams of samples.

Examples of this 'natural fit' principle can be found in literature. For example, in [18], the CSP model of computation is used for describing applications that are mapped onto asynchronous hardware. In [19], the cyclo-static dataflow (CSDF) is used for describing applications that are mapped on one or more VSP processors, which are real-time programmable video processors. The most well know example of the presented principle is the imperative C-language that is mapped onto a micro-processor [5].

Other examples of the 'natural fit' at higher levels of abstraction, can be found in the ORAS work [8,10] and SPADE work [13]. In both cases, process networks are mapped onto abstract models of stream-oriented architectures. Another example is the POLIS work [9]. It maps a special kind of Finite State Machines (FSMs) onto abstract models of microprocessor architectures.

6   Processor Design

In the introduction, we described the problem of finding the correct parameters to instantiate an architecture instance that satisfies a number of constraints for a given set of applications. This problem has already been researched for decades in the realm of general-purpose processor (GPP) design. In this domain, complex architectures called *instruction-set processors* or *microprocessors* are designed that execute a word-processor application as easily as a spreadsheet

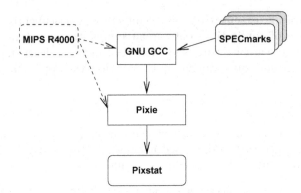

Fig. 9. The Y-chart used in the construction of the MIPS R4000.

application or even simulate some complex physical phenomenon. Therefore, designers working in this domain know what programmability implies in terms of (complex) trade-offs between hardware, software, and compilers. In this section, we will show that the design of GPPs fits into our Y-chart approach.

6.1   Design of General-Purpose Processors

In the beginning of the 1980s, revolutionary GPPs emerged that were called RISC microprocessors [20]. These processors were developed in a revolutionary way; namely, designers used extensive quantitative analysis of a suite of *benchmarks*, which is a set of applications. As a result, these architectures were smaller, faster, cheaper and easier to program than conventional architectures of that time. With the advent of the RISC microprocessors, the design of GPPs in general began to swing away from focusing purely on hardware design. Designers started to focus more on the quantitative analysis of difficulties encountered in architecture, mapping (or compiling), and the way benchmarks are written. This quantitative approach has become the de-facto development technique for the design of general-purpose processors [21,5].

As we will show, we can in retrospect cast the design of general-purpose processor architectures in terms of our Y-chart approach as presented in this article. We do this first by looking at the design of the MIPS R4000 microprocessor [22] as depicted in Figure 9. In this Y-chart, the set of applications is described in the C-language by the *SPECmark* programs. Using a C-compiler, tuned especially to reflect the R4000 architecture, and a special architecture simulator called *Pixie*, Hennessy et al., evaluated the performance of the applications mapped onto an instance of the R4000. The *Pixstat* program interprets the produced performance numbers. In the given Y-chart, the dashed box represents the fact that the architecture is not specified as a separate entity, but that it is hard coded into the GNU GCC compiler and architecture simulator Pixie.

According to Hennessy et al., the design space of the MIPS R4000 is extremely large and evaluating alternatives is costly for three reasons: construction

Table 1. Different Levels of Simulation used in the MIPS R4000 design [22].

Simulator	Level of Accuracy	Sim. Speed
Pixie	Instruction Set	$> 10^6$ cycles/sec
Sable	System Level	$> 10^3$ cycles/sec
RTL (C-code)	Synchronous Register Transfer	> 10 cycles/sec
Gate	Gate/Switch	< 1 cycles/sec

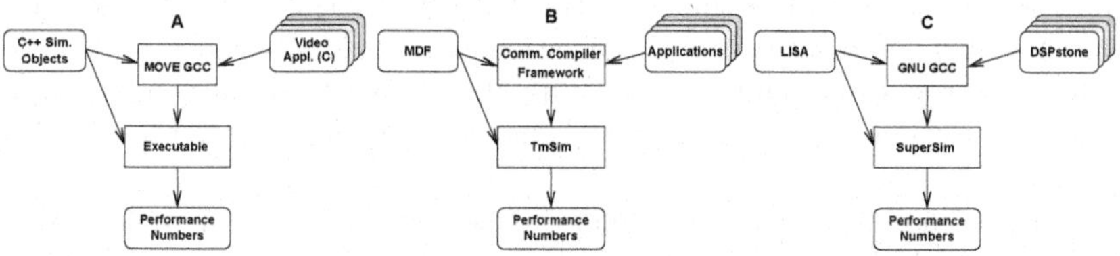

Fig. 10. Y-chart environments used in various design projects.

of accurate performance models, long simulation runs, and tuning of the compiler to include architectural changes. Precisely these three issues are expressed in the Abstraction Pyramid in figure 5.

To narrow down the design space of the R4000, in a stepwise fashion as shown in Figure 7(b), four different simulators are used at increasing levels of detail, as shown in Table 1. One can clearly see that the simulation speed drops dramatically as more detail is added. Interestingly, Hennessy et al. consider the top two levels of simulation to be the most critical levels in the design of processors. It allowed for the exploration of a large part of the design space of the MIPS R4000, helping the designers to make better trade-offs.

6.2   Design of Application-Specific Processors

Next, we show three processor designs that we have put in context of the Y-chart methodology. In these Y-charts, the selection of benchmarks results in more application-specific processor architectures.

Wilberg et al. [23] used a Y-chart, as shown in Figure 10(a) for designing application-specific VLIW (Very Long Instruction Word) architectures for low-speed video algorithms like JPEG, H.262 and MPEG1. The video applications written in C are compiled into generic RISC-instructions using the GCC/MOVE compiler developed by Corporaal et al. [24].

Sijstermans et al. [25] used a Y-chart, as shown in Figure 10(b) to design the *TriMedia* programmable multi-media processor TM1000. They compiled a set of applications that were written in C into object-code, using a commercial compiler framework. The architecture simulator *tmsim* can simulate this object-code clock-cycle accurately. Both the compiler and the simulator are *retargetable* for a class of TriMedia architectures that they describe using a Machine Description File (MDF).

Živojnović et al. [26] used a Y-chart, as shown in Figure 10(c) to develop DSP processors. As a benchmark, they used a special set of C functions called DSPstone. They mapped the benchmarks onto the retargetable simulator called *SuperSim* using a retargetable version of the GNU GCC-compiler. They described a class of DSP-architectures using the special language *LISA*.

So, if the benchmark suite contains very different programs like a word processor application, a spreadsheet application and a compiler application, a general-purpose architecture results that is optimized for a broad range of applications. If, on the other hand, the set of applications contains only video applications, a dedicated processor architecture results that is optimized for video applications. The selection of the benchmarks is hence a key decision step in the design process.

In all the cases presented, designers make refinements to a well-known architecture template commonly referred to as *load-store architectures* [5]. For these architectures, good detailed models exist as well as good compiler frameworks. The model of computation underlying the C-language, e.g., imperative languages, fits naturally with the model of architecture of load-store architectures. Consequently, designers of microprocessors use applications written in the C-language. To design architectures, they resort to tuning known compiler frameworks to include architectural changes, to change mapping strategies, or to rewrite applications.

7   Conclusions

We believe that programmable embedded systems will more and more be designed by means of an architecture template for which designers needs to select the proper set of parameter values. We assume that different architecture templates will emerge for different domains like mobile communication, automotive, and high-performance signal processing. The domain specific templates will become the models of architecture that match the typical characteristics of the applications that execute within those domains.

As a design approach for programmable embedded systems, we presented the Y-chart approach. It is a methodology in which designers use quantitative data that provides them with a sound basis on which to make decisions and motivate particular design choices. This leads to an environment in which a systematic exploration of the design space of the architecture template can be performed, leading to solid engineered systems. Since the design space of an architecture template is in general huge, a stepwise refinement of the design space is needed. This leads to the concept of a stack of Y-chart environments, in which each Y-chart models the system at a different level of abstraction.

In the design of programmable embedded systems, the current practice is still the golden point design (See Figure 7(a)). Quantifying architectural choices in architectures is unfortunately by no means current practice. Yet the RISC architecture development has unmistakably shown that quantifying design choices leads to well engineered architectures. As shown in this article, the design methodology of RISC processors and other application-specific processors can be cast into the presented Y-chart approach.

We believe, that the Y-chart approach presents a general and solid methodology for designing programmable embedded system architectures. This is reinforced by the fact that the methodology has already effected other research in embedded system design [27,28,29]. Furthermore, at Philips research, the Y-chart approach has led to the development of YAPI [30], which stands for *Y-chart application programming interface*. In addition, the Y-chart approach has influenced, and has been influenced by, the system level design work described in [31].

Before we can fully perform design space exploration at various levels of abstraction, there are still some tough research issues to be tackled. Especially performing mappings at high abstraction levels is difficult. For some dedicated systems, we can relay on applications written in 'C', compilers and architecture models developed in the realm of general-purpose processors to construct Y-chart environments. Nonetheless, we believe that new systems on a chip require new architectural models, new application models, and mapping techniques. The new systems will for example exploit both task-level parallelism and instruction level parallelism. Furthermore, they should operate under real-time constraints and use heterogeneous architectural components (e.g. CPUs, DSPs, dedicated co-processors, distributed memories). The notion of models of computation and models of architectures should help us to pave the way to the exploration of systems at higher levels of abstraction.

Acknowledgement

This research has been performed at both Philips Research and Delft University of Technology, as part of their "cluster program". Philips Research, Ministry of Economic affairs, and Delft University of Technology have supported this research and are hereby acknowledged.

References

1. Claasen, T.: Technical and industrial challenges for signal processing in consumer electronics: A case study on TV applications. In: Proceedings of VLSI Signal Processing, VI. (1993) 3–11
2. Richards, M.A.: The rapid prototyping of application specific signal processors (RASSP) program: Overview and status. In: 5th International Workshop on Rapid System Prototyping, IEEE Computer Society Press (1994) 1–6
3. De Micheli, G., Sami, M.: Hardware/Software Co-Design. Volume 310 of Series E: Applied Sciences. NATO ASI Series (1996)
4. Kalavade, A., Subrahmanyam, P.: Hardware/software partioning for multi-function systems. In: Proc. of ICCAD'97. (1997) 516–521
5. Hennessy, J.L., Patterson, D.A.: Computer Architectures: A Quantitative Approach. second edn. Morgan Kaufmann Publishers, Inc. (1996)

6. Kienhuis, B., Deprettere, E., Vissers, K., van der Wolf, P.: An approach for quantitative analysis of application-specific dataflow architectures. In: Proceedings of 11th Int. Conference of Applications-specific Systems, Architectures and Processors (ASAP'97), Zurich, Switzerland (1997) 338–349
7. Gajski, D.: Silicon Compilers. Addison-Wesley (1987)
8. Kienhuis, B., Deprettere, E., Vissers, K., van der Wolf, P.: The construction of a retargetable simulator for an architecture template. In: Proceedings of 6th Int. Workshop on Hardware/Software Codesign, Seattle, Washington (1998)
9. Balarin, F. abd Giusto, P., Jurecska, A., Passerone, C., Sentovich, E., Tabbara, B., Chiodo, M., Hsieh, H., Lavagno, L., Sangiovanni-Vincentelli, A.L., Suzuki, K.: Hardware-Software Co-Design of Embedded Systems: The POLIS Approach. Kluwer Academic Publishers (1997)
10. Kienhuis, B.A.: Design Space Exploration of Stream-based Dataflow Architectures: Methods and Tools. PhD thesis, Delft University of Technology, The Netherlands (1999)
11. Lavenberg, S.S.: Computer Performance Modeling Handbook. Acadamic Press (1983)
12. van Gemund, A.J.: Performance Modeling of Parallel Systems. PhD thesis, Laboratory of Computer Architecture and Digital Techniques, Delft University of Technology (1996)
13. Lieverse, P., van der Wolf, P., Vissers, K., Deprettere, E.F.: A methodology for architecture exploration of heterogeneous signal processing systems. Journal of VLSI Signal Processing for Signal, Image and Video Technology 29 (2001) 197–207
14. Kruijtzer, W.: Tss: Tool for system simulation. IST Newsletter, Philips Research Laboratories (1997) 5–7 Issue 17.
15. Liao, S., Tjiang, S., Gupta, R.: An efficient implementation of reactivity for modeling hardware in the scenic design environment. In: Proceedings of DAC-97. (1997)
16. Lee, E.A., et al.: An overview of the Ptolemy project. Technical report, University of California at Berkeley (1994)
17. Chang, W.T., Ha, S., Lee, E.A.: Heterogeneous simulation - mixing discrete-event models with dataflow. VLSI Signal Processing 15 (1997) 127–144
18. van Berkel, K.: Handshake Circuits: an asynchronous architecture for VLSI programming,. Cambridge University Press (1993)
19. Vissers, K., Essink, G., van Gerwen, P., Janssen, P., Popp, O., Riddersma, E., Veendrick, J.: Architecture and programming of two generations video signal processors. In: Algorithms and Parallel VLSI Architectures III. Elsevier (1995) 167–178
20. Patterson, D.: Reduced instruction set computers. Comm. ACM 28 (1985) 8–21
21. Bose, P., Conte, T.M.: Performance analysis and its impact on design. IEEE Computer 31 (1998) 41–49
22. Hennessy, J., Heinrich, M.: Hardware/software codesign of processors: Concepts and examples. In Micheli, G.D., Sami, M., eds.: Hardware/Software Codesign. Volume 310 of Series E: Applied Sciences. NATO ASI Series (1996) 29–44
23. Camposano, R., Wilberg, J.: Embedded system design. Design Automation for Embedded Systems 1 (1996) 5–50
24. Corporaal, H., Mulder, H.: Move: A framework for high-performance processor design. In: Proceedings of Supercomputing, Albuquerque (1991) 692–701
25. Sijstermans, F., Pol, E., Riemens, B., Vissers, K., Rathnam, S., Slavenburg, G.: Design space exploration for future trimedia CPUs. In: ICASSP'98. (1998)
26. Živojnović, V., Pees, S., Schläger, C., Willems, M., Schoenen, R., Meyr, H.: DSP Processor/Compiler Co-Design: A Quantitative Approach. In: Proc. ISSS. (1996)

27. Rabaey, J., Potkonjak, M., Koushanfar, F., li, S., Tuan, T.: Challenges and opportunities in broadband and wireless communication designs. In: Proceedings of ICCAD. (2000)
28. Hekstra, G., La Hei, G., Bingley, P., Sijstermans, F.: Trimedia cpu64 design space exploration. In: ICCD. (1999)
29. Marculescu, R., Nandi, A.: Probabilistic application modeling for system-level performance analysis. In: Proceedings Design, Automation and Test in Europe (DATE'01), Munich, Germany (2001) 190–196
30. de Kock, E., Essink, G., Smits, W., van der Wolf, P., Brunel, J., Kruijtzer, W., Lieverse, P., Vissers, K.: Yapi: Application modeling for signal processing systems (2000)
31. Keutzer, K., Malik, S., Newton, A.R., Rabaey, J.M., Sangiovanni-Vincentelli, A.: System-level design: Orthogonalization of concerns and platform-based design. IEEE Transactions on Computer-Aided Design of Integrated Circuits and Systems **19** (2000) 1523–1543

Flexibility/Cost-Tradeoffs
of Platform-Based Systems[*]

Christian Haubelt[1], Jürgen Teich[1], Kai Richter[2], and Rolf Ernst[2]

[1] DATE, University of Paderborn, Paderborn, Germany
{haubelt,teich}@date.upb.de
http://www-date.upb.de
[2] IDA, Technical University of Braunschweig, Braunschweig, Germany
{richter,ernst}@ida.ing.tu-bs.de
http://www.ida.ing.tu-bs.de

Abstract. This paper provides a quantitative characterization of an embedded system's capability to implement alternative behaviors. This new objective in system-level design is termed *flexibility* and is most notable in the field of adaptive and reconfigurable systems, where a system may change its behavior during operation. Different behaviors are also taken into consideration while implementing platform-based systems. Based on a *hierarchical graph model* which permits formal modeling of flexibility and implementation cost of a system, an efficient exploration algorithm to find the *optimal flexibility/cost-tradeoff-curve* is proposed. The feasibility of our approach is demonstrated by a case study concerning the design of a family of Set-Top boxes.

1 Introduction

Multi-dimensional optimization of a system for a given, single application is challenging, but has been formalized already by methods of graph-based allocation and binding (see [1]) which are used in commercial systems such as VCC by Cadence [2].

In platform-based design, however, a system should be dimensioned such that it is able to implement not only one particular application optimally, but a complete set of different applications or variants of a certain application. Hence, the task is to find a tradeoff between cost and flexibility of an architecture which is able to implement several alternative behaviors.

In adaptive systems which have to react to environmental changes, the definition of flexibility is of utmost importance. Here, it is also necessary to implement different behaviors. Unfortunately, this may cause additional cost. For this purpose, reconfigurable architectures seem to be an adequate choice.

As far as we are concerned, there is no approach that quantitatively tradeoffs implementational cost in terms of additional memory, hardware, network, etc. and the flexibility of a system which implements multiple behaviors. Here,

---

[*] This work was supported by the German Science Foundation (DFG), SPP 1040.

E.F. Deprettere et al. (Eds.): SAMOS 2001, LNCS 2268, pp. 38–56, 2002.

we introduce *flexibility* as a tentative to quantitatively describe the functional richness that the system under design is able to implement (Section 3). In order to describe a set of applications, a hierarchical specification is useful, e.g., see [3,4]. In this paper, we introduce a *hierarchical graph model* for describing alternatives of the behavior of a system. The same idea may be used in order to describe reconfigurable architectures on the implementation side, i.e., systems that change their structure over time.

With this model, we are then able to define the problem of dimensioning a system that is able to dynamically switch its behavior and/or structure at run-time. Basically, this problem extends previous approaches such as [1] to reconfigurable, platform-based systems that implement time-dependent functionality.

Finally, an efficient exploration algorithm for exploring the flexibility/cost-tradeoff-curve of a system under design is presented that efficiently prunes solutions that are not optimal with respect to both criteria (Section 4). The example of a flexible video Set-Top box is used as the guiding example throughout the paper.

2   Hierarchical Specification Model

Each embedded system is developed to cover a certain range of functionality. This coverage depends on the different types of tasks as well as on the scope every task is able to process. A specification of such an embedded system is depicted in Fig. 1.

The specification shows interacting processes of a digital television decoder. There are four top-level processes, P_A to handle the authentification process, P_C to control channel selection, frequency adjustment, etc., I_D which performs decryption, and I_U for uncompression. Here, the uncompression process requires input data from the decryption process. Furthermore, the controller and authentification process are well known and are most likely to be implemented equally in each decoder.

The main difference between TV decoders consists of the implemented combinations of decryption and uncompression algorithms. As shown in Fig. 1, we use hierarchical refinement to capture all alternative realizations. There are three decryption and two uncompression processes used in this decoder. Obviously, if we implement even more of these refinements, our decoder will support a greater number of TV stations. Consequently, the decoder possesses an increased flexibility.

Before defining the flexibility of a system formally, we have to introduce a specification model that is able to express flexibility. As shown in Fig. 1, our specification model is based on the concept of hierarchical graphs, where a hierarchical graph possesses vertices that can be refined by subgraphs. If it is possible to replace such hierarchical vertices by a set of alternative subgraphs, we call these subgraphs *clusters* and the hierarchical vertices are termed *interfaces*. Definitions 1 to 3 declare this basic structure of hierarchical graphs.

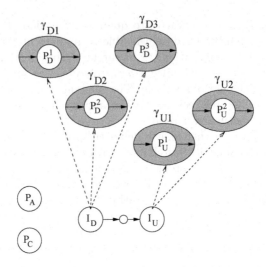

Fig. 1. Specification of a Digital TV Decoder

Definition 1 (cluster). *A cluster* $\gamma(I, O, V, E, \Psi)$ *contains a directed non-hierarchical graph* $G = (V_G, E_G)$, *where* V *and* Ψ *define a partitioning of the set of vertices* V_G *and* E_G *is the set of edges* E. *Furthermore, we define:*

> $I = \{i_1, i_2, \ldots, i_{N_I}\}$ *is the set of inputs,*
> $O = \{o_1, o_2, \ldots, o_{N_O}\}$ *is the set of outputs,*
> $V = \{v_1, v_2, \ldots, v_{N_V}\}$ *is the set of non-hierarchical vertices or* leaves,
> $E \subseteq (I \times \{V \cup I_\Psi\}) \cup (V \times \{V \cup I_\Psi\}) \cup (O_\Psi \times \{V \cup O\}) \cup (V \times O)$ *is the set of edges, where* I_Ψ *and* O_Ψ *denote the unions of the inputs and outputs of the interfaces (see Def. 2), respectively, and*
> $\Psi = \{\psi_1, \psi_2, \ldots, \psi_{N_\Psi}\}$ *is the set of hierarchical vertices or* interface *as defined by Definition 2.*

While leaves can not be refined, interfaces are used as placeholders to embed subgraphs. Since the in-degree and out-degree of an interface is not limited, we need the notion of *ports*. Interfaces are connected with vertices or other interfaces via ports. These ports are used to embed clusters into a given interface. In the sequel, we use the term *ports* for the union of the in- and outputs ($I \cup O$).

An *interface* is defined as follows:

Definition 2 (interface). *An interface* $\psi(I, O, \Gamma, \Phi)$ *is a 4-tuple* (I, O, Γ, Φ), *where*

> $I = \{i_1, i_2, \ldots, i_{N_I}\}$ *denotes the set of inputs,*
> $O = \{o_1, o_2, \ldots, o_{N_O}\}$ *denotes the set of outputs,*
> $\Gamma = \{\gamma_1, \gamma_2, \ldots, \gamma_{N_\Gamma}\}$ *is the set of associated clusters, and*
> $\Phi : I_\Gamma \cup O_\Gamma \to I \cup O$ *is a function which maps the ports of all associated clusters* $\gamma \in \Gamma$ *onto the ports of this interface, where* I_Γ *and* O_Γ *denote the unions of the inputs and outputs of the associated clusters (see Def. 1), respectively. In the following, we term this function as* port mapping.

With the Definition 1 and 2 we are able to define *hierarchical graphs*.

Definition 3 (hierarchical graph). *A hierarchical graph is a cluster (defined by Def. 1) where the set of in- and outputs are empty, i.e., $I = O = \emptyset$.*

Figure 1 shows a digital TV decoder as a hierarchical graph with its top-level graph depicted at the bottom. The top-level graph consists of two non-hierarchical vertices, $V = \{P_A, P_C\}$ and two interfaces ($\Psi = \{I_D, I_U\}$). The decryption interface I_D itself can be refined by three clusters γ_{D1}, γ_{D2}, and γ_{D3}, where each cluster represents an alternative refinement of I_D. The set of clusters is given by $\Gamma = \{\gamma_{D1}, \gamma_{D2}, \gamma_{D3}, \gamma_{U1}, \gamma_{U2}\}$. For simplicity, we omit the ports of the vertices, interfaces, and clusters.

All clusters associated with the interface ψ represent *alternative refinements* of ψ. The process of *cluster-selection* associated with each interface ψ determines exactly one cluster to implement ψ at each instant of time. In order to avoid a loss of generality, we do not restrict cluster-selection to system start-up. Thus, reconfigurable and adaptive systems may be modeled via time-dependent switching of clusters.

The set of leaves of a hierarchical graph G is defined by the recursive equation[1]:

$$V_l(G) = G.V \cup \bigcup_{\psi \in G.\Psi} \bigcup_{\gamma \in \psi.\Gamma} V_l(\gamma) \qquad (1)$$

As defined by Equation (1), the set of leaves $V_l(G)$ of graph G shown in Figure 1 computes to $V_l(G) = \{P_A, P_C\} \cup \{\gamma_{D1}.P_D^1, \gamma_{D2}.P_D^2, \gamma_{D3}.P_D^3\} \cup \{\gamma_{U1}.P_U^1, \gamma_{U2}.P_U^2\}$.

So far, we only considered the behavioral part of the specification. For implementation, we also require information about the possible structure of our system, i.e., the underlying architecture. This leads to a graphical model for embedded system specification, the so called *specification graph* $G_S = (G_P, G_A, E_M)$. It mainly consists of three components: a *problem graph*, an *architecture graph*, and *user-defined mapping* edges (see also [1]). The respective graphs G_P and G_A are based on the concept of hierarchical graphs as defined in Def. 3.

Problem Graph. The *problem graph* G_P is a directed hierarchical graph $G_P = (V_P, E_P, \Psi_P, \Gamma_P)$ for modeling the required system's behavior (see Fig. 1). Vertices $v \in V_P$ and interfaces $\psi \in \Psi_P$ represent processes or communication operations at system-level. The edges $e \in E_P$ model dependence relations, i.e., define a partial ordering among the operations. The clusters $\gamma \in \Gamma_P$ are possible substitutions for the interfaces $\psi \in \Psi_P$.

Architecture Graph. The class of possible architectures is modeled by a directed hierarchical graph $G_A = (V_A, E_A, \Psi_A, \Gamma_A)$, called *architecture graph*. Functional or communication resources are represented by vertices $v \in V_A$ and interfaces $\psi \in \Psi_A$, interconnections are specified by the edges $e \in E_A$. Again, the clusters $\gamma \in \Gamma_A$ represent potential implementations of the associated interfaces. All the resources are viewed as potentially allocatable components.

---

[1] The $G.V$ notation is used as decomposition operation, e.g., to access the set of vertices V inside the graph G.

Mapping Edges. *Mapping edges* $e \in E_M$ indicate user-defined constraints in the form of a "can be implemented by"-relation. These edges link leaves $V_l(G_P)$ of the problem graph G_P with leaves $V_l(G_A)$ of the architecture graph G_A.

Additional parameters, like priorities, power consumption, latencies, etc., which are used for formulating implementational and functional constraints, are annotated to the components of G_S. For simplicity, a specification graph can also be represented only by its vertices and edges: $G_S = (V_S, E_S)$. The set of vertices V_S covers all non-hierarchical vertices, interfaces, and clusters contained in the problem or architecture graph. The set of edges E_S consists of all edges and port mappings in the specification graph.

An example of a specification graph is shown in Figure 2. Again, the problem graph specifies the behavior of our digital TV decoder. The architecture graph is depicted on the right. It is composed of a μ-Controller (μP), an ASIC (A), and an FPGA. There are two busses C_1 and C_2 to handle the communication between the μ-Controller and FPGA and ASIC, respectively. Figure 2 also shows the allocation cost for each resource in the architecture graph.

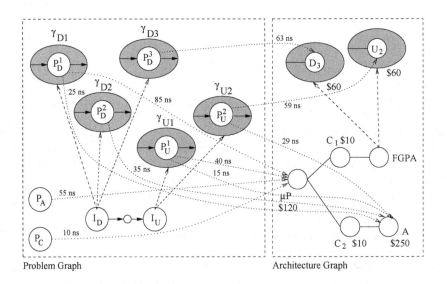

Problem Graph   Architecture Graph

Fig. 2. Hierarchical Specification Graph

The mapping edges (dotted edges in Fig. 2) outline the possible bindings of processes of the problem graph to resources of the architecture graph. The latencies to execute a given process on a specific resource are annotated to the respective mapping edges. For example, the uncompression process P_U^1 is executable on resource μP with a latency of 40 ns or on resource A with a latency of 15 ns.

As shown in Figure 2, the hierarchical specification graph permits modeling of adaptive systems by interchanging clusters in the problem graph. In our example, we have to select a certain decryption and uncompression process to match the requirements imposed by the TV station. Generally, an adaptive system responds to environmental changes by selecting clusters according to the requirements of input/output data at runtime. Therefore, clusters with various parameters or perhaps totally different functionality are activated in the problem graph. On the other hand, interchanging clusters in the architecture graph modifies the structure of the system. If this cluster-selection is performed at runtime, the architecture model characterizes reconfigurable hardware. For example, in order to execute process P_D^3, we have to configure the FPGA with the respective design D_3 (see Figure 2).

In order to specify an *implementation*, i.e., a concrete mapping, Blickle et al. [1] introduce the concept of *activation* of vertices and edges. The activation of a specification graph's vertex or edge describes its use in the implementation. Since we use hierarchical graphs, we have to define *hierarchical timed activation* or, for short, *hierarchical activation*:

Definition 4 (hierarchical activation). *The* hierarchical activation *of a specification graph* $G_S = (V_S, E_S)$ *is a function* $a : \{V_S \cup E_S\} \times T \to \{0,1\}$ *that assigns to each edge* $e \in E_S$ *and to each vertex* $v \in V_S$ *the value 1 (activated) or 0 (not activated) at time* $t \in T (= \mathbb{R})$.

Hierarchical activation should support synthesis in such a way that no infeasible implementations are caused by the following rules. Here we summarize the *hierarchical activation rules*:

1. The activation of an interface at time t implies the activation of exactly one associated cluster at the same time:

$$a(\psi, t) = \begin{cases} 1 \text{ if } t \in T^1 \\ 0 \text{ if } t \in T^0 \end{cases} \Leftrightarrow \sum_{\gamma \in \psi.\Gamma} a(\gamma, t) = \begin{cases} 1 \text{ if } t \in T^1 \\ 0 \text{ if } t \in T^0 \end{cases} \quad (2)$$

2. The activation of a cluster γ at time t activates all embedded vertices and edges in γ:

$$a(\gamma, t) = \begin{cases} 1 \text{ if } t \in T^1 \\ 0 \text{ if } t \in T^0 \end{cases} \Leftrightarrow \forall x \in \{\gamma.V \cup \gamma.\Psi\} : a(x, t) = \begin{cases} 1 \text{ if } t \in T^1 \\ 0 \text{ if } t \in T^0 \end{cases} \quad (3)$$

3. Each activated edge $e \in E_S$ has to start and to end at an activated vertex. This must hold for all times $t \in T$:

$$a(e, t) = \begin{cases} \{0, 1\} \text{ if } & a(v_i, t) = a(v_j, t) = 1 \\ 0 & \text{else} \end{cases} \quad (4)$$

4. Due to (perhaps implied) timing constraints, the activation of all top-level vertices and interfaces in the problem graph G_P is required, i.e., $\forall t \in T :$ $a(G_P, t) = 1$.

For a given selection of clusters, the hierarchical model can be flattened. With the formalism of hierarchical activation rules, we are able to determine the overall activation of the specification graph. The result is a non-hierarchical specification.

With the definition of hierarchical activation, we formally define the term *implementation*, where a feasible implementation consists of a feasible *allocation* and a corresponding feasible *binding*.

Definition 5 (timed allocation). *A* timed allocation $\alpha(t)$ *of a specification graph* G_S *is the subset of all activated vertices and edges of the problem and architecture graph at time t, i.e.,*

$$\alpha(t) \ = \alpha_V(t) \cup \alpha_E(t)$$
$$\alpha_V(t) = \{v \in \{V_l(G_P) \cup V_l(G_A)\} \mid a(v,t) = 1\}$$
$$\alpha_E(t) = \{e \in E_S \backslash E_M \mid a(e,t) = 1\}.$$

$\alpha_V(t)$ denotes the set of activated leaves in the specification graph at time t. $\alpha_E(t)$ is the set of activated edges in the problem and architecture graph at time t.

Definition 6 (timed binding). *A* timed binding $\beta(t)$ *is the subset of all activated mapping edges at time t, i.e.,*

$$\beta(t) = \{e \in E_M \mid a(e,t) = 1\}.$$

In order to restrict the combinatorial search space, it is useful to determine the set of feasible timed allocations and feasible timed bindings.

Definition 7 (feasible timed binding). *Given a specification graph* G_S *and a timed allocation* $\alpha(t)$, *a feasible timed binding is a timed binding* $\beta(t)$ *that satisfies the following requirements:*

1. *Each activated edge* $e \in \beta(t)$ *starts and ends at a vertex, activated at time t, i.e.,*
$$\forall e = (v, \tilde{v}) \in \beta(t) : v, \tilde{v} \in \alpha(t)$$

2. *For each activated leaf* $v \in \{V_l(G_P) \cap \alpha(t)\}$ *of the problem graph* G_P, *exactly one outgoing edge* $E \in E_M$ *is activated at time t, i.e.,*
$$|\{e \in \beta(t) \mid e = (v, \tilde{v}), v \in \{V_l(G_P) \cap$$
$$\alpha(t)\} \wedge \tilde{v} \in V_l(G_A)\}| = 1$$

3. *For each activated edge* $e = (v_i, v_j) \in E_P \cap \alpha_E(t)$:
   - *either both operations are mapped onto the same vertex, i.e.,*
   $$\tilde{v}_i = \tilde{v}_j \quad with \quad (v_i, \tilde{v}_i), (v_j, \tilde{v}_j) \in \beta(t),$$
   - *or there exists an activated edge* $\tilde{e} = (\tilde{v}_i, \tilde{v}_j) \in \{E_A \cap \alpha_E(t)\}$ *to handle the communication associated with edge e, i.e.,*
   $$(\tilde{v}_i, \tilde{v}_j) \in \{E_A \cap \alpha_E(t)\}$$
   $$with \quad (v_i, \tilde{v}_i), (v_j, \tilde{v}_j) \in \beta(t).$$

Definition 8 (feasible timed allocation). *A feasible timed allocation is a timed allocation $\alpha(t)$ that allows at least one feasible timed binding $\beta(t)$ for all times t.*

In Figure 2, an infeasible binding would be caused by binding decryption process P_D^2 onto the ASIC A and the uncompression process P_U^1 onto the FPGA. Since no bus connects the ASIC and the FPGA, there is no way to establish the communication between these processes.

Note that our hierarchical model extends the specification model proposed in [1] by two important features:

1. modeling of alternative refinements in the problem graph (behavior) as well as in the architecture graph (structure)
2. time-variant allocations and bindings.

These major extensions are necessary to model flexibility (reconfigurability) of the behavior (architecture).

With the hierarchical refinements, one has to know exactly what happens if a cluster's execution is interrupted by its own displacement. The request for interchanging clusters while in execution can cause two possible reactions (see also [4]):

1. *safe termination* ensures that a subsystem terminates in a known state without information about the time needed for this.
2. *explicit kill* immediately starts the interchanging process by ignoring the state of computation of a subsystem.

In both cases, the system may become unpredictable. In the following, we neglect the impact of reconfiguration times, context switches, etc.

So far, we have not accounted for system performance. Whether or not the implementation meets the application's performance requirements in terms of throughput (e. g. frames per second) and latencies, depends on the existence of a *feasible schedule*. Although it is possible to schedule any feasible implementation as defined above, the resulting schedule may fail performance requirements. Such scheduling or performance analysis is complex, especially for distributed systems, and is not the scope of this paper. Thus, we do not include a complete analysis in the exploration in Section 4. Rather, we quickly estimate the processor utilization and use the 69% limit as defined in [5] to accept or reject implementations due to performance reasons.

3   Definition of Flexibility

With the hierarchical specification model described above, we are able to quantify the amount of implemented functionality. Subsequently, we denote this objective *flexibility*.

For example, consider the problem graph G_P shown in Figure 3. This graph is an extension of the TV decoder example in Figure 1. Here, our goal is to design a Set-Top box family which supports multiple applications. Besides the already known digital TV decoder, there are two more possible applications:

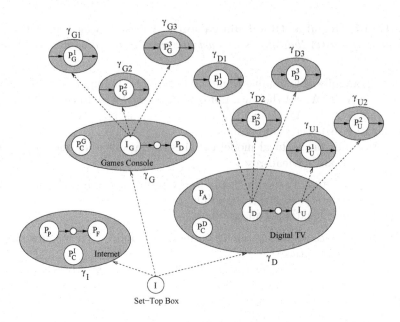

Fig. 3. Example for System's Flexibility

1. An Internet browser, consisting of a controller process P_C^I, parser process P_P for parsing HTML pages and a formatter process P_F for formatting the output.
2. A game console, modeled by a controller process P_C^G, the game's core interface I_G, and the graphics accelerator P_D. The game's core interface can be refined by three different game classes denoted P_G^1, P_G^2, and P_G^3 in Fig. 3. Since the output is constrained to a minimal frame period and the graphic accelerator depends on data produced by the game core process, also the game's core process has to obey some timing constraints.

It should be clear that implementing only one of the three possible applications results in an inflexible system. Furthermore, implementing a digital TV decoder with a great number of decryption algorithms (supported TV stations) is desirable.

So, the basic idea, as stated here, is to enumerate the possible interchanges of implementing clusters in the whole system's problem graph. For example, the flexibility of a trivial system with just one activated interface directly increases with the number of activatable clusters.

The key concepts of *flexibility* are as follows:

– Since each cluster represents an alternative for the same functionality, we know that implementing more clusters for a given interface increases system flexibility in the sense that the system may switch at runtime to select a different cluster.

– A cluster itself can contain interfaces, which can be implemented with different degrees of flexibility.
– Although flexibility depends on the implementation, we neglect the impact of the underlying architecture on flexibility, e.g., we do not distinguish whether the flexibility of a system is obtained by the use of either reconfigurable or dedicated hardware components.

With these assumptions, flexibility can be defined as follows:

Definition 9 (flexibility). *The flexibility f_{impl} of a given cluster γ is expressed as:*

$$f_{\text{impl}}(\gamma) = a^+(\gamma) \cdot \begin{cases} \left[\sum_{\psi \in \gamma.\Psi} \sum_{\hat{\gamma} \in \psi.\Gamma} f_{\text{impl}}(\hat{\gamma})\right] \\ -(|\gamma.\Psi| - 1) \quad \text{for} \quad \gamma.\Psi \neq \emptyset \\ 1 \qquad\qquad\qquad\quad \text{otherwise} \end{cases}$$

where the term $a^+(\gamma)$ describes the activation of the cluster γ in the future. If cluster γ will be selected at any time in the future then $a^+(\gamma) = 1$. Otherwise $a^+(\gamma) = 0$, meaning it will not be implemented at all.

In other words: The flexibility of a cluster γ, if ever activated, is calculated by the sum of all its interfaces' flexibilities minus the number of its interfaces less 1, and 1 if there is no interface in the given cluster. The flexibility of an interface is the sum of flexibilities of all its associated clusters. If a cluster will never be activated, its flexibility is 0.

The flexibility $f(G_{\text{P}})$ of this problem graph shown in Figure 3 is computed as follows:

$$\begin{aligned} f(G_{\text{P}}) &= a^+(G_{\text{P}}) \cdot [f(\gamma_{\text{I}}) + f(\gamma_{\text{G}}) + f(\gamma_{\text{D}})] \\ &= a^+(G_{\text{P}}) \cdot [a^+(\gamma_{\text{I}}) + a^+(\gamma_{\text{G}}) \cdot [a^+(\gamma_{\text{G1}}) + \\ &\quad a^+(\gamma_{\text{G2}}) + a^+(\gamma_{\text{G3}})] + a^+(\gamma_{\text{D}}) \cdot \\ &\quad [a^+(\gamma_{\text{D1}}) + a^+(\gamma_{\text{D2}}) + a^+(\gamma_{\text{D3}}) + \\ &\quad a^+(\gamma_{\text{U1}}) + a^+(\gamma_{\text{U2}}) - 1]] \end{aligned}$$

Based on this equation, the system's flexibility is obtained by specifying the utilization of each cluster γ in the future, denoted by $a^+(\gamma)$. If all clusters can be activated in future implementations, system's flexibility calculates to $f(G_{\text{P}}) = 8$. This is also the maximal flexibility $f_{\max}$. If, e.g., cluster γ_{G} is not used in future implementations the flexibility will decrease to $f(G_{\text{P}}) = 5$.

For the sake of simplicity, we have omitted the architecture graph and the mapping edges. Obviously, a cluster only contributes to the total flexibility if it is bindable as per Def. 7. A more sophisticated definition of flexibility can established by using weighted sums in Definition 9. The weight associated with each cluster shows the cluster's inherent functionality.

4   Design Space Exploration

Because of the accepted use of tools on lower design levels of abstraction, exploration becomes the next step in order to prevent under- or over-designing

a system. Typically, a system has to meet many constraints and should optimize many different design objectives and constraints simultaneously such as
execution time, cost, area, power consumption, weight, etc.

A single solution that optimizes all objectives simultaneously is very unlikely
to exist. Instead, it should be possible to first explore different optimal solutions
or approximations, and subsequently select and refine one of those solutions.

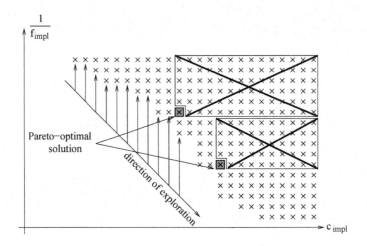

Fig. 4. Flexibility/Cost-Design Space

4.1   The Flexibility/Cost-Design-Space and the Optimization Goal

In this paper, we consider the two objectives *flexibility* $f_{\text{impl}}(\alpha(t))$, as described
in Section 3, and *cost* $c_{\text{impl}}(\alpha(t))$. Here we use the so-called *allocation cost model*
$c_{\text{impl}}(\alpha(t))$, where $c_{\text{impl}}(\alpha(t))$ is the sum of all realization cost of resources in the
allocation $\alpha(t)$.

Figure 4 shows a typical tradeoff-curve between cost and the reciprocal value
of flexibility. As already mentioned we are concerned with a MOP (Multiob-
jective Optimization Problem). Our MOP consists of two objective functions
$c_{\text{impl}}(\alpha(t))$ and $\frac{1}{f_{\text{impl}}(\alpha(t))}$, where the parameter $\alpha(t)$ is the decision vector. The
optimization goal is to minimize $c_{\text{impl}}(\alpha(t))$ and $\frac{1}{f_{\text{impl}}(\alpha(t))}$ simultaneously, i.e.,
to maximize system's flexibility for minimal cost implementations.

Definition 10 (feasible set). *Let allocation $\alpha(t)$ denote our decision vector.
The* feasible set $\mathbf{X}_f$ *is defined as the set of allocations $\alpha(t)$ that satisfy the
definition for feasible allocation (Def. 8) for all times $t \in T$.*

Definition 11 (Pareto-optimality). *For any two decision vectors $\mathbf{a}(t), \mathbf{b}(t) \in$
$\mathbf{X}_f$, $\mathbf{a}(t)$ dominates $\mathbf{b}(t)$ iff* $\left(c_{\text{impl}}(\mathbf{a}(t)) < c_{\text{impl}}(\mathbf{b}(t)) \wedge \frac{1}{f_{\text{impl}}(\mathbf{a}(t))} \leq \frac{1}{f_{\text{impl}}(\mathbf{b}(t))} \right) \vee$

$\left(c_{\mathrm{impl}}(\mathbf{a}(t)) \leq c_{\mathrm{impl}}(\mathbf{b}(t)) \wedge \frac{1}{f_{\mathrm{impl}}(\mathbf{a}(t))} < \frac{1}{f_{\mathrm{impl}}(\mathbf{b}(t))} \right)$. *A decision vector* $\mathbf{x}(t) \in \mathbf{X}_f$
is said to be non-dominated *with respect to a set* $\mathbf{A} \subseteq \mathbf{X}_f$ *iff* $\nexists \mathbf{a}(t) \in \mathbf{A} : \mathbf{a}(t)$
dominates $\mathbf{x}(t)$. *Moreover,* $\mathbf{x}(t)$ *is said to be* Pareto-optimal *iff* $\mathbf{x}(t)$ *is non-dominated regarding* $\mathbf{X}$ *(see also [6]).*

Figure 4 shows two Pareto-optimal design points. The goal of design space exploration is to find *all* Pareto-optimal design points that also fulfill all timing requirements. The points in Figure 4 represent possible solutions, where not every solution has to be feasible in the sense of Def. 7, and not every feasible solution has to meet the timing requirements. If we have found a Pareto-optimal solution x that meets all requirements, the class of all design points dominated by x can be pruned. This is shown in Figure 4 by boxes. In the following, we will introduce an algorithm for efficiently exploring flexibility/cost-tradeoff-curves.

4.2   The Exploration Algorithm

Figure 4 shows the general distribution of design points. At this stage, we do not distinguish between feasible and non-feasible solutions. Our objective is to find all Pareto-optimal solutions that meet all timing constraints. At a glance, a good strategy for design space exploration is to investigate each design point at the front, where we use the order of increasing implementation cost (direction of exploration). If a point represents an infeasible implementation or it misses some performance requirements, we discard it and pick up the next one on the front.

The problem of this idea is, that the set of possible implementations is unknown. A possible modification of this strategy would be to determine all points in advance, i.e., to determine all possible $2^{|V_S|}$ activations. Since binding is a NP-complete problem (see [1]), this exhaustive search approach seems not to be a viable solution.

To avoid superfluous computation of non-Pareto-optimal solutions, we propose two methods for search space reduction:

1. **Possible Resource Allocations.** A *possible resource allocation* is a partial allocation of resources in the architecture graph which allows the implementation of *at least one* feasible problem graph activation by neglecting the feasibility of binding first. Usually, we have to investigate all $2^{|V_S|}$ design points. But only the elements covering a possible resource allocation represent meaningful activations in the sense that at least a required minimum of problem graph vertices is bindable.
2. **Flexibility Estimation.** With the possible resource allocations we are able to sort the remaining design points by increasing cost. If we inspect the elements of this sorted list by increasing cost, a new calculated solution is Pareto-optimal, iff it possesses a greater flexibility than each solution that has been already implemented, as defined in Def. 11.

As shown in our case study (see Section 5), by using these two techniques, we dramatically reduce the invocations of the solver for the NP-complete binding problem.

With our approach of hierarchical specification and activations, we are able to first determine the set of possible resource allocations: For each vertex v_i inside a given cluster γ_j, we determine the set R_{ij} of reachable resources. A resource r is reachable if a mapping edge between v_i and r exists. Derived from the hierarchical activation rules, only leaves $v \in G_A.V$ of the top-level architecture graph or whole clusters of the architecture graph are considered. Next, we set up the outer conjunction R_j of all power sets $2^{R_{ij}}$. Consequently, the set R_j describes *all* combinations of resource activations for implementing the non-hierarchical vertices $v \in \gamma_j.V$ of cluster γ_j by ignoring the feasibility of binding.

Finally, we have to inspect all hierarchical components $\gamma_j.\Psi$ of cluster γ_j. Since all clusters associated with an interface $\psi \in \gamma_j.\Psi$ represent alternative refinements of ψ, we compute the union of possible resource allocations for the associated clusters.

The elements of the resulting set are the possible resource allocations, which we sort by increasing implementation cost. The algorithm PRA to determine this set of **P**ossible **R**esource **A**llocations $\mathcal{A}(\gamma)$ for a given cluster γ is listed below:

PRA
    IN: specification graph G_S
    IN: current cluster γ_{cur}
    OUT: set of possible resource allocations $\mathcal{A}$
    BEGIN
      $\mathcal{A} = \emptyset$
      FOR each vertex $v \in \gamma_{\mathrm{cur}}.V$ DO
        $\mathcal{A}_v = \{v_a \mid (v_i, v_a) \in E_M \wedge v_a \in V_A\}$
        $\mathcal{A}_\gamma = \{\gamma_a \mid (v, v_a) \in E_M \wedge v_a \in \gamma_a.V\}$
        $\mathcal{A} = \mathcal{A} \times 2^{\mathcal{A}_v \cup \mathcal{A}_\gamma} \backslash \epsilon$
      ENDFOR
      FOR each interface $\psi \in \gamma_{\mathrm{cur}}.\Psi$ DO
        $\mathcal{X} = \emptyset$
        FOR each cluster $\gamma \in \psi.\Gamma$ DO
          $\mathcal{X} = \mathcal{X} \cup$ PRA(γ)
        ENDFOR
        $\mathcal{A} = \mathcal{A} \times \{2^{\mathcal{X}} \backslash \epsilon\}$
      ENDFOR
    END

Here, ϵ denotes the element representing the empty set $\{\emptyset\}$. For example, the set $\mathcal{A}$ of possible resource allocations for the specification given in Figure 2 computes to:

$$\mathcal{A} = \{\mu P, \mu PC_1, \mu PC_2, \mu PC_1 C_2, \mu PD_3, \mu PU_2,$$
$$\mu PC_1 D_3, \mu PC_2 D_3, \mu PC_1 U_2, \mu PC_2 U_2,$$
$$\mu PC_1 C_2 D_3, \dots, \mu PC_1 C_2 D_1 U_2 A\}$$

The elements of the ordered set of possible resource allocations are inspected in ascending order of their allocation cost c_{impl} (see Fig. 4). For each possible resource allocation, we remove all resources that are not activated from the architecture graph G_A. By removing these elements, also mapping edges are removed from the specification graph. Next, we delete all vertices in the problem graph with no incident mapping edge. This results in a reduced specification graph.

In order to avoid superfluous computation of non-Pareto-optimal solutions, we use a lower bound to restrict our search space: With Definition 9, the maximal flexibility f_{max} of the reduced specification graph can be calculated. Since we explore flexibility/cost-objective-space by increasing cost (see Figure 4), we are only interested in design points with a greater flexibility than already implemented. So we use the already maximal implemented flexibility as lower bound for pruning the search space. With the known maximal implemented flexibility, we therefore may skip specifications with a lower implementable flexibility. Only for specifications with greater expected flexibility, we try to construct a feasible implementation next.

Generally, more than one activatable cluster for a problem graph's interface remains in the specification graph. Consequently, we have to identify so-called *elementary cluster-activations*, which are defined as follows. Let Γ_{act} denote the set of activatable clusters which is computed by traversing the problem graph and checking the existing of at least one mapping edge per leaf. Only if all leaves are incident to at least one mapping edge, the cluster is meant to be activatable. An elementary cluster-activation ecs is a set $ecs = \{\gamma_i \mid \gamma_i \in \Gamma_{act}\}$, where exactly one cluster is selected per activated interface. Since every activatable cluster has to be part of the implementation to obtain the expected flexibility, we have to determine a coverage [7] of Γ_{act} by elementary cluster-activations.

Given an elementary cluster-activation, we can select these clusters for implementation. Furthermore, we must determine valid cluster activations in the architecture graph, e.g., it is possible that two problem graph clusters are mapped on different configurations of the same FPGA. So, we have to guarantee that each elementary cluster-activation can be bound to a non-ambiguous architecture, i.e., there is exactly one activated cluster for every activated interface in the architecture graph, e.g., one activated configuration for an FPGA.

Finally, we validate all timing constraints that are imposed on our implementation. Here, we use a statistical analysis method to check for fulfillment. Only if a new calculated implementation

1. is feasible as defined in Def. 7,
2. possesses a greater flexibility as already implemented, and
3. obeys all performance constraints,

it is Pareto-optimal.

With these basic ideas of pruning the search space, we formulate our exploration algorithm based on a branch-and-bound strategy [7,8]. For the sake of clarity, we omit details for calculating a coverage of activatable problem graph clusters or successive flexibility estimation, etc. The following code should be self-explanatory with the previous comments.

<u>EXPLORE</u>
    IN: specification graph G_S
    OUT: Pareto-optimal set $\mathcal{O}$
    BEGIN
        $f_{cur} = 0$
        $\mathcal{A} = G_S$.possibleResourceAllocations()
        $f_{max} = G_S$.computeMaximumFlexibility()
        FOR each candidate $a \in \mathcal{A}$ DO
            $f = a$.computeMaximumFlexibility()
            WHILE $f_{cur} < f_{max}$ THEN
                $\alpha = G_S$.computeAllocation(a)
                $\beta = G_S$.computeBinding(α)
                $i = $ new Implementation(α, β)
                IF i.isFeasibleImplementation() THEN
                    IF i.meetsAllConstraints() THEN
                        IF i.flexibility() $> f_{cur}$ THEN
                            $\mathcal{O} = \mathcal{O} \cup i$
                            $f_{cur} = i$.flexibility()
                        ENDIF
                    ENDIF
                ENDIF
            ENDWHILE
        ENDFOR
    END

In the worst case, this algorithm is not better than an exhaustive search algorithm. But, a typical search space with 10^5-10^{12} design points can be reduced by the EXPLORE-algorithm to a few 10^3-10^4 possible resource allocations. Since we only try to implement design points with a greater expected flexibility than the already implemented flexibility, again, only a small fraction of these point has to be taken into account, typically less than 100.

5   Case Study

In our case study we investigate the specification of our Set-Top box depicted in Figure 5. Again, we increased the complexity of our example. The architecture graph is now composed of two processors (μP_1 and μP_2), three ASICs (A_1 to A_3), and an FPGA. The ASICs are used to improve performance for the decryption, uncompression, game's core, and graphic acceleration processes. The FPGA can also be used as coprocessor for the third decryption, the second uncompression, or the first game core class. The allocation cost of each component are annotated in Fig. 5.

In Figure 5, we have omitted the mapping edges. Possible mappings and respective core execution times are given in Table 1. Furthermore, we assume that all communications can be performed on every resource. No latencies for

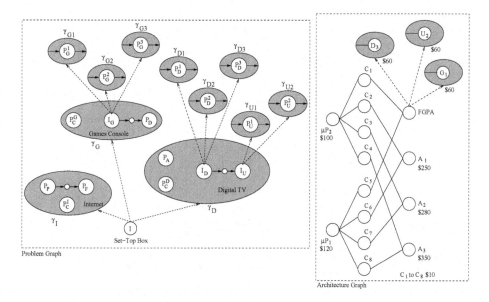

Fig. 5. Specification of a Set-Top Box

external communications are taken into account. Timing constraints for the game console and digital TV are given by the minimal periods of the output processes (P_D, P_U^1, and P_U^2). P_D has to be executed every 240 ns. The output for the digital TV box is less restrictive: P_U^1 and P_U^2 should be executed at least every 300 ns if activated.

As described above, our algorithm starts with the determination of the set of all possible resource allocations. Here, elements that are obviously not Pareto-optimal or no feasible implementations are left out, e. g., all combinations of a single functional component and an arbitrary number of communication resources. The beginning of the ordered subset $\mathcal{A}$ of possible resource allocations is given by:

$$\begin{aligned}
\mathcal{A} = \{&\mu P_2, \mu P_1, \mu P_2 D_3 C_1, \mu P_2 U_2 C_1, \mu P_2 G_1 C_1, \\
&\mu P_1 D_3 C_5, \mu P_1 U_2 C_5, \mu P_1 G_1 C_5, \mu P_2 D_3 U_2 C_1, \\
&\mu P_2 D_3 G_1 C_1, \mu P_2 U_2 G_1 C_1, \mu P_1 D_3 U_2 C_5, \\
&\mu P_1 D_3 G_1 C_5, \mu P_1 U_2 G_1 C_5, \mu P_1 \mu P_2, \ldots\}
\end{aligned}$$

Next, we determine all elementary cluster activations that can be activated under the given resource allocation. For the first resource allocation (μP_2), we find the elementary cluster activations γ_I, γ_{G1}, and $\gamma_{D1}\gamma_{U1}$. The estimated flexibility as defined by Def. 9 calculates to $f_{impl} = 3$. Since our already implemented flexibility is 0 (there is no feasible implementation yet), we try to find feasible implementations for the given elementary cluster activations. With Figure 5 and Table 1, we are able to find a feasible allocation and binding for all elementary cluster activations.

Table 1. Possible Mappings in Figure 5

Process	μP_1	μP_2	A_1	A_2	A_3	D3	U2	G1
P_C^1	$10ns$	$12ns$	-	-	-	-	-	-
P_P	$15ns$	$19ns$	-	-	-	-	-	-
P_F	$50ns$	$75ns$	-	-	-	-	-	-
P_C^G	$25ns$	$27ns$	-	-	-	-	-	-
P_G^1	$75ns$	$95ns$	$15ns$	$15ns$	$15ns$	-	-	$20ns$
P_G^2	-	-	$25ns$	$22ns$	$22ns$	-	-	-
P_G^3	-	-	$50ns$	$45ns$	$35ns$	-	-	-
P_D	$70ns$	$90ns$	$30ns$	$30ns$	$25ns$	-	-	-
P_C^D	$10ns$	$10ns$	-	-	-	-	-	-
P_A	$55ns$	$60ns$	-	-	-	-	-	-
P_D^1	$85ns$	$95ns$	$25ns$	$22ns$	$22ns$	-	-	-
P_D^2	-	-	$35ns$	$33ns$	$32ns$	-	-	-
P_D^3	-	-	-	-	-	$63ns$	-	-
P_U^1	$40ns$	$45ns$	$15ns$	$12ns$	$10ns$	-	-	-
P_U^2	-	-	$29ns$	$27ns$	$22ns$	-	$59ns$	-

Next, we have to check all timing constraints. Therefore, we define a maximal processor utilization of 69%. If the estimated utilization exceeds this upper bound, we reject the implementation as infeasible. Since the Internet browser need not meet any timing constraints, this particular implementation is indeed feasible.

For the validation of the digital TV application, we need some more information. As we know the timing constraint imposed on the uncompression and the decryption process, we only need information about how often the authentification and controller processes are executed. The execution of the authentification is scheduled once at system start up. Statistically, the controller process makes up about 0.01% of all process calls in the digital TV application. So, we neglect the authentification and controller process in our estimation. For fulfillment of the performance constraint, the sum of the core execution times of process P_D^1 and P_U^1 ($95ns + 45ns$) must be less than $0.69 \cdot 300ns$. Evidently, this constraint is met.

Unfortunately, we have to reject the implementation of the application of the game console violating the upper utilization bound ($95ns + 90ns \not\leq 0.69 \cdot 240ns$). So our implemented flexibility calculates to $f_{\text{impl}} = 2$ which is still greater than the already implemented flexibility.

Now, we continue with the next possible resource allocation, i.e., μP_1. Due to space limitations, we only present the results. The set of Pareto-optimal solutions for this example is shown in Table 2. At the beginning, our search space consisted of 2^{25} design points. By calculating the set of possible resource allocations, this design space was reduced to 2^{14} design points. That is, by traversing our specification graph and setting up one boolean equation we are able to reject about 99.9% of our design points as non-Pareto-optimal. After investigating approx. 7000 design points, we have found all 6 Pareto-optimal solutions. For

Table 2. Pareto-Optimal Solutions

Resources	Clusters	c	f
μP_2	γ_I, γ_{D1}, γ_{U1}	\$100	2
μP_1	γ_I, γ_{G1}, γ_{D1}, γ_{U1}	\$120	3
μP_2, G_1, U_2, C_1	γ_I, γ_{G1}, γ_{D1}, γ_{U1}, γ_{U2}	\$230	4
μP_2, D_3, G_1, U_2, C_1	γ_I, γ_{G1}, γ_{D1}, γ_{D3}, γ_{U1}, γ_{U2}	\$290	5
μP_2, A_1, C_2	γ_I, γ_{G1}, γ_{G2}, γ_{G3}, γ_{D1}, γ_{D2}, γ_{U1}, γ_{U2}	\$360	7
μP_2, A_1, D_3, C_1, C_2	γ_I, γ_{G1}, γ_{G2}, γ_{G3}, γ_{D1}, γ_{D2}, γ_{D3}, γ_{U1}, γ_{U2}	\$430	8

these design points, we estimated the implementable flexibility by solving a single boolean equation. In only approx. 1050 cases (0.0032% of the original search space) the estimated flexibility was greater than the already implemented flexibility. Only for these points, we needed to try to construct an implementation. Hence, our exploration algorithm typically prunes the search space so much that industrial size applications can be efficiently explored within minutes.

Conclusions and Future Work

Based on the concept of hierarchical graphs, we have introduced a formal definition of system flexibility. Furthermore, an algorithm for exploring the flexibility/cost design space was presented. Due to the underlying branch-and-bound strategy, we are able to prune about 99.9% of a typical search space, while still finding all Pareto-optimal implementations. Hence, industrial size applications can be explored efficiently.

In the future, we would like to extend the proposed approach by an exact scheduling method to check performance constraints. In [9], first results in scheduling hierarchical dataflow graphs are presented.

References

1. Blickle, T., Teich, J., Thiele, L.: System-Level Synthesis Using Evolutionary Algorithms. In Gupta, R., ed.: Design Automation for Embedded Systems. Number 3. Kluwer Academic Publishers, Boston (1998) 23–62
2. Cadence: Virtual Component Co-design (VCC). (2001) http://www.cadence.com.
3. Chatha, K.S., Vemuri, R.: MAGELLAN: Multiway Hardware-Software Partitioning and Scheduling for Latency Minimization of Hierarchical Control-Dataflow Task Graphs. In: Proc. CODES'01, Ninth International Symposium on Hardware/Software Codesign, Copenhagen, Denmark (2001)
4. Richter, K., Ziegenbein, D., Ernst, R., Thiele, L., Teich, J.: Representation of Function Variants for Embedded System Optimization and Synthesis. In: Proc. 36th Design Automation Conference (DAC'99), New Orleans, U.S.A. (1999)

5. Liu, C.L., Layland, J.W.: Scheduling Algorithm for Multiprogramming in a Hard-Real-Time Environment. Journal of the ACM **20** (1973) 46–61
6. Pareto, V.: Cours d'Économie Politique. Volume 1. F. Rouge & Cie., Lausanne, Switzerland (1896)
7. Hachtel, G.D., Somenzi, F.: Logic Synthesis and Verification Algorithms. 2 edn. Kluwer Academic Publishers, Norwell, Massachusetts 02061 USA (1998)
8. Micheli, G.D.: Synthesis and Opimization of Digital Circuits. McGraw-Hill, Inc., New York (1994)
9. Bhattacharya, B., Bhattacharyya, S.: Quasi-static Scheduling of Reconfigurable Dataflow Graphs for DSP Systems. In: Proc. of the International Conference on Rapid System Prototyping, Paris, France (2000) 84–89

Towards Efficient Design Space Exploration of Heterogeneous Embedded Media Systems

A.D. Pimentel, S. Polstra, F. Terpstra, A.W. van Halderen,
J.E. Coffland, and L.O. Hertzberger

Dept. of Computer Science, University of Amsterdam
Kruislaan 403, 1098 SJ Amsterdam, The Netherlands
{andy,spolstra,ftrpstra,berry,jcofflan,bob}@science.uva.nl

Abstract. Modern signal processing and multimedia embedded systems increasingly have heterogeneous system architectures. In these systems, programmable processors provide flexibility to support multiple applications, while dedicated hardware blocks provide high performance for time-critical application tasks. The heterogeneity of these embedded systems and the varying demands of their growing number of target applications greatly complicate the system design.

As part of the Artemis project, we are developing a modeling and simulation environment which aims at efficient design space exploration of heterogeneous embedded systems architectures. In this paper, we present an overview of the modeling and simulation methodology used in Artemis. Moreover, using a case study in which we have applied an initial version of our prototype modeling and simulation environment to an M-JPEG encoding application, we illustrate the ease with which alternative candidate architectures can be modeled and evaluated.

1 Introduction

Modern embedded systems, like those for media and signal processing, increasingly need to be multifunctional and must support multiple standards. A high degree of *programmability*, which can be provided by applying microprocessor technology as well as reconfigurable hardware, is key to the development of such advanced embedded systems. However, performance requirements and constraints on cost and power consumption still require substantial parts of these systems to be implemented in dedicated hardware blocks. As a result, modern embedded systems often have a *heterogeneous system architecture*, i.e., they consist of components in the range from fully programmable processor cores to dedicated hardware components for the time-critical application tasks. Increasingly, such heterogeneous systems are integrated on a single chip. This yields heterogeneous multi-processor systems-on-a-chip (*SoCs*) that exploit task-level parallelism in applications.

For these modern embedded systems, it becomes more and more important to have good tools available for exploring different design choices at an early stage in the design. This is because the heterogeneity of the embedded systems and the varying demands of their target applications greatly complicate the system design, which already affects the very first design decisions. Common simulation practice for the design space exploration of heterogeneous embedded systems architectures is unable to cope with this increase in

E.F. Deprettere et al. (Eds.): SAMOS 2001, LNCS 2268, pp. 57–73, 2002.

complexity and is especially becoming unsuited for the early design stages. Designers typically use only relatively detailed, often cycle-accurate, simulators for design space exploration of embedded systems architectures. For complex embedded systems, the effort required to build such detailed simulators can be high, making it impractical to use those simulators in early design stages. Moreover, their low simulation speeds significantly hamper the architectural exploration.

In the scope of the Artemis (ARchitectures and meThods for Embedded MedIa Systems) project [17], we are developing an architecture workbench which provides modeling and simulation methods and tools for the efficient design space exploration of heterogeneous embedded multimedia systems [16]. This architecture workbench should allow for rapid evaluation of different architecture designs, application to architecture mappings, and hardware/software partitionings and it should do so at multiple levels of abstraction *and* for a wide range of multimedia applications. By allowing simulation at multiple abstraction levels, the speed, required modeling effort, and attainable accuracy of the architecture simulations can be controlled. This enables a stepwise refinement approach in which abstract simulation models are used to efficiently explore the large design space in the early design stages, while in a later stage more detailed models can be applied for focused architectural exploration.

Another important requirement for our architecture design space exploration environment is that it should be open to reuse of intellectual property, thereby allowing for reducing the time-to-market of products. For example, simulation models of architecture components, such as microprocessors, busses and memories, must be reusable with relative ease. This calls for a high degree of modularity when building system architecture models and, as we show later on, a clear separation between specifying application behavior and architectural performance constraints.

In this paper, we present an overview of the modeling and simulation methodology used in Artemis and the open research problems it addresses. Using a case study with an M-JPEG encoding application we illustrate the ease with which different architectural design choices can be evaluated at a high level of abstraction. To this end, we have used an initial version of our prototype modeling and simulation environment, called Sesame, to evaluate three alternative multi-processor target architectures with different memory interconnects.

The next section describes how Artemis relates to other efforts in the field of simulation of embedded systems architectures. In Section 3, we describe the modeling and simulation methodology applied in Artemis. In Section 4, the Sesame modeling and simulation environment is described. Section 5 presents the case study with an M-JPEG application and Section 6 concludes the paper.

2   The Limitations of Traditional Co-simulation

System architecture modeling and simulation of heterogeneous systems is a relatively new research field which has received a lot of attention in recent years. The key concept in most efforts in this field is *co-simulation*. Like its name already suggests, co-simulation implies that the software parts (which will be mapped onto a programmable processor) and the hardware components and their interactions are simulated together in one simulation [18]. Traditional co-simulation frameworks (e.g., Seamless VCE [11], Virtual CPU [2], and the work of [7,4]) often combine two simulators, one for simulating the programmable components running the software and one for the dedicated hardware. For software simulation, instruction-level processor simulators, host code execution or bus-functional processor models [18] are typically used. To simulate the hardware components, HDLs such as VHDL are a popular choice.

A major drawback of such co-simulation is its inflexibility: because an explicit distinction is made between software and hardware simulation, it must already be known which application components will be performed in software and which ones in hardware before the system model is built. This significantly complicates the performance evaluation of different hardware/software partitionings since a whole new system model may be required for the assessment of each partitioning. For this reason, the co-simulation stage is often preceded by a stage in which the application is studied in isolation by means of a functional (behavioral) software model written in a high level language. This typically results in rough estimations of the application's performance requirements, which are subsequently used as guidance for the hardware/software partitioning. In that case, the co-simulation stage is mainly used as verification of the chosen hardware/software partitioning and not as a design space exploration vehicle.

A number of exploration environments, such as VCC [1], Polis [3] and eArchitect [2], facilitate more flexible system-level design space exploration by providing support for mapping a behavioral application specification to an architecture specification. However, in contrast to these efforts, Artemis pushes the separation of modeling application behavior and modeling architectural constraints at the system level to its extremes. As will be shown in the next section, such separation leads to efficient exploration of different design alternatives while also yielding a high degree of reusability.

3   Modeling and Simulation Methodology

We strongly believe that for the design of programmable embedded systems a clear distinction should be made between *applications* and *architectures*, and that an explicit *mapping* step must be supported. This permits multiple target applications to be mapped one after the other onto candidate architectures for evaluation of their performance. This approach is referred to as the *Y-chart* of system design [10,3]. Typically, the designer studies the target applications, makes some initial calculations, and proposes an architecture. The performance of this architecture is then quantitatively evaluated and compared against alternative architectures. For such performance analysis, each application is mapped onto the architecture under investigation and the performance of each application-architecture combination is evaluated. Subsequently, the resulting performance numbers may inspire the designer to improve the architecture, restructure the application(s) or modify the mapping of the application(s).

The Artemis modeling and simulation environment facilitates the performance analysis of embedded systems architectures in a way that directly reflects the Y-chart design approach: Separate application and architecture models are recognized for system simulation. An *application model* describes the functional behavior of an application, including both computation and communication behavior. The *architecture model* defines architecture resources and captures their performance constraints. Essential in this modeling methodology is that an application model is independent from architectural specifics, assumptions on hardware/software partitioning, and timing characteristics. As a result, a single application model can be used to exercise different hardware/software partitionings and can be mapped onto a range of architecture models, possibly representing different system architectures or simply modeling the same system architecture at various levels of abstraction. This clearly demonstrates the strength of decoupling application models and architecture models: it enables the *reuse* of *both* types of models. After mapping, an application model is co-simulated with an architecture model allowing for evaluation of the system performance of a particular application, mapping, and underlying architecture.

3.1 Trace-Driven Co-simulation

To co-simulate application models and architecture models, an interface between the two must be provided, including a specification of the mapping. For this purpose, we apply trace-driven simulation. In our approach, the application model is structured as a network of *concurrent communicating processes*, thereby expressing the inherent task-level parallelism available in the application and making communication explicit. Each process, when executed, produces a trace of events which represents the application workload imposed on the architecture by that particular process. Thus, the trace events refer to the computation and communication operations performed by an application process. These operations may be coarse grain, such as "*compute a Discrete Cosine Transform (DCT)*".

Since application models represent the functional behavior of applications, the traces correctly reflect data dependent behavior. Consequently, the architecture models, which are driven by the application traces, do not need to represent functional behavior but only need to account for the performance consequences of the application events.

3.2 Application Modeling

For modeling of applications, we use the Kahn Process Network (KPN) model of computation [9]. To obtain a Kahn application model, a sequential application (written in a high-level language) is restructured into a program consisting of parallel processes communicating with each other via unbounded FIFO channels. In the Kahn paradigm, reading from channels is done in a blocking manner, while writing is non-blocking.

The computational behavior of an application can be captured by instrumenting the code of each Kahn process with *annotations* which describe the application's computational actions. The reading from or writing to Kahn channels represents the communication behavior of a process within the application model. By executing the Kahn model, each process records its actions in order to generate a trace of application events, which is necessary for driving an architecture model.

In the field of application modeling, a lot of research has been done on models of computation (e.g., [6]). We decided to use KPNs for application modeling because they fit nicely with the multimedia application domain and are deterministic. The latter means that the same application input always results in the same application output, i.e., the application behavior is architecture independent. This automatically guarantees the validity of event traces when the application and architecture simulators are executed independently of each other [8]. However, because of the semantics of KPNs which disallow, for example, the modeling of interrupts, we are currently not able to model applications with time dependent behavior.

A beneficial side effect of using a separate application model is that it also makes it possible to analyze the computational/communication needs and the potential performance constraints of an application in isolation from any architecture. This can be a benefit as it allows for investigation of the upper bounds of the performance and may lead to early recognition of bottlenecks within the application itself.

3.3   Architecture Modeling

A model of an architecture is based on components representing (co)processors, memories, buffers, busses, and so on. A performance evaluation of an architecture can be achieved by simulating the performance consequences of the incoming computation and communication events from an application model. This requires an explicit mapping of the processes and channels of a Kahn application model onto the components of the architecture model. The generated trace of application events from a specific Kahn process is routed towards a specific component inside the architecture model by using a trace-event queue. The Kahn process dispatches its application events to this queue while the designated component in the architecture model consumes them. This is illustrated in Figure 1. Mapping the FIFO channels between Kahn processes (shown by the dashed arrows) defines which communication medium at the architecture level is used for the data exchanges. In Figure 1, one application channel stays unmapped since both its application tasks are mapped onto the same processing component. Mapping the trace-event queues from multiple Kahn processes onto a single architecture component occurs when, for example, several application tasks are executed on a microprocessor. In this case, the events from the different queues need to be scheduled.

We reiterate that the underlying architecture model solely accounts for architectural (performance) constraints and therefore does not need to model functional behavior. This is possible because the functional behavior is already captured in the application model, which subsequently drives the architecture simulation. An architecture model is constructed from generic building blocks provided by a library. This library contains performance models for processing cores, communication media (like busses) and different types of memory. Evidently, such a library-based modeling approach greatly simplifies the reuse of architecture model components.

At a high level of abstraction, the model of a processing core is a *black box* which can model timing behavior of a programmable processor, a reconfigurable component or a dedicated hardware unit. Modeling such a variety of architectural implementations is accomplished by the fact that the architecture simulator assigns parameterizable latencies to the incoming application events. For example, to model software execution of an application event, a relatively high latency can be assigned to the event. Likewise, to model the application event being executed by dedicated or reconfigurable hardware one only needs to tag the event with a lower latency. So, by simply varying the latencies for computational application events, different hardware/software partitionings can rapidly

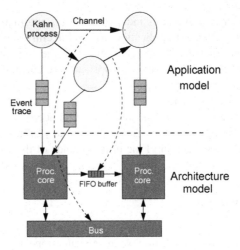

Fig. 1. Mapping a Kahn application model onto an architecture model.

be evaluated at a high level of abstraction. The latencies themselves can be obtained either from a lower level model of an architecture component, from performance estimation tools, or they can be estimated by an experienced designer.

In this approach, the communication events from the application model are used for modeling the performance consequences of data transfers and synchronizations at the architecture level. These events cause the appropriate communication component within the architecture model (onto which the communicating Kahn channel is mapped) to account for the latencies associated with the data transfers. Unlike in the application model where all FIFO channels are unbounded, writes at the architecture level may also be blocking dependent on the availability of resources (e.g., buffer space).

As design decisions, such as hardware/software partitioning, are made, components of the architecture model may be refined. This implies that the architecture model starts to reflect the characteristics of a particular implementation (e.g., dedicated versus programmable hardware). To facilitate the process of model refinement, the architecture model library should include models of common architecture components at several levels of abstraction. For example, there may be multiple instances of a microprocessor model such as a black box model, a model which accounts for the performance consequences of the processor's memory hierarchy (e.g., translation lookaside buffers and caches), and a model which accounts for the performance impact of both its memory hierarchy and datapath (e.g., pipelining and instruction-level parallelism). Moreover, to support architecture model refinement, events from the application model should also be refined to match the level of detail present in the architecture model. Providing flexible support for such event refinement is still largely an open problem [13,5].

The process of model refinement may continue to the level at which detailed simulators for certain architecture components, e.g., instruction-level simulators or Register Transfer Level (RTL) simulators, are embedded into the overall system architecture simulation. For instance, consider the example in which it is decided that a certain application task will be implemented in software. In that case, instead of using an abstract architecture model of a processor core onto which the Kahn process in question is mapped, a detailed instruction-level simulator can be used which emulates the actual code of the application task. The process of embedding more detailed simulators can be continued such that more and more functionality is gradually incorporated into an architecture model. In the end, the architecture model can then be used as a starting point for more traditional hardware/software co-simulation composed of instruction-level simulators and RTL simulators.

4   The Sesame Modeling and Simulation Environment

For the development of the Artemis architecture modeling and simulation environment, we currently are developing and experimenting with two prototype simulation frameworks: *Spade* (System-level Performance Analysis and Design space Exploration) [14] and *Sesame* (Simulation of Embedded System Architectures for Multi-level Exploration) [20]. Both frameworks act as technology drivers in the sense that they allow for testing and evaluating new simulation models and simulation methods to gain insight into their suitability for the Artemis modeling and simulation environment. Only those simulation models and simulation methods that have proven to be effective will be incorporated in Artemis. In this paper, we limit our discussion to Sesame only.

The Sesame framework aims at studying the potentials of simulation at multiple levels of abstraction and the concepts needed to refine simulation models across different abstraction levels in a smooth manner. For example, refinement of one component in an architecture model should not lead to a completely new implementation of the entire model. This means that the modeling concepts being studied should also include support for refining only parts of an architecture model, thus creating a *mixed-level simulation model*. The resulting mixed-level simulations allow for more detailed evaluation of a specific architecture component within the context of the behavior of the whole system. They therefore avoid the need for building a complete detailed architecture model during the early design stages. Moreover, mixed-level simulations do not suffer from deteriorated system evaluation efficiency caused by unnecessarily refined parts of the architecture model.

Sesame currently only provides a library of black box architecture models. In the near future, the library will be extended with models for architecture components at several levels of abstraction in order to facilitate the performance evaluation of architectures from the black box level towards the level of cycle-accurate models. This library will eventually be supplemented with techniques and tools to assist the modeler in gradually refining the models and performing mixed-level simulations. Currently, these issues are still largely open research problems.

The architecture models in Sesame are implemented using a small but powerful discrete-event simulation language, called Pearl, which provides easy construction of the models and fast simulation [15]. Evidently, these characteristics greatly improve the scope of the design space that can be explored in a reasonable amount of time. The architecture library components in Sesame are not meant to be fixed building blocks with pre-defined interfaces but merely template models which can be freely extended

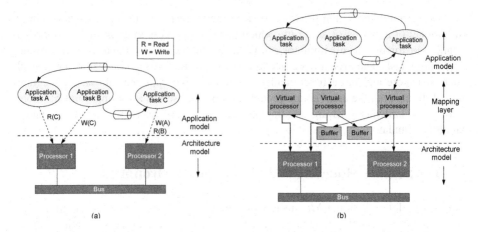

Fig. 2. Figure (a) shows a potential deadlock situation due to scheduling of communication events. The Sesame solution, using virtual processors, is illustrated in Figure (b).

and adapted. With this approach, a high degree of flexibility is achieved (which can be helpful when refining models) at the cost of a slightly increased effort required to build architecture models. This effort will however still be relatively small due to the modeling ease provided by Pearl.

As we have described, multiple Kahn processes of the application model can be mapped onto a single processing component in the architecture model. In this case, the incoming event traces need to be scheduled. Scheduling of communication events is, however, not straightforward as it may cause deadlocks. Such a situation is illustrated in Figure 2(a). In this example, Kahn process A reads data from Kahn process C, Kahn process B writes data for process C and Kahn process C first reads the data from B after which it writes the data for A. Since Kahn processes A and B are mapped onto a single processor, their read and write events need to be scheduled. Assume that the read event from Kahn process A is dispatched first to processor 1. Processor 2 receives the read event from Kahn process C. In this case, a deadlock occurs since both dispatched read events cannot be carried out as there are no matching write events. As a result, the processors block.

In Figure 2(b), Sesame's solution to the above problem is depicted. Between the application and architecture layers, we distinguish an extra mapping layer. This mapping layer, which is implemented in the Pearl language and which can be automatically generated from an application model, consists of virtual processor components and FIFO buffers for communication between the virtual processors. A virtual processor reads in an application trace from a Kahn process and dispatches the events to a processing component in the architecture model. The mapping of a virtual processor onto a processing component in the architecture model is parameterized and thus freely adjustable. The FIFO buffers in the mapping layer have a one-to-one relationship with the FIFO channels in the Kahn application model but they are limited in size. Their size is parameterized and dependent on the modeled architecture.

As can be seen from Figure 2(b), multiple virtual processors can be mapped onto a single model of an actual processor. In this scheme, computation events are directly forwarded by a virtual processor to the processor model. The latter subsequently schedules the events in a FCFS fashion and models their timing consequences. However, for communication events, the appropriate buffer at the mapping layer is first consulted to check whether or not a communication is safe to take place. Only if it is found to be safe (e.g., data is available when performing a read event), then communication events may be forwarded to the actual processor model.

5 The M-JPEG* Case Study

To demonstrate the flexibility of modeling in Sesame we have applied its current version to a modified M-JPEG encoding application, referred to as M-JPEG*. This application has already been studied in the scope of the Spade environment [12,19], which demonstrated that the modeling and simulation methodology of Artemis facilitates efficient evaluation of different application to architecture mappings and hardware/software partitionings. In this section, we use the Sesame environment to show the capability to quickly evaluate different architecture designs.

The M-JPEG* application slightly differs from traditional M-JPEG as it can operate on video data in both YUV and RGB formats on a per-frame basis. In addition, it includes dynamic quality control by means of on-the-fly generation of quantization and Huffman tables. The application model of M-JPEG* is shown in Figure 3.

The data received in the Video-in Kahn process, which is either in RGB or YUV format, is sent to the DMUX in blocks of 8 × 8 pixels. The DMUX first determines the format and then forwards data from RGB frames to the RGB2YUV converter process, while YUV data is sent directly to the DCT Kahn process. Once the data has been transformed by the DCT process the blocks are quantized by the Q Kahn process. The next step, performed by the VLE process, is the variable length encoding of the quantized DCT coefficients followed by entropy encoding, such as Huffman encoding. Finally, the resulting bitstream is sent to the Video-out process.

In M-JPEG*, the tables for Huffman encoding[1] and those required for quantization are generated for each frame in the video stream. The quality control process (Q-Control) computes the tables from information gathered about the previous video frame. For this purpose, image statistics and obtained compression bitrate are transmitted by the VLE to the Q-Control Kahn process. When the calculations by the Q-Control process are finished, updated tables are sent to both the Q and VLE Kahn processes.

5.1 The Base Architecture and Mapping

The base M-JPEG* target architecture has five processing components connected via a common bus to a shared memory. In Figure 3, this architecture is shown together with the mapping of the M-JPEG* application onto it. Of the five processing components

---

[1] In M-JPEG*, we assume that Huffman encoding is the default entropy encoding scheme.

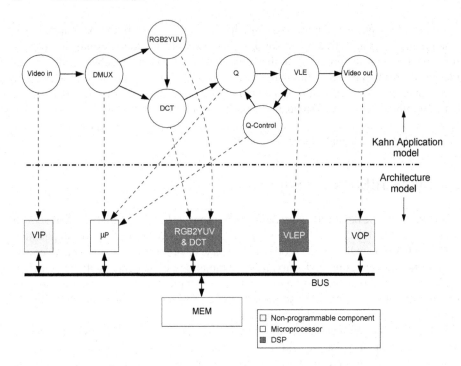

Fig. 3. M-JPEG*'s application to architecture mapping

in the architecture, one is a general purpose microprocessor (assumed to be a MIPS R4000), two are DSPs (assuming Analog Devices' ADSP-21160s) and two are non-programmable components. The non-programmable components are used for input and output processing and are referred to as respectively the VIP (Video In Processor) and VOP (Video Out Processor). The two DSPs are used for computationally intensive tasks. One of them is used for RGB to YUV conversion and the DCT transform. We refer to this component as the RGB2YUV & DCT component. The other DSP is used for variable length encoding and is referred to as the VLEP. For the memory we assume DRAM, while the bus is assumed to be 64 bits wide. Communication between components is performed through buffers in shared memory. A detailed description of the M-JPEG* application, its application model, and the base architecture model can be found in [19].

To demonstrate the ease of modeling in Pearl (Sesame's simulation language), Figure 4 shows the Pearl code of the bus model for the M-JPEG* target architecture. This bus model simulates transactions at the granularity of message transfers of abstract data types. Extending this model to account for 64-bit transactions is trivial. As Pearl is an object-based language and architecture components are modeled by objects, the code shown in Figure 4 embodies the class of bus objects.

A bus object has two object variables, mem and setup. These variables are initialized at the beginning of the simulation, and more specifically, at the instantiation of a bus object. The mem variable references the memory object that is connected to the bus, while the setup time of a connection on the bus is specified by setup. A bus object has two

```
class bus

mem   : memory
setup : integer

load : (nbytes:integer, address:integer)->void
{
    blockt( setup );
    mem ! load(nbytes, address);
    reply();
}

// [ store method is omitted ]

{
  while(true) {
    block(load, store);
  };
}
```

Fig. 4. Pearl code for the common bus object.

methods: load and store. The store method is not shown here since it is identical to the load method. To explain how the load method works we first need to give some background on the blockt() function. Pearl is equipped with a virtual clock that holds the current simulation time. When an object wants to wait for an interval in simulated time it uses the blockt() function. In our example, the bus object uses the blockt() function to wait for setup time units in order to account for the connection setup latency. The statement "mem ! load(nbytes, address)" calls the load method of the memory object mem by sending it a synchronous message. Since it is synchronous the bus has to wait until the memory has explicitly returned a reply message. The latter is done by the reply() primitive. In our example, the synchronous message passing also causes the virtual clock to advance in time, because the memory object accounts for the time it takes to retrieve the requested data before replying to the bus. After having received a reply from the memory object, the bus itself executes a reply() to return control to one of the processor objects (which are connected to the bus object) that has called the load method. At the bottom of Figure 4 is the main loop of the object which does nothing until either the load or store method is called (by one of the processor objects).

In the bus model of the M-JPEG* case study, we have not explicitly modeled bus arbitration. Instead, we use Pearl's internal scheduling, which applies a FCFS strategy to incoming method calls for the bus object. We note, however, that an arbiter component which implements other strategies than FCFS can be added to the model with relative ease.

In the Pearl language, the instantiation of objects and the specification of the connections between objects are done using a so-called *topology file*. In Sesame, this file is also used for specifying the mapping of the incoming application traces from the Kahn model to the components in the architecture model. Figure 5 shows the topology file for the M-JPEG* base architecture and mapping as shown in Figure 3. For the purpose of brevity, we left out a number buffer specifications. The first column of the topology file contains the names of the objects that need to be instantiated, while after the colon

```
commonbus() {
    vidin   : virt_proc(6,2,[header,buf1],vip)
    rgbyuv  : virt_proc(4,2,[buf2,buf3],rgbdct)
    dct     : virt_proc(1,4,[buf3,xx,type,buf4],rgbdct)
    dmux    : virt_proc(2,7,[header,buf1,fsize,buf2,xx,type,numof],mp)
    quant   : virt_proc(3,4,[buf4,qtable,qcmd,buf5],mp)
    control : virt_proc(0,7,[numof,stats,qtable,qcmd,hcmd,htable,info],mp)
    vle     : virt_proc(5,6,[buf5,hcmd,htable,stats,flag,stream],vlep)
    vidout  : virt_proc(7,4,[fsize,flag,info,stream],vop)
    vip     : processor(bus,10,[0,0,20,0,0,0,0,0,0])
    rgbdct  : processor(bus,10,[0,200,0,0,0,0,0,192,0,0])
    mp      : processor(bus,10,[180,0,0,0,154,1,23,0,2,154])
    vlep    : processor(bus,10,[0,0,0,0,154,0,0,0,0,154])
    vop     : processor(bus,10,[0,0,0,20,0,0,0,0,0,0])
    header  : buffer(1,    7, 1)
    info    : buffer(1,  672, 2)
    qtable  : buffer(1,  128, 2)
    qcmd    : buffer(0,    1, 150)
    hcmd    : buffer(0,    1, 150)
    htable  : buffer(1, 1536, 2)
    stats   : buffer(1,  514, 1)
        [ ... ]
    bus     : bus(mem, 1)
    mem     : memory(10,8)
}
```

Fig. 5. Topology definition for the M-JPEG* simulation: this shows how Pearl objects are instantiated and connected.

the object class is specified. Together with this class-name, a number of parameters are specified. The different classes and their parameters are explained below.

- The `virt_proc` class implements the virtual processor components as described in Section 4. This class has four parameters of which the first one is an identifier used for identifying the event trace queue to read from. The second one gives the number of FIFO buffers connected to a `virt_proc` object, after which these FIFO buffers are specified in an array. The last parameter defines to which actual processor a virtual processor is linked: this is the application to architecture mapping.
- The `processor` class has three parameters. The first one describes to which memory interconnect it is connected. The second parameter gives the size of the instruction set, being the different application events for which the timing behavior needs to be modeled. This is followed by the latencies of each of these instructions. By adapting these latencies, one can easily change the speed of a processor.
- The `buffer` class has three parameters. The first one specifies whether communication is performed over the interconnect or internally. When a buffer connects two virtual processors which are mapped onto the same (actual) processor, communication is assumed to be performed internally. When the two virtual processors are mapped on different processors, communication is performed through shared memory, resulting in bus traffic. The second parameter of the `buffer` class specifies the size of the tokens in the buffer while the third parameter specifies the maximum number of these tokens that can be in the buffer at one time.
- The `bus` class has two parameters. The first one specifies the memory it is connected to and the second one defines the time for setting up a connection.

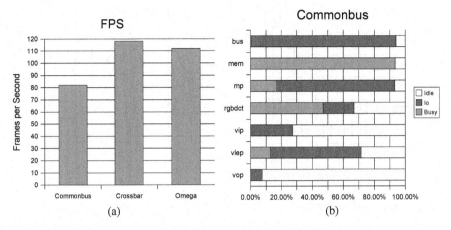

Fig. 6. Fig. (a) shows the measured frames per second for all three interconnects. Fig. (b) depicts a breakdown for the common bus showing busy/io/idle statistics for all architecture components.

- The memory class takes two parameters. The first specifies the delay for reading or writing one word and the second specifies the width in bytes of the memory interconnect it is attached to.

Obviously, the topology file allows for easy configuration of a Pearl simulation. It is simply a matter of changing a few numbers to change the application architecture mapping or to change the characteristics of a processor. For example, replacing a DSP for a dedicated hardware component in our M-JPEG* base architecture model can be achieved by reducing the instruction latencies of the processor object in question.

5.2 Design Space Exploration

To illustrate that Sesame and its Pearl simulation language facilitate efficient evaluation of different candidate architectures, we have performed an experiment [20] in which we modeled, simulated and briefly studied two alternative communication structures for the M-JPEG* architecture: a crossbar and an Omega network. To avoid confusion, the original M-JPEG* architecture will be referred to as the common bus architecture.

In our experiments, the input video stream consists of images captured in a resolution of 128 × 128 pixels with RGB color encoding. For the architecture, we have assumed conservative timings: The bus-arbitration overhead when a request (at the level of abstract data types) is granted access to the bus equals to 10ns, while it takes 100ns to read/write a 64-bit word from/to DRAM. The instruction latencies for the microprocessor and DSP components were estimated using technical documentation. Figure 6(a) shows the simulation results in terms of the measured number of frames per second for all three candidate architectures (using a common bus, crossbar or Omega network). Below, the results for each of the communication structures are explained in more detail.

In Figure 6(b), a description is given of the activities of the various architecture components during simulation of the common bus architecture. For each component, a bar shows the breakdown of the time each component spends on I/O, being busy and

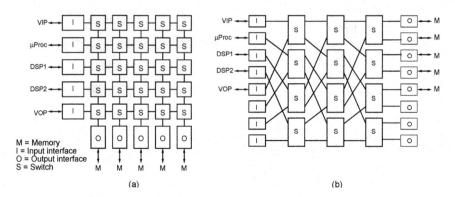

Fig. 7. The crossbar (a) and Omega (b) memory interconnects used in our experiments.

being idle. As Figure 6(b) shows, the common bus architecture has a high memory utilization while the various processors have low utilization and spend a lot of time doing I/O. Figure 6(a) shows that the common bus architecture obtains a framerate of 82 frames per second. While this is more than enough for real time operation, this is for a low resolution. Such performance is roughly equivalent to only 3 frames per second in full resolution PAL television (720×576). The common bus interface to the memory is clearly a bottleneck and therefore a candidate for further exploration. Similar conclusions about the M-JPEG* architecture were drawn from experiments using the Spade environment [12].

To reduce the communication bottleneck of our M-JPEG* architecture, we have implemented a Pearl simulation model of a 5×5 crossbar switch, shown in Figure 7(a), and replaced the common bus model in M-JPEG* with this crossbar model. The memory in this architecture is distributed over five banks. Therefore, a mapping of buffers to memories is defined in the topology file. This mapping is, like the application to architecture mapping, easy to configure. In our crossbar model, the delay to set up a connection is identical to the bus-arbitration delay in the common bus model (10ns).

As the results in Figure 6(a) show, there is a substantial gain in frames per second compared with the common bus. When we look at the architecture component statistics in Figure 8(a) we see that all the components spend more time doing work and less time waiting for I/O. Since the memory load is now divided over five memories, the memory utilization is at about 20% for most memories. Note that memory 5 is still busy for almost 80% of the time. The reason for this is that one buffer takes 53% of memory bandwidth. This buffer contains the statistics needed for the (re)calculation of the Huffman and quantization tables. For every block of image data in the M-JPEG* application, these statistics are sent from the VLE process to the Q-control process.

As an alternative to the crossbar we have also modeled the Omega network as shown in Figure 7(b). The main difference is that the crossbar is a single-stage network whereas the Omega network is a multi-stage network. This means that the Omega network does not provide a direct connection between a processor and the memory, and thus requires routing. The Omega network is generally cheaper to implement than a crossbar because it has less switches, but the setup of a connection costs more (we account for a setup

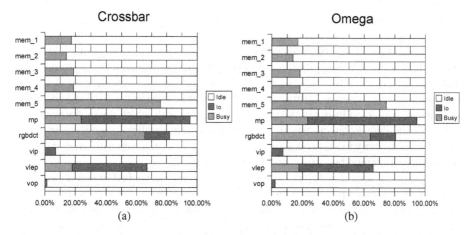

Fig. 8. Results for the crossbar (a) and Omega network (b) showing busy/io/idle statistics for all architecture components.

latency of 10ns per hop) and connections may be blocking. The latter means that it is not always possible to connect an idle input to an idle output.

The results in Figure 6(a) show that the Omega network is about 5% slower than a crossbar. Detailed statistics show that the processing cores spend a little more time waiting for I/O compared to the crossbar, leading to a slightly lower utilization. This is, however, hardly noticeable in Figure 8(b). So, when considering both cost and performance, the Omega network might be the better choice for replacing the common bus. Nevertheless, the simulation results indicate that, with the applied (multi-processor) architecture and mapping, the performance is highly communication bound. Therefore, mapping more application tasks to a single processing component (thereby reducing communication) or reducing the memory latency will certainly lead to improvements, which has already been demonstrated in [12,19].

5.3   A Note on Modeling and Simulation Efficiency

Due to the simplicity and expressive power of Sesame's Pearl simulation language, modeling and simulating the three candidate architectures was performed in only a matter of days. This includes the construction of the crossbar and Omega network models, which had to be implemented from scratch, as well as the realization of a run-time visualization of the architecture simulations. Pearl is an object-based language, which means that we could exploit features such as "class sub-typing" to easily exchange the models for the different communication/memory architecture components. Making these models a sub-type of a generic interconnect type, the models could be replaced in a plug-and-play manner.

Models are not only constructed quickly in Pearl, but the actual simulation is also fast. For example, the simulation of M-JPEG* mapped onto the crossbar-based architecture takes just under 7 seconds. This was done on a 270Mhz Sun Ultra 5 Sparcstation with a video input stream of 16 frames of 128×128 pixels with RGB encoding.

6 Conclusions

In this paper, we have described a modeling and simulation methodology that allows for the efficient architectural exploration of heterogeneous embedded media systems. The presented methods and techniques are currently being realized in the Sesame modeling and simulation environment. Using an initial version of Sesame and an M-JPEG encoding application, we have illustrated the ease and swiftness with which the performance of different candidate architectures can be evaluated. More specifically, we have explored three shared-memory multi-processor target architectures, each with a different memory interconnect (common bus, crossbar and Omega network).

Research on Sesame will be continued along the lines described in this paper, with an emphasis on techniques for model refinement. In particular, the support for mixed-level simulation introduces many new research problems that need to be addressed. In addition, we intend to perform more case studies with industrially relevant applications to further demonstrate the effectiveness of the methods and tools we are developing.

Acknowledgments

This research is supported by PROGRESS, the embedded systems research program of the Dutch organization for Scientific Research NWO, the Dutch Ministry of Economic Affairs and the Technology Foundation STW. We thank Paul Lieverse, Todor Stefanov, Pieter van der Wolf and Ed Deprettere for their invaluable contributions to this work. In addition, we acknowledge Bart Kienhuis and Kees Vissers for their contribution to the modeling methodology.

References

1. Cadence Design Systems, Inc., http://www.cadence.com/.
2. Innoveda Inc., http://www.innoveda.com/.
3. F. Balarin, E. Sentovich, M. Chiodo, P. Giusto, H. Hsieh, B. Tabbara, A. Jurecska, L. Lavagno, C. Passerone, K. Suzuki, and A. Sangiovanni-Vincentelli. *Hardware-Software Co-design of Embedded Systems – The POLIS approach.* Kluwer Academic Publishers, 1997.
4. M. Bauer and W. Ecker. Hardware/software co-simulation in a VHDL-based test bench approach. In *Proc. of the Design Automation Conference*, 1997.
5. J.-Y. Brunel, E.A. de Kock, W.M. Kruijtzer, H.J.H.N. Kenter, and W.J.M. Smits. Communication refinement in video systems on chip. In *Proc. 7th Int. Workshop on Hardware/Software Codesign*, pages 142–146, May 1999.
6. J. Buck, S. Ha, E. A. Lee, and D. G. Messerschmitt. Ptolemy: A framework for simulating and prototyping heterogeneous systems. *Int. Journal of Computer Simulation*, 4:155–182, Apr. 1994.
7. S.L. Coumeri and D.E. Thomas. A simulation environment for hardware-software codesign. In *Proceedings of the Int. Conference on Computer Design*, pages 58–63, Oct. 1995.
8. M. Dubois, F.A. Briggs, I. Patil, and M. Balakrishnan. Trace-driven simulations of parallel and distributed algorithms in multiprocessors. In *Proc. of the Int. Conference in Parallel Processing*, pages 909–915, Aug. 1986.
9. G. Kahn. The semantics of a simple language for parallel programming. In *Proc. of the IFIP Congress 74*, 1974.

10. B. Kienhuis, E.F. Deprettere, K.A. Vissers, and P. van der Wolf. An approach for quanti-
    tative analysis of application-specific dataflow architectures. In *Proc. of the Int. Conf. on
    Application-specific Systems, Architectures and Processors*, July 1997.
11. R. Klein and S. Leef. New technology links hardware and software simulators. Electronic
    Engineering Times, June 1996. http://www.mentorg.com/seamless/.
12. P. Lieverse, T. Stefanov, P. van der Wolf, and E.F. Deprettere. System level design with spade:
    an M-JPEG case study. In *Proc. of the Int. Conference on Computer Aided Design*, November
    2001.
13. P. Lieverse, P. van der Wolf, and E.F. Deprettere. A trace transformation technique for com-
    munication refinement. In *Proc. of the 9th Int. Symposium on Hardware/Software Codesign*,
    pages 134–139, Apr. 2001.
14. P. Lieverse, P. van der Wolf, E.F. Deprettere, and K.A. Vissers. A methodology for architecture
    exploration of heterogeneous signal processing systems. *Journal of VLSI Signal Processing
    for Signal, Image and Video Technology*, 29(3):197–207, November 2001. Special issue on
    SiPS'99.
15. H.L. Muller. *Simulating computer architectures*. PhD thesis, Dept. of Computer Science,
    Univ. of Amsterdam, Feb. 1993.
16. A.D. Pimentel, P. Lieverse, P. van der Wolf, L.O. Hertzberger, and E.F. Deprettere. Exploring
    embedded-systems architectures with Artemis. *IEEE Computer*, 34(11):57–63, Nov. 2001.
17. A.D. Pimentel, P. van der Wolf, E.F. Deprettere, L.O. Hertzberger, J.T.J. van Eijndhoven, and
    S. Vassiliadis. The Artemis architecture workbench. In *Proc. of the Progress workshop on
    Embedded Systems*, pages 53–62, Oct. 2000.
18. J. Rowson. Hardware/software co-simulation. In *Proc. of the Design Automation Conference*,
    pages 439–440, 1994.
19. T. Stefanov, P. Lieverse, E.F. Deprettere, and P. van der Wolf. Y-chart based system level
    performance analysis: an M-JPEG case study. In *Proc. of the Progress workshop on Embedded
    Systems*, pages 113–124, Oct. 2000.
20. F. Terpstra, S. Polstra, A.D. Pimentel, and L.O. Hertzberger. Rapid evaluation of instantiations
    of embedded systems architectures: A case study. In *Proc. of the Progress workshop on
    Embedded Systems*, pages 251–260, Oct. 2001.

An Overview of Methodologies and Tools
in the Field of System-Level Design

Vladimir D. Živković[1] and Paul Lieverse[2]

[1] Leiden Institute of Advanced Computer Science (LIACS), Leiden University,
Niels Bohrweg 1, 2333 CA Leiden, the Netherlands
lale@liacs.nl
http://www.liacs.nl/~cserc/
[2] Delft University of Technology, Information Technology and Systems,
Delft, the Netherlands
lieverse@ieee.org

Abstract. In this paper we present an overview of system level design methodologies and tools. Eight tools and their underlying methodologies are analysed. We give a short description of each of them and point out some of their strengths and weaknesses. We conclude that there still is a lot of room for research on the design of embedded systems-on-a-chip, especially in the areas of mixed-level simulation, verification, and synthesis.

1 Introduction

The increasing interest in embedded systems has heightened the need for methodologies and tools suitable for modelling, simulation and design of embedded systems. We focus on heterogeneous embedded systems, i.e., those that mix programmable and dedicated components. These systems are of particular interest since they are used as underlying platforms in multimedia and communication-oriented products. In order to deal with the complexity of such systems, designers rely more and more on methodologies and tools that allow them to explore their designs at the system-level. In this document, we report on today's research in the area of system-level methodologies and tools for heterogeneous signal processing systems. We discuss eight tools and their underlying methodologies. Apart from a short description, we also point out some of their strengths and weaknesses. They are: Ptolemy, UC San Diego/NEC, POLIS, VCC, COSY, PAMELA, SystemC, and SPADE. Our choice of methodologies and tools was based on the availability of either the methodologies and tools or information about them.

This paper is organised as follows. First, we give some general remarks about directions in today's methodologies and tools in Section 2. Then we briefly describe each of the methodologies and tools in Sections 3 through 10. Finally, we draw some conclusions in Section 11.

E.F. Deprettere et al. (Eds.): SAMOS 2001, LNCS 2268, pp. 74–88, 2002.

2   General Observations

As we have indicated, modern embedded systems become increasingly complex and not easy to design. They typically have to meet real-time constraints, must be reliable and fault tolerant, and have a low power consumption. Designers have to verify each of these constraints in a model of an embedded system. Models become more accurate when more details are added. However, this also increases the time needed for system model development and simulation. In order to reduce the time needed for modelling and simulation, the evaluation of design choices should move to the early phases of the design process. This can be illustrated in terms of the abstraction pyramid [15] in Figure 1. The cost of model construction and model evaluation is higher at the more detailed levels of abstraction, while the opportunities to explore alternative realizations is significantly reduced at these levels. Therefore, methodologies to deal with the exploration of embedded systems at the system level are of interest.

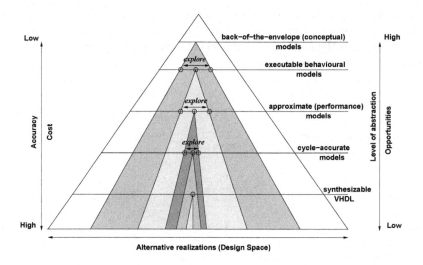

Fig. 1. The abstraction pyramid

In the past embedded system designers were almost exclusively operating at the VHDL level. In Figure 2 this is represented with the black dotted arrow. Skipping intermediate levels between high and low levels is only acceptable when a few low level parameters have to be explored. Otherwise, the lower levels are too detailed to explore larger design spaces. Indeed, the complexity of embedded systems grows constantly, and the design approach labelled as 'guru' in Figure 2 is no longer feasible for these complex system-on-a-chip designs. In order to cut time-to-market, embedded system design is now widely believed to benefit from a step-by-step design. This approach is represented by the white dotted arrow

in Figure 2. At each level the alternatives are explored before going to the next
level.

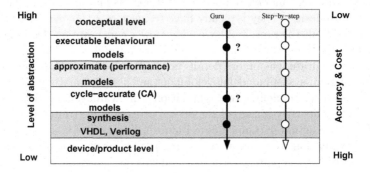

Fig. 2. Guru vs. Step-by-step approach

An interesting abstraction level is the approximate-accuracy level in Figure
1, otherwise known as time-approximate [13], or performance model level [11].
This level bridges the gap between models at behavioural or un-timed [13] level
and models at cycle-accurate level.

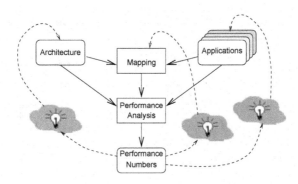

Fig. 3. The Y-chart [16]

Another approach to cut time-to-market is to allow reusability. The *Y-chart*
approach [15], [18] is a general scheme that uses reusability for an efficient design-
space exploration. It enables reuse by separating architecture and application
modelling. This approach is illustrated in Figure 3. The Y-chart approach permits multiple target applications to be mapped one after another onto candidate
architectures in order to evaluate performance. The resulting performance numbers may inspire an architecture designer to improve the architecture. The designer may also decide to restructure the application(s) or to modify the mapping
of the application(s).

Different methodologies have a different view on how application modelling and architecture modelling in Figure 3 can be performed. Some promote hardware/software co-design based on Models of Computation (MoC) ([4], [12]) and Models of Architecture (MoA) ([18], [2], [12]). Others do not distinguish between MoCs and MoAs but model both the application and the architecture with MoCs. Which MoC or combination of MoCs to chose depends on the nature of the application domain at hand. Many MoC choices are available: Communicating Sequential Processes (CSP), Continuous Time (CT), Discrete Events (DE), Distributed Discrete Events (DDE), Discrete Time (DT), Finite State Machines (FSM), Process Networks (PN), Synchronous Data Flow (SDF), and Synchronous/Reactive (SR) models, or a mixture of these models. While MoCs are well formalised, MoAs have not received that much attention. Architecture features, such as time, types of resources, and resource contention are not easily captured in the formalisms of a single MoC. Figure 4 illustrates how multiple MoCs could be used to model an architecture. In this figure, the application is modelled as a Kahn Process Network (KPN) [17], and the architecture, onto which the application is to be mapped, is modelled in terms of three MoCs: a KPN-like model (with blocking writes in addition to blocking reads), a CSP-like model (with *rendezvous*), and the FSM model. While the application model is homogeneous, the architecture model is not. One can say that both the application and the architecture are specified in terms of MoCs. However, one can also call the combination of MoCs for modelling the architecture a MoA.

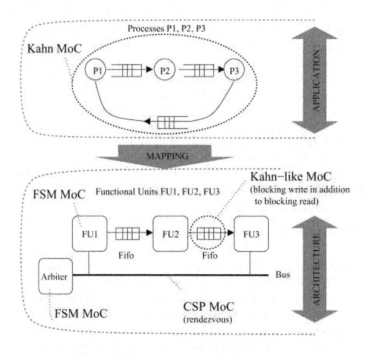

Fig. 4. MoA as an union of different MoCs

In the following sections we briefly present some of the available methodologies and tools in system-level design. A global overview is given for each methodology/tool, and the presence or absence of particular features is pinpointed.

3   Ptolemy

The Ptolemy framework provides methods and tools for the modelling, simulation, and design of complex computational systems [4]. It focuses on heterogeneous system design using MoCs for modelling both hardware and software. Important features are:

1. The ability to construct a single system model using multiple MoCs which are interoperable, and
2. The introduction of disciplined interactions between components, where each of them is governed by a MoC.

The interoperability between different MoCs is based on *domain polymorphism*, which means that components can interact with other components within a wide variety of domains (MoCs). Also, the Ptolemy methodology does not have the objective to describe existing interactions, but rather imposes structure on interactions that are being designed. Components do not need to have rigid interfaces, but they are designed to interact in a possible number of ways. Particularly, instead of verifying that a particular protocol in a single port-to-port interaction can not deadlock, Ptolemy tends to focus on whether an assemblage of components can deadlock. Designers are supposed to think about an overall pattern of interactions, and to trade off expressiveness for uniformity.

Ptolemy does not explicitly support the Y-chart approach, neither does it strictly separate application features and architecture features. There exists only a single implementation of a specified system, which is on top of a Java Virtual Machine. Also, it does not have a layered abstraction approach like, for example, VCC has (see Section 6). However, because of its excellent features, some projects that deal with deriving methodologies for system design use Ptolemy as a kernel for the implementation of a particular methodology into a tool-set. For example, an extension of the Ptolemy kernel in the direction of a Y-chart oriented tool for evaluation of architecture trade-offs, is described in [5].

4   UC San Diego/NEC Methodology

A design space exploration methodology of communication architectures is presented in [6]. The aim of the methodology is to obtain an optimal and automatic mapping of various communication mechanisms among system components onto a target communication architecture template. This is a sensible objective because the volume and diversity of data and control traffic exchanged among System-on-Chip (SoC) components imply that on-chip communication could have severe impediment to system performance and power consumption. What is needed, is SoC communication protocols that efficiently transport large volumes of heterogeneous communication traffic.

The methodology supports an efficient performance analysis of inter-component communication in a bus oriented system. It also supports accurate modelling of communication resources. The method assumes that a communication architecture template is given (see Figure 5), but communication protocols are not.

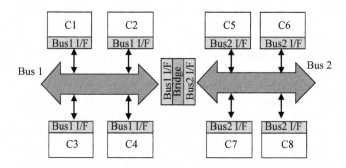

Fig. 5. Predetermined architecture topology in the methodology described in [6]

The methodology consists of two steps:

1. A constructive algorithm, that determines an initial architecture for mapping various SoC communications onto specific paths in a template communication topology.
2. An iterative improvement strategy, that generates optimised mappings, as well as carefully configured communication protocols.

In order to support accurate modelling of dynamic effects, e.g., resource contention, a trace-based approach is employed. First, all computational and communication events that originate from a hardware-software co-simulation of a specified system, are captured in traces. Second, these traces are converted into a communication analysis graph. This graph is the data-structure on which all algorithms used in the methodology are performed.

The methodology provides efficient performance analysis to drive the exploration algorithms of communication architectures. The resulting solutions are characterised by a significant improvement over the initial solutions. The methodology is narrowed to a particular architecture template, but it could be extended to more general architecture template. Also, it could be used as a source of ideas for extending more general methodologies that have problems with communication mapping and optimisation.

5   Polis

Polis is a design environment for *control-dominated* embedded systems [12]. It supports designers in the partitioning of a design and in the selection of a microcontroller and peripherals. It can generate C-code for the software part, including a simple Real-Time Operating System for the microcontroller, and HDL code for synthesis of hardware. It also provides an interface to verification and simulation tools, as well as an embedded (software) simulator.

The underlying MoC used for representation of applications in Polis is the Co-design Finite State Machines (CFSMs). A CFSM is a specialised FSM that incorporates the unbounded delay assumption: In a classic FSM, only the idle phase can have any duration between zero and infinity, the other phases have a duration of zero. The CFSM model can also be described as globally asynchronous/locally synchronous. A system is modelled as a network of interacting CFSMs communicating through events. The events are broadcasted to all connected CFSM.

A system specification is given either using a graphical FSM editor, or using the synchronous language Esterel. The specification is composed of separate modules. Each module is a CFSM. The analysis of a system at the behavioural level can be carried out either with formal tools or by simulation. In the latter case the Ptolemy simulation environment is used.

The Polis environment supports system partitioning by providing useful figures about the partitions. For example, for each module in the software partition, it provides estimations of the execution time and code size. For the hardware modules it gives the number of primary inputs and outputs and the number of latches.

Polis offers several options for simulation:

1. A basic CFSMs simulator that gives all signals and internal states, and that can track the sources of the signals,
2. A simulation of the software partition, where only external signals can be watched,
3. The Ptolemy DE[1] domain simulation of the software partition, and
4. A number of different output formats, such as behavioural VHDL, that can be used for simulation in other simulators.

On the other hand, Polis does not offer the following:

1. Representation of system specification in terms of any other MoC except CFSM,
2. Estimation techniques for more complex processor models, other than simple micro-controllers,
3. Non-dedicated type of communication among components, and
4. Multiple hardware and software partitions (there are only 2 partitions in Polis: one hardware and one software)

Items 1. and 2. imply that the POLIS system can not be used efficiently for designing embedded systems that are not control dominated.

---

[1] see Section 2

6   VCC – Virtual Component Co-design

The Cadence VCC (Virtual Component Co-design) toolset is built on top of the toolset in the Polis framework. The toolset is intended to support communication refinement. The VCC approach is illustrated in Figure 6. First, the functional behaviour of the entire system is captured and verified, thereby re-using elements from behavioural libraries and algorithmic fragments. Similarly, target architecture is captured by re-using existing architecture IP components (DSP cores, micro-controllers, buses, and RTOSs). The next step involves a manual mapping of behavioural functions and communication channels onto the appropriate architecture resources. The system is evaluated in terms of, e.g., speed, power consumption, and cost. This is a performance analysis step. Then, architecture, behaviour, and mapping for the given system specification are explored until an optimal solution is obtained. Finally, the target architecture is refined into a detailed hardware and/or software implementable architecture. The refined target architecture can be passed to external environments for hardware and software implementations. One important step which is not visible in Figure 6 is co-verification. Co-verification is performed between the architecture and the functional levels and is used for detecting timing problems and bugs.

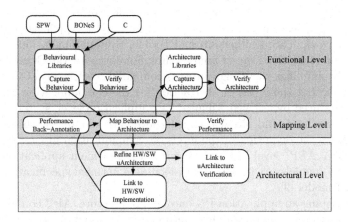

VCC by Cadence Design Systems

Fig. 6. POLIS/VCC related methodology [7]

VCC can be used together with SPW (Cadence's Signal Processing Worksystem) and BONeS (Cadence's system simulation kernel), as it is shown in Figure 6. SPW and BONeS are useful for specifying behaviour and simulating performance models, respectively. For more information, see [8].

VCC integrates a number of technologies. It provides several input formats for system behaviour, including C/C++. Also, it unifies heterogeneous control and data-flow models. The system behaviour can be given using many different

MoCs, but all of them are actually implemented on top of CFSMs, that plays a dominant role as meta-model in VCC. Moreover, system architecture and system behaviour are well separated. The main VCC features are:

1. Higher abstraction level of architectural estimation models than the current cycle-accurate simulation models,
2. Evaluation of an architecture via mapping of a system behaviour onto an architecture implementation, followed by performance analysis,
3. Interface based communication design.

The third feature has been exploited by the COSY project (see next Section). Also, VCC follows the Y-chart approach. However, a specification of a system behaviour can be simulated only jointly with a system performance model. This means that independent functional simulation, i.e., independent of lower performance related levels of abstraction, is not possible.

7 COSY

In the COSY (COdesign Simulation and SYnthesis) methodology [10], VCC is used in order to obtain an infrastructure for mixing and matching software and hardware components (IPs). Focus is on communication refinement. The input behavioural specification is given using YAPI, Y-chart Application Programmer's Interface [9]. TSS, Philips' internal Tool for System Simulation, is used for the simulation of a refined target architecture. Furthermore, the COSY approach substantially simplifies the design process compared to Polis or VCC. One reason for this is that the levels of abstraction for the communication mechanism that are introduced by the VSI Alliance, i.e., application level, system level, virtual component level, and physical transfer level, are adopted by this approach. Figure 7 shows the definition of the levels of communication in COSY.

The COSY APP[2] level in Figure 7 serves to implement application Process Network (PN) models. At this level an executable untimed specification is used, i.e., a YAPI model [9].

After mapping an application PN onto an architecture, APP communication transfers (or transactions) are refined into system transactions (the COSY SYS level in Figure 7). Functionally, APP, SYS, VCI, and PHY transactions are equivalent. In contrast with APP level the SYS level designers can implement certain functions either as software tasks on a programmable processor core, or as a dedicated coprocessor. However, at the SYS level, transactions still operate on abstract data-types, e.g., video-frames. Hence, the SYS level can be seen as the timed-functional abstraction level used in SystemC (see Section 9). In order to map the high-level I/O semantics and to refine them into the more detailed on-chip communication interfaces, a new level is required. At this VCI level, the interfaces work with addresses and split data in chunks managable by a bus or a switching network. The COSY system integration flow relies on the simple VCI

---

[2] see Figure 7 for the meaning of acronyms in this section

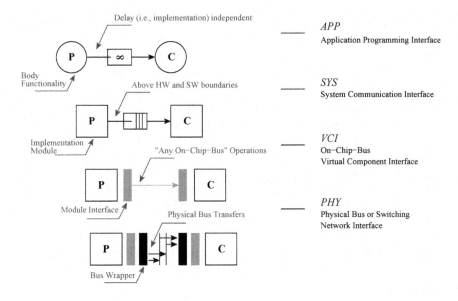

Fig. 7. COSY related transaction levels [10]

wrappers that translate the protocol used by VCI compliant interfaces into the physical protocol of the selected bus. The final level deals with physical bus size, signalling, and arbitration protocols. This level is marked as PHY in Figure 7. A simulation model at this level can be used to calibrate the estimation models at higher levels of abstraction.

The benefit of COSY is that a designer can, starting from pure behavioural/functional specification, do communication refinement and design-space exploration using generic performance models, and efficiently get to an optimal implementation. Furthermore, he can effectively exchange IPs because of clear separation of functionality and architecture, as well as the separation of IP behaviour and communication.

8 PAMELA

System performance modelling can be also done using a modelling language. In this section we discuss the tool PAMELA (Performance Modelling Language) [11]. The objectives of PAMELA are:

1. Improving model accuracy by allowing dynamic behaviour, and
2. Providing a source language for a static performance modelling that yields an analytic (compile-time) model.

In order to cope with these conflicting goals, PAMELA imposes some restrictions in particular with respect to the modelling of synchronisation, so that the objectives can at least partly be achieved. It uses highly structured language operations to describe four factors that determine parallel system performance modelling: conditional synchronisation (CS), mutual exclusion (ME), conditional control flow (CCF), and basic calibration of performance models (BC).

There are few features that should be observed:

1. PAMELA gives priority to static compile-time analysis, which goes at the cost of possible reduced accuracy. So, PAMELA could be seen as an analysis method and not as a performance modelling method. However, the PAMELA model does not fully exclude dynamic behaviour and does give more accurate performance measures than fully static models. See [11].
2. PAMELA does not distinguish separate formalisms to model programs and machines - there is no distinction between MoC and MoA. The Y-chart approach is thus not supported explicitly.
3. PAMELA does not support re-usability and extension of models clearly. In contrast to SPADE or Ptolemy, PAMELA was not designed to do so.

9   SystemC

Originally intended for software design, neither C nor C++ are suited to model hardware [14]. There are two ways to remedy this lack: either to build syntax extensions, or to introduce specific class libraries. The second approach has been taken by the developers of SystemC. Currently, SystemC has wide support both from commercial and academic side, and tends to become a standard as a language based modelling tool for System-level design.

With SystemC, embedded systems can be described by means of multiple concurrent processes. The underlying simulation kernel of SystemC is built on top of a co-routine based multithreading library.

By providing a C++ class library almost all kind of communication mechanisms can be modelled. The remote procedure call mechanism is used to model master-slave communication at the high abstraction level. Moreover, version 2.0, which is supposed to be available at the second half of 2001, is going to support user defined types of communication.

SystemC uses modules, which usually encapsulate some component, either a processing element or a communication block, and which can contain other modules or processes. Processes serve to capture functionality, and can be reactive either to any input signal or to a clock. Also, processes can be either synchronous, meaning they include timing control statements or conditional synchronisation, e.g., *wait*(*delay*), and instructions between *waits* are timeless, or asynchronous, meaning instructions are timeless, and local variables are redefined each time the process is invoked [13].

Another benefit of the library based implementation of hardware objects is that SystemC is ANSI C++ compliant; hence, an application and an architecture (whole system) can be modelled within one and the same simulation environment.

System C distinguishes several levels of abstraction:

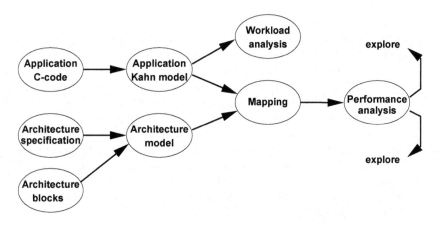

Fig. 8. The SPADE methodology flow

1. *Untimed functional*: control/dataflow MoCs
2. *Timed functional*: behavioural processes,
3. *BCA/CA functional*: bus-cycle-accurate/cycle-accurate architecture modules.

Modelling is possible at all levels of abstraction. Furthermore, SystemC provides interoperability among different levels of abstractions. That helps in dealing with large scale system complexity - simply we are allowed to model certain parts at the CA level, while others are at higher functional levels.

Specifications given within the SystemC context are executable. As a result, model verification is possible. It supports modelling of both hardware and software, and has support for low level hardware models. Because of a broad support, SystemC tends to become a standard, which would empower re-use and sharing of models.

SystemC itself should not be considered as a methodology; it is a modelling language. But as such, it may have impact on the exchange and interoperability of IP's at the various levels of abstraction.

10   Spade

In this section we present a concise description of the Spade methodology [1], [16]. Spade stands for System-level Performance Analysis and Design-space Exploration. It is both a methodology and an implementation for high level system modelling and evaluation. The Spade methodology follows the Y-chart approach introduced in Section 2. The methodology flow is illustrated in Figure 8. In this flow we recognise the aspects of Y-chart application modelling, architecture modelling, mapping and performance analysis. We now briefly comment on the various parts in Figure 8.

For application modelling Spade uses Kahn Process Network MoC [17] in order to make task level parallelism and communication explicit. The Kahn processes can run in parallel, but internally each of them is sequential. They communicate by token-exchange via unbounded channels. The application model represents the workload that is imposed on an architecture. The workload consists of two parts: communication workload and computation workload. Communication workload is seen through actions on channels, while computation workload is annotated explicitly. If an application model is run independently of an architecture model, a designer can do workload analysis.

Spade uses a building block approach for architecture modelling. Each architecture component is instantiated according to an architecture specification. Also, architecture components are generic building blocks. They describe only a timing behaviour, and not a functional behaviour. A set of parameters that is given in the architecture specification, is directly related to the timing behaviour of a particular component.

Spade supports an explicit mapping step, where each application process is mapped on a particular architecture component. Spade uses trace-driven execution to map the workload on an architecture model. In other words, application processes generate traces which drive architecture components. Traces contains stamps of communication and computation activities for each process.

When the application model, architecture model, and mapping are available, then Spade can perform simulation. After the execution, Spade provides some performance numbers: number of cycles processor was executing, was switching context, was busy with I/O or stalling or was idle, bus utilisation, and many others. These numbers should give guidelines to a designer of what are the bottlenecks or which parts of the architecture are under-utilised. The performance numbers can later on be visualised, analysed, and used for generating metrics information.

Since Spade has to obtain some hardware performance numbers, a hardware simulator tool has been included. Currently, this simulator is TSS (see Section 7), which is a BCA-level simulator. BCA-level simulators are typically slower than DE simulators at the higher levels of abstraction. While this is a drawback, an advantage is that in this environment it may be possible to easily perform mixed level simulation and exploration.

11   Conclusion

We have reported on a study that we conducted to evaluate and compare different features of some embedded system design methodologies and tools that are available today. Although they are all intended to be used in the field of system-level design, they are very diverse.

We studied eight different methodologies and tools: Ptolemy, UC San Diego/-NEC methodology, POLIS, Cadence VCC, COSY, PAMELA, SystemC, and Spade. In Table 1 we summarise their most interesting properties.

We conclude that the presented methodologies and tools differ from each other in their approach to hardware/software co-synthesis, e.g., Y-chart support

Table 1. Simultaneous overview of properties of presented methodologies & tools.

Methodologies & Tools ↦	Ptolemy	UCSD/NEC	POLIS	VCC	COSY	PAMELA	SystemC	SPADE
Commercial	-	-	-	+	+/-	-	-	-
Available	+	-	+	+	-	+	+	+/-
Y-chart supported	-	+	+	+	+	o	-	+
MoC variety supported	+	-	-	o/-	o	-	o	-
MoA support	-	o	o	+	+	-	o	+
Dynamic aspects modelling	+	+	+	+	+	+	+	+
Formal analysis & verification	-	o	+	o	o	+	-	-
Reusability	+	+	+	+	+	-	+	+
Complex designs	o	o	-	+	+	-	+	+
Multiple abstraction levels	-	o	+	+	+	-	+	o
Mixed level simulation	-	-	o	-	o	-	+	o
Support for Synthesis	-	o	+	o	o	-	-	-

in the third row in Table 1, as well as in their use of MoCs, e.g., in the fourth row in Table 1, and their use of MoAs, in the fifth row in Table 1.

Although most of the methodologies and tools share some common features, the overview shown in Table 1 indicates that from our selection of methodologies and tools COSY is the most complete one. The features shown in Table 1 also do suggest that (1) today's embedded system design methodologies and tools do not yet solve all design problems, and thus, (2) there is plenty of room for further research, e.g., support for synthesis, multiple abstraction levels, and formal analysis and verification. Specifically, there is more work to be done to master complexity in designs and to support mixed abstraction levels (rows 9 and 11 in Table 1).

Acknowledgements

This study was performed in part in the Archer project, funded by Philips Semiconductors. We want to thank Ed Deprettere (Leiden University), and Pieter van der Wolf (Philips Research Laboratories) for their contributions to this paper.

References

1. P. Lieverse et al.: A methodology for architecture exploration of heterogeneous signal processing systems. In Proc. 1999 Workshop on Signal Processing Systems, Taipei, Taiwan, Oct. 1999.
2. W. Wolf: Hardware/Software Co-Synthesis Algorithms. In System-Level Synthesis, A.A. Jerraya and J. Mermet (eds.), pp. 189-217, Kluwer Academic Publishers, 1999.
3. J.S. Davis II: Order and Containment in Concurrent System Design. In PhD thesis, University of California at Berkeley, Fall, 2000.
4. E.A. Lee et al.: Overview of The Ptolemy Project. Technical memorandum UCB/ERL M01/11, University of California at Berkeley, March, 2001.
5. E. Pauer, J.B. Prime: An Architectural Trade Capability Using The Ptolemy Kernel. In Proc. of the 1996 IEEE Int. Conf. on Acoustics, Speech, and Signal Processing (ICASSP), 1996.
6. K. Lahiri, A. Raghunathan, S. Dey: Performance analysis of systems with multi-channel communication architectures. In Proc. Int. Conf. VLSI Design, pp. 530-537, January 2000.

7. G. Martin, B. Salefski: Methodology and Technology for Design of Communications and Multimedia Products via System-Level IP Integration. In Proc. of DATE 98, February 1998.
8. http://www.cadence.com/articles/vcc_meth_backgrounder.html
9. De Kock et al.: YAPI: Application modeling for signal processing systems. In Proceedings of DAC'2000, Los Angeles, USA, 2000, June.
10. Jean-Yves Brunel et al.: COSY Communication IP's. In Proceedings of DAC'2000, Los Angeles, USA, 2000, June.
11. Arjan van Gemund: Performance Modeling of Parallel Systems. In PhD thesis, Technische Universiteit Delft, the Netherlands, 1996.
12. F. Balarin, et al.,: Hardware/Software Co-Design Of Embedded Systems - The POLIS Approach. Kluwer Academic Publishers, 2nd printing, 1999.
13. Synopsys, Inc., CoWare, Inc., Frontier Design, Inc. and others: Functional Specification For SystemC 2.0 - Final. January 17th, 2001.
14. D. Verkest, J. Kunkel, F. Schirrmeister: System Level Design Using C++. white paper, IMEC - Synopsys - Cadence.
15. A.C.J. Kienhuis: Design Space Exploration of Stream-based Dataflow Architectures *Methods and Tools*. In PhD thesis, Technische Universiteit Delft, the Netherlands, 1999.
16. Paul Lieverse, Todor Stefanov, Pieter van der Wolf, Ed Deprettere,: System Level Design with Spade: an M-JPEG Case Study. In Proc. of Int. Conference on Computer Aided Design (ICCAD'01), San Jose CA, USA, Nov. 4-8, 2001.
17. G. Kahn: The semantics of a simple language for parallel programming. Information processing 74 - North-Holland Publishing Company, 1974.
18. B. Kienhuis, E. Deprettere, K. Vissers and P. van der Wolf: An Approach for Quantitative Analysis of Application-Specific Dataflow Architectures. In Proc. 11-th Int. Conf. on Application-specific Systems, Architectures and Processors, Zurich, Switzerland, July 14-16 1997.

Translating Imperative Affine Nested Loop Programs into Process Networks

Ed F. Deprettere[1], Edwin Rijpkema[1,2], and Bart Kienhuis[1]

[1] Leiden Institute of Advanced Computer Science (LIACS), Leiden University,
Niels Bohrweg 1, 2333 CA Leiden, the Netherlands
{edd,kienhuis}@liacs.nl
http://www.liacs.nl/~cserc/
[2] Philips Research,
Eindhoven, the Netherlands
edwin.rijpkema@philips.com

Abstract. Specification of signal processing applications in terms of executable process networks is indispensable when these applications are to be mapped on parallel running processing units. The specifications are typically not given as process networks but as imperative programs. Translating imperative programs to process networks is thus necessary. This can be done, be it that some restrictions on the imperative programs have to be imposed: they have to be affine nested loop programs.

1 Introduction

Research efforts in processor design on high levels of abstraction are steadily growing. This is particularly so in the system-on-chip design research community where mastering the complexity of embedded systems design is now being a major challenge. Although no generally accepted definition of what an embedded system is has been given so far, its properties are well agreed upon and the different categories of embedded systems are well documented [1]. On the system level of abstraction, an embedded system can be specified in terms of three models, [2], [3]. One model specifies the functional behavior and structure of one or more applications, typically taken from some application domain. A second model specifies timing behavior and structure of an architecture. The third model specifies the relation between the other two models, i.e., the mapping of an application onto an architecture. Both application and architecture models can be expressed in terms of so-called *models of computation* (MoC) [4], Generally speaking, at the system level of abstraction, both the application and the architecture will be networks of communicating processes and processors, respectively. These networks will also be heterogeneous in the sense that neither the computations nor the communications will be uniformly modeled across the network. These two models must *match* in the sense that a mapping of the application model onto the architecture model must yield a meaningful system model, as is e.g., the case with the classical model {*C-program, GNU compiler, Instruction*

E.F. Deprettere et al. (Eds.): SAMOS 2001, LNCS 2268, pp. 89–111, 2002.

set Architecture}. This model is not appealing when dealing with the application domain of signal and multimedia processing, in which most applications are composed of tasks that operate on streams of data, and the architectures are typically composed of a number of processing units embedded in a communication network. The way the relation between the application and the architecture is modeled in this case may depend on what is to be done with the resulting system model. In [5], for example, where the objective is quantitative performance analysis through simulation, the relation between application and architecture is modeled by means of execution traces between application tasks and architecture processor units. These traces abstract the application and model the mapping of the application onto the architecture; they contain information that is generated by the tasks and used by the processor units in a co-simulation of application (functional behavior) and architecture (timing behavior). In embedded systems design, it is a fact of life that almost all applications are specified in terms of the executable imperative model of computation. Being strictly sequential, these specifications are, in general, unsuitable for a direct mapping on multi-processor architectures. In such an architecture, the processors are executing tasks and, therefore, a specification of the application in terms of communicating tasks or processes is much more appealing. Deriving a model of the second kind from a model of the first kind need not be difficult to perform; in general though the derived model is neither unique nor architecture impartial. The obvious question, then, is whether it would be possible to convert imperative models into models that express interaction of concurrent tasks, as well as converting such models into functionally equivalent models of the same type. To the best of our knowledge, this is not in general possible. It is, however, possible for a restricted class of static nested loop applications. Specifications of such algorithms in C or in Matlab can be converted automatically to a process network, either a Kahn Process Network (KPN) or one of its specializations that are collectively known as Dataflow Process Networks (DPN). The restriction imposed on the applications is that they must be affine Nested Loop Programs (NLP). Such programs appear frequently (as subprograms) in signal processing and multimedia applications. Moreover, PNs are natural models of computation for such applications because they elegantly model the concurrent execution of tasks operating on streams of data, as well as the communication of data streams between the tasks.

Figure 1 illustrates the problem and the route to be taken to solve this problem. The top-left part of the figure displays a sample algorithm that is executable in the Matlab algorithm development environment. The bottom-left part depicts a typical high-level architecture organization. It consist of a micro processor/memory pair, and a number of autonomous processing elements connected to some sort of interconnection network. The application is to be mapped onto this architecture. Clearly, the specifications (or models) will not match and, therefore, another (executable) application specification is what is needed. The desired model is shown in the bottom-right part of the figure. It is a Kahn Process Network, in which the nodes (circles) represent sequential processes and the arcs represent unbounded FIFO queues. The processes communicate over these

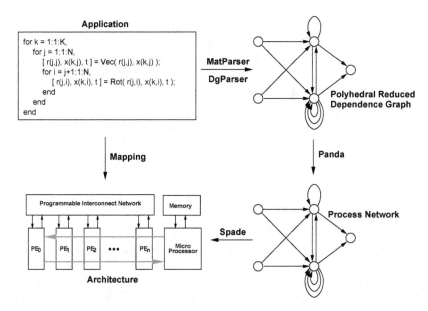

Fig. 1. Mapping the application onto an architecture is difficult because the Model of Computation of the application does not match the way the architecture operates.

channels using a blocking read synchronization. Converting the given application specification into a behaviorally equivalent process network may seem to be as troublesome as mapping that application to the given architecture. That is (almost) so and, therefore, that conversion needs an intermediate model that is shown in the top-right part of the figure. This so-called Polyhedral Reduced Dependence Graph (PRDG) which has a structure that is (almost) identical to the process network is derived from the Matlab code by means of an aggressive array dataflow analysis procedure, denoted MatParser and DgParser in the figure. The conversion from the PRDG to the PN model (denoted Panda in the figure) is the main focus of this chapter. As the figure indicates, the direct Mapping is replaced by a compiling chain consisting of MatParser/DgParser, Panda, and Spade. These are the names of the tools in our toolset Compaan. In this set, SPADE is a simulation tool in which the application network and the architecture network are co-simulated for performance analysis and exploration, [5]. This step will not be elaborated upon in this paper.

2   From the Imperative MoC to the PRDG

The *Polyhedral Reduced Dependence Graph* MoC is built on a polyhedral partitioning of a *single assignment program* (SAP) version of the given Imperative MoC specification. In the *Uniform Modeling Language* [15], the PRDG has a data structure as shown in Figure 2.

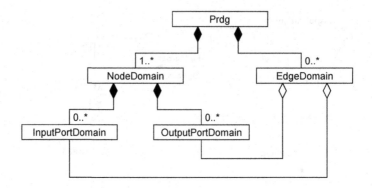

Fig. 2. The data structure of the PRDG

Thus, a PRDG is a graph consisting of *Nodes*, and *Edges* between *Output Ports* and *Input Ports* of Nodes, all having specific properties. These entities are actually *polyhedral domains* - Port Domains, Node Domains, and Edge Domains which have behavioral, topological and geometrical constituents, as shown in Table 1.

Table 1. Elements of the PRDG and their behavioral, topological, and geometrical constituents.

type	behavior	topology	geometry
P	p		$\mathcal{I}_P$
Q	q		$\mathcal{I}_Q$
N	f_N	(I_N, O_N)	$\mathcal{I}_N$
E		(Q, P)	$\mathcal{I}_E$

In this table, $\mathcal{I}_P$, $\mathcal{I}_Q$, $\mathcal{I}_N$, and $\mathcal{I}_E$ are the *domains* of an input port (P), an output port (Q), a node (N), and an edge (E), respectively, and are defined in terms of lattices and (integral points in) polytopes. The entries in the second column are atomic *input ports* (p), atomic *output ports* (q) and atomic *node functions* (f), respecttively, defined on each and every integer point in their domains. Finally, (I_N, O_N) is the pair of input and output port sets of a node $N = (I_N, O_N, f_N, \mathcal{I}_N)$. Thus, the PRDG is a graph $G = (\mathcal{N}, \mathcal{E})$, specialized in the following sense:

- $P \in I$ is an input port $P = (p, \mathcal{I}_P)$,
- $Q \in O$ is an output port $Q = (q, \mathcal{I}_Q)$,
- $N \in \mathcal{N}$ is a node $N = (I_N, O_N, f_N, \mathcal{I}_N)$, and
- $E \in \mathcal{E}$ is an edge $E = (e, \mathcal{I}_E)$, where $e = (Q, P)$.

Figure 3 shows a portion of a PRDG as a graph together with some of the associations made to the elements of this graph. The graph (bottom) has one producer node connected to two consumer nodes.

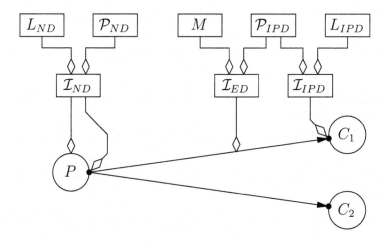

Fig. 3. A PRDG viewed as an graph

Node P has the domain $\mathcal{I}_{ND}$ associated with it. A node domain and an input port domain are defined by means of a Polytope $\mathcal{P}$ and a Lattice matrix L. An edge domain is defined by an affine Mapping M from an input port to an output port. An output port of a node has the domain of the node associated with it. The reason for this is that the single assignment program from which the PRDG is derived is in *output normal form*. The way in which we convert an imperative program to a single assignment program has been described elsewhere [6], [7]. We deal with that part of the compilation chain in the next section, but only for as far as our needs for the present paper go.

2.1 Representation of Single Assignment Programs

Single assignment programs (SAP) may be written by hand or may be the result of an *array dataflow analysis* of an imperative program. An array dataflow analysis is the analysis that finds all flow dependencies in a program [8]. One such array dataflow analysis tool is MATPARSER [6]. The input of MATPARSER is an imperative program that follows the MATLAB syntax; its output is either a single assignment program or a parse tree representing a single assignment program. In this paper we presume that a single assignment program is generated with MATPARSER, and that the nested loop programs (NLP) to be analised are *piecewise affine* NLPs, which are precisely the programs accepted by the MAT-PARSER tool. An example of a piecewise affine NLP and its corresponding SAP are given in the following two programs[1].

---

[1] The SAP for the sample program in Figure 1 can be found in [9].

Program   SAP
%parameter N 10 20;
%parameter M 10 20;
for $i = 1 : 1 : N$,
  for $j = 1 : 1 : M$,
    if $i - 2 \geq 0$,
      if $j \leq M - 1$,
        $[in_0] = $ **ipd** $(a_1(i - 1, j + 1))$;
      else
        $[in_0] = $ **ipd** $(a(i + j))$;
      end
    else
      $[in_0] = $ **ipd** $(a(i + j))$;
    end
    $[out_0] = f(in_0)$;
    $[a_1(i, j)] = $ **opd** (out_0);
  end
end

Program   NLP
%parameter N 10 20;
%parameter M 10 20;
for $i = 1 : 1 : N$,
  for $j = 1 : 1 : M$,
    $[a(i + j)] = f(a(i + j))$;
  end
end

Piecewise affine NLPs have piecewise affine SAPs. SAPs contain assignment and control statements.

Assignment statements occur in the functional part of the program, they deal with the assignment of values to variables, the binding of variables to arguments of functions, and function calls. There are three types of assignment statements.

- **ipd** statement, $[arg] = $ **ipd** $(var(index))$; where arg is an input argument of a function, var is the variable array name, and $index$ is a vector of affine expressions, called the *indexing function*.
- **opd** statement, $[var(index)] = $ **opd** (arg); where arg is a result of a function, var is the variable array name, and $index$ is a vector of affine expressions, the indexing function.
- **node** statement, $[arg, arg, \cdots, arg] = function(arg, arg, \cdots, arg)$; where $[arg, arg, \cdots, arg]$ is the list of result arguments of the function with name $function$ and where $(arg, arg, \cdots, arg)$ is the list of input arguments of the function.

Control statements describe the structure of a SAP. There are four types of control statements.

- **for** statement. **for** $var = expression : integer : expression \ body$ **end**. i specifies a set of index points $\mathcal{I} = \{\ell + ks\}_{k=0}^{p}$, where p is the largest integer for which $\ell + ps \leq u$. For every $i \in \mathcal{I}$, $body$ is executed once.
- **conditional** statement. **if** $expression \geq 0$ *if-body* **else** *else-body* **end**. al.
- index **transformation** statement. $var = expression;$, where $expression$ is a pseudo-affine expression (see below).

– **parameter** declaration statement. %**parameter** *var integer integer;*, where
the two integers specify the range of values the parameter can have.

All statements except the **node** statement contain expressions. There are two
types of expressions, *affine expressions* and *pseudo-affine expressions*, and the
type of expression allowed in the statements differs per statement [7]. Pseudo-
affine expressions are found in lower and upper bounds of **for** statements, conditions in **conditional** statements, and expressions in index **transformation**
statements. All other expressions are affine expressions.

Parse Tree. In the parse tree representation of a SAP, the statements are
associated with the nodes in the parse tree [10]. For the complete grammar of the
parse trees see [6]. The topology of the parse tree represents the control structure
of the program. The parse tree representation of program **ProgramSAP** is given
in Figure 4.

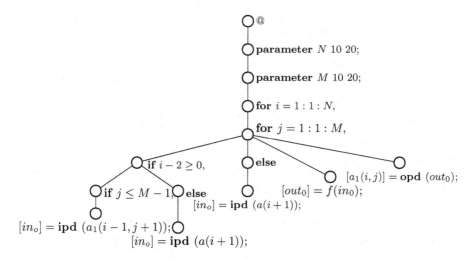

Fig. 4. Parse tree of Program **ProgramSAP**.

The node labeled with the @-symbol is the *root* of the tree. The parse tree is an
ordered tree and must be interpreted depth first, left to right.
From now on the term NLP is used to denote piecewise affine nested loop programs and the term SAP is used to denote the single assignment program of
an NLP generated with MATPARSER as code or parse tree. The next step is to
convert a SAP into a polyhedral reduced dependence graph.

2.2   From SAP to PRDG

Converting a SAP to a PRDG comprises the extraction of the PRDG's behavior,
topology and geometry (see Table 1) from the SAP.

- The elements in the column *geometry* in Table 1 are encoded in the SAP in its control statements and the indexing functions of its **ipd** and **opd** statements.
- The elements in the column *behavior* in Table 1 are encoded in the leaf nodes of the parse tree. Depending on the type of the statement, an atomic node, atomic input port, or atomic output port has to be constructed.
- The elements in the column *topology* in Table 1 are also encoded in the leaf nodes of the parse tree. Now their relative position and the variable array name, in case of **ipd** or **opd** statement, are of importance.

First the Geometry, or Domain Construction. The *iteration vector* or *index vector* of a statement is defined as the vector composed of the index variables of the **for** statements in the path from the root of the parse tree to the parent of the statement. An *iteration* of a statement is a specific value of its iteration vector. The set of all iterations for which a statement is executed is called the *iteration domain* of that statement. Besides the index vector of a statement two more vectors play a role. The *control vector* of a statement is defined as the vector composed of all control variables of the statements in the path from the root of the parse tree to the parent of that statement. The *parameter vector* of a statement is defined as the vector composed of all parameters of the statements in the path from the root of the parse tree to the parent of that statement. When specifying the iteration domain of a statement, a set of affine constraints is associated with every control statement. This is done in three steps: First a set of (possibly pseudo-affine) constraints are associated with every statement, second all pseudo-affine constraints are rewritten into a set of affine constraints, third the set of affine constraints from the root of the parse tree to the statement are collected in one single system of constraints. As to the last step, for a statement, the vector composed of its index vector $\mathbf{i}$, its control vector $\mathbf{c}$, the parameter vector $\mathbf{p}$, and the homogeneous constant $t = 1$ is called the *data-parameter vector*, often denoted by the vector $\mathbf{k} = [\mathbf{i} \quad \mathbf{c} \quad \mathbf{p} \quad t]^t$, where the superscript t denotes vector transposition. Indexing functions in the SAP, then, lead to the mappings $M\mathbf{k}$ from **ipd** statements to **opd** statements, where M is called the *mapping matrix* of the indexing function, see Figure 3. Let s be a statement, and let $(@, s_1, s_2, \cdots, s_n)$ be the path from the root of the parse tree to the parent of s. Let $\mathbf{k}$ be the data-parameter vector of s, and let $\{A_i \mathbf{k} = \mathbf{0} \wedge C_i \mathbf{k} \geq \mathbf{0}\}$ be the sets of constraints associated with s_i, $i = 1, 2, \cdots, n$. Then, the iteration domain of s is given by $\mathcal{I} = (L, \mathcal{P})$, where the number of rows of L equals the dimension of the index vector of s and where $\mathcal{P}$ is the polytope

$$\mathcal{P} = \{\mathbf{x} \in \mathbb{Q}^d \mid \begin{bmatrix} A_1 \\ A_2 \\ \vdots \\ A_n \end{bmatrix} \mathbf{x} = \mathbf{0} \wedge \begin{bmatrix} C_1 \\ C_2 \\ \vdots \\ C_n \end{bmatrix} \mathbf{x} \geq \mathbf{0}\}$$

in which d is the dimension of the data-parameter vector. The construction of the SAP is such that the **opd** statements are direct siblings at the right hand side of the **node** statements, and consequently they have the same iteration domain.

Second the Behavior and Topology. The conversion of the parse tree to a PRDG $G = (\mathcal{N}, \mathcal{E})$ encompasses the conversion of the **node,ipd**, and **opd** statements to node domains, input port domains, output port domains, and edge domains. Let s be a leaf node of the parse tree and let its domain $\mathcal{I}$ be given by $(L, \mathcal{P})$. Depending on the type of s one of the following must be done for each leaf node s.

- if s is an **opd** statement and if Q is the corresponding output port, $Q = (q, \mathcal{I}_q)$, then $\mathcal{I}_q = \mathcal{I}$ and q is the atomic output port $q = (arg, var, \texttt{double})$ with arg and var parsed from s.
- if s is an **ipd** statement and if P is the corresponding input port, $P = (p, \mathcal{I}_p)$, then $\mathcal{I}_p = \mathcal{I}$ and p is the atomic input port $p = (arg, var, \texttt{double})$ with arg and var parsed from s.
- if s is an **ipd** statement and if E is the corresponding edge, $E = ((Q, P), \mathcal{I}_e)$, then P is the input port associated with s and Q is the output port that has the same variable in its atomic port as P has. Further, $\mathcal{I}_e$ is the domain $(M, \mathcal{P}_e)$ where $\mathcal{P}_e = \mathcal{P}$, and M is the mapping matrix.
- if s is an **node** statement and if N is the corresponding node, $N = (I_N, O_N, f_n, \mathcal{I}_n)$, then $\mathcal{I}_n = \mathcal{I}$ and f_n is the *function* parsed from s. Further, I_N and O_N are the sets of input ports and output ports constructed from the **ipd** and **opd** statements directly preceding and following the **node** statement in the parse tree, respectively.

For the sample program in Figure 1, part of the lower most node and edges in the corresponding PRDG (top-right) can be found in [9]. We are now ready to move on to the Process Network that goes with the PRDG.

3   From the PRDG to the Process Network MoC

The graphical structure of the Kahn Process Network is very close to that of the PRDG: PRDG nodes become KPN nodes and PRDG arcs become KPN channels. KPN channels are unbounded FIFO queues. KPN nodes are sequential processes that communicate over the channels. Writing to a channel is unconditional, and reading from a channel is blocking. There are three steps involved in the conversion from a PRDG to a KPN.

1. The first step is the identification of the actual output port domains. Recall that every output port of a node has the domain of the node associated with it. The actual domain of an output port of a producing node can be reconstructed from the input port of the corresponding consuming node and the mapping M from the consumer's input port domain to the producer's node domain. We call this first step the *domain matching* step.
2. The second step is the ordering of the operations in the node domains. One possible ordering is the default ordering that is included in the SAP output by MATPARSER (which is directly borrowed from the original Matlab program). Of course, the PRDG is impartial with respect to the ordering of the function calls within a node[2], and many orderings, other than the default one can be conceived of. We call this ordering step the *domain scanning* step.

---

[2] Taking the dependence relations into account, of course.

3. The third and last step is to structure the processes in such a way that higher dimensional data structures can be elegantly scheduled over the one-dimensional communication (FIFO) channels. This step, we call the *linearization step*.

The following example illustrates the three steps in the conversion of a PRDG into a KPN. Both have the same graphical structure shown in 5.

3.1   Example 1

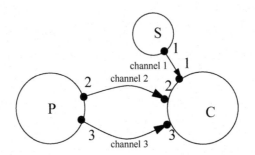

Fig. 5. PRDG and KPN graph for the example

The nodes **P**, **C**, and **S** have domains $\mathcal{P} = \{(j,i) \mid 1 \leq j \leq N \ \wedge j \leq i \leq N\}$, $\mathcal{C} = \{(l,k) \mid 1 \leq l \leq N \ \wedge l \leq k \leq N\}$, and $\mathcal{S} = \{m \mid 1 \leq m \leq N\}$, respectively. Node **C** has input port domains $\mathcal{C}_1 = \{(l,k) \mid 1 \leq k \leq N \wedge l = 1\}$ through which tokens (variables with name **x** from channel 1 between nodes **S** and **C** enter node **C**; $\mathcal{C}_2 = \{(l,k) \mid 1 \leq l \leq N \wedge l \leq k \leq N\}$ and $\mathcal{C}_3\{(l,k) \mid 2 \leq l \leq N \wedge l \leq k \leq N\}$, both receiving tokens (variables with name **r_** and **x_**, respectively), from node **P**, through channel 2 and channel 3, respectively.

domain matching. The output port domains of nodes **S** and **P** are made explicit through the mappings $m = k$ from $\mathcal{C}_1$ to $\mathcal{S}$, $(j,i) = (l,k)$ from $\mathcal{C}_2$ to $\mathcal{P}$, and $(j,i) = (l-1,k)$ from $\mathcal{C}_3$ to $\mathcal{P}$.

domain scanning. The atomic functions f_P, f_S, and f_C in the nodes **P**, **S**, and **C** are lexicographically ordered. For example, the ordering in $\mathcal{P}$ could be **for** $(j = 1; \ j \leq N; \ j++)$, **for**$(i = j; \ i \leq N; \ i++)$. The ordering in $\mathcal{S}$ could be **for** $(m = 1; \ m \leq N; \ m++)$, and the ordering in $\mathcal{C}$ could be **for** $(k = 1; \ k \leq N; \ k++)$, **for**$(l = 1; \ l \leq k; \ l++)$.

linearization. The tokens (variables) produced by the atomic functions in the nodes **P** and **S** are written to the channels *in order*, that is in the (scanning) order in which they are produced. Notice that some of the variables $\mathbf{x}_-(j,i)$ do not belong to the output port $\{(j,i) \mid 1 \leq j \leq N - 1 \ \wedge j + 1 \leq i \leq N\}$ of the variable with name **x_** and are, therefore, not put on channel 3. Because the channel is a FIFO channel, node **C** must read the tokens from channel 3 in the same order as they are produced by node **P**. However, the order in which *the atomic functions* in node **C** actually *consume* these tokens may be in a different order (as is the case in our example). As a result, tokens read from the channel will in general have to be stored temporary in a *private memory* that we require to be linear and such that 1) writing to this memory follows an auto-increment addressing policy. and 2) the size of this memory must be minimal. Taking again channel 3, **P** will produce $\frac{1}{2}N \times (N-1)$ tokens (implicitly) labeled 1, 2, 3, 4, 5, 6 (N=3) and **C** will consume them in the order 1, 2, 4, 3, 5, 6, hence token 3 will have to be stored temporary and loaded from private memory when the atomic function at node index $(k, l) = (4, 2)$ has to consume it.

The above example is merely an illustration of *what* is to be done, it does not give any insight in *how* all this is done. We shall disclose the methods in the subsections to follow. Before doing so, however, we have to digress for a while to introduce the underpinning property that integer points in a polytope can be *counted* and *ranked* by means of *(pseudo) polynomials*.

3.2   Ehrhart Polynomials

Let be given a parameter vector $\mathbf{p} \in \mathbb{Q}^m$ and a convex polytope

$$\mathcal{P}(\mathbf{p}) = \{\mathbf{x} \in \mathbb{Q}^n \mid A\mathbf{x} = B\mathbf{p} + \mathbf{b} \wedge C\mathbf{x} \geq D\mathbf{p} + \mathbf{d}\}$$

where A is an integral $k \times n$ matrix, $\mathbf{b}$ is an integral vector of size k, C is an integral $\ell \times n$ matrix, $\mathbf{d}$ is an integral vector of size ℓ, k and ℓ are the number of equalities and inequalities, and where B and D are integral $k \times m$ and $\ell \times m$ matrices, respectively. There are two questions that we want to answer: First, how many points are contained in the set $\mathcal{P}(\mathbf{p}) \cap \mathbb{Z}^n$, and second, can these points be ranked in a one-to-one correspondence with the natural numbers (not including 0). These enumerative combinatorial problems have been considered in great detail in [12] and [13]. Here, we give a concise summary with reference to the example in Subsection 3.1. To begin with, the polytope $\mathcal{P}$ can be partitioned into polytopes for each of which the number of integer points it contains (*counting*) as well as a linear lexicographical ordering of these integer points (*ranking*) can be expressed as a *pseudo polynomial*. Let p be an integer. A one-dimensional pseudo polynomial $f(p)$ of degree k is a 'polynomial' $f(p) = c_k(p)p^k + c_{k-1}(p)p^{k-1} + \cdots + c_0(p)$ that is integral for all p, and whose coefficients are periodic, that is, $c_l(p)$ is either constant, $c_l(p) = c_l$, or equal to $c_{l,p \bmod P}$ where P is the period. Thus the number of integer points in a polytope of dimension k and parameterized in a single parameter p is expressed in terms of pseudo-polynomial in p of degree k. In the example given in Subsection 3.1, the number of points in the domains $\mathcal{P}$ (and $\mathcal{C}$) and $\mathcal{S}$ are $\frac{1}{2}N^2 + \frac{1}{2}N$, and N respectively. Likewise, the ranking of the integer points in the domains $\mathcal{P}$, $\mathcal{C}$ and $\mathcal{S}$ are $rank(j, i) = -\frac{1}{2}j^2 + (N + \frac{1}{2})j + i - N$, $rank(k, l) = \frac{1}{2}k^2 - \frac{1}{2}k + l$, and $rank(m) = m$, respectively, for the lexicographical scanning orders given earlier. We rely on the tool POLYLIB[16] for deriving pseudo polynomials. This tool has

```
process P(double out wp₁)        process C(double in rp₁)
   for j = 1 to N                   for k = 1 to N
      for i = j to N                   for l = 1 to  k
                                          if ( 2 ≤ l )
                                             while ( l < r(k,l) )
                                                x(l++) = read (rp₁);
                                             end
                                             in =  x(r(k,l)) ;
                                          end
                                          ··· = g ( in);
      [ out] =  f(···) ;
      if ( j + 1 ≤ i )
         write( wp₁, out);
      end
   end
      end                                  end
   end                                  end
end                                   end


                      Network N
                double channel ch₃ ;
                  P(ch₃) par C(ch₃);
```

Fig. 6. The two processes for the example in Subsection 3.1. Only channel 3 is considered

been developed partially in Rennes and partially in Strasbourg[3], France. The polynomial counting and ranking concept is a key method in all three steps of our procedure to convert a PRDG into a KPN and. Before going into the specifics of deriving Kahn Processes from PRDG nodes, we give in the next subsection, as an example, (part of) the KPN processes $P()$ and $C()$ in the nodes **P** and **C** of the producer-consumer example in Subsection 3.1.

3.3   Kahn Processes for Example 1

Restricting ourselves to communication channel 3, the two processes are given in Figure 6.

Processes $P()$ and $C()$ start with a declaration of the process (where rp and wp mean *read port* and *write port*, respectively). The declarations are followed by a set of loops that give the scanning order of the node domain. For every output port of the process, there is a block of code containing a **write** statement. For every input port of the process, there ia a block of code containing a **read** statement and a **while** statement. The **while** statement in this block models the *blocking read synchronization* between the two processes $P()$ and $C()$. $r(k,l)$ is a read function: It refers to the $r(k,l)$-th token that was sent by the producer. When that token is not at the head of the channel, the tokens preceding it are stored in the *private memory* of process $C()$ until the requested token comes

---

[3] http://icps.u-strasbg.fr/~loechner/polylib/

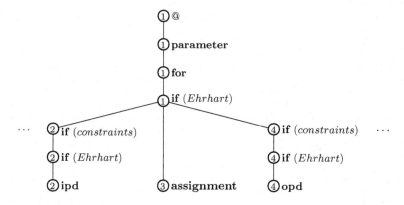

Fig. 7. The structure of the parse tree generated from the PRDG.

available. This read function is actually a *(pseudo) polynomial*. We come back to that in Subsection 3.7 to come.

We now go into a more formal description of the derivation of Kahn processes.

3.4 Parse Tree Representation of a Kahn Process

The structure of a Kahn process parse tree is shown in Figure 7. All nodes in the tree, except for the root and the leaves, represent a number of nodes of the same type on top of each other. For example the **if** (*Ehrhart*) node represents a set of nested **if** (*Ehrhart*) statements. The dots "···" on the left and right hand side of the figure represent repetitions of the left most branch and right most branch, respectively. An **if** (*constraints*) statement has an equality or inequality condition that narrows down a (polytope) domain. An **if** (*Ehrhart*) statement has a condition of the form $E \geq 1$, where E is an Ehrhart polynomial, to filter out points in a domain (to create holes). The four numbers in the nodes of the parse tree refer to four partitions the nodes belong to.

partition 1. The nodes here define the parameters and the iteration space.

a) Every **parameter** statement in the set defines one parameter together with its lower and upper bound.
b) The **for** statements define a set of index variables and an iteration domain that is a dense (strides equal to one) integer domain that contains the PRDG node domain.
c) The **if** (*Ehrhart*) statements filter out all points that do not belong to the original PRDG node domain. No **if** (*Ehrhart*) statements are found in the code example in Figure 6, because the two processes in our example are themselves dense.

partition 2. The nodes here define the iterations at which a **read** operation from a specific channel must be done. See e.g., the block of code containing the **read** statement in process $C()$ in Figure 6.

a) The **if** (*constraint*) statements narrows down the iteration domain to that part of it that contains an input port domain. See e.g., the constraint $2 \leq \ell$ in process $C()$ in Figure 6.
b) The **if** (*Ehrhart*) statements filter out points from the (input port) iteration domain for which no input is to be read from the specific channel.
c) The **ipd** statement represents the block of code that contains the **read** operation, except for the **if** statement; see e.g., the consumer process in Figure 6.

partition 3. The **assignment** statement represents the function call in the body of the Kahn process. Its input arguments get values assigned in partition 2. The results are written to the channels in partition 4.

partition 4. The nodes here define the points of the iteration domain at which a **write** operation to a specific channel must be done. See e.g., the block of code containing the **write** statement in process $P()$ in Figure 6.

a) The **if** (*constraint*) statements narrow down the iteration domain to a part of it that encloses the PRDG input port domain. In our example, this corresponds to the constraint $j + 1 \leq 1$ in process $P()$ in Figure 6.
b) The **if** (*Ehrhart*) statements filter out points from the iteration domain for which no output is to be written to the specific channel.
c) The **opd** statement represents the **write** operation as e.g., in the producer process in Figure 6.

The problem of how to convert the PRDG model into such a parse tree can be divided in three sub-problems which are exactly those we have touched upon in Subsection 3.1. They are *domain scanning*, covering nodes 1a, 1b, and 1c in the parse tree; *domain matching*, covering nodes 2a, 2b, 4a, and 4b in the parse tree; and *linearization*, covering node 2c in the parse tree. The creation of node 3 is simple: it is the conversion of a function in the PRDG model into an assignment statement.

Before delving into these three steps, we introduce a test that plays a crucial role in what follows. The test is to answer the question whether or not a particular integral point belongs to a domain. We call this test the *Ehrhart test*.

The Ehrhart Test. Let be given a domain $\mathcal{J} = (M, \mathcal{P}), \mathcal{J} \subset \mathbb{Z}^d$, with $\mathcal{P}$ a polytope. Let $\mathbf{j} \in \mathbb{Z}^d$ be a vector. The problem is to count the number of integral points $\mathbf{k} \in \mathcal{P}$ for which $\mathbf{j} = M(\mathbf{k})$. We call this number the *multiplicity* of $\mathbf{j}$ with respect to the domain $(M, \mathcal{P})$. Thus the problem is to count the number of integral points in $\mathcal{K}(\mathbf{j}) = \{\mathbf{x} \in \mathcal{P} \mid \mathbf{j} = M(\mathbf{x})\}$. This number is given by the following theorem, [14].

Theorem *Let be given the domain* $\mathcal{J} = (M, \mathcal{P}), \mathcal{P} \subset \mathbb{Z}^n, \mathcal{J} \subset \mathbb{Z}^d$. *Let for* $\mathbf{j} \in \mathbb{Z}^d$, $\mathcal{P}(\mathbf{j})$ *be the parameterized polyhedron* $\{\mathbf{x} \in \mathbb{Q}^n \mid M(\mathbf{x}) = \mathbf{j}\}$. *Then the multiplicity of* $\mathbf{j}$ *in* $\mathcal{J}$ *is given by* $\mathcal{M}(\mathbf{j}) = EP(\mathcal{P} \cap \mathcal{P}(\mathbf{j}))$, *where* EP *denotes the Ehrhart polynomial (enumerator) parametrized in the entries of the vector.*

Example (Ehrhart test).
Let the domain $\mathcal{J} = (M, \mathcal{P}(N))$ be given by $\mathcal{P}(N) = \{(x_1, x_2) \in \mathbb{Q}^2 \,|\, 0 \leq x_1 \leq N \ \wedge\ x_1 \leq x_2 \leq N\}$ and $M(\mathbf{k}) = \begin{bmatrix} 2 & 1 \end{bmatrix} \mathbf{k} + 3, \mathbf{k} \in \mathcal{P}(N) \cap \mathbb{Z}^2$. Then

$$\mathcal{K}(N, j) = \mathcal{P}(N) \cap \mathcal{P}(j) = \{ \begin{bmatrix} x_1 \\ x_2 \end{bmatrix} \,|\, 0 \leq x_1 \leq N \wedge x_1 \leq x_2 \leq N \wedge j = 2x_1 + x_2 + 3\}.$$

The enumerator of $\mathcal{K}(j)$ is

$$\mathcal{M}(N, j) = EP(\mathcal{P}(N) \cap \mathcal{P}(N, j))$$
$$= \begin{cases} \frac{1}{3}j + [0, -\frac{1}{3}, -\frac{2}{3}]_j, & \text{if } 3 \leq j \leq N+3 \\ \frac{1}{2}N + [-\frac{1}{6}j + [1, \frac{7}{6}, \frac{1}{3}, \frac{3}{2}, \frac{2}{3}, \frac{5}{6}]_j, -\frac{1}{6}j + [\frac{3}{2}, \frac{2}{3}, \frac{5}{6}, 1, \frac{7}{6}, \frac{1}{3}]_j]_N \\ \quad \text{if } N+3 \leq j \leq 3N+3 \end{cases}$$

In this example, the domain $\mathcal{J}$ is not a polytope since there is a "hole" at $j = 17$. Because the hole structure is not regular, the Ehrhart pseudo-polynomial[4] is rather complex. Of course, if the question is whether or not there is a point in the domain, rather than how many, then the integer valued multiplicity is mapped onto a boolean. We rely on the tool POLYLIB for performing the test. Let us now look at the three basic steps.

3.5 Domain Scanning

The problem is to convert a domain that is defined as a *polyhedral image* $\mathcal{I} = \{\mathbf{i} = M\mathbf{k} \,|\, \mathbf{k} \in \mathcal{P} \cap \mathbb{Z}^d\} = (M, \mathcal{P})$, where M is an integral matrix and $\mathcal{P}$ a polyhedron, to a nested loop structure. There are three cases to be considered as shown in Figure 8.

The first case is illustrated by the polytope $\mathcal{P}_1 \subset \mathbb{Q}$, and domain $\mathcal{I}_1$ that is obtained through the mapping $i = Lk, k \in \mathcal{P}_1 \cap \mathbb{Z}$ onto $\mathbb{Z}$. In this case the domain consists of just the integral points contained in the polytope, hence the scanning of the points can be performed in the polytope. The second case is illustrated by the polytope $\mathcal{P}_2 \subset \mathbb{Q}^2$, and domain $\mathcal{I}_2$ that is obtained through the mapping $i = L(x, c), (x, c) \in \mathcal{P}_2 \cap \mathbb{Z}^2$ onto $\mathbb{Z}$. In this case the domain is still a dense domain and contains the same points as $\mathcal{I}_1$. The main difference is that its defining polytope is in $\mathbb{Q}^2$ rather than in $\mathbb{Q}$. The third case is illustrated by the polytope $\mathcal{P}_3 \subset \mathbb{Q}^2$, and domain $\mathcal{I}_3$ that is obtained through the mapping $i = L(x, c), (x, c) \in \mathcal{P}_3 \cap \mathbb{Z}^2$ onto $\mathbb{Z}$. In this case the domain differs from the domains $\mathcal{I}_1$ and $\mathcal{I}_2$ in that there are "holes" in the domain.

The lexicographical scanning of a polytope $\mathcal{P}(\mathbf{p})$ (case 1) to obtain a set of nested **for** loops can be easily done using the tool POLYLIB mentioned before. The lexicographical order is specified by a vector $(i_1, i_2, \cdots, i_d)$ where d is the dimension of the space that contains the domain. We also rely on the tool POLYLIB for the other two cases which are, however, more involved and will not be elaborated upon here. See [14] for the details.

---

[4] Here, the periodic coefficients $c_{l, p \bmod P}$ introduced earlier are expressed in terms of arrays $[c_l(0) \ c_l(1) \ \ldots c_l(P-1)]_p$ from which $c_l(k)$ has to be selected if $p \bmod P$ is k.

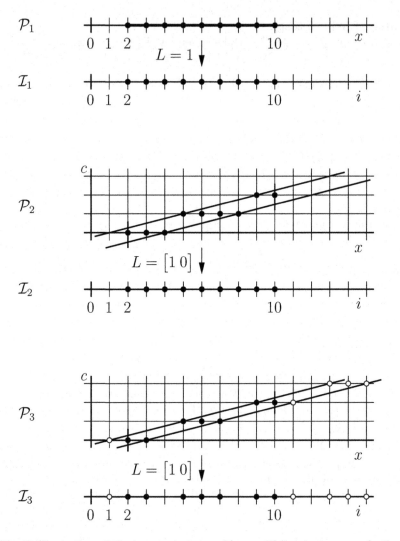

Fig. 8. Illustration of the tree scanning problems with increasing complexity.

3.6   Domain Matching

Recall that input port domains are explicit in the PRDG whilst output port domains are to be identified as part of their node domain through the mapping from input to output port domains.

We have said earlier that the structures of a PRDG and the corresponding KPN are almost the same. The difference may be that an output port domain of a PRDG node communicates data to input port domains of more than one other PRDG nodes, see Figure 3. This is not allowed in a KPN in which every output port connects only to a single input port. If an output port domain connects to multiple input port domains, then the output port domain have to

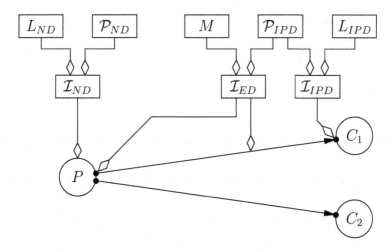

Fig. 9. PRDG of Figure 3 after the matching of port domains

be duplicated for the different edge domains and the domains associated with the duplicates have to be set to the domains of their associating edges. After this transformation, if applicable, the communication input/output port domain pair is said to *match*. Thus, after port matching, the PRDG shown in Figure 3 becomes as shown in Figure 9. We now have that for every $\mathbf{j} \in \mathcal{I}_{OPD}$ there is at least one $\mathbf{i} \in \mathcal{I}_{IPD}$ at which the data produced at $\mathbf{j}$ is to be consumed, and, fore ever $\mathbf{i} \in \mathcal{I}_{IPD}$ there is exactly one $\mathbf{j} \in \mathcal{I}_{OPD}$ that produces that data to be consumed at iteration $\mathbf{i}$. What remains is the construction of the parse nodes.

Let node $N = (I_N, O_N, f_n, \mathcal{I}_n)$ be given, and let $IP \in I_N$ and $OP \in O_N$ be an input port and an output port, respectively. IP and OP must be converted to an input port and an output port, respectively, of the Kahn process. The domain scanning procedure described in the previous subsection scans domain $\mathcal{I}_n$. So, for every iteration $\mathbf{i} \in \mathcal{I}_n$ data must be read from the port that is derived from IP when $\mathbf{i} \in \mathcal{I}_{IPD}$. Similarly, data must be written to the port derived from OP when $\mathbf{i} \in \mathcal{I}_{OPD}$. The problem, then, is that for every $\mathbf{i} \in \mathcal{I}_n$ it must be decided whether $\mathbf{i} \in \mathcal{I}_{IPD}$ and/or $\mathbf{i} \in \mathcal{I}_{OPD}$. This leads to the following tests: For every $IP \in I_N$, $\mathbf{i} \in \mathcal{I}_{IPD}$, if $\mathcal{M}_{\mathcal{I}_{IPD}}(\mathbf{i}) = 1$, where $\mathcal{M}_{\mathcal{I}_{IPD}}()$ is the *multiplicity* with respect to domain $\mathcal{I}_{IP}$, and for every $OP \in O_N$, $\mathbf{i} \in \mathcal{I}_{OPD}$, if $\mathcal{M}_{\mathcal{I}_{OPD}}(\mathbf{i}) \geq 1$, where $\mathcal{M}_{\mathcal{I}_{OPD}}()$ is the *multiplicity* with respect to domain $\mathcal{I}_{OPD}$. See the **Ehrhart test** paragraph. For lack of space, we can not go into details here. We instead give two examples, [14].

Example (input port domain code generation). Let be given a node domain with iteration domain $\mathcal{I}_n = (L_n, \mathcal{P}_n)$. Let $\mathcal{P}_n = \{(x_1, x_2) \in \mathbb{Q}^2 \mid 0 \leq x_1 \leq 100 \wedge x_1 = 2x_2\}$ and $L_n = \begin{bmatrix} 1 & 0 \end{bmatrix}$. Further, let an input port domain with iteration domain $\mathcal{I}_{IPD} \in \mathcal{I}_n$ be given by $\mathcal{I}_{IPD} = (L_{IPD}, \mathcal{P}_{IPD})$ with $\mathcal{P}_{IPD} = \{(x_1, x_2, x_3) \in \mathbb{Q}^3 \mid 10 \leq x_1 \leq 100 \wedge x_1 = 2x_2 \wedge x_1 = 3x_3$ and $L_{IPD} = \begin{bmatrix} 1 & 0 & 0 \end{bmatrix}$. The resulting program is as follows.

```
for i = 1 : 1 : 100,
    if i ≥ 10,
        if [1 0 0 0 0 0]_i ≥ 1,
            body
        end
    end
end
```

Lines 1,2,3, and 4 correspond with the parse nodes 1b, 2a, 2b, and 2c, respectively (See Figure 7 in Subsection 3.4).

Example (output port domain code generation). Let be given a node domain with iteration domain $\mathcal{I}_n = (I, \mathcal{P}_n)$, where I is the identity matrix and $\mathcal{P}_n = \{x_1 \in \mathbb{Q} \mid 0 \le x_1 \le 3N + 3\}$. Let the output port domain be $\mathcal{P}(N) = \{(x_1, x_2) \in \mathbb{Q}^2 \mid 0 \le x_1 \le N \ \wedge \ x_1 \le x_2 \le N\}$, and let $M\mathbf{k}) = \begin{bmatrix} 2 & 1 \end{bmatrix} \mathbf{k} + 3, \mathbf{k} \in \mathcal{P}(N) \cap \mathbb{Z}^2$. The resulting program is as follows.

```
parameter N 16 8;
for j = 1 : 1 : 3N + 3,
    w = false;
    if  − j + N + 3 ≥ 0,
        if j − 3 ≥ 0,
            if ⅓j + [0, −⅓, −⅔]j ≥ 1,
                w = true;
            end
        end
    end
    if w == false,
        if j − N − 3 >= 0,
            if ½N + [−⅙j + [1, 7⁄6, ⅓, 3⁄2, ⅔, 5⁄6]j, −⅙j + [3⁄2, ⅔, 5⁄6, 1, 7⁄6, ⅓]j]N ≥ 1,
                w = true;
            end
        end
    end
    if w == true,
        body
    end
end
```

3.7   Linearization

Let $E = (Q, P, \mathcal{J})$ be an edge that is mapped on the channel that connects the two processes onto which Q and P are mapped. The scanning of the node domain that contains Q also imposes a scanning of Q itself. For every point in the domain of Q the rank is determined. Let $\mathcal{J}$ be the domain $\mathcal{J} = (M, \mathcal{P})$. The *rank* of point $\mathbf{j} \in \mathcal{J}$ is defined as the number of points in $\mathcal{J}$ that are lexicographically preceding $\mathbf{j}$. The expression that ranks all point s $\mathbf{j} \in \mathcal{J}$ is called the *ranking function* and is denoted by rank($\mathbf{j}$). The procedure that finds ranking function is called *ranking*. We have given examples of ranking functions in Subsection 3.2. Recall that tokens are put on the channel in the same order as they are produced. Thus the ranking function of an output port (domain) gives an implicit label to the tokens that are put on the channel, and is, therefore, called the *write polynomial*. The consuming process gets the tokens from the channel, and either consumes a token from the head of the channel or stores the tokens in its private memory for later consumption. Moreover, a token that is read from the channel may have to be consumed multiple times (multi cast). The consumer's token reading management is controlled by the read function (see Subsection 3.3. This function is likewise a (pseudo)polynomial that we call the *read polynomial*. This polynomial is in principle obtained by substituting in the producer's *write polynomial* the consumer-to-producer port mapping. Even when the write polynomial is not available, the read polynomial can still be obtained from the polytope in the input port domain definition and the mapping. The polynomials are obtained by *counting* points in domains and *ranking* points in domains according to a given scanning order. Thus let a domain $\mathcal{I} = (M, \mathcal{P})$ be given. When M is a bijection from $\mathcal{P}$ to $\mathcal{I}$, the points in $\mathcal{I}$ are in one-to-one correspondence with the integral points in $\mathcal{P}$. So, for this case the number of points contained in $\mathcal{I}$ is equal to the number of points in $\mathcal{P} \cap \mathbb{Z}^n$ and, thus, $|\mathcal{I}| = EP(\mathcal{P})$. When M is not a bijection from $\mathcal{P}$ to $\mathcal{I}$, the *multiplicity* of some of the points $\mathbf{i} \in \mathcal{I}$ is greater than one, and counting the number of integral points in $\mathcal{P}$ would count some iterations $\mathbf{i}$ more than once. In this case the number of points in $\mathcal{I}$ is given by $|\mathcal{I}| = |\mathcal{P} - \mathcal{P}_{br}|$ where "-" is the polyhedral difference and $\mathcal{P}_{br}$ is any polyhedral subset of $\mathcal{P}$ that meets the following two requirements:

1. $\mathcal{I} = (M, \mathcal{P} - \mathcal{P}_{br})$
2. for every $\mathbf{i} \in \mathcal{I}$, $\mathcal{M}_{\mathcal{P}_u}(\mathbf{i}) \in \{0, 1\}$, where $\mathcal{P}_u = \mathcal{P} - \mathcal{P}_{br}$ and $\mathcal{M}_{\mathcal{P}_u}(\mathbf{i})$ is the multiplicity with respect to the polytope $\mathcal{P}_u$.

We call $\mathcal{P}_{br}$ and $\mathcal{P}_u$ the *multicast* and *unicast* polytopes of $\mathcal{P}$, respectively. In case of broadcast, the read polynomial is obtained from the unicast polytope and the multiplicities are obtained from the multicast polytope. For example, let $j = M\mathbf{i}$ be the mapping from an input port domain $\mathcal{I}$ to an output port domain $\mathcal{J}$, where M is a 1×3 integral co-prime vector. Let U be a unimodular matrix such that $MU = [1 \; 0 \; 0]$. The second and third columns of U span the null-space of M, which itself is the first row of U^{-1}. Define $\mathbf{j} = U^{-1}\mathbf{i}$. The domains $\mathcal{I}$ and $\mathcal{J}$ are now represented in the three-dimensional $\mathbf{j}$-space whose natural basis $[1 \; 0 \; 0]$, and $[0 \; 1 \; 0]$, $[0 \; 0 \; 1]$ correspond to the original output port domain, and the two vectors that span the null-space of M, respectively. In this new representation, all integral points in the intersection of the input port domain and any plane parallel to the $j_1 = 0$ plane are mapped onto a single point on the j_1 axis. A single point in that plane belongs to the unicast polytope and all others belong to the multicast polytope.

Ranking is always done in polytopes, even when the domain is not dense.

Before going on, we return to the example processes given in Subsection 3.3.

The *write polynomial* of the producer's output port is its ranking polynomial - for the given scanning order of the atomic nodes in its node domain - and is given by $w(j, i) = -\frac{1}{2}j^2 + (N - \frac{1}{2})j + i - N$. The consumer's *read polynomial* is obtained by substituting in the producer's write polynomial the mapping $(j, i) = (l - 1, k)$, and is given by $r(k, l) = w(j = l - 1, i = k) = -\frac{1}{2}l^2 + (N + \frac{1}{2})l + k - 2N$. This polynomial is not identically equal to the ranking polynomial of the consumer's input port domain -for the given scanning order of the atomic nodes in its node domain - and, therefore, the consuming of tokens from the channel will be out of order. A *reordering* (private) memory in the consumer is thus be needed.

Coming back to the main part of this subsection, two interesting properties are worthwhile mentioning. The first one is that an out of order consuming of tokens read from the channel will occur if and only if the mapping matrix M in the **ipd** to **opd** mapping $\mathbf{k} \to \mathbf{i} = M\mathbf{k} + \mathbf{o}$, where $\mathbf{o}$ is a constant vector, is not a lower triangular matrix, provided the entries in $\mathbf{k}$ and $\mathbf{i}$ are ordered in the given ranking orders of the consumer and producer, respectively. In the example we have been working out so far, the mapping matrix is the antidiagonal matrix and, hence, the out of order consumption of channel tokens is no surprise. The second property is that the minimum size of the private memory that is needed for the out of order consumption mechanism is given by $max(r(\mathbf{k}) - rank(\mathbf{k}))$ over all $\mathbf{k}$ in the consumer's input port domain. Here $rank(\mathbf{k})$ is the ranking polynomial of the input port domain - given the scanning order of the port domain. In our example, $rank(k, l) = \frac{1}{2}k^2 - \frac{3}{2}k + \ell$, hence the minimum size of the consumer's private memory is 1 (for $N = 4$), as we know already from the example. However, this memory is not, in general, of the type we have assumed it should be, so that its size will in general be larger than this absolute lower bound. Ranking, write and read polynomials, as well as multiplicities are all derived in our tool PANDA.

4   Converting a KPN to Behaviorally Equivalent KPNs

Our definition of a Process Network that is a translation of an imperative program is such that the Process Network that is generated by the toolchain COMPAAN:{MATPARSER, DGPARSER, PANDA} is *unique* in that it is composed of a minimal number of processes and channels. Because an imperative program is translated to a process network in order to express task-level concurrency, the unique minimal version we have obtained so far will in general not be the preferred one. Many process networks that are behaviorally equivalent to that reference network do exist. An interesting question is whether the alternatives should be obtained by operating on the KPN itself or on the PRDG the KPN originates from. The answer is that operating on the PRDG is what is to be done. However, it turns out that for a number of possible transformations of the reference KPN to alternatives, the best approach is to operate on the original imperative program. For that reason, we have developed a tool MATSOURCE that generates from a given Matlab program alternative programs that can then be taken through COMPAAN to obtain the corresponding process networks. Matlab source to source translations that are possible so far are the following.

4.1   Unfolding

The operation of *unfolding* is to increase the number of processes in a given KPN by unrolling part of the program that KPN was obtained from. For example, to unfold the KPN in Figure 1, MATSOURCE takes the sample program and an unfolding factor, of 3 say, and generates the following code.

```
for k = 1:1:K,
    if mod(k,3) = 1,
        body;
    if mod(k,3) = 2,
        body;
    if mod(k,3) = 0,
        body;
end
```

where *body* is a copy of the original program, except for the outer loop. The KPN translation will now have three processes (in a loop) where the original one had only a single one (except for the source and sink nodes), as well as the associated channels.

4.2   Skewing

The operation of *skewing* is to break dependencies. For example, to skew the KPN in Figure 1, MATSOURCE takes the sample program and a skewing matrix, say with rows $[1 \ 1 \ 0]$, $[0 \ 1 \ 0]$, and $[0 \ 0 \ 1]$, and generates the following code.

```
for k = 2:1:T+N,
    for j = max(1, k-T) :1:1 min(k-1,N),
        [r(j,j), x(k-j,j), t] = Vec(r(j,j), x(k-j,j));
        for i = j+1 :1: N,
            [ r(j,i), x(k-j,i),t] = Rot(r(j,i), x(k-j,i), t);
        end
    end
end
```

The effect of skewing is that input and output port domains, as well as mapping matrices get modified.

Figure 5 is actually part of an unfolded and skewed version of the sample program in Figure 1.

4.3   Lookahead

The operation *lookahead* is to skip some steps in the algorithm and making sure that the remaining part is still correct. For example, to generate a lookahead version for the KPN in Figure 1, MATSOURCE takes the sample program and a lookahead factor, say of 3, and generates the following code.

```
for k = 1:3:3*T,
   for j = 1:1:N,
      for i = j:1:N,
         if i ≤ j,
            [x(k+1,j), x(k+2,j), t1] = Vec(x(k+1,j), x(k+2, j));
            [x(k,j), x(k+1,j), t2] = Vec(x(k,j), x(k+1, j));
            [r(j,j), x(k,j), t] = Vec(r(j,j), x(k, j));
         else
            [x(k+1,i), x(k+2,i), t1] = Rot(x(k+1,i), x(k+2, i), t1);
            [x(k,i), x(k+1,i), t2] = Rot(x(k,i), x(k+1, i), t2);
            [r(j,i), x(k,i), t] = Rot(r(j,i), x(k, i), t);
         end
      end
   end
end
```

Notice that lines 5, 6, 9, and 10 are simply added to the original code lines 7 and 11. The new program leads to a KPN in which the main node-pair (not counting the source and sink nodes) appearing in the original KPN appears three times, the two additional pairs not having the r-channels (which are selfloops in the graph), and communication channels between the three node-pairs only being unidirectional and not forming a loop.

4.4   Partitioning

The operation of *partitioning* is to split processes by decomposing PRDG node domains using domain cutting hyperplanes. The Matlab program that should lead to such partitioning is straightforwardly generated by the tool MATSOURCE.

4.5   Loop Transformation

The operation of loop transformation is to modify the default lexicographical ordering in the SAP program. This will lead to different rankings of the domains, hence to different read and write relationships.

5   Conclusion

The extraction of task-level parallelism from imperative programs is more difficult than extracting instruction level parallelism. However, in high-level system design, one of the first steps is to map concurrent tasks onto autonomous processing units that communicate over an interconnection network. In this paper, we have considered special imperative programs, i.e., affine nested loop programs, and their translation to Kahn process networks. For the mapping of applications specified in the form of process networks into parallel architectures, and a subsequent performance analysis and exploration, we use our tool SPADE, [5],

[17], see Figure 1. This tool implements the so-called Y-chart approach which can be found in [2]. Before we map the Kahn Process Network onto an architecture, we perform an additional translation on the Kahn Processes to provide a specification which better matches the models of architecture components. This translation converts the Kahn Process into the stream based function model SBF, which we have presented in [11].

References

1. Special Issue on Hardware/Software Co-Design. In Proceedings of the IEEE, Mar. 1997.
2. B. Kienhuis et al.: A Methodology to Design Programmable Embedded Systems. In Lecture Notes in Computer Science, this Volume.
3. V. Zivkovic, P. Lieverse: An Overview of Methodologies and Tools in the Field of System-level Design. In Lecture Notes in Computer Science, this Volume.
4. S. Edwards et al.: Design of Embedded Systems: Formal Models, Validation, and Synthesis. In Proceedings of the IEEE, pp. 366-390, Mar. 1997.
5. P. Lieverse et al.: A methodology for architecture exploration of heterogeneous signal processing systems. In Journal of VLSI Signal Processing, Vol. 29, No. 3, pp. 197-207, Nov. 2001.
6. B. Kienhuis: MatParser, An Array Dataflow Analysis Compiler. Technical Report UCB/ERL M00/9, 2000.
7. P. Held, B. Kienhuis: Div, Floor, Ceil, Mod and Step Functions in Nested Loop Programs and Linearly Bounded Lattices. In Algorithms and Parallel Vlsi Architectures III, M. Moonen and F. Catthoor (eds.), pp. 271-282, Kluwer, 1995.
8. F. Feautrier: Compiling for massively parallel architectures: A perspective. In Algorithms and Parallel VLSI Architectures III, M. Moonen and F. Catthoor (eds.), pp. 259-270, Kluwer, 1995.
9. E. Rijpkema: Deriving Process Networks from Nested Loop Algorithms. In Parallel Processing Letters, Vol. 10, Nos. 2 & 3, pp. 165-176, 2000.
10. W. Barnier, J. Chan: Discrete Mathematics with Applications. West Publishing Company, 1989.
11. B. Kienhuis, E. Deprettere: Modeling Stream-Based Applications using the SBF model of computation. In Proc. IEEE Workshop on Signal Processing Systems, SIPS, pp. 385-394, Sep. 2001.
12. E. Ehrhart: Sur les polyèdres rationnels homothétiques à n dimsions. In "C.R. Acad. Sci. Paris, Vol. 254, pp. 616-618, 1962.
13. Ph. Clauss, V. Loechner: Parametric Analysis of Polyhedral Iteration Spaces. In Proc. IEEE Int. Conf. on Application Specific Array Processors, ASAP, pp. 415-424, Chicago, 1996.
14. E. Rijpkema: Modeling Task Level Parallelism in Piecewise Regular Programs. PhD Dissertation, Leiden University, Leiden, The Netherlands, 2002.
15. G. Booch et al.: The Unified Modeling Language User Guide. Addison-Wesley, 1999.
16. D. Wilde: A Library for Doing Polyhedral Operations. IRISA technical report PI 785, Rennes, France, 1993.
17. T. Stefanov et al.: System Level Design with Spade: an M-JPEG Case study. In Proceedings Int. Conf. on Computer Aided Design, pp. 384-388, San Jose, 2001.

Structured Scheduling of Recurrence Equations: Theory and Practice

Patrice Quinton[1] and Tanguy Risset[2]

[1] Irisa, Campus de Beaulieu, 35042 Rennes Cedex, France
quinton@irisa.fr
[2] LIP, ENS Lyon, 46 allée d'Italie
69364 Lyon Cedex 07
trisset@ens-lyon.fr

Abstract. We present new methods for scheduling structured systems of recurrence equations. We introduce the notion of structured dependence graph and structured scheduling. We show that the scheduling of recurrence equations leads to integer linear programs whose practical complexity is $O(n^3)$, where n is the number of constraints. We give new algorithms for computing linear and multi-dimensional structured scheduling, using existing techniques for scheduling non-structured systems of affine recurrence equations. We show that structured scheduling is more than one order of magnitude more efficient than the scheduling of corresponding inlined systems.

Keyword: parallelization of loop nests, structured recurrence equations, scheduling, automatic synthesis of parallel architectures, parallel VLSI architectures.

1 Introduction

The synthesis of parallel programs or of architectures for the execution of loops has two main applications: the generation of parallel programs in order to accelerate applications, or the design of special purpose architectures for embedded systems. In both cases, the method is basically the same: isolate the loops which are good candidate to parallel implementation, extract the parallelism available in the loop, transform the loop into a parallel program, and finally, generate either a program or the description of a parallel architecture.

Loop analysis and transformation can be carried out either by keeping the imperative form of the code, or by transforming it into a single assignment program before applying the transformations. In the latter case, imperative code is rewritten as a set of recurrence equations, a formalism that was introduced by Karp, Miller and Winograd [1]. This approach has been taken in [2,3,4,5] in the context of the automatic parallelization of programs, and in [6,7,8,9] for the synthesis of regular arrays. Recurrence equations is also the basis of several applicative languages: Lucid [10], Lustre [11], Signal [12], Crystal [13], Pei [14] and Alpha [15], for example. All these languages aim at better supporting the

E.F. Deprettere et al. (Eds.): SAMOS 2001, LNCS 2268, pp. 112–134, 2002.

formal derivation of a system from high level specification. Throughout this paper, we will consider Systems of Affine Recurrence Equations (SARE) and express them using the Alpha language, a precise description of which can be found in [16,17].

Since recurrence equations are not imperative, their evaluation order relies upon a scheduler. This problem has been extensively studied [18,19,8,3,20] and results have been used in many parallelizing compilers such as Ape [21], Pips [22], Paf [23], Loopo [24], or in high level synthesis tools for the design of special-purpose architectures such as Arrest [25], Cathedral IV [26], Compaan [27], and MMAlpha [28]. Methods proposed all rely upon expressing the problem as an Integer Linear Program (ILP).

Structured specifications based on recurrence equation are obviously needed in order to deal with large, real-world applications. Primarily addressing the need for program structuring, the extension of recurrences to structured systems of recurrences described in [29] allows one to write and manipulate large specifications in a structured form. Therefore, to fully benefit from structuring, one needs to adapt existing analysis methods to structured systems, and this raises some new issues.

In order to find out a schedule for a structured system of recurrence equations, one can inline this system to obtain a single set of recurrence equations, and then schedule it using classical methods. But this approach has two drawbacks: it looses the information on the structure of the program, and it leads to ILPs which become difficult to solve, as we shall see in this paper.

The other approach, which is taken in this paper, is to look for a *structured scheduling*. Basically, the idea is to use existing scheduling techniques to find out in several steps a schedule for the complete system. In this sense, we are looking for methods which extend the scheduling of SAREs to structured SAREs.

There are several ways to do so. For example, one can first schedule the called subsystems, then reuse the obtained schedules in the calling system. This approach corresponds to a divide and conquer strategy for scheduling. It has many advantages:

- The structure of the specifications, often meaningful from the point of view of the design flow, is kept unchanged.
- If some components of the system have already been designed, one can try to use their schedule and integrate them as such in the global design.
- The scheduling process is faster, as the problems to be solved are smaller.
- Finally, the schedules obtained in such a way are often easier to use in a design process. For instance, we can easily obtain a pipe-line between successive uses of the same system as shown in [30].

However, this raises new questions. For instance, when a SARE is used in several different contexts, it is not always possible to define a single schedule of this SARE suitable for all these contexts. For this reason, the scheduling of structured SAREs cannot be directly deduced from the scheduling techniques dealing with unstructured SAREs.

There are very few contributions reporting research on structured scheduling. A preliminary research to this paper [16] gives some theoretical results on structured scheduling. Later, Crop and Wilde [31] adressed the problem of scheduling structured SAREs. Although it was not formally defined, the notion of a structured scheduling considered is their paper corresponds to the definition of *linear* structured scheduling that we provide here, but they do not handle multidimensional scheduling.

The particularity of the methods proposed here is that they use classical scheduling techniques (solving a linear programming problem) and hence can be directly implemented on top of a tool for the scheduling of SAREs.

The paper is organized as follows. Section 2 reviews the main results on scheduling of recurrence equations, and introduces the notion of a structured dependence graph as an extension of the classical reduced dependence graph. In section 3, we recall how a linear schedule can be modelled as an ILP, and we show on a set of benchmark programs that the practical complexity of this problem is $O(n^3)$, where n is the number of constraints or variables. Section 4 addresses linear scheduling, and provides a systematic method for computing a structured linear schedule for a structured SARE. Then, in section 5, this method is extended to find multi-dimensional structured scheduling. Finally, section 6 shows the practical efficiency of the structured scheduling by comparing it to the schedule of the corresponding inlined systems.

2   Background and Definitions

In this section, we introduce the main notions and definitions needed to formalize the problem: affine recurrence equations, Alpha programs, scheduling, reduced dependence graphs, and the extensions of these notions to structured systems of recurrence equations.

2.1   Affine Recurrence Equations

A System of Affine Recurrence Equation (SARE), is a finite number of equations of the form:
$$z \in \mathcal{D} \quad : \quad V_0(z) = f(V_0(I_0(z)), \dots, V_p(I_p(z)))$$
where:

1. $\mathcal{D}$ is the *domain* of the equation: it is the set of points with integral coordinates included in a convex domain of Z^n.
2. n is the *dimension* of variable V_0.
3. For all i, I_i, the *dependency function*, is an integral affine function from Z^n to Z^p, where p is the dimension of variable V_i.

For example

$$\{k \mid k = 0\} : \mathsf{Acc}(k) = 0 \tag{1}$$
$$\{k \mid 1 < k \le N\} : \mathsf{Acc}(k) = \mathsf{Acc}(k-1) + \mathsf{V1}(k) * \mathsf{V2}(k) \tag{2}$$

is a SARE which computes the dot product of two N-vectors V1 and V2.

For a given variable V, we denote as $\mathrm{Dom}(V)$ the definition domain of this variable.

2.2 Alpha Systems

The Alpha language [15] allows SAREs to be expressed. Fig. 1 show an Alpha program for the dot product of equations (1-2), with the addition of a variable res which isolates the result. In the remaining of this paper, we will describe SAREs as Alpha systems.

```
system dot : {N | N >= 2}
  (V1,V2 : {k | 1<=k<=N} of integer)
returns (res:  integer);
var
  Acc : {k | 0<= k <= N } of integer;
let
  Acc[k] =
     case
        {| k = 0 } : 0[];
        {| k > 0 } : Acc[k-1]+V1[k]*V2[k];
     esac;
  res[] = Acc[N];
 tel;
```

Fig. 1. Alpha program for the dot product of two vectors

2.3 Scheduling SAREs

Scheduling a SARE aims at assigning an execution time to the computations specified by the system. As there are usually a very large number of such computations, we look for a closed form in order to express the schedule of a possibly infinite number of computations in a finite manner.

The formalism of recurrence equations naturally leads to the notion of a *linear schedule*: for each variable V of the system, the computation date is expressed as an affine function $T_V(z) = \tau_V \cdot z + \alpha_V$ of its indices. A linear schedule is valid if it is positive and respects dependencies between the computations. For instance, in equation (2), $\mathrm{Acc}(k)$ depends on $\mathrm{Acc}(k-1)$ for all k in $\{k \mid 1 < k \leq N\}$, hence a valid schedule T_{Acc} must satisfy the constraint $T_{\mathrm{Acc}}(k) - T_{\mathrm{Acc}}(k-1) > 0$. Therefore, $T_{\mathrm{Acc}}(k) = k$ is a valid linear schedule for this SARE, and a valid schedule for the whole system dot is:

$$T_{\mathrm{V1}}^{\mathrm{dot}}(k) = 0 \quad T_{\mathrm{V2}}^{\mathrm{dot}}(k) = 0 \quad T_{\mathrm{Acc}}^{\mathrm{dot}}(k) = k \quad T_{\mathrm{res}}^{\mathrm{dot}} = 1 + N \quad . \tag{3}$$

2.4   Reduced Dependence Graph

Scheduling techniques base their analysis on the data dependencies. For a SARE, the data dependency information is usually represented in the form of a reduced dependence graph.

Definition 1. *(reduced dependence graph) The reduced dependence graph (DG) of an Alpha system is a graph $G = (V, E)$ whose vertices V are Alpha variables and edges E represent dependencies between variables. Vertices are labeled by the variable names and domains, and edges are labeled by the dependency function and the definition domain of this function.* ■

As an example, Fig. 2 shows the reduced dependence graph of the Alpha system of Fig. 1.

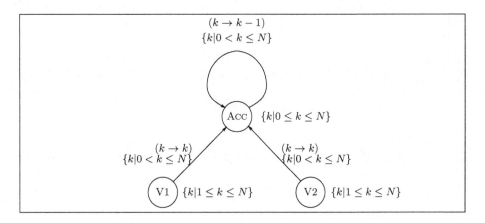

Fig. 2. Reduced dependence graph of the Alpha system for the dot product

2.5   Structured Systems of Recurrence Equations

The Alpha language provides a means to describe Structured Systems of Affine Recurrences Equations (SSARE) [29]. For instance, Fig. 3 shows the definition of a matrix multiplication MM by means of N^2 dot products. The third equation, called a **use** statement, instanciates N^2 times the dot product for all points (i, j) such that $1 \leq i, j \leq N$. The general form of a use statement in Alpha is the following:

$$\text{use } \{J|AJ \leq b\} \text{ sub}[f(J, N)] \ (U_1, \ldots, U_n) \text{ return } (V_1, \ldots, V_m) \ . \qquad (4)$$

This statement represents a multiple instantiation of the **sub** Alpha system, and it is made out of the following elements:

```
system MM : {N | N >= 2}
  (M1,M2 : {i,j | 1<= i,j <= N} of integer)
returns (Mres : {i,j | 1<= i,j <= N} of integer);
var
  Mdup1,Mdup2: {k,i,j | 1<= i,j,k <= N} of integer;
let
  Mdup1[k,i,j] = M1[i,k];
  Mdup2[k,i,j] = M2[k,j];
  use {i,j| 1<= i,j <= N} dot[N] (Mdup1,Mdup2) returns (Mres);
tel;
```

Fig. 3. Structured Alpha specification of the matrix product using N^2 dot products.

- The domain $\mathcal{E} = \{J|AJ \leq b\}$ is called the *extension domain* of the statement. It represents the instances of sub used. Note that, as the formal input of dot is one-dimensional and $\mathcal{E} = \{i,j \mid 1 \leq i,j \leq N\}$ is two-dimensional, the actual inputs of the use of dot are three-dimensional. In system MM, i and j are *extension indices*.
- The function $f(J,N)$, the *parameter assignment* function, gives the value of the size parameters of the called subsystem sub in terms of the parameters of the caller system. In system MM, the parameter assignment function $f(i,j,N) = N$ simply transmits the size parameter N from MM to dot.

2.6 Structured Scheduling

As the research on scheduling recurrence equations has always focused on unstructured recurrence equations, we have to give a formal definition of a *structured scheduling*. The notion that we introduce here allows one to reuse components of libraries of (already scheduled) systems.

Definition 2. *(structured scheduling) Consider an Alpha system* sys, *and a schedule T^{sys} of* sys. *Let*

$$\text{use } \{J|AJ \leq b\} \text{ sub}[f(J,N)] \ (U_1,\ldots,U_n) \text{ return } (V_1,\ldots,V_m) \qquad (5)$$

be a use statement in sys, *calling a subsystem* sub. *Denote by u_i (resp. v_i) the formal input (resp. output) variable of* sub *corresponding to U_i (resp. V_i). We say that T^{sys} is structured with respect to this use statement if there exists a schedule T^{sub} of* sub, *and a linear function $c(J)$ such that:*

$$\forall U_i, \forall (I,J) \in \text{Dom}(U_i), \ T_{U_i}^{sys}(I,J) = c(J) + T_{u_i}^{sub}(I)$$
$$\forall V_i, \forall (I,J) \in \text{Dom}(V_i), \ T_{V_i}^{sys}(I,J) = c(J) + T_{v_i}^{sub}(I)$$

We say that T^{sys} is a structured schedule if it is structured with respect to all use statements in sys. ∎

The key property of a structured schedule is that the c function is the same for all input and output parameters of a use statement.

To illustrate this definition, consider the example of the MM Alpha program shown in Fig. 3.

We have seen that a schedule for the dot system is

$$T_{\text{V1}}^{\text{dot}}(k) = 0 \quad T_{\text{V2}}^{\text{dot}}(k) = 0 \quad T_{\text{Acc}}^{\text{dot}}(k) = k \quad T_{\text{res}}^{\text{dot}} = 1 + N \quad . \tag{6}$$

In program MM, there are N^2 calls to dot, each one being attached to a unique pair (i, j) in the extension domain $\{i, j \mid 1 \leq i, j \leq N\}$. For a given dot instance, say instance (i_1, j_1), scheduling this instance at time $c(i_1, j_1)$ means exactly that the inputs Mdup1$[k,i_1,j_1]$ and Mdup2$[k,i_1,j_1]$, $1 \leq k \leq N$ are available at time $c(i_1, j_1)$ and that, according to (3), the output Mres$[i_1,j_1]$ is available at time $c(i_1, j_1) + N + 1$. Therefore, the schedule

$$\begin{aligned}
T_{\text{Mdup1}}^{\text{MM}}(k, i, j) &= i + j \\
T_{\text{Mdup2}}^{\text{MM}}(k, i, j) &= i + j \\
T_{\text{Mres}}^{\text{MM}}(i, j) &= i + j + N + 1
\end{aligned} \tag{7}$$

is a valid structured scheduling for system MM.

2.7   Structured Dependence Graph

We propose now an extension of the notion of reduced dependence graph to structured SARES.

Definition 3. *(structured dependence graph,* SDG*) The structured dependence graph of a structured Alpha system is a graph $G = (V, E)$ whose vertices V are labeled by the variables of the system and their domains, and edges E represent either:*

1. *dependencies between variables, these edges being labeled by the dependency function and the domain on which it applies;*
2. *dependencies between actual inputs and actual outputs of a use statement, these edges being labeled with the name of the instanciated system, the extension domain and the parameter assignment function.* ∎

The structured dependence graph of the system of Fig. 3 is shown in Fig. 4. Note that, unlike the dependence graph, the structured dependence graph does not represent all the information contained in the program. For example, in the SDG of Fig. 4, the dependency between inputs Mdup1, Mdup2 and output Mres is not explicitly expressed. This is fair because this information could only be extracted by analyzing the body of the dot system.

3   The Complexity of Scheduling SARES

In this section, we briefly explain how to find a schedule for a SARE, and we describe the complexity, both theoretical and practical, of this problem.

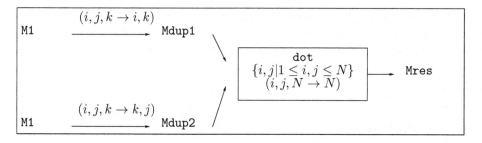

Fig. 4. Structured dependence graph of the Matrix product MM of Fig. 3. The rectangular box corresponds actually to 2 edges from Mdup1 to Mres and Mdup2 to Mres.

3.1 Method

Scheduling SARE has been addressed in two contexts: the synthesis of systolic arrays [7,8,9] and the automatic parallelization of programs [3,20,4,5,32]. Scheduling uniform recurrences was first considered by Karp, Miller and Winograd [1]. Later on, extensions to linear recurrences [3,19,9] were examined. All these methods are based on results of linear programming. For instance, the method depicted in [3] uses the affine form of Farkas Lemma, and the one of [19] uses the duality theorem of linear programming.

In all cases, the problem is to solve an ILP, obtained in the following way. Consider a recurrence equation

$$z \in \mathcal{D} \quad : \quad V_0(z) = f(V_0(I_0(z)), \dots, V_p(I_p(z))) \quad . \tag{8}$$

To find a linear schedule T_{V_0}, two types of constraints should be met:

- First, T_{V_0} must be positive on the domain $\mathcal{D}$. As $\mathcal{D}$ is a convex polyhedron, this property amounts to satisfy a finite set of linear inequalities, whose variables are the coefficients of the T_{V_0} function.
- Second, for all pair of dependent variables (V_0, V_j) in equation (8), the schedule of T_{V_0} and T_{V_j} must be such that $T_{V_0}(z) \geq T_{V_j}(I_j(z))$, for all points $z \in \mathcal{D}$. Again, this property is satisfied if a set of linear inequalities whose variables are the coefficients of T_{V_0} and T_{V_j} are met.

Finding a schedule consists therefore of building the system of linear inequalities, and solving it using an ILP solver. In practice, one chooses between all the valid schedules the one that minimizes the total computation time for a system.

3.2 Complexity of Scheduling

To solve the ILP, one uses methods based on the simplex algorithm. The method of choice to solve this problem is the Parametric Integer Programming (PIP) method of Feautrier [33]: in all the experiments reported in this paper, this is the software that was used. It is well known that the number of pivoting steps of the integral simplex method is exponential in the number of variables (or linear contraints) of the problem [34], but when the simplex is run to find out a rational solution, the number of pivoting steps is in practice linear. Although we solve the scheduling ILP using an integral simplex, we shall see here that the behaviour of the algorithm is the same as the rational one. The reason is that most polyhedra we are dealing with have integral vertices.

To have a more precise idea of this complexity, we have run this method on a set of Alpha systems.

Table 1. Result of a flat scheduler on a set of Alpha systems.

Program	#vertices	#constraints	Time (s)
Dot product Vector	74	82	0.14
Fir filter	84	80	0.25
Forward substitution	85	88	0.28
Full adder	40	32	0.03
Binary addition	181	174	1.48
Sum	99	90	0.26
ROM	131	136	0.94
Gaussian elimination	165	162	1.40
Givens rotations	388	434	30.13
Lower matrix vector	69	64	0.14
Matrix multiplication	92	80	0.19
Two matrix multiplication	142	144	0.72
Three matrix multiplication	270	240	6.39
Multiplexer	132	154	0.98
Fuzzy set22	1119	1218	542.56
Neural Network	545	620	67.21

Table 1 gives the list of systems considered, and the number of vertices, constraints, and total scheduling time. These programs were run on a Sun Workstation. Fig. 5 gives a plot of the number of contraints in terms of the number of variables, and shows that there is a very strong linear relationship between these variables. Fig. 6 gives a plot of the scheduling time in terms of the number of variables. This curve was fitted to a cubic expression with a very high significance.

The conclusions of this experiment are three-fold:

1. First, the practical complexity of the scheduling fits near perfectly to that of the rational simplex algorithm. This shows that the problem has a very good behaviour.
2. Second, the $0(n^3)$ complexity is a very strong incentive to find out structured methods for solving the scheduling of systems, as we may save in practice a lot of time.
3. Finally, we can see that the scheduling time is reasonable for small systems, but becomes prohibitive in the context of automatic design of circuits for large systems.

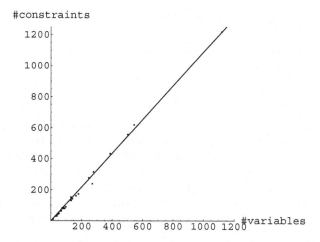

Fig. 5. Plot of the number of constraints against the number of variables for the scheduling ILP of the Alpha system of Table 1, together with the line $y = 1.087x$ which represents the best linear fit.

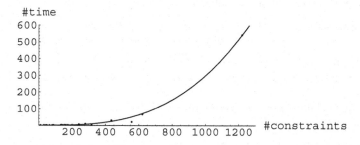

Fig. 6. Plot of the execution time of the scheduler against the number of constraints for the Alpha systems of Table 1, together with the curve $y = 2.9810^{-7}x^3$ which is the best cubic fit.

4   Linear Scheduling of Structured SARES

In this section we study the following problem: given an Alpha structured program, how can we find a structured linear scheduling for this program using the same technique as that used for finding linear schedules for recurrence equations?

A necessary condition for this scheduling to exist is obviously that the inlined system has a linear schedule, but this condition is not sufficient. Indeed, our definition of structured scheduling imposes that any output of a use statement depends on any input of it; some of these constraints may not be necessary when one knows the exact structure of the called subsystem.

In this section, we propose an algorithm for finding structured linear scheduling using a linear scheduler such as the one presented in section 3 [3]. We provide necessary and sufficient conditions to find a structured linear scheduling in the case of a bottom-up approach, i.e. when the called subsystems are scheduled before the calling system.

We consider successively two cases: when the SDG has no cycle with a use statement, and then the general case.

4.1 The SDG Has no Cycle with a Use Statement

In the program of Fig. 3 whose reduced dependence graph is depicted in Fig. 4, the structured dependence graph does not have dependence cycles with use statements: it corresponds to N^2 independent uses of the system dot. A natural method to obtain a structured schedule is therefore to schedule the dot system first, and then to deduce constraints for the schedule of the MM system.

Based on these ideas, we propose a method for finding structured schedules for a system sys whose cycles of the reduced dependence graph do not contain use statements:

- First decompose the SDG into strongly connected components, each one of which contains at most one system call to sub.
- Then solve the scheduling problem for each component, in the topological order of the components of the graph.

Let us examine first the constraints that a linear structured scheduling of sys must satisfy. Given an edge of the SDG, two cases may occur:

- The edge is not labeled with a system name. In this case, the scheduling constraints are defined in the usual way, as defined for example by Feautrier in [3].
- The edge is labeled by a system name, i.e., the edge is part of a use statement of the form

$$\texttt{use } \{J | AJ \leq b\} \texttt{ sub}[\texttt{f(J,N)}] \ (U_1, \ldots, U_n) \texttt{ return } (V_1, \ldots, V_m) \quad . \quad (9)$$

Let u_i and v_j be the formal arguments of system sub corresponding to U_i and V_j, respectively. Because of the restricted information contained in the SDG, the corresponding dependencies are: each output $V_j(I, J)$ of sub depends on each input $U_i(I', J)$, for all J in the extension domain $\mathcal{E}$ and for all $I \in \text{Dom}(v_j)$ and $I' \in \text{Dom}(u_i)$.

The following theorem shows that these constraints are exactly those needed to define a structured scheduling.

Theorem 1. *Let* sys *be an Alpha program with a call to subsystem* sub. *Let* T^{sub} *be a schedule of* sub. *Then the following constraints are necessary and sufficient to obtain a valid structured schedule* T^{sys}:

$$\forall u_i, v_j :$$

$$\forall I \in \text{Dom}(u_i), \ T^{sys}_{U_i}(I, 0) = T^{sub}_{u_i}(I)$$

$$\forall I \in \text{Dom}(v_i), \ T^{sys}_{V_i}(I, 0) = T^{sub}_{v_i}(I) \tag{10}$$

$$\forall J \in \mathcal{E}, \qquad T^{sys}_{U_i}(0, J) - T^{sys}_{V_j}(0, J) = T^{sub}_{u_i}(0) - T^{sub}_{v_j}(0)$$

The proof of this theorem is given in appendix A.   ∎

To illustrate this result, consider again the example of Fig. 3. The constraints deduced from schedule (3) are:

$$\forall k, 1 \leq k \leq N, T^{MM}_{Mdup1}(k,0,0) \quad = T^{MM}_{Mdup2}(k,0,0) = 0$$
$$T^{MM}_{Mres}(0,0) \quad\quad\quad\quad\quad = N+1,$$
$$\forall i, j, 1 \leq i, j \leq N, T^{MM}_{Mdup1}(0,i,j) = T^{MM}_{Mdup2}(0,i,j) = T^{MM}_{Mres}(i,j) - N - 1$$

The schedule of (7) meets these constraints. Another valid structured schedule is:

$$\begin{aligned} T^{MM}_{Mdup1}(k,i,j) &= 0 \\ T^{MM}_{Mdup2}(k,i,j) &= 0 \\ T^{MM}_{Mres}(i,j) \quad &= N+1 \end{aligned} \tag{11}$$

If the SDG does not contains cycles with use statements, the method presented here can be applied even if the schedule of the called system sub has not already been computed. In that case, when the computation dates of the actual inputs U_i to sub are known, one just computes the schedule of sub with the additional constraints on formal inputs u_i inherited from the computation dates of the actual inputs U_i. This top-down approach always provides a linear structured schedule whenever there exists one and, moreover, it chooses the fastest linear schedule if we minimize the execution time. Indeed, if there is no use statement in a cycle, each strongly connected component can be scheduled in minimum time and the total time is the sum of the execution times of the components. The interested reader may find more details in [16].

4.2   The SDG Has Cycles with Use Statements

In most reasonably complex structured programs, use statements will appear in cycles, i.e., there will be a repetitive use of a subsystem. An example of such program is shown in Fig. 7; this program computes the product of P square matrices using P-1 times the MM matrix-matrix product of Fig. 3.

If we want to schedule such a program, and if we restrict ourselves to linear schedules, then the method is very similar to the one explained above:

- First compute the schedules of all called subsystems.
- Then schedule the calling system with the additional constraints given by equation (10).

This bottom-up approach has one drawback: depending on the schedule choosen for the subsystems, the calling system may or may not have a linear schedule. Hence, the scheduling algorithm would have to be a trial and error process where the scheduling of the called subsystem is changed until a satisfying solution is obtained for the calling system. However, one can cut this trial and error process with the result presented in Theorem 2 below.

```
system MMM: {M,P |P,M>=2}
  (matList : {i,j,p | 1<=i,j<=M; 1<=p<=P} of real)
returns
  (res : {i,j | 1<=i,j<=M } of real);
var
  matAcc:        {i,j,p | 1<=i,j<=M; 2<=p<=P} of real;
  matAccNext:    {i,j,p | 1<=i,j<=M; 2<=p<=P} of real;
let
  matAcc[i,j,p] = case
        {|p=2} : matList[i,j,p-1];
        {|p>2} : matAccNext[i,j,p-1];
     esac;
  use {p| 2<=p<=P} matmult[M] (matList,matAcc) returns (matAccNext);
  res[i,j] = matAccNext[i,j,P];
tel;
```

Fig. 7. Structured Alpha specification of the product of a series of P square matrices

But first, we need to introduce the notion of separate dependencies. Consider again a calling system sys and a subsystem sub used in sys (use equation in 5). Consider a dependency from an output of sub to an input of sub:

$$U_i[I, J] \leftarrow V_j[f(I, J), g(I, J)] \tag{12}$$

where J denotes the vector of extension indices (we have splitted the dependency into two parts, f and g, where g corresponds to the extension indices introduced in section 2.6). If $f(I, J)$ really depends upon J, then the time-shift between different inputs to sub may vary with the instance executed, as it may depend on J. Similarly, if $g(I, J)$ really depends upon I, then a single variable U_i input to one subsystem may depend on several other instances of the same subsystem. In both cases, it may be impossible to use the same schedule for all instances of sub.

There is a situation where this problem disappears. Consider dependencies of the form:

$$U_i[I, J] \leftarrow V_j[f(I), g(J)] \quad . \tag{13}$$

where $f(I)$ depends only on I and $g(J)$ only on J. If all dependencies from outputs to inputs of called subsystems have this form, then we say that the system has the *separated dependency property*. In practice, all the Alpha structured programs have this property, as this is the most intuitive way of expressing structuring. The following theorem indicates exactly when a linear structured schedule exists.

Theorem 2. *Let* sys *be a system which has the separated dependency property for all its calls. Then* sys *admits a linear structured scheduling only if, for each subsystem call to sybsystem* sub *contained in a cycle c of the* SDG, *the time delay in cycle c from an input to an output of subsystem* sub *is constant.*

The proof of this theorem is given in appendix B. ■

This condition is very restrictive, but this is not surprising because most of the programs containing a **use** statement in a cycle have a linear time schedule. Indeed, consider the program of Fig. 7, and say that the schedule of system MM is the one presented in equation (10), i.e., an earliest time schedule. Computing P such matrix products in succession will last P*(N+1) unit of times, which is impossible with a linear schedule.

We now propose an algorithm for computing a linear structured scheduling of an Alpha system **sys**.

Algorithm A

(Given: a system **sys**, and a call to subsystem **sub** *)*
*Perform a topological sort of the structured dependence graph of **sys***
for each strongly connected component c (in topological order) do
    determine the constraints of the input to the component
    *for each call C to a subsystem **sub** in c (written as (5)) do*
        build the set $\mathcal{IO}_C$ of pairs (U_i, V_j) such
            *that there is a dependence from V_j to U_i in **sys** as in (12)*
            *schedule **sub** by Algorithm A, with constraints from input to the*
                component and minimization of the latency between
                the consumption of U_i and the production of V_j for $(U_i, V_j) \in \mathcal{IO}_C$
        *If no schedule is found **then return** fail*
    endfor
    *schedule c using the schedule found for **sub** in constraints (10)*
    *If no schedule is found **then return** fail*
endfor

This algorithm is valid, because we have proven that constraints (10) are sufficient to provide a structured linear schedule.

Algorithm A can easily be modified in order to use the same schedule for different calls to the same system **sub**. To do so, we replace the second schedule of **sub** in algorithm A by the first schedule found for **sub**, thus giving priority to the first call in the SDG.

As already said, algorithm A may fail, for instance, if the schedule is non-linear. In the next section, we look for non-linear structured scheduling.

5   Structured Multi-dimensional Scheduling

In the context of loop parallelization, non-linear scheduling has been studied through *multi-dimensional* scheduling. In this section, we present methods to obtain structured multi-dimensional schedules, after introducing the background material necessary to formalize this notion.

5.1   Multi-dimensional Scheduling

The principles of multi-dimensional scheduling were settled down by Karp, Miller and Winograd [1] and explored further in [20,35]. The idea is as follows. Consider an Alpha system which does not have a linear schedule. This means that no linear expression on the indices provides a partial order that respects the dependencies of the system. Instead of looking for a unique linear expression T_V associated with each variable, we look for a vector of linear expressions on the indices in order to represent the computation date. Let $\ll$ denote the lexicographic order between vectors, i.e.:

$$X \ll Y \text{ if there exists } i \text{ such that } \begin{cases} x_k = y_k, \forall k < i \\ x_k < y_k, \text{if } k = i \end{cases} .$$

Then, if U depends on V in the SARE, we impose that $\forall z \in \text{Dom}(U)$, $T_U(z) \ll T_V(z)$.

For instance, the following multi-dimensional schedule is valid for the program of Fig. 3:

$$T_{\texttt{Mdup1}}(i,j,k) = T_{\texttt{Mdup2}}(i,j,k) = \begin{pmatrix} i \\ k \end{pmatrix} \quad ,$$

$$T_{\texttt{Mres}}(i,j) = \begin{pmatrix} i \\ N+1 \end{pmatrix} \quad .$$

This schedule has two dimensions. It does not really give an absolute date of computation for each variable but merely a relative order: first compute the coefficients of the first row of $\texttt{Mres}$ ($i = 1$), then when this is finished, compute the coefficients of the second row ($i = 2$, because $\forall j, k$, $T_{\texttt{Mres}}[1,j] \ll T_{\texttt{Mdup1}}[2,j,k]$) and so on. As an intuitive explanation of what a multi-dimensional schedule represents, one can interpret the components of the time vector as hours, minutes, seconds, etc. (Notice however that this interpretation is realistic only if all the variables have the same rectangular domains, which is not always the case.)

5.2   Computing Multi-dimensional Schedules

Computing multi-dimensional schedules is based on the following idea. If a dependency, say for instance

$$\forall i,j,k, \quad T_{\texttt{Mres}}(i,j) - T_{\texttt{Mdup1}}(i,j,k) \geq 1 \qquad (14)$$

cannot be met using a linear schedule, then we introduce an additional dimension in the timing vector; T becomes thus $\begin{pmatrix} T^1 \\ T^2 \end{pmatrix}$. Then we try to satisfy the relaxed constraint

$$\forall i,j,k, \quad T^1_{\texttt{Mres}}(i,j) - T^1_{\texttt{Mdup1}}(i,j,k) \geq 0$$

by means of the first component of T and leave it up to T^2 to *strictly satisfy* the strict dependency (14). We say that this dependency is *satisfied at level 2*.

The schedule shown in (14) respects these constraints on T^1 and T^2. Hence, computing multi-dimensional schedules can be done with a linear scheduler provided that we implement the process described here. Feautrier [20] does this by minimizing the number of dimensions of the resulting schedule.

Multi-dimensional scheduling provides a lot of flexibility in the loop parallelization process. However, the space of possible valid multi-dimensional schedules is huge and few strategies have yet been proposed. This is why the practical use of such methods is limited.

In the next paragraph, we propose a strategy for finding structured multidimensional scheduling.

5.3   Multi-dimensional Schedule and Structuring

In section 4, we were looking for linear schedules by enforcing constraints on the computation dates of inputs and outputs of system calls. In the multi-dimensional case, we do not know in advance which dependency is satisfied at which level. Hence, it is impossible to enforce values for timing vectors, and we must propose another method.

One way of doing so is to assume that each call to a subsystem takes no time with respect to the schedule of the calling system: in other words, the inputs and outputs are assumed to be available at the same time instant. Then, in order to satisfy the dependency constraints inside the subsystem, it suffices to add extra dimensions to the time vector. This method is always applicable to Alpha programs: indeed, as two systems cannot call each other, the graph of the system calls of an Alpha program is always acyclic.

Let us formalize this idea. Assume that we have a procedure (Algorithm A for example) that computes a linear structured schedule. Given an Alpha system, the following algorithm tries to find out a structured multidimensional scheduling.

Algorithm B

1.   Decompose the SDG *of sys in strongly connected components*
2.   for each strongly connected component c of the SDG   *do*
        determine the constraints on the inputs of the component
        compute a schedule T_c for this component with Algorithm A
        if no schedule is found   then do
            for each system call to s_i of the component   do
                schedule s_i with Algorithm B and get a k_i-dimensional
                schedule T_c^i
            end for
        get a k-dimensional schedule T_c' of the component c
            with the constraints that inputs and outputs of a system call
            have exactly the same schedule
        Build a $k + \max_i(k_i)$-dimensional schedule $T_c = \begin{pmatrix} T_c' \\ T_c^i \end{pmatrix}$ (padd
            T_c^i with 0's if needed)
        end if
    enddo
3.   If the T_c schedules have different dimensions for different c, padd
        the smaller ones with 0's.

Notice that in this algorithm, each call to a subsystem may have a different schedule.

5.4   Validity of Algorithm B

In this section, we prove that the schedules obtained by algorithm B are valid structured schedules, i.e., that all dependencies are met by the schedule found. We have already proven that algorithm A provides valid linear schedules. Thus, it remains to prove that the schedule found with algorithm B, when algorithm A fails, satisfies the dependencies inside a strongly connected component and that dependencies between strongly connected components are satisfied.

Inside a strongly connected component c, dependencies in a subsystem sub (from inputs to outputs) are satisfied because all variables have the same coefficients in T'_c, and the recursive use of algorithm B provides coefficients of T^i_c that satisfy dependencies (a simple induction argument would be needed to prove this, but we assume that this property is clear enough to not need a formal proof). Inside a strongly connected component c, a dependency occurring in the sys system is ensured by T'_c. As all our dependence constraints are *strict* (i.e., we forbid computation which last 0 unit of time, except for the calls), appending T^i_c (and possibly 0's) at the end, will not change the lexicographic order.

Dependencies between strongly connected components are satisfied because, before scheduling one component, we compute the constraints (on the first level of schedule) derived from the schedules of all previous (in the topological order sense) components. Hence, the addition of 0's performed in step *3* of Algorithm B concern variables for which dependency constraints have been (strictly) satisfied at a higher level.

Algorithm B provides one possible strategy for structured multi-dimensional scheduling. Of course this approach has drawbacks. First, as for the linear case of section 4, this will not work on all Alpha programs which admit multi-dimensional schedules. Again, this is due to the way our SDG models dependencies inside a system call: some outputs may not depend on some inputs, hence a cycle in the SDG may not be a real cycle. For instance, if the dependency occurring from an output to an input is the identity, algorithm B will fail. But, let us point out that writing a call where inputs depend on outputs is not coherent with the usual notion of structuring: this will never happen when, for instance, the SAREs come from imperative code which has been automatically translated.

Another limitation of our approach is that it forbids possible pipelining between successive instances of a call of the same (or different) system: the output of a system cannot be used before the system is completely executed. This is a limitation in VLSI synthesis since pipelining is very often used there. In our approach, pipelining can only be achieved with linear schedules obtained by algorithm A.

6   Practical Efficiency of Structured Scheduling

To establish the practical performance of structured scheduling, we have run the structured scheduler on 6 benchmark programs, and we have run the non structured scheduler on the sames programs after fully inlining the called subsystems.

In all cases, the schedules obtained by both techniques were the sames, up to a factor which is due to the difference of structuration of the programs. Indeed, the default option of our scheduler is that the computation of each equation costs one unit of time, and therefore, splitting an equation may introduce extra artificial delays: a careful setting of the delays allows such differences to disappear. Table 2 gives the time needed to schedule these programs. It clearly shows that there is a gain of more than one order of magnitude when running a structured scheduling.

Table 2. Comparizon of the time needed to schedule structured programs and inlined programs. Times are given in seconds.

Program	Structured scheduling	Inlined scheduling
Binary adder	0.26	1.48
Gaussian elimination	0.42	1.40
Three matrix multiplications	0.42	6.39
Neural network	5.36	67.21
Fuzzy set	9.48	542.56
One step of SVD	4.21	21.59

7   Conclusion

We have presented the basic concepts of structured scheduling for recurrence equations. We have given a precise definition of the structured dependence graph for a structured SARE, and of the notion of structured scheduling. With respect to these definitions, we have presented an algorithm for finding a valid (linear or multi-dimensional) structured scheduling. The main interest of this approach is that it permits a scheduling tool for unstructured SAREs to be reused, and thus can be implemented very quickly.

We have also proven that, if we are looking for linear structured scheduling with a "bottom-up" approach, our algorithm is *optimal* in the sense that if there exists a linear structured scheduling, then we will find it.

We have shown that a structured scheduler gives in practice the same results as scheduling the inlined program, with a much lower complexity.

Structured scheduling allows the structuring information to be kept and reduces the scheduling computation complexity. It also provides more readable and natural schedulings.

This work has been done in order to provide a strategy for scheduling large Alpha systems in the MMAlpha environment. Many open questions remain. First, we do not know if it is possible to statically determine all the cases where a structured SARE admits a structured linear scheduling (neither for structured multidimensional scheduling of course). Algorithm B proposed for multi-dimensional structured scheduling is one possible method among many variants, and it remains to compare it to other approaches. In particular, in this work, we wanted to use an existing scheduler as the basis for structured scheduling. If we get rid of this implementation constraint, it may be possible to define completely different scheduling algorithms.

Acknowledgments

The authors would like to thank the referees for their help in improving this document.

References

1. Karp, R., Miller, R., Winograd, S.: The organization of computations for uniform recurrence equations. Journal of the ACM **14** (1967) 563–590
2. Lamport, L.: The Parallel Execution of DO Loops. Communications of The ACM **17** (1974) 83–93
3. Feautrier, P.: Some efficient solutions to the affine scheduling problem, part I, one dimensional time. Int. J. of Parallel Programming **21** (1992) 313–348
4. Wolf, M., Lam, M.: Loop transformation theory and an algorithm to maximize parallelism. IEEE Transactions on Parallel and Distributed Systems **2** (1991) 452–471
5. Darte, A., Khachiyan, L., Robert, Y.: Linear scheduling is nearly optimal. Parallel Processing Letters **1** (1991) 73–81
6. Kung, H.: Why systolic architectures? Computer **15** (1982) 37–46
7. Lee, P., Kedem, Z.: Mapping nested loop algorithms into multidimensional systolic arrays. IEEE Transaction On Parallel and Distributed System **1** (90) 64–76
8. Moldovan, D.: On the analysis and synthesis of VLSI systolic arrays. IEEE Transactions on Computers **31** (1982) 1121–1126
9. Mauras, C., Quinton, P., Rajopadhye, S., Saouter, Y.: Scheduling affine parameterized recurrences by means of variable dependent timing functions. In Kung, S., E.E. Swartzlander, J., Fortes, J., Przytula, K., eds.: Application Specific Array Processors, IEEE Computer Society Press (1990) 100–110
10. Ashcroft, E., Wadge, W.: Lucid, a formal system for writing and proving programs. SIAM j. Comp. **3** (1976) 336–354
11. Caspi, P., Halbwachs, N., Pilaud, D., Plaice, J.: Lustre: a declarative language for programming synchronous systems. In: 14th Symposium on Principles of Programming Languages, ACM, Munich (1987)
12. Le Guernic, P., Benveniste, A., Bournai, P., Gautier, T.: SIGNAL: A data flow oriented language for signal processing. In: IEEE Workshop on VLSI 1984. (1984)
13. Chen, M., Choo, Y., Li, J. In: Crystal: Theory and Pragmatics of Generating Efficient Parallel Code. ACM Press (1991) Chapter 7
14. Perrin, G., Genaud, S., Violard, E.: PEI: a theoretical framework for data-parallel programming. Technical report, ICPS, Strasbourg (1994)

15. Mauras, C.: Alpha : un langage équationnel pour la conception et la programmation d'architectures parallèles synchrones. Thèse de doctorat, Ifsic, Université de Rennes 1 (1989)
16. Dupont De Dinechin, F., Robert, S., Risset, T.: Structured scheduling of recurrence equations. Technical Report 1140, Irisa, Rennes, France (1997)
17. Wilde, D.: The Alpha language. Technical Report 827, Irisa, Rennes, France (1994)
18. Saouter, Y.: A propos de systèmes d'équations récurrentes. Thèse de doctorat, Ifsic, Université de Rennes 1 (1992)
19. Darte, A.: Techniques de parallélisation automatique de nids de boucles. Thèse de doctorat, LIP ENS-Lyon (1993)
20. Feautrier, P.: Some efficient solution to the affine scheduling problem, part II, multidimensional time. Int. J. of Parallel Programming **21** (1992)
21. Chaudhary, V., Xu, C.Z., Roy, S., Ju, J., Sinha, V., , Luo, L.: Design and evaluation of an environment ape for automatic parallelization of programs. In: Int. Symp. on Parallel Architectures, Algorithms, and Networks. (1996) 77–83
22. Irigoin, F., Jouvelot, P., R.Triolet: Overview of the PIPS project. In: Procs of the Int. Workshop on Compiler for Parallel Computers, Paris. (1990) 199–212
23. Raji-Werth, M., Feautrier, P.: On parallel program generation for massively parallel architectures. In Durand, M., Dabaghi, F.E., eds.: High Performance Computing II, North-Holland (1991)
24. Griebl, M., Lengauer, C.: The loop parallelizer LooPo. In Gerndt, M., ed.: Proc. Sixth Workshop on Compilers for Parallel Computers. Volume 21 of Konferenzen des Forschungszentrums Jülich. Forschungszentrum Jülich (1996) 311–320
25. Burleson, W.: Using regular array methods for DSP module synthesis. In: 27th Hawaii Int. Conf. System Science Vol 1: Architecture. (1994) 58–67
26. Catthoor, F., Danckaert, K., Kulkarni, C., Omnes, T.: Data transfer and storage architecture issues and exploration in multimedia processors. In: Programmable Digital Signal Processors: Architecture, Programming, and Applications. Marcel Dekker, Inc, New York (2000)
27. Kienhuis, B., Rijpkema, E., Deprettere, E.: Compaan: Deriving process networks from matlab for embedded signal processing architectures. In: 8th International Workshop on Hardware/Software Codesign (CODES'2000). (2000)
28. Dupont de Dinechin, F., Quinton, P., Risset, S.R.T.: First steps in alpha. Publication Interne 1244, Irisa (1999)
29. De Dinechin, F.D., Quinton, P., Risset, T.: Structuration of the Alpha language. In Giloi, W., Jahnichen, S., Shriver, B., eds.: Massively Parallel Programming Models, IEEE Computer Society Press (1995) 18–24
30. Dupont De Dinechin, F.: Libraries of schedule-free operators in Alpha. In: Application Specific Array Processor. (1997)
31. Crop, J., Wilde, D.: Scheduling Structured Systems. In: Fifth International Europar Conference. LNCS, Toulouse, France, Springer Verlag (1999) 409–412
32. Darte, A., Robert, Y.: Scheduling uniform loop nests. Technical Report 92-10, Laboratoire de l'Informatique du Parallélisme, Ecole Normale Supérieure de Lyon, France (1992)
33. Feautrier, P.: Parametric integer programming. RAIRO Recherche Opérationnelle **22** (1988) 243–268
34. Schrijver, A.: Theory of Linear and Integer Programming. John Wiley and Sons, New York (1986)
35. Darte, A., Vivien, F.: Revisiting the decomposition of Karp, Miller and Winograd. In: Application Specific Array Processor. (1997) 13–25

A   Proof of Theorem 1

In the following, we will call *degenerated* a domain which contains equalities in its definition (e.g. $\mathcal{D} = \{i, j \mid i = j; i \geq 0\}$ is degenerated). We have to prove two lemmas. The first one deals with the case when there are no degenerated domains concerned with the call, the other one is a generalization of the first one to any situations.

Lemma 1. *Consider the call (15) to* sub *in* sys *where domains of input/output variables and the extension domain are not degenerated:*

$$\textbf{use } \{J|AJ \leq b\} \text{ sub[F(J,N)] } (U_1, \ldots, U_n) \textbf{ return } (V_1, \ldots, V_m) \quad . \quad (15)$$

Let u_i and v_j be the formal arguments of system sub *corresponding to U_i and V_j. If the schedule T^{sub} of* sub *is given, the constraints (16) added to the usual dependency constraints between variables of* sys *are sufficient to obtain a valid structured scheduling T^{sys} of* sys. *Moreover these constraints are necessary, in the sense that they are satisfied by every structured scheduling.*

$$
\begin{aligned}
T_{U_i}^{sys}(I, 0) &= T_{u_i}^{sub}(I) & \forall I \in Dom(u_i) \\
T_{V_j}^{sys}(I, 0) &= T_{v_i}^{sub}(I) & \forall I \in Dom(v_i) \qquad (16) \\
T_{U_i}^{sys}(0, J) - T_{V_j}^{sys}(0, J) &= T_{u_i}^{sub}(0) - T_{v_i}^{sub}(0) \; \forall J \in \{J|AJ \leq b\}
\end{aligned}
$$

Proof: we look for structured scheduling (definition 2), hence T^{sys} must meet the following conditions:

$$
\begin{aligned}
&\text{for all actual input } U_i[I, J]: \\
&\quad \forall (I, J) \in Dom_{U_i} \qquad T_{U_i}^{sys}(I, J) = c(J) + T_{u_i}^{sub}(I) \\
&\text{for all actual output } V_i[I, J]: \\
&\quad \forall (I, J) \in Dom_{V_i} \qquad T_{V_i}^{sys}(I, J) = c(J) + T_{v_i}^{sub}(I)
\end{aligned}
$$

These equalities hold for all $(I, J) \in \text{Dom}(U_i)$ (resp. $(I, J) \in \text{Dom}(V_i)$). Unless these domains are degenerated, these equalities can be extended to the whole space (any value of (I, J)). Hence, for non-degenerated domains, we can deduce (setting I then J to 0):

- $T_{U_i}^{sys}(0, J) - T_{V_j}^{sys}(0, J) = T_{u_i}^{sub}(0) - T_{v_j}^{sub}(0)$ and,
- $T_{U_i}^{sys}(I, 0) = T_{u_i}^{sub}(I), \qquad T_{V_j}^{sys}(I, 0) = T_{v_i}^{sub}(I) \quad .$

As a consequence, conditions (16) are necessary when the domains are not degenerated.

We must now show that, for each dependence d_1 between input and output of sub, constraints (16), impose that d_1 is satisfied by T^{sys}. Here, we will note $\mathcal{D}(N)$ to express the fact that domain $\mathcal{D}$ is parameterized by N.

Consider the following dependence constraints occuring from a dependence path d_1 in subsystem sub:

$$\forall I \in \mathcal{D}_{d1}(M), T_{v_i}^{sub}(I) - T_{u_j}^{sub}(d_1(I, M)) \geq d(I, M) \quad , \qquad (17)$$

where M represents the parameters of sub, d_1 is the value of the dependence and d is the *duration* (affine function of I and M). As T^{sub} is a valid schedule of sub, this constraint is met by T^{sub}. From the definition of the structuring mechanism (see [29]) in Alpha, the corresponding constraint that must be respected by the schedule T^{sys} of sys, which contains the call (15), is:

$$\forall J \in \{J | AJ \le b\}, \forall I \in \mathcal{D}_{d1}(F(J,N)),$$
$$T_{V_i}^{\text{sys}}(I,J) - T_{U_j}^{\text{sys}}(d_1(I,F(J,N),J) \ge d(I,F(J,N)) \quad,$$

where N represents the parameters of sys and $F(J,N)$ is the parameter assignment function in (15). As we have $\mathcal{D}_{d_1}(F(J,N)) \subset \mathcal{D}_{v_i}(F(J,N))$, from the constraints (16) we can deduce:

$$\forall J \in \{J | AJ \le b\}, \forall I \in \mathcal{D}_{d1}(F(J,N))$$
$$T_{V_i}^{\text{sys}}(I,J) - T_{U_j}^{\text{sys}}(d_1(I,F(J,N),J) = T_{v_i}^{\text{sub}}(I) - T_{u_j}^{\text{sub}}(d_1(I,F(J,N)))$$

By the construction of the use, if J is in the extension domain: $\{J | AJ \le b\}$ and if N is in the parameter domain of sys, $F(J,N)$ is in the parameter domain of sub. Hence we can use the inequality (17) to bound the right hand side of the above equality, and we get the result:

$$\forall J \in \{J | AJ \le b\}, \forall I \in \mathcal{D}_{d1}(F(J,N)),$$
$$T_{V_i}^{\text{sys}}(I,J) - T_{U_j}^{\text{sys}}(d_1(I,F(J,N),J) \ge d(I,F(J,N)) \quad.$$

Hence the constraints generated by dependence d_1 is respected by a scheduling of sys provided it respect respects constraints (16).   ∎

Lemma 2. *Consider a call to* sub *in* sys *(see (15)) in which degenerated domains occur. Then the constraints (16) are still sufficient, but may not be satisfied by a valid structured scheduling T^{sys} of* sys. *However, if this is the case, it is always possible to find another expression of the same schedule in which constraints (16) are met.*

Proof: the second part of the previous proof can be repeated here, and we obtain that the dependency constraints are respected if constraints (16) are added to the schedule. The problem with degenerated domains come from the fact that we may not be able to extend the relation of definition (2) to $J = 0$.

Say we have this relation happening on the domain of U_i:

$$T_{U_i}^{\text{sys}}(I,J) = c(J) + T_{u_i}^{\text{sub}}(I) \quad \forall(I,J) \in Dom_{U_i} \quad.$$

This relation can be extended to the affine space containing Dom_{U_i} that we note $\text{Aff}(Dom_{U_i})$. By hypothesis this space contains equalities but one important property (due to the structuring mechanism) is that none of these equalities involve together extension indices (J) and local indices (I). Hence, this set of equalities can be splitted in two sets: n_J equalities occurring on extension indices and n_I equalities occurring on local indices. The real dimension of $\text{Aff}(Dom_{U_i})$ is therefore $n - n_J - n_I$ (where n is the dimension of the global space).

Let us note m_J the number of extension indices, i.e., the length of J, and $\{eq_1, \ldots, eq_{n_J}\}$ the set of equalities occurring on J. Without loss of generality, we can suppose that this set of equalities has been simplified, and the J components have been permuted in such a way that equality eq_i defines J_i in terms of $\{J_{n_J+1}, \ldots, J_{m_J}\}$. Suppose, for instance, that we cannot extend the relation along the first component of J. Then we have: $T_{U_i}^{\mathbf{sys}}(I, j_1, \ldots, j_m) = c(j_1, \ldots, j_m) + T_{u_i}^{\mathbf{sub}}(I)$ and $T_{U_i}^{\mathbf{sys}}(I, 0, j_2, \ldots, j_{m_J}) \neq c(0, j_2, \ldots, j_{m_J}) + T_{u_i}^{\mathbf{sub}}(I)$. This means that the first equality holds *only* in the context of the relation between j_1 and $\{J_{n_J+1}, \ldots, J_{m_J}\}$. In that case, it sufficies to replace j_1 in c by its definition in terms of $\{J_{n_J+1}, \ldots, J_{m_J}\}$ as defined by eq_1, we will obtain a new expression of the timing function of U_i which take the same value as $T_{U_i}^{\mathbf{sys}}$ on $\mathrm{Aff}(Dom_{U_i})$ and which respects the equality wanted along one the j_1 dimension (obviously because j_1 is no more involved in c) . Just by counting the number of dimension added, one can check that we will use at most n_j equality on J to obtain a timing function $\mathcal{T}_{U_i}^{\mathbf{sys}}$ which is equal to $T_{U_i}^{\mathbf{sys}}$ on $\mathrm{Aff}(Dom_{U_i})$ and respects: $\mathcal{T}_{U_i}^{\mathbf{sys}}(I, 0) = T_{u_i}^{\mathbf{sub}}(I) \; \forall I \in Dom(u_i)$

The same transformation can be done with the n_I equalities on I to obtain the other equality: $\mathcal{T}_{U_i}^{\mathbf{sys}}(0, J) = c(J) + T_{u_i}^{\mathbf{sub}}(0) \; \forall J \in \{J | AJ \leq b\}$ And we have the result. ∎

B   Proof of Theorem 2

$$U_i[I, J] \leftarrow V_j[f(I), g(J)] \quad . \tag{18}$$

We have two dependence paths, $p_1 : U_i[I, J] \leftarrow V_j[f(I), g(J)], \forall (I, J) \in Dom_{p_1}$ and also $p_2 : V_j[I, J] \leftarrow U_i[h(I), J], \forall I \in Dom_{p_2}, \forall J \in \mathcal{E}$. Suppose that the condition is not respected, i.e. $T_{V_j}^{\mathbf{sub}}(I) - T_{U_i}^{\mathbf{sub}}(I') >= k(I, J, N)$ (N is the parameter of sys, J are the extension indices, k is *not* a constant function). We have the constraints:

$$T_{U_i}^{sys}[I, J] \geq T_{V_j}^{sys}[f(I), g(J)] \geq k(f(I), g(J), N) + T_{U_i}^{sys}[h(f(I)), g(J)] \geq$$
$$k(f(I), g(J), N) + k(f(h(f(I))), g^2(J), N) + T_{U_i}^{sys}[h(f(h(f(I)))), g^2(J)] \geq$$
$$\underbrace{\cdots}_{P \text{ cycles unrolled}} \geq \sum_{l=1}^{P} k((f \circ h)^l \circ f(I), g^l(J), N) + T_{V_j}^{sys}[(f \circ h)^{(P)}(I), g^{P+1}(J)]$$

None of the terms of the above sum is constant, hence, unless the cycle is not a real cycle (i.e. it can only be unrolled a constant number of time), the above constraint is not linear but quadratic. Thus, there is no hope to find a linear schedule (for sake of clarity we have assumed that the parameter assignment function $\mathcal{F}$ was simply $(J, N \rightarrow N)$, the computation above can be carried out with any parameter assignment function). ∎

Exact Partitioning
of Affine Dependence Algorithms

Jürgen Teich[1,*] and Lothar Thiele[2]

[1] University of Paderborn, D-33100 Paderborn, Germany
teich@date.upb.de, http://www-date.upb.de
[2] ETH Zürich, CH-8092 Zürich, Switzerland
thiele@tik.ee.ethz.ch, http://www.tik.ee.ethz.ch

Abstract. This paper presents a first approach to *partition affine dependence algorithms* (e.g., sets of affine recurrence equations, loop programs with affine data dependences) when mapped onto reduced/fixed size processor arrays with local interconnect. Existing approaches start with localized dependence algorithms (e.g., sets of uniform reccurence equations, uniform loop programs). These give up optimality with respect to 1) freedom of scheduling processor tiles, 2) memory requirements due to copy operations introduced by localization of data dependences prior to partitioning, and 3) they cause unnecessary control overhead due to intermediate statements. Our partitioning approach is able to partition affine dependence algorithms and therefore represents a substantial extension of previous partitioning approaches such as described in [10,14,15,11]. 4) We also propose the concept and methodology of *partial localization* that only localizes intra-tile or inter-tile data dependences, respectively, for the partitioned affine dependence algorithm.

1 Introduction

This paper deals with techniques for partitioning affine dependence algorithms (e.g., sets of affine recurrence equations, loop programs) onto processor arrays, e.g., VLSI processor arrays or distributed memory multiprocessors. These architectures are distinguished by the properties of distributed memory and computing power, simple and regular communication, locality in time and space, and intensive pipelining and parallelism. They are considered the most promising architectures for computationally intensive applications.

In the domain of *systolic array* processing, a typical design flow is shown in Fig. 1. Starting with a parallelized loop program with affine data dependences, or directly with a set of affine recurrence equations (AREs), data dependences are localized first. This step converts global into local data dependences. These result in local, nearest-neighbor interprocessor communications as imposed by a given interconnection topology or as a result of the mapping of operations in space and time. Transformation techniques like [13], [2] are applied that convert affine

* This work was supported by the Deutsche Forschungsgemeinschaft (DFG), SFB 376.

E.F. Deprettere et al. (Eds.): SAMOS 2001, LNCS 2268, pp. 135–153, 2002.
© Springer-Verlag Berlin Heidelberg 2002

dependences between variables into local data propagations, see, e.g., in Fig. 2b) for the simple affine recurrence equation $x[i, j] = y[0, 0]$ for all $i, j : 0 \leq i, j, < N$. The result is a (piecewise) regular algorithm (PRA) [17] or a set of uniform recurrence equations [8] (URE).

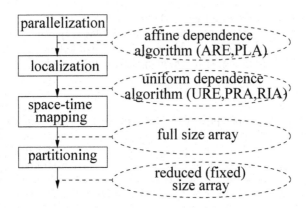

Fig. 1. Conventional design flow for mapping algorithms to processor arrays

After localization, linear [9] or piecewise linear [17] scheduling and allocation techniques are applied to derive a full size array. Finally, in order to match re-source constraints such as limited number of processing elements, partitioning techniques have been investigated. Most of these have in common that the index space of computations is tiled using hyperplane [18], boxes [4], or parallelepiped shapes [6], [14], [1], [11]. Techniques have been proposed to either sequentially execute tiles (LPGS - local parallel, global sequential partitioning) or to se-quentialize operations within a tile (LSGP - local sequential, global parallel) [7], or intermediate schemes [14]. In [3], Eckhardt and Merker propose a tech-nique called co-partitioning that is basically a combination of LPGS and LSGP techniques for balancing memory and I/O-rate requirements while maintaining problem size independence.

The main motivation and idea of the hereafter presented *affine partitioning* solution will be explained using the following simple introductory example. In Fig. 2b), it can be seen that in case of a) where each tile is replaced by a physi-cal processor (LSGP-scheme, see d) for the resulting array), localization of data dependences within tiles would introduce unnecessary copy operations as oper-ations within the tile are by definition executed sequentially on the reduced size array. Also, the order of sequentially executing the operations within a tile would be unnecessarily restricted when partitioning the localized algorithm shown in Fig. 2b). Indeed, dependences between tiles need not to be localized because the physical array has the form of one tile (see d)). Localization before partitioning would unnecessarily reduce the order and amount of overlap, different tiles may be executed on the reduced size array.

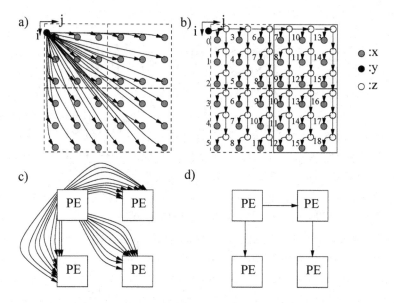

Fig. 2. Dependence graph of the simple affine recurrence equation $x[i,j] = y[0,0]$ and of an equivalent regular algorithm obtained by localization, tiling, and annotated schedule for LSGP partitioning. The nodes correspond to the variables x, y, and an intermediate propagation variable z caused by localization, respectively. The arcs denote data dependences. In case of LSGP partitioning, each tile corresponds to one physical processor that executes its operations sequentially. c) shows the resulting processor array for the algorithm in a), d) shows the resulting processor array for the localized regular algorithm shown in b).

Localization prior to partitioning is thus inefficient in the sense that 1) many unnecessary copy operations are introduced and 2) the optimality of remaining schedules after partitioning may be greatly restricted. In the following examples, we quantify these inefficiencies concerning latency and memory overhead resulting from previous partitioning approaches for regular (localized) dependence algorithms[1].

Example 1. Consider the dependence graph of the regular algorithm in Fig. 2b) that is the localized version of the affine dependence algorithm $x[i,j] = y[0,0]$ for all $i,j : 0 \leq i,j, < N$ shown in Fig. 2a). The transformed algorithm looks as follows: $x[i,j] = z[i,j]$ for all $0 \leq i,j < N$, $z[i,j] = z[i,j-1]$ for all $i = 0, 1 \leq j < N$, $z[i,j] = z[i-1,j]$ for all $1 \leq i < N, 0 \leq j < N$, and $z[i,j] = y[0,0]$ for $i = j = 0$. Note that the value of $y[0,0]$ is propagated first to each j at index points $i = 0$ using the propagation direction $\begin{pmatrix} 0 & 1 \end{pmatrix}^{\mathrm{T}}$ and from there in

---

[1] The examples introduced throughout Section 1 to 4 are on purpose chosen to be as simple as possible in order to be able to understand the problem and to quantify the advantages of our methodology to partition affine dependence algorithms. A complex case study is given in Section 5.

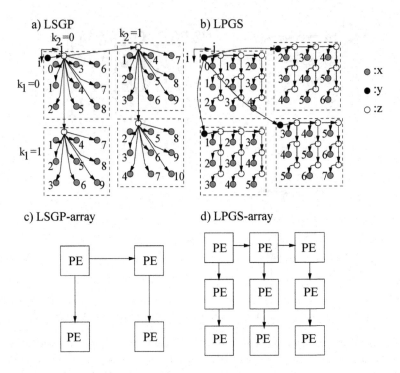

Fig. 3. Dependence graph of the simple affine recurrence equation $x[i,j] = y[0,0]$ during partitioning using new affine partitioning methodology: a) LSGP partitioning, b) LPGS partititioning; included: annotated schedule. In case of LPGS partitioning, each index point within one tile corresponds to one physical processor that executes the index points at the same position of other tiles sequentially. Only dependences resulting in inter-processor communication should be localized, i.e., inter-tile data dependences in case of LSGP, and intra-tile-dependences in case of LPGS partitioning. The resulting interconnections are shown in c) for the LSGP mapping, and in d) for the LPGS-mapping.

the direction $\left(1\ 0\right)^T$ by introducing an intermediate variable z. Now, assume this graph is tiled using tiles of square size M by M as shown in Fig. 2) for $M = 3$. In case a) we decide to replace each tile by a physical processor that executes each operation within a tile sequentially (LSGP-scheme), resulting in a reduced size array of size $\lceil \frac{N}{M} \rceil \times \lceil \frac{N}{M} \rceil$, we can easily see that localization prior to partitioning introduces $M \times M$ unnessary copy operations of $y[0,0]$ (white nodes in Fig. 2b)). Hence, the local memory overhead is $\mathcal{O}(M^2)$ with respect to the solution proposed in Fig. 3a) where only one copy of $y[0,0]$ must be stored within each tile (white node). Lets look at the freedom for scheduling tiles: It can be seen in Fig. 2b) that the first time step a neighbor processor (tile $\left(1\ 0\right)^T$ or tile $\left(0\ 1\right)^T$) may start executing its first operation is at least M time steps after the first time step of operation of tile processor $\left(0\ 0\right)^T$. As can be seen in out solution

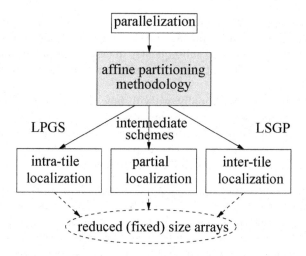

Fig. 4. Affine dependence algorithm partitioning methodology

in Fig. 3a), such a schedule overhead may be greatly avoided if localization is not done prior to partitioning: Obviously, only the dependences between tiles must be localized (see Fig. 3a)) allowing considerably faster schedules.

Example 2. In case of LPGS partitioning, the reduced size array has $M \times M$ processor elements. Correspondingly, the tiles have to executed sequentially or in a pipelined mode. Again, deficiencies in terms of redundant copy operations and restrictions in the freedom of scheduling result from localization prior to partitioning: As can be seen in Fig. 2b), the physical processor at index $\left(0\ 0\right)^{\mathrm{T}}$ may start executing an operation at index points $\left(kM\ lM\right)^{\mathrm{T}}$, $k, l \in \mathbf{N}$ not before time step kM, lM, respectively. In Fig. 3b), our solution is shown that avoids this inefficiency by localization of intra-tile dependences only, however not across tiles.

A major drawback of the design flow shown in Fig. 1 is therefore that localization prior to partitioning leads to unoptimal results with respect to the latency of schedules of the reduced size array, and introduces unnecessary copy operations (additional memory requirements). In order to overcome these major drawbacks, we present to our knowledge the first systematic partitioning methodology for affine dependence algorithms. Resulting is the main message of this paper is to apply this affine partitioning methodology prior to localizing data dependences, see Fig. 4. The main results presented in this paper are summarized as follows.

- *Exact[2] partitioning of affine dependence algorithms* by definition of two transformations called EXPAND and REDUCE.

---

[2] Exact means that the transformed algorithm has the same number of computations as the original algorithm even in the existence of non-perfect tilings and that the input/output behavior of the transformed algorithm stays the same.

- *Partial localization*: By a small adaption of the EXPAND transformation, i.e., a splitting of variable transformation, only equations with inter-tile dependences must be localized subsequently in case of LS-partitioning schemes. Or, only equations with intra-tile dependences must be localized in case of a GS-partitioning scheme.
- *Hierarchical partitioning*: Finally, we will show that intermediate and hierarchical partitioning, see e.g., [4] becomes possible as special cases of how the parameters of the above transformations are chosen. This includes recent extensions to cover LPGS and LSGP partitioning schemes simultaneously such as Eckhardts [3] co-partitioning methodology.

In Section 2, we introduce the considered class of algorithms. In Section 3, the partitioning transformations EXPAND and REDUCED are introduced. It is also shown how these transformations may be used to avoid subsequent localization of intra-tile, inter-tile dependences, respectively in Section 4 (partial localization). Experimental results are reported in Section 5 for a real (FIR) digital filter design.

2   Regular and Affine Dependence Algorithms

In order to explain the background of our optimization methodology, we review the definitions of regular algorithms and of partitioning.

2.1   Regular and Affine Dependence Algorithms

The class of algorithms we are using to explain our partitioning methodology is given by extensions of the class of *Regular Iterative Algorithms* [12] which are similar to the class of *Piecewise Regular Algorithms* (PRAs), (see [17], [14]), however, with a more complex index domain, namely a *linearly bounded lattice* [16] will be named *Regular (Dependence) Algorithms* here. In case data dependences are extended to be affine, we speak of *Affine (Dependence) Algorithms*.

Definition 1 (Affine/Regular Algorithm). *An affine/regular algorithm consists of a set of $|V|$ quantified indexed equations $S_l[I]$*

$$S_1[I] \quad \cdots \quad S_l[I] \quad \cdots \quad S_{|V|}[I] \qquad \forall\, I \in \mathbf{I} \tag{1}$$

where $I \in \mathbf{Z}^n$ is the index vector and the index domain $\mathbf{I} \subseteq \mathbf{Z}^n$ is a linearly bounded lattice that is defined below.
An algorithm is called affine *if each equation $S_l[I]$ is of the form*

$$x_j[P_l I + f_l] = \mathcal{F}_j(\cdots x_i[Q_{ij} I - d_{ij}] \cdots) \quad \text{if } I \in \mathbf{I}_l \tag{2}$$

where $x_i[I]$ are indexed variables, $\mathcal{F}_i$ are arbitrary functions and P_l, Q_{ij}, f_l, d_{ij} are constant matrices and vectors of appropriate dimensions, respectively.
An algorithm is called regular *if each equation $S_i[I]$ is of the form*

$$x_j[I] = \mathcal{F}_j(\cdots x_i[I - d_{ij}] \cdots) \quad \text{if } I \in \mathbf{I}_l \tag{3}$$

where $d_{ij} \in \mathbf{Z}^n$ are constant dependence vectors. In Eq. (3) and Eq. (2), $\mathbf{I}_l$ is a linearly bounded lattice called condition space *of equation $S_l[I]$.*

Definition 2 (Linearly Bounded Lattice). *A linearly bounded lattice is an index space of the form $\mathbf{I} = \{I : I = L\kappa + m \;\wedge\; A\kappa \geq b \;\wedge\; \kappa \in \mathbf{Z}^l\}$ where $L \in \mathbf{Z}^{n \times l}$, $m \in \mathbf{Z}^n$, $A \in \mathbf{Z}^{m \times l}$ and $b \in \mathbf{Z}^m$.*

$\{\kappa : A\kappa \geq b \wedge \kappa \in \mathbf{Z}^l\}$ defines the set of all integer vectors within a polytope. The integral points in this polytope are mapped to index vectors I using an affine function, i.e., $I = L\kappa + m$. For reasons of simplicity of notation, we assume L and m in the description of the index space $\mathbf{I}$ in Eq. (1) to be the unity matrix and the zero vector respectively[3], i.e., the index space can be written as $\mathbf{I} = \{I \in \mathbf{Z}^s : AI \geq b\}$.

3 Partitioning of Affine Dependence Algorithms

The partitioning procedure consists of two algorithm transformations called EX-PAND and REDUCE. Whereas the first transformation describes the tiling and embedding of tiles in a $2n$-dimensional space, the REDUCE transformation is an affine transformation that describes a multiprojection that is able to realize all well-known and combinations of well-known partitioning schemes such as LPGS, LSGP. Later, we will also show how co-partitioning [3] can be realized.

EXPAND-Transformation: First, the given global iteration space $\mathbf{I}$ is decomposed into the direct sum of two subspaces $\mathbf{J}$ and $\mathbf{K}$ such that $\mathbf{I} \subseteq \mathbf{J} \oplus \mathbf{K}$. The subspace $\mathbf{J} \in \mathbf{Z}^n$ represents one of the tiles and the subspace $\mathbf{K} \in \mathbf{Z}^n$ accounts for their regular repetition. Here, we consider tiles $\mathbf{J}$ that are parallelepipeds. These may be described by n linearly independent tiling directions $p_i \in \mathbf{Z}^n$, $i = 1, \cdots, n$, combined in a tiling matrix $P = (p_1, \cdots, p_n)$, and a tiling offset $q \in \mathbf{Z}^n$ that describes the point where the tesselation starts.

Example 3. An example of a tiling of an iteration space is shown in Fig. 3 for the simple affine dependence algorithm $x[i,j] = y[0,0]$ and a tiling matrix $P = \begin{pmatrix} 3 & 0 \\ 0 & 3 \end{pmatrix}$, $q = \begin{pmatrix} 0 \\ 0 \end{pmatrix}$. The two tiling vectors $p_1 = \begin{pmatrix} 3 \\ 0 \end{pmatrix}$ and $p_2 = \begin{pmatrix} 0 \\ 3 \end{pmatrix}$ span a rectangular tile (shown surrounded by dashed lines in Fig. 3). The tiling offset q denotes at which index point the tesselation starts covering the index space.

As tiling is not different from whether regular or affine algorithms are partitioned, we refer to [14] for details on how to compute the index space of a tile

---

[3] This assumption does not by any means restrict the generality of the approach: I.e., an equivalence transformation called *distribution of iteration and condition spaces* [14] may be applied to distribute the lattice mapping into the condition spaces $\mathbf{I}_l$ of each of the indexed equations in Eq. (2), and Eq. (3), respectively. As we have not formulated any restrictions on these, the approach is therefore the most general.

J and the linearly bounded lattice **K** containing all origins of non-empty tiles covered by the tiling described by tiling matrix P and offset q:

$$\mathbf{J} = \{J \in \mathbf{Z}^n : A_J J \geq b_J\} \tag{4}$$

$$\mathbf{K} = \{K : K = P\kappa + q \,\wedge\, A_K \kappa \geq b_K \,\wedge\, \kappa \in \mathbf{Z}^n\} \tag{5}$$

Example 4. Consider again the tiling shown in Fig. 3. With $\mathbf{I} = \{i, j : 0 \leq i, j < N\}$, and P, q taken from Example 3, we obtain

$$A_J = A_K = \begin{pmatrix} 1 & 0 \\ -1 & 0 \\ 0 & 1 \\ 0 & -1 \end{pmatrix}, b_J = \begin{pmatrix} 0 \\ -2 \\ 0 \\ -2 \end{pmatrix}, b_K = \begin{pmatrix} 0 \\ \lceil N/3 \rceil - 1 \\ 0 \\ \lceil N/3 \rceil - 1 \end{pmatrix}$$

Next, all variables are *embedded* in a $2n$-dimensional index space according to the chosen tiling. In particular, the iteration vector of the given algorithm $I \in \mathbf{I} = \mathbf{J} \oplus \mathbf{K}$ [4] will be replaced by $\hat{I} = \begin{pmatrix} J \\ K \end{pmatrix}$, $J \in \mathbf{J}$, and $K \in \mathbf{K}$. This transformation must introduce new equations with new dependences in case dependences origin from different tiles as follows. This part is much more difficult as for regular algorithms because we have to preserve affine data dependences that cross tiles instead of simple, regular dependences. Without loss of generality, we assume that equations $S_l[I]$ are all given in output normalized form:

$$x[I] = \mathcal{F}(\cdots y[QI - d] \cdots) \quad \forall I \in \mathbf{I}_l$$

In order to be able to analyze dependences between tiles easily, the above equation is transformed into the set of equivalent equations

$$x[I] = \mathcal{F}(\cdots z[I] \cdots) \quad \forall I \in \mathbf{I}_l \tag{6}$$
$$z[I] = x[QI - d] \quad \forall I \in \mathbf{I}_l$$

such that dependences between different tiles may only be caused by simple equations of the form of the second equation. Now, the embedding transformation replaces the above two equations by

$$\hat{x}[J, K] = \mathcal{F}(\cdots \hat{z}[J, K] \cdots) \quad \forall I \in \mathbf{I}_l \tag{7}$$
$$\hat{z}[J, K] = \hat{x}[QJ - d - R, QK + R] \quad \forall J + K \in \mathbf{I}_l \,\wedge\, QJ - d - R \in \mathbf{J}$$

where an equation of the second form is generated for all different vectors $R \in \mathbf{Z}^n$ which are solutions of the following systems of equations: In the above equation, we can write $QI - d = Q(J + K) - d = (QJ - d - R) + (QK + R)$ and we must find all possible values of R for which a) $QJ - d - R \in \mathbf{J}$ and b) $QK + R \in \mathbf{K}$. From b), $K \in \mathbf{K}$ and Eq. (5), we deduce $K = P\kappa_1 + q \,\wedge\, A_K \kappa_1 \geq b_K$ and $QK + R = P\kappa_2 + q \,\wedge\, A_K \kappa_2 \geq b_K$. Hence, R must satisfy:

$$R = P\kappa_2 + q - QP\kappa_1 - Qq \,\wedge\, A_K \kappa_{1,2} \geq b_k \tag{8}$$

---

[4] $\mathbf{J} \oplus \mathbf{K} = \{I = J + K : J \in \mathbf{J} \,\wedge\, K \in \mathbf{K}\}$.

From a) and $J \in \mathbf{J}$, we deduce $A_J J \geq b_J$ and $A_J(QJ - d - R) \geq b_J$. Hence, we must introduce an equation for any distinct value R in Eq. (8) obtained for any solution κ_1, κ_2 of the constraint polytope:

$$A_J(QJ - d - P\kappa_2 - q + QP\kappa_1 + Qq) \geq b_J$$
$$A_J J \geq b_J \tag{9}$$
$$A_K \kappa_{1,2} \geq b_K$$

The above polytope has $3n$ variables, and one must enumerate all its integral points to find all different solutions of R for each of which a different equation is to be generated[5].

Example 5. Given the affine recurrence equation $x[i, j] = y[0, 0]$. With the tiling as described in the previous example, and $Q = \mathbf{0}$, $d = \mathbf{0}$, we obtain the transformed recurrence equation $\hat{x}[j_1, j_2, k_1, k_2] = \hat{y}[0, 0, 0, 0] \quad \forall J = \begin{pmatrix} j_1 \\ j_2 \end{pmatrix} \in \mathbf{J}$,
$K = \begin{pmatrix} k_1 \\ k_2 \end{pmatrix} \in \mathbf{K}$ as there is only one R that satisfies the system of inequalities above: First, as $Q = \mathbf{0}$, the first set of inequalities in Eq. (9) reduces to $-A_J P \kappa_2 \geq b_J$ and is independent on J. Next, one can see using Eq. (8) that κ_1 has no influence on R and that $\kappa_2 = \begin{pmatrix} 0 & 0 \end{pmatrix}^{\mathrm{T}}$ leads to the only solution $R = \mathbf{0}$.

REDUCE-Transformation: Linear transformations of the index space after embedding can now be used to permute indices, normalize lattices, etc. Using these, all known partitioning schemes can be realized, see e.g., [14] for regular algorithms:

$$I' = \begin{pmatrix} p \\ t \end{pmatrix} = \begin{pmatrix} P_J & P_K \\ \lambda_J & \lambda_K \end{pmatrix} \tag{10}$$

where $P_J \in \mathbf{Z}^{(n-s) \times n_J}$, $P_K \in \mathbf{Z}^{(n-s) \times n_K}$, $\lambda_J \in \mathbf{Z}^{1 \times n_J}$, $\lambda_K \in \mathbf{Z}^{1 \times n_K}$, and $n_J + n_K = n$. The REDUCE transformation reduces the dimension of the iterations space by $s - 1$. Variable t becomes the sequencing index (time) of operations, p becomes the processor index. If the decomposition $I = \begin{pmatrix} J \\ K \end{pmatrix}$ is the same as in the EXPAND transformation, then λ_J represents the schedule of operations inside a tile, λ_K represents the schedule of the tiles.

The freedom in the REDUCE transformation according to Eq. (10) can now be used in order to realize different partitioning schemes, i.e.

- Multiprojection: $s > 1$.
- LS (Local Sequential)-partitioning: The sequentialization of operations inside a tile leads to $P_J = \mathbf{0}$. In particular, the well-known LSGP-clustering scheme is realized if $P_J = \mathbf{0}$, $P_K = E$ [6], $n - s = n_K$.

---

[5] This can be done quite efficiently by computing the vertices of the polytope in Eq. (9), and by testing for each integral point in its rectangular hull whether it is inside or on the border of the polytope or not. Among many investigated test cases, only very few solutions were typically detected.

[6] Let E denote the unity matrix.

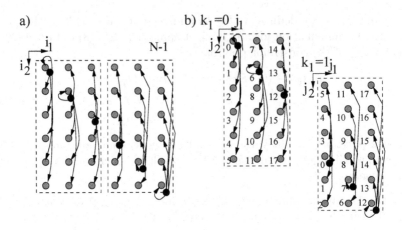

Fig. 5. Partitioning of an affine dependence algorithm

- GS (Global-Sequential)-partitioning: The sequentialization of the execution of different tiles leads to $P_K = \mathbf{0}$. In particular, the well-known LPGS-clustering is realized if $P_K = \mathbf{0}$, $P_J = E$, $n - s = n_J$.

Any intermediate partitioning scheme can be realized.

Example 6. Consider the simple affine dependence algorithm $y[i_1, i_2] = \mathcal{F}(z[i_1, i_1])$ with $\mathbf{I} = \{i_1, i_2 : 0 \leq i_1, i_2 < N\}$. The algorithm is already in the form that embedding may be applied directly. We have $Q = \begin{pmatrix} 1 & 0 \\ 1 & 0 \end{pmatrix}$ and $d = \begin{pmatrix} 0 \\ 0 \end{pmatrix}$ (tiling shown in Fig. 5). Assume we want to map the algorithm onto a processor array of fixed size 2, we choose the tiling matrix to be $P = \begin{pmatrix} \lceil \frac{N}{2} \rceil & 0 \\ 0 & N \end{pmatrix}$, $q = \begin{pmatrix} 0 \\ 0 \end{pmatrix}$ and obtain the transformed algorithm $\hat{y}[j_1, j_2, k_1] = \mathcal{F}(\hat{z}[j_1, j_1, k_1])$ if $j_1 + \lceil \frac{N}{2} \rceil k_1 < N$ as $R = \mathbf{0}$ is the only solution to the set of inequalities in Eq. (9), and as $k_2 = 0$, this index may be omitted[7]. The transformed index space is $\{ \begin{pmatrix} J \\ K \end{pmatrix} \mid 0 \leq j_1 < \lceil \frac{N}{2} \rceil, 0 \leq j_2 < N, 0 \leq k_1 < 2\}$. Fig. 5b) shows the dependence graph of the embedded affine algorithm.

Finally, when applying LSGP partitioning, we see that there is no communication between the tiles. Therefore, any sequential schedule of operations within a tile would be a feasible schedule for the transformed algorithm. We choose $P_K = 1$ and $P_J = 0$ in the corresponding REDUCE transformation. Unfortunately, there is no linear schedule λ for executing the operations within a tile. Although any sequential schedule of operations will do (see the annotated schedule times of operations in Fig. 5b)), we might want to find a linear schedule instead. Therefore, we carry out an affine transformation of variable $\hat{z}$ replacing

---

[7] Such a tiling is called *degenerated* [14].

$\hat{z}[j_1, j_1, k_1]$ by $z[j_1, 0, k_1]$. Now, a linear schedule such as $\lambda_J = \left(j_1 + \lceil \frac{N}{2} \rceil j_2\right)$, $\lambda_K = 0$ becomes feasible.

4   Partial Localization

In Fig. 3, we have tried to explain that in order to have local inter-processor communication in the array resulting from partitioning, the localization of data dependences is only necessary for intra-tile dependences in case of GS-partitioning and for inter-tile dependences in case of LS-partitioning schemes.

Here, we show how the embedding transformation can be modified in order to split a dependency into intra-tile dependences and inter-tile dependences, respectively. Let the embedding transformation for the second equation $z[I] = x[QI - d]$ in Eq. (6) be modified as follows:

$$\hat{z}[J, K] = \hat{x}[Q(J + K) - d, 0] \quad \forall J + K \in \mathbf{I}_l \tag{11}$$

Therefore, the indexing matrix of $\hat{x}$ becomes $Q' = \begin{pmatrix} Q & Q \\ 0 & 0 \end{pmatrix}$, and $d' = \begin{pmatrix} d \\ 0 \end{pmatrix}$. This means that $\hat{x}$ is embedded in the space $K = 0$, and therefore, no case-dependent consideration of dependences is necessary as all dependences origin from the tile at $K = 0$.

The last operation is a two-fold *splitting of inputs* transformation that transforms Eq. (11) into the equivalent system of three equations:

$$\begin{aligned} \hat{z}[J, K] &= z_1[QJ, K] \quad \forall J + K \in \mathbf{I}_l \\ z_1[QJ, K] &= z_2[QJ, QK] \quad \forall J + K \in \mathbf{I}_l \\ z_2[QJ, QK] &= \hat{x}[Q(J + K) - d, 0] \quad \forall J + K \in \mathbf{I}_l \end{aligned} \tag{12}$$

Explanations:

- The three sets of equations satisfy the single-assignment condition if variables z_1 and z_2 are names of so-far not existing variables, and as $\mathbf{N}(P_{\hat{z}}) \subseteq \mathbf{N}(Q_{z_1}) \subseteq \mathbf{N}(Q_{z_2}) \subseteq \mathbf{N}(Q_{\hat{x}})$ [8].
- LS-partitioning: In case of local sequential partitioning, intra-tile dependences must not be localized. In terms of Eq. (12) and variables $\hat{z}, z_1, z_2$, and $\hat{x}$, the dependences between z_2 and z_1 (second equation) must be localized only.
- GS-partitioning: Here, only intra-tile dependences must be localized. As the interconnection structure between PEs is given by the dependences caused by the first equation (between z_1 and $\hat{z}$), only this equation must be localized. The third equation describes copies of variables $\hat{x}$ from the border.

Example 7. Consider the equation $x[i, j] = y[0, 0]$ with the dependence graph shown in Fig. 2a). When applying the modified embedding transformation as described in Eq. (12), we obtain the sets of equations:

---

[8] Let $\mathbf{N}(M)$ denote the right null space of a matrix M.

$$\hat{x}[J,K] = z[0,K] \quad \forall J+K \in \mathbf{I}_l$$
$$z[0,K] = w[0,0] \quad \forall J+K \in \mathbf{I}_l$$
$$w[0,0] = \hat{y}[0,0] \quad \forall J+K \in \mathbf{I}_l$$

Obviously, the introduction of variable w is not necessary here such that 2nd and 3rd equation may be replaced by the equation $z[0,K] = \hat{y}[0,0] \quad \forall J+K \in \mathbf{I}_l$.
In case of LSGP partitioning, only this second equation must be localized. Therefore, $z[0,K] = \hat{y}[0,0]$ is replaced by $z[0,K] = z[0,K-(1\,0)^{\mathrm{T}}]$ if $k_1 > 0$, $z[0,K] = z[0,K-(0\,1)^{\mathrm{T}}]$ if $k_2 > 0 \wedge k_1 = 0$, $z[0,K] = z[0,0]$ if $K = \mathbf{0}$. The dependence graph of the resulting algorithm has already been shown in Fig. 3a)[9]. A feasible REDUCE-transformation resulting in a fixed size array of $\lceil \frac{N}{M} \rceil \times \lceil \frac{N}{M} \rceil$ processing elements is given in Eq. (13).

$$\begin{pmatrix} p \\ t \end{pmatrix} = \overbrace{\begin{pmatrix} 0 & 0 & 1 & 0 \\ 0 & 0 & 0 & 1 \\ 1 & M & 1 & 1 \end{pmatrix}}^{LSGP} \cdot \begin{pmatrix} j_1 \\ j_2 \\ k_1 \\ k_2 \end{pmatrix} \tag{13}$$

Finally, in case of LPGS partitioning, only the first equation must be localized. Therefore, $\hat{x}[J,K] = z[0,K]$ is replaced by $\hat{x}[J,K] = \hat{x}[J-(1\,0)^{\mathrm{T}},K]$ if $j_1 > 0$, $\hat{x}[J,K] = [J-(0\,1)^{\mathrm{T}},K]$ if $j_2 > 0 \wedge j_1 = 0$, $\hat{x}[0,K] = z[0,0]$ if $J = \mathbf{0}$. The dependence graph of the resulting algorithm is shown in Fig. 3b)[10]. A feasible REDUCE-transformation resulting in a fixed size array of $M \times M$ processing elements is given in Eq. (14):

$$\begin{pmatrix} p \\ t \end{pmatrix} = \overbrace{\begin{pmatrix} 1 & 0 & 0 & 0 \\ 0 & 1 & 0 & 0 \\ 1 & 1 & 1 & 2 \end{pmatrix}}^{LPGS} \cdot \begin{pmatrix} j_1 \\ j_2 \\ k_1 \\ k_2 \end{pmatrix} \tag{14}$$

5   Hierarchical Partitioning and Case Study

In [3], Eckhardt and Merker introduce the term *co-partitioning* based on the idea to combine LPGS partitioning and LSGP partition by applying them one after the other with the goal to balance local memory and communication.

Using the example of an FIR-filter algorithm, we show that this hierarchical partitioning approach can be also handled as a special case of our affine partitioning methodology.

---

[9] Corresponding schedule times of operations are also annotated to the nodes in Fig. 3a).

[10] Corresponding schedule times of operations are also annotated to the nodes in Fig. 3b).

Example 8. The equation $y_{i_2} = \sum_{i_1=0}^{\min\{i_1, N-1\}} A_{i_1} \cdot U_{i_2-i_1}$ with $0 \leq i_2 < T$ is the difference equation of a finite impulse response (FIR)-digital filter. The functionality of this equation can be captured by the following affine algorithm:

$$y[i_1, i_2] = y[i_1 - 1, i_2] + a[i_1, i_2] * u[i_1, i_2] \tag{15}$$
$$a[i_1, i_2] = a[i_1, 0] \tag{16}$$
$$u[i_1, i_2] = u[0, i_2 - i_1] \tag{17}$$

with the index domain $\mathbf{I} = \{(i_1, i_2) : 0 \leq i_1 \leq N - 1 \wedge 0 \leq i_2 \leq T - 1\}$. Let us assume we want to partition this algorithm such that the operations are executed on a fixed size processor array with $\#PEs = 4$ processing elements (PEs).

5.1   Co-partitioning of Affine Dependence Algorithms

We apply co-partitioning by performing an LPGS-tiling P_{LPGS}, followed by a subsequent LSGP-tiling P_{LSGP} (see Fig. 6a)) with

$$P_{\text{LPGS}} = \begin{pmatrix} N & 0 \\ 0 & x \end{pmatrix}; \quad P_{\text{LSGP}} = \begin{pmatrix} N & 0 & 0 \\ 0 & y & 0 \\ 0 & 0 & z \end{pmatrix} \tag{18}$$

with $x = 8$, $y = 2$, and $z = \lceil T/x \rceil$.

The transformed algorithm obtained after these two subsequent EXPAND transformations is:

$$y[j_1, j_2, k, l] = y[j_1 - 1, j_2, k, l] + a[j_1, j_2, k, l] * u[j_1, j_2, k, l] \tag{19}$$
$$a[j_1, j_2, k, l] = a[j_1, 0, 0, 0] \tag{20}$$
$$u[j_1, j_2, k, l] = u[0, j_2 - j_1 + 4k + 2l, 0, 0] \tag{21}$$

Obviously, the data dependences of Eq. (19) do not cause any global communication. The data dependency in Eq. (20), however, must be localized partially. l denotes the processor index of the final array obtained by co-partitioning, so we see that variables at processors $l > 0$ have to read data from the processor at location $l = 0$ (border), hence the equation causes inter-processor communication.

Following our methodology of partial localization presented in Section 4, we therefore localize these data dependencies. Let $J = (j_1, j_2, k)^{\text{T}}$ and $K = l$, we obtain the transformed set of equations:

$$a[j_1, j_2, k, l] = z_1[j_1, 0, 0, l] \tag{22}$$
$$z_1[j_1, 0, 0, l] = z_2[j_1, 0, 0, 0] \tag{23}$$
$$z_2[j_1, 0, 0, 0] = a[j_1, 0, 0, 0] \tag{24}$$

Obviously, we can simplify this set of equations as follows: 1) There is no need for introducing the variable z_2. Instead, we just delete Eq. (24) and replace

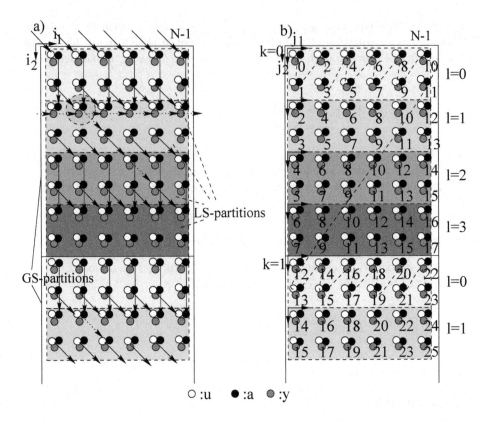

Fig. 6. Example of co-partitioning the depencence graph (only arcs at some index points shown) of an FIR-filter by applying two subsequent tilings after another. The first one is an LPGS-based partitioning (tiles surrounded by solid lines), the second is an LSGP-based scheme (tiles bounded by dotted lines) (a). In b), the embedded algorithm as well as a schedule is shown for each of the 4 resulting processing elements.

z_2 in Eq. (23) by a. Now, only this 2nd equation (Eq. (23)) leads to interprocessor communication and must be localized leading to the set of transformed equations:

$$a[j_1, j_2, k, l] = z_1[j_1, 0, 0, l] \tag{25}$$

$$z_1[j_1, 0, 0, l] = z_1[j_1, 0, 0, l-1] \quad \text{if } l > 0 \tag{26}$$

$$= a[j_1, 0, 0, 0] \quad \text{if } l = 0 \tag{27}$$

A final simplification is possible here by renaming z_1 by a such that the final result after partial localization is the set of equations:

$$y[j_1, j_2, k, l] = y[j_1 - 1, j_2, k, l] + a[j_1, j_2, k, l] * u[j_1, j_2, k, l] \tag{28}$$

$$a[j_1, j_2, k, l] = a[j_1, 0, 0, l-1] \quad \text{if } l > 0 \tag{29}$$

$$= a[j_1, 0, 0, 0] \quad \text{if } l = 0 \tag{30}$$

$$u[j_1, j_2, k, l] = u[j_1 - 1, j_2 + 1, k, l - 1] \quad \text{if } j_1 > 0 \wedge l > 0 \wedge j_2 = 0 \quad (31)$$
$$= u[j_1 - 1, j_2 - 1, k, l] \quad \text{if } j_1 > 0 \wedge l \geq 0 \wedge j_2 > 0 \quad (32)$$
$$= u[j_1 - 1, j_2 + 1, k - 1, l + 3] \quad \text{if } j_1 > 0 \wedge l = 0 \wedge j_2 = 0 (33)$$
$$= u[0, j_1 - j_2 + 4k + 2l, 0, 0] \quad \text{if } j_1 = 0 \quad (34)$$

In Eq. (31)-(34), the same idea of only partially localizing dependencies for variable u has been carried out. A final REDUCE transformation leading to an array with a fixed number of $\lceil x/y \rceil = 4$ PEs ($l = 0, 1, 2, 3$) is

$$I = \begin{pmatrix} p \\ t \end{pmatrix} = \begin{pmatrix} P_J & P_K & P_L \\ \lambda_J & \lambda_K & \lambda_L \end{pmatrix} ; P_L = 1, P_J = P_K = 0.$$

with the feasible schedule (see Fig. 6b)) $\lambda_J = \begin{pmatrix} y & 1 \end{pmatrix} = \begin{pmatrix} 2 & 1 \end{pmatrix}$, $\lambda_K = 2N = 12$, and $\lambda_L = y = 2$. The resulting processor array with 4 PEs (that sequentially computes the operations at $k = 0, k = 1, \ldots$, is shown in Fig. 7. The black boxes denote registers.

The number of registers in each inter-processor connection is obtained by multiplying the dependency vector of the corresponding dependency in Eq. (28)-Eq. (34) by the schedule vector $\lambda = (\lambda_J \ \lambda_K \ \lambda_L)$, e.g., the vector $d_{yy} = (1 \ 0 \ 0 \ 0)$ results in a connection with $\lambda d_{yy} = (2 \ 1 \ 12 \ 2) d_{yy} = 2$ registers in a feed-back path. Similarly, the dependency $d_{aa} = (0 \ 0 \ 0 \ 1)$ results in 2 registers. Finally, variable u is either a) read in from the external or b) passed from the previous processor (Eq. (31)) where $d_{uu} = (1 \ -1 \ 0 \ 1)$ results in a link with 3 registers, or c) read internally from a feedback interconnection (Eq. (32)) where $d_{uu} = (-1 \ 1 \ 0 \ 0)$ results in a link with 3 registers, or d) where the processor at index $l = 0$ reads data from the processor at $l = 3$ leading to a wrap-around interconnection with $\lambda (-1 \ 1 \ 1 \ -3) = 7$ registers. The control circuitry for controlling the multiplexers is not shown in Fig. 7.

5.2   Optimization

For given N and T, we finally would like to explore the influence of the sizes of parameterized tiling matrices in Eq. (18) during co-partitioning, i.e., of x and y on the number of PEs of the resulting array and on the timing, i.e., on the maximum and average computation rate of filter outputs.

The number of PEs of the resulting array, denoted $\#PEs$, is given by the number of LS-partitions:

$$\#PEs = \lceil x/y \rceil \quad (35)$$

It turns out that depending on x and y, the schedule of the REDUCE transformation may be written also in a parameterized way:

$$\lambda = (\lambda_J \ \lambda_K \ \lambda_L) = (y \ 1 \ yN \ y)$$

Now filter outputs are computed at index points $j_1 = N - 1$. From Fig. 6, it can be seen that for the chosen values $x = 8, y = 4$ of the co-partitioning

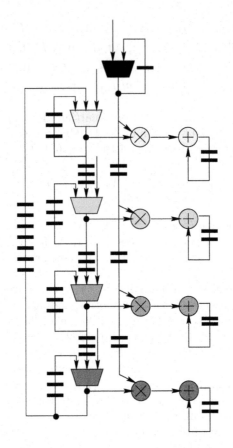

Fig. 7. Fixed size processor array for the FIR-filter algorithm with 4 processing elements corresponding to the 4 LS-partions shown in Fig. 6a) (control circuitry not shown)

tiling matrices, the time between successive filter outputs is minimally 1 and maximally 5 clock cycles. The maximum delay is caused by the last output of one LPGS partition at index $k, l = l_{\max} = \#PEs - 1$ and the first output of a valid output at the subsequent partition $k + 1$. This happens at index $j_1 = N - 1$, $j_2 = 0$, $l = 0$. Hence, the maximum distance in time between two successive inputs, denoted $L_{\max}$ in the following, arises between scheduling of an index point $I = (N - 1\ 0\ k + 1\ 0)^{\mathrm{T}}$ and point $I' = (N - 1\ \ y - 1\ \ k\ \ l_{\max})^{\mathrm{T}}$. Therefore, the distance in time is $\lambda(I - I') = (y\ 1\ yN\ y)(0\ (1 - y)\ 1\ (-l_{\max}))^{\mathrm{T}} = y(N - l_{\max} - 1) + 1$. We obtain

$$L_{\max} = y(N - \lceil x/y \rceil - 2) + 1 \tag{36}$$

The final objective, we would like to compute in dependence on the tiling is the *average latency per output* of the array, denoted L_{avg} in the following. Obviously, with the parameterized schedule above, the array outputs $x - 1$ outputs

Table 1. Design space exploration of $\#PEs$, $L_{\max}$, and L_{avg} in dependence of the parameters of the co-partitioning tiling matrices in Eq. (18) for the FIR-filter algorithm and problem size $N = 6$.

x	y	x/y	$\#PEs$	$L_{\max}$	L_{avg}
2	2	1	1	11	6.0
4	2	2	2	9	3.0
4	4	1	1	21	6.0
6	2	3	3	7	2.0
6	4	1.5	2	9	2.6
6	6	1	1	36	6.8
8	2	4	4	5	1.5
8	4	2	2	17	3.0
8	6	1.3	2	25	49.0
8	8	1	1	49	7.0
10	2	5	5	3	1.2
10	4	2.5	3	13	2.2
10	6	1.6	2	25	3.4
10	8	1.25	2	33	4.2
10	10	1	1	51	6.0
12	2	6	6	1	1.0
12	4	3	3	13	2.0
12	6	2	2	25	3.0
12	8	1.5	2	33	3.67
12	10	1.2	2	41	4.3
12	12	1	1	61	6.0

in successive cycles and then requires $L_{\max}$ cycles for the next sample, and so on. Hence, L_{avg} is given as follows:

$$L_{\mathrm{avg}} = ((x - 1)1 + L_{\max})/x \qquad (37)$$

In Table 1, we report the computed objectives $\#PEs$, $L_{\max}$, and L_{avg} for different tile size parameters x and y for $N = 6$ as shown in Fig. 6. First, it can be seen from these numbers that for any fixed value of the size x of the LPGS partition, $L_{\max}$ and L_{avg} monotonically increase for increasing values of y (parameter in the LSGP partitioning matrix). Hence, for each value of x, a small value for y gives the best latencies. However, this comes at the prices of having the largest number of PEs for small values of y. Secondly, it can be observed that there is an upper limit for the number of PEs that are useful in the sense to decrease the latency. With $x = 12$ and $y = 2$, we obtain the smallest array with a size of $\#PEs = 6$ that is able to output one filter output at each clock cycle.

6   Conclusions

In this paper, we presented a first approach to exactly partition affine dependence algorithms. With the major advantage to avoid a) unnessary copy oper-

ations created by localization prior to partitioning and b) to restrict the freedom of scheduling in early design phases of processor arrays, the message of
the paper for algorithm and parallel architecture designer is to *do partitioning first!* in the design flow using the here presented transformations for tiling,
embedding and partial localization. The presented transformations have been
implemented for non-parameterized index spaces in the PARO design system
for mapping computation intensive algorithms to hardware, see **http://www-
date.upb.de/RESEARCH/PARO/**.

In the future, we would like to work out formulas for quantifying the savings obtained by our new design flow as shown in Fig. 4 in terms of latency and
memory. Also, we would like to work on automatic design space exploration techniques for partitioning schemes like co-partitioning. First results on automatic
exploration of space time mappings have been described in [5].

References

1. A. Darte. Regular partitioning for synthesizing fixed size systolic arrays. *INTE-
   GRATION, the VLSI Journal*, 14:293–304, 1991.
2. V. V. Dongen and P. Quinton. Uniformization of linear recurrence equations: A
   step towards the automatic synthesis of systolic arrays. In *Proc. Int'l Conf. Systolic
   Arrays*, pages 403–412, San Diego, 1988.
3. U. Eckhardt and R. Merker. Co-partitioning - a method for hardware/software
   codesign for scalable systolic arrays. In R. Hartenstein and V. Prasanna, editors,
   Reconfigurable Architectures, pages 131–138, IT Press, Chicago, IL, 1997.
4. U. Eckhardt and R. Merker. Hierarchical algorithm partitioning at system level for
   an improved utilization of memory structures. *IEEE Trans. on Computer-Aided
   Design*, 18(1):14–24, Jan. 1999.
5. Frank Hannig and Jürgen Teich. Design Space Exploration for Massively Parallel
   Processor Arrays. In *Sixth International Conference on Parallel Computing Technologies (PaCT-2001)*, volume 2125 of *Lecture Notes in Computer Science*, pages
   51–65, Novosibirsk, Russia, September 2001. Springer-Verlag.
6. F. Irigoin and R. Triolet. Supernode partitioning. In *Proc. SIGPLAN*, pages
   319–329, San Diego, Jan. 1988.
7. K. Jainandunsing. Optimal partitioning scheme for wavefront/systolic array processors. In *Proc. IEEE Symp on Circuits and Systems*, 1986.
8. R. M. Karp, R. E. Miller, and S. Winograd. The organization of computations for
   uniform recurrence equations. *Journal of the ACM*, 14:563–590, 1967.
9. R. H. Kuhn. Transforming algorithms for single-stage and VLSI architectures.
   Workshop Interconnection Networks for Parallel and Distributed Processing, 1980.
10. D. I. Moldovan and R. A. B. Fortes. Partitioning and mapping of algorithms into
    fixed size systolic arrays. *IEEE Trans. Computers*, C-35:1–12, 1986.
11. T. P. Plaks. *Multidimensional Piecewise Regular Arrays*. PhD thesis, School
    of Electrical and Computer Engineering, Chalmers University of Technology,
    Göteborg, Sweden, 1997.
12. S. K. Rao. *Regular iterative algorithms and their implementations on processor
    arrays*. PhD thesis, Stanford University, 1985.
13. V. Roychowdhury, L. Thiele, S. K. Rao, and T. Kailath. On the localization of
    algorithms for VLSI processor arrays. *in: VLSI Signal Processing III, IEEE Press,
    New York*, pages 459–470, 1989.

14. J. Teich and L. Thiele. Partitioning of processor arrays: A piecewise regular approach. *INTEGRATION: The VLSI Journal*, 14(3):297–332, 1993.

15. J. Teich, L. Thiele, and L. Zhang. Partitioning processor arrays under resource constraints. *Int. Journal of VLSI Signal Processing*, 17(1):5–20, September 1997.

16. L. Thiele. On the hierarchical design of VLSI processor arrays. In *IEEE Symp. on Circuits and Systems*, pages 2517–2520, Helsinki, 1988.

17. L. Thiele. On the design of piecewise regular processor arrays. In *Proc. IEEE Symp. on Circuits and Systems*, pages 2239–2242, Portland, 1989.

18. M. W. Wolf and M. S.Lam. A loop transformation theory and an algorithm to maximize parallelism. *IEEE Transactions on Parallel and Distributed Systems*, 2:452–471, 1991.

Generation of Distributed Loop Control*

Marcus Bednara, Frank Hannig, and Jürgen Teich

University of Paderborn, D-33098 Paderborn, Germany
{bednara,hannig,teich}@date.upb.de
http://www-date.upb.de

Abstract. We present a new methodology for controlling the space-time
behavior of VLSI and FPGA-based processor arrays. The main idea is to
generate simple local control elements which take control over the active-
ness of each attached processor element. Each control element thereby
propagates a "start" and a "stop execution" signal to its neighbors. We
show that our control mechanism is much more efficient than existing
approaches because 1) only two control signals (start/stop) are required,
2) no extension of the computation space is necessary. 3) By the local
propagation of just one start/stop signal, energy is saved as processing
elements are only active between the time they have received the start
signal and the time they have received the stop signal. Our methodology
is applicable to one- and multi-dimensional processor arrays and is based
on local control signal propagation. We provide a theoretical analysis of
the overhead caused by the control structure.

1   Introduction

Parallel processor arrays and mapping methodology for such architectures are
becoming more and more important, especially due to the advent of reusable
reconfigurable hardware such as FPGAs [20,1], and due to the increasing amount
of computing power implementable on a single chip (SoC-technology). Only if
we are able to map computation intensive algorithms onto such architectures
efficiently are we able to exploit the benefit of the given technology.

This paper is a contribution to implement computation intensive algorithms
as specified by loop-like algorithms such as *piecewise regular algorithms* [17,16]
or *uniform recurrence equations* [7] in hardware, see also [2,6].

The major task of mapping a given algorithm with indexed computations
onto hardware is to assign space (processor index) and time to each computation
in a computational domain that is often called *index space*. In the area of VLSI
processor arrays, linear index transformations [8,11,10] are typically used and
known as *space-time mappings*. Similar approaches are also used in the area of
parallelizing compilers for supercomputers with linear transformations such as
loop skewing, *loop tiling*, and *loop permutation* [19].

---

* Supported in part by the German Science Foundation (DFG) Project SFB 376 "Massively Parallel Computation".

E.F. Deprettere et al. (Eds.): SAMOS 2001, LNCS 2268, pp. 154–170, 2002.
© Springer-Verlag Berlin Heidelberg 2002

The problem addressed in this paper is in the context of controlling the operations of a given algorithm when being linearly transformed by a space-time mapping. Let the index space be described by a bounded polyhedron (polytope), then a space-time mapping leads to a skewed polytope. In such a polytope, the operations assigned to each processing element do not necessarily start executing at the same time 0. Hence, one could either apply techniques of control generation such as described in [14, 13, 21] that have in common that the index space is extended by dummy operations such that all processors start at the reset time $t = 0$. In order to control correct execution, a control signal is generated for each bounding hyperplane of the transformed index space such that predicates in control signals help a processing element to identify whether and what operation it has to perform at each time step.

This is, however, inefficient in the sense that the number of control signals generated depend on the number of bounding hyperplanes of the algorithm and that much energy is consumed by extension of index spaces and by the introduction of propagated control signals.

Here, we present a new idea of efficient controlling the boundaries of a space-time transformed index space polytope that introduces only two additional signals that indicate at each processing element the first time step and the last time step it will have to execute an operation. These two signals are propagated locally to neighbor processing elements. The approach is energy-efficient in the sense that a processing element only consumes energy during the time interval between reception of its start and its stop signal.

The rest of the paper is structured as follows. First, in Section 2, we show how the principle works for 1-D arrays (2-D index spaces). In Section 3, we extend this generation of boundary control hierarchically to higher dimensions including optimization techniques to reduce the control overhead in terms of number of control elements. Finally, results are presented in Section 4.

2   Control Mechanism for Linear Processor Arrays

First, we present our approach to controlling the activity of linear processor arrays. Let $\mathcal{I}$ denote a two-dimensional convex index space defined as follows:

$$\mathcal{I} = \{I \in \mathbb{Z}^d \mid AI \geq b\}, \quad A \in \mathbb{Z}^{m \times d}, \ b \in \mathbb{Z}^m \tag{1}$$

and let $d = 2$. Hence, $\mathcal{I}$ is the set of integral points in the intersection of m two-dimensional halfspaces: $\mathcal{I} = \bigcap_{i=0}^{m-1} H_i$. For each halfspace $H_i = \{I \in \mathbb{Z}^2 \mid A_i I \geq b_i\}$, $i = 0 \ldots m-1$, its *bounding hyperplane* P_i is $P_i = \{I \in \mathbb{Z}^2 \mid A_i I = b_i\}$ where $A_i = (A_{i,p} \ A_{i,t})$ is the i-th row vector of matrix A and b_i is the i-th element of vector b. For each index vector $I = (p \ t)^\mathrm{T} \in \mathcal{I}$, p denotes the *processor index* and t the (discrete) *time index* or simply time. Hence, a space-time mapping of the operations inside the polytope is assumed to be given.

If the element $A_{i,t} \neq 0$, P_i can be written as a linear equation:

$$t = T_i(p) := -\frac{A_{i,p}}{A_{i,t}} p + \frac{b}{A_{i,t}} \tag{2}$$

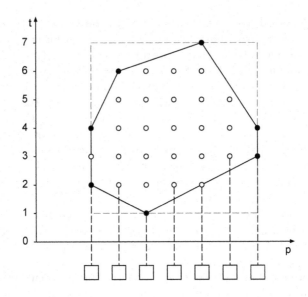

Fig. 1. Index space $\mathcal{I}$ with bounding hyperplanes. Each integer point corresponds to the computation of a loop body.

In Eq. (2), t denotes the time at which the bounding hyperplane P_i is crossed in dependence of the processor index p. If $A_{i,t} = 0$, then p is constant.

Fig. 1 shows an index space $\mathcal{I}$ with 7 bounding hyperplanes. Each integral point inside or on the border of the index space corresponds to a computation of a loop-body of a given algorithm. For the purpose of this paper, it does not matter how complex and what type of computation is specified at each index point. In Fig. 1, we have already given a space-time mapping: The p-axis denotes the processor index, and t denotes the time of a computation. By the projection of the polytope along the time-axis, it can be seen that the corresponding processor arrays consists of 7 processing elements.

2.1   Boundary Control

It can be seen in Fig. 1 that some processor elements start their first computation at different times than others. A similar observation holds for the last time, a processor performs a computation inside the index space polytope. Hence, control is necessary that tells each processing element when to start executing and when to stop executing.

In previous approaches to *control generation* such as [14, 15, 13], it was discovered that the space-time-transformed index space of an algorithm that corresponds to a synchronously clocked processor array reset at time 0 must be in the shape of a *right prism* as indicated by dashed lines in Fig. 1 for the index space shown there. The authors proposed to specify an *extension of index space* to such a right prism hull and to provide control signals that propagate control signals from the border of the array that provide a processing element with the information whether it computes an operation inside $\mathcal{I}$ or not. The complexity of this kind of boundary control in terms of the number of control signals is m. Another disadvantage of the control proposed in [14, 21] is that the m generated control signals are propagated in the complete space $\mathcal{I}$, hence causing an overhead of $m|\mathcal{I}|$ propagations that cause a lot of energy consumption.

In the following, we develop our main idea of *boundary control* by propagating just a signal start and a single stop signal to the processing elements, and only once during the complete algorithm execution. Before that, some definitions are in order.

We assume that $\mathcal{I}$ is an integral polytope. In this case, all its vertices of $\mathcal{I}$ are integral points. Otherwise, we may apply the *cutting plane algorithm* according to [12] to compute the integer hull[1]. The *vertex set* V of $\mathcal{I}$ is defined as follows:

$$V = \mathcal{I} \cap \left\{ \bigcup_{0 \le i,j < m, i \ne j} (P_i \cap P_j) \right\}. \tag{3}$$

For example, the vertex set of the index space shown in Fig. 1 is highlighted by black dots.

In the following, let the processor index of $v_i \in V$ be denoted p_i and the time index be denoted t_i $(v_i = (p_i \ t_i)^{\mathrm{T} \in \mathcal{I}})$. We define

$$\mathcal{I}_{t_{\min}} = \{v_i \in V : \forall v_j \in V, v_j \ne v_i : t_i \le t_j\}$$
$$\mathcal{I}_{t_{\max}} = \{v_i \in V : \forall v_j \in V, v_j \ne v_i : t_i \ge t_j\}$$
$$\mathcal{I}_{p_{\min}} = \{v_i \in V : \forall v_j \in V, v_j \ne v_i : p_i \le p_j\}$$
$$\mathcal{I}_{p_{\max}} = \{v_i \in V : \forall v_j \in V, v_j \ne v_i : p_i \ge p_j\}$$

Hence, $\mathcal{I}_{t_{\min}}$ denotes the set of vertices with the property that there is no vertex with a smaller time step, and so on. Let $I_{t_{\min}}$ $(I_{t_{\max}}, I_{p_{\min}}, I_{p_{\max}})$ be an arbitrary element of $\mathcal{I}_{t_{\min}}$ $(\mathcal{I}_{t_{\max}}, \mathcal{I}_{p_{\min}}, \mathcal{I}_{p_{\max}})$. Finally, we define two predicates TLO and THI on index vectors as follows:

$$\mathrm{TLO}(I) \quad \Leftrightarrow \quad I = \begin{pmatrix} p \\ t \end{pmatrix} \in \mathcal{I} \wedge \forall \begin{pmatrix} p \\ t' \end{pmatrix} \in \mathcal{I} : t \le t'$$

$$\mathrm{THI}(I) \quad \Leftrightarrow \quad I = \begin{pmatrix} p \\ t \end{pmatrix} \in \mathcal{I} \wedge \forall \begin{pmatrix} p \\ t' \end{pmatrix} \in \mathcal{I} : t \ge t'$$

In other words, $\mathrm{TLO}(I)$ $(\mathrm{THI}(I))$ is true for an index point $I = (p \ t)^{\mathrm{T}}$ iff $I \in \mathcal{I}$ and there is no point $I' = (p \ t')^{\mathrm{T}}$ in $\mathcal{I}$ at the same processor index p with a smaller (bigger) time step than t.

We use these predicates in order to define the *boundary control graph* $G(\mathcal{I}) = (V_G(\mathcal{I}), E_G(\mathcal{I}))$ with vertices $V_G(\mathcal{I})$ and edges $E_G(\mathcal{I})$:

---

[1] Although the cutting plane algorithm has exponential complexity, it is in general possible to apply the algorithm for low-dimensional index spaces (e.g., $d = 2, 3$), and the number of half-spaces is small in practical applications.

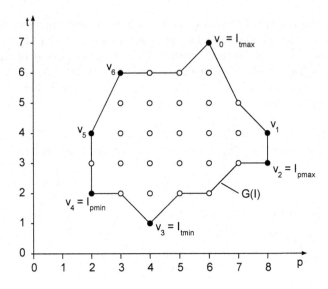

Fig. 2. Index space $\mathcal{I}$ with vertex set $V = \{v_0, \ldots, v_6\}$ and boundary control graph $G(\mathcal{I})$.

$$V_G(\mathcal{I}) = \{I \in \mathcal{I} \mid \text{TLO}(I) \vee \text{THI}(I)\}$$

$$E_G(\mathcal{I}) = \left\{ \left(I_1 = \begin{pmatrix} p_1 \\ t_1 \end{pmatrix} \in V_G(\mathcal{I}), I_2 = \begin{pmatrix} p_2 \\ t_2 \end{pmatrix} \in V_G(\mathcal{I}) \right) \mid \right.$$
$$((|p_2 - p_1| = 1 \wedge (\text{TLO}(I_1) = \text{TLO}(I_2))) \vee$$
$$\left. (p_2 = p_1 \wedge ((\text{TLO}(I_1) = \text{THI}(I_2)) \vee (t_1 = t_2)))) \right\}$$

In Fig. 2, a sample index space $\mathcal{I}$ and the corresponding graph $G(\mathcal{I})$ is shown. Since $\text{TLO}(I_{t_{\min}})$ and $\text{THI}(I_{t_{\max}})$ holds, $I_{t_{\min}}, I_{t_{\max}} \in V_G(\mathcal{I})$.

The idea of boundary control is now to traverse the boundary control graph node by node, starting in a node $I_{t_{\min}} \in \mathcal{I}_{t_{\min}}$ in two directions (L for left and R for right) as indicated in Fig. 3 until a node $I_{t_{\max}} \in \mathcal{I}_{t_{\max}}$ is reached. These two paths can be represented as vectors, where each vector component is a pair $(I_i, I_j) \in V_G(\mathcal{I}) \times V_G(\mathcal{I})$ that denotes a *directed* edge from I_i to I_j:

$$L = (l_0, \ldots, l_{k-1}) \; : \; \forall i \in \{0, \ldots, k-1\} \; : \; l_i = (I_{i,1}, I_{i,2})$$
$$\wedge \; \{I_{i,1}, I_{i,2}\} \in E_G(\mathcal{I}) \wedge I_{i+1,1} = I_{i,2} \wedge I_{0,1} = I_{t_{\min}}$$
$$\wedge \; I_{k-1,2} = I_{t_{\max}} \wedge \exists j \in \{0, \ldots, k-1\} \; : \; I_{j,1} = I_{p_{\min}};$$

$$R = (r_0, \ldots, r_{k'-1}) \; : \; \forall i \in \{0, \ldots, k'-1\} \; : \; r_i = (I_{i,1}, I_{i,2})$$
$$\wedge \; \{I_{i,1}, I_{i,2}\} \in E_G(\mathcal{I}) \wedge I_{i+1,1} = I_{i,2} \wedge I_{0,1} = I_{t_{\min}}$$
$$\wedge \; I_{k'-1,2} = I_{t_{\max}} \wedge \exists j \in \{0, \ldots, k'-1\} \; : \; I_{j,1} = I_{p_{\max}}.$$

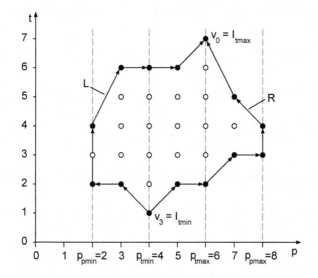

Fig. 3. Index space $\mathcal{I}$ with boundary control paths L and R.

The traces L and R are called *boundary control paths*. Each vector element of a boundary control path represents the flow of a control signal from a *control element* to the next. The implied hardware structure of control elements is defined in the next subsection.

2.2   Control Hardware

All index vectors $I = (p\ t)^{\mathrm{T}}$ with the same p-coordinate are mapped on the same processor element. Thus, the processor elements of operations at index points $I_{t_{\min}}$, $I_{t_{\max}}$, $I_{p_{\min}}$, $I_{p_{\max}}$ are mapped onto processor indices $p_{t_{\min}}$, $p_{t_{\max}}$, $p_{p_{\min}}$, $p_{p_{\max}}$, respectively.

The hardware structure of our control methodology is defined as follows: To each processing element, we associate a dedicated controller called *control element* (CE). Each control element has exactly two control input/output pairs. Control elements are interconnected locally with neighbor control elements in the form of a *control chain* as indicated in Fig. 4, showing the control chain for the index space in Fig. 2.

Thereby, each trace L and R represents a control signal flow from $p_{t_{\min}}$ to $p_{t_{\max}}$. A control signal that initiates the execution of a processing element is passed from $p_{t_{\min}}$ to $p_{p_{\min}}$ and $p_{p_{\max}}$. Each processor element in between starts its operation once receiving this start signal. When a control signal is passed back from $p_{p_{\min}}$ and $p_{p_{\max}}$ to $p_{t_{\max}}$, the processor elements in between stop their execution (stop signal).

The CE at location $p_{t_{\min}}$ has a start-input which must be set active for one clock cycle when the computation of the array starts. Two control signals are duplicated from the start signal and propagated to the first and the last CE

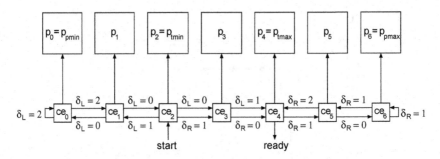

Fig. 4. Control chain for the index space in Fig.2. The data links between the processor elements are not shown here.

in the control chain (at $p_{p_{\min}}$ and $p_{p_{\max}}$) and then back to the CE $p_{t_{\max}}$. The control signals are delayed in each CE, and both control signals must arrive at $p_{t_{\max}}$ at the same time step. Thus, the sum of the delays must be the same for both control signal paths. By determining an appropriate delay for both control signals when passing from one CE to the next, we obtain a control mechanism for controlling the boundary of an index space $\mathcal{I}$.

Each CE thus handles two control signals, thus it has two control input/ output pairs, except for the CEs connected to $p_{t_{\min}}$ and $p_{t_{\max}}$ which are slightly different. A control signal on an input is passed to the corresponding output after a delay of δ cycles. An additional control output (*enable*) is connected to the attached processor element. This enable signal is set active when the first (start) control signal arrives and is reset when the second control signal (stop) arrives. The processor element is active as long as the enable signal is set and stopped else.

2.3   Computation of δ-Delays

The number δ of time steps a control signal must be delayed before passed to the next CE depends on the number of isotemporal hyperplanes the corresponding edge $e = (v, w) \in E_G(\mathcal{I})$ crosses the index space $\mathcal{I}$. Thus, we define functions $delay_L : 0, \ldots, k - 1 \rightarrow \mathbb{N}^3$ and $delay_R : 0, \ldots, k' - 1 \rightarrow \mathbb{N}^3$ that return the triples (i, j, δ_L) and (i, j, δ_R) with the following semantics: A control signal passed from the CE at p_i to the CE at p_j must be delayed for δ_L (δ_R) time steps. Remember that each vector element l_i (r_i) of the vector L (R) is of the form $((p_{i,2}\ t_{i,2})^{\mathrm{T}}, (p_{i,1}\ t_{i,1})^{\mathrm{T}})$.

$$delay_L(i) = (p_{i,1}, p_{i,2}, (t_{i,2} - t_{i,1}))$$
$$delay_R(j) = (p_{j,1}, p_{j,2}, (t_{j,2} - t_{j,1}))$$

Computing both $delay_L$ and $delay_R$ on their whole domains gives us the complete structure of the control chain and all necessary δ_L and δ_R delays of the CEs.

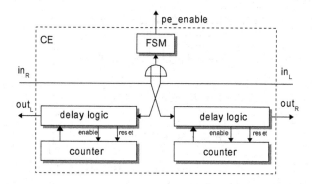

Fig. 5. Internal logic of a control element

2.4   Architecture of the Control Elements

A refinement of the internal circuitry of a control element is shown in Fig. 5. The CE consists of two binary counters used for realizing the delay of the control signals. Each counter is controlled by a delay logic that starts the counter when a control signal event occurs at the in_L (in_R) input. The counter is stopped and reset after δ_L (δ_R) clock cycles and the out_L (out_R) output is set active for one clock cycle. A small state machine (FSM) is used to generate the signal pe_enable, which is set active when the in_L (in_R) signal arrives and is reset when the in_R (in_L) signal arrives.

The CE architecture differs from that shown in Fig. 5 at processor locations $p_{t_{\min}}$ and $p_{t_{\max}}$ since they have an additional start input or ready output. In the case of $p_{t_{\min}} = p_{t_{\max}}$, we use another type of control element that has both start and stop signals.

The computed delays for the space-time transformed index space introduced in Fig. 2 are represented by the slope of the edges of the boundary control paths in Fig. 3. I.e., the number of isotemporal hyperplanes crossed by each edge corresponds to the δ-delay. The δ-delays are also annotated to the interconnect of the control elements in Fig. 4.

3   Boundary Control for Multi-dimensional Arrays

The methodology of boundary control presented in Section 2 is applicable only to two-dimensional index spaces (1-D arrays). Here, we show how the concept may be extended to multi-dimensional arrays by a hierarchical application of the principle introduced earlier.

3.1   Multi-dimensional Control

An extension of our model to algorithms with index spaces of higher dimensions is possible due to the observation that each n-dimensional convex polytope can

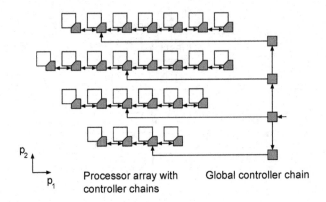

p_2

p_1

Processor array with   Global controller chain
controller chains

Fig. 6. Controller structure of a two-dimensional processor array. The data links between the processor elements are not shown here.

be decomposed into a finite set of $n-1$-dimensional convex polytopes by slicing it using a hyperplane partitioning. Such a slicing algorithm will be used in this section to extend the method of boundary control to higher-dimensional index spaces.

For example, a space-time mapped 3-D index polytope corresponds to a two-dimensional processor array. A hyperplane partitioning in 3-D space divides the 2-D processor space into a set of 1-D (linear arrays), see, e.g., in Fig. 6. For each of the partitions, we may apply the boundary control of the 2-D polytopes as introduced in Section 2. Finally, an additional controller is required that generates the *start*-signal for each of the linear control chains. For this purpose, we introduce another global controller chain. A sample control structure of a two-dimensional processor array is shown in Fig. 6.

The number of required additional control elements obviously depends on the orientation of the slices of the original polytope. If the slices were oriented in vertical direction, in Fig. 6, 8 additional control elements instead of 4 would be required. Other hyperplane directions used for slicing the 3-D space would lead to different directions of controller chains and different numbers of required global control elements.

3.2   Hyperplane Partitioning Algorithm

Our slicing algorithm is applicable for any convex index space of arbitrary dimension $d > 1$. Actually, for illustrative reasons, the algorithm is described here only for $d = 3$. The algorithm decomposes a given index space $\mathcal{I}$ into a finite number of parallel, $d - 1$ dimensional hyperplanes, such that

- the hyperplane normal vector chosen is not equal to the time axis, and
- the number of hyperplane partitions is minimal[2].

The last condition minimizes the number of additional control elements.

---

[2] In the following, we denote the intersection of a hyperplane with a given index space *slice*.

Optimal Hyperplane Direction

Given an index space $\mathcal{I}$ according to Def. 1. Let the index space be space-time transformed. This means that without loss of generality, we may assume that the index points $I = (p_0 \; p_1 \; \ldots \; p_{d-1} \; t)^{\mathrm{T}}$ have $d-1$ leading processor indices and the time t as the d-th coordinate.

The first step in our algorithm is to find the slice-minimal orientation of the hyperplanes. Let $v = (v_0 \; v_1 \; \ldots \; v_{d-1} \; v_t)$ be the normal vector of feasible hyperplanes (being orthogonal to the time axis). This problem is very similar to finding an optimal schedule vector for processor arrays, see [4, 18], and can be solved as follows: Find a vector v that minimizes the maximum number of hyperplanes, i.e., that minimizes $\max\{v(I_2 - I_1) \mid AI_1 \geq b \; \wedge \; AI_2 \geq b\}$. This problem can be represented in its dual form as one single linear program as follows:

$$
\begin{aligned}
\text{minimize } & -(y_2 + y_1)b \\
\text{subj. to } & y_1 A = -v \quad y_1 \geq 0 \quad y_1 \in \mathbb{Q}^{1 \times m} \\
& y_2 A = +v \quad y_2 \geq 0 \quad y_2 \in \mathbb{Q}^{1 \times m} \\
& v_t = 0.
\end{aligned}
\tag{4}
$$

This linear program may be solved in polynomial time.

For example, for the processor space shown in Fig. 6, the optimal hyperplane obtained is $v = (0\ 1\ 0)$ leading to a hyperplane with 4 control elements.

The purpose of the top-level linear array of control elements is to inject only start signals to the local linear control chains that are obtained by the hyperplane partitioning. This is due to the fact that the control elements at the lowest level generate stop signals to finish operations which are not needed at higher levels. Hence, the control hierarchy is obtained by having one processing element at which the start signal is injected. This element, see e.g., in Fig. 6, is obtained as belonging to a hyperplane with a processing element that starts at a globally minimal time step. All neighbor elements obtain a delayed start signal. On the top-level, this delay is given by the difference between the minimal time step of one hyperplane and the minimal time step of the index space in the neighbor partition.

In case of more than 3 dimensions, the hyperplane method can be applied iteratively to obtain a control hierarchy with one linear array at the top-level, each element starts a linear control array at the next lower level, and so on, until a control chain at the lowest level is started.

For completeness, we only specify next how we obtain the description of the slices.

Description of Slices

With a found hyperplane direction v, we can process on the next lower hierarchical level by a) computing all non-empty slices, and b) for each slice, apply the boundary control to each slice of dimension $d-1$.

In the following, we simply present an algorithm for computing the descriptions of each slice, given an index space $\mathcal{I}$ and a hyperplane partitioning vector v.

All non-empty slices satisfy:

$$vI = z$$
$$AI \geq b.$$

The first slice is obtained by solving the linear program

$$z_{\min} = \min\{vI \mid AI \geq b\}.$$

The last slice is obtained by solving the linear program

$$z_{\max} = \max\{vI \mid AI \geq b\}.$$

By the convex nature of the index space, there is a non-empty slice for each value $z_{\min} \leq z \leq z_{\max}$. Each hyperplane description is given by $\{I \in \mathbb{Z}^d \mid vI = z \wedge AI \geq b\}$. In order to apply the control to the next lower level of hierarchy, we need to eliminate a variable of I to obtain a description with $d-1$ variables. This can be done easily by choosing an arbitrary variable of the index vector I, e.g., p_0, solve $vI = z$ for p_0, i.e.,

$$p_0 = -\frac{v_1}{v_0}p_1 - \frac{v_2}{v_0}p_2 - \cdots - \frac{v_{d-1}}{v_0}p_{d-1},$$

and replace p_0 in $AI \geq b$ with the right hand side of the above equation.

4   Results

In this section, the methodology of our approach is shown for a realistic example. As instance, we consider the well-known problem of LU-decomposition. In the LU-decomposition, a given matrix $C \in \mathbb{R}^{N \times N}$ is decomposed into $C = A \cdot B$, where $A \in \mathbb{R}^{N \times N}$ is a lower triangular and $B \in \mathbb{R}^{N \times N}$ is an upper triangular matrix. This problem may be formulated by a recursive algorithm [9]. A corresponding piecewise regular algorithm is given by the following set of quantified equations

$$b\,[i,j,k] \quad \leftarrow \quad \begin{cases} c\,[i,j,k-1] & \text{if } i = k \\ b\,[i-1,j,k] & \text{else} \end{cases}$$

$$a\,[i,j,k] \quad \leftarrow \quad \begin{cases} c\,[i,j,k-1]\,/b\,[i,j,k] & \text{if } j = k \\ a\,[i,j-1,k] & \text{else} \end{cases}$$

$$c\,[i,j,k] \quad \leftarrow \quad c\,[i,j,k-1] - a\,[i,j,k] \cdot b\,[i,j,k]$$

where the index space is given by

$$\mathcal{I} = \left\{ I = \begin{pmatrix} i \\ j \\ k \end{pmatrix} \in \mathbb{Z}^3 \ \middle| \ \begin{pmatrix} 0 & 0 & 1 \\ 0 & 0 & -1 \\ 1 & 0 & -1 \\ -1 & 0 & 0 \\ 0 & 1 & -1 \\ 0 & -1 & 0 \end{pmatrix} \begin{pmatrix} i \\ j \\ k \end{pmatrix} \geq \begin{pmatrix} 0 \\ 1 - N \\ 0 \\ 1 - N \\ 0 \\ 1 - N \end{pmatrix} \right\}.$$

For illustration purposes let be $N = 5$ in the following. As mentioned before, linear transformations as in Equation (5) are used as *space-time mappings* [11,10] in order to assign a *processor index* $p \in \mathbb{Z}^{n-1}$ (space) and a *sequencing index* $t \in \mathbb{Z}$ (time) to index vectors $I \in \mathcal{I}$.

$$\begin{pmatrix} p \\ t \end{pmatrix} = \begin{pmatrix} Q \\ \lambda \end{pmatrix} I \tag{5}$$

In Eq. (5), $Q \in \mathbb{Z}^{(n-1) \times n}$ and the *schedule vector* $\lambda \in \mathbb{Z}^{1 \times n}$.

Now, consider that we have obtained an optimal space-time mapping by exploring the design space in terms of cost and performance. In [6], we have presented efficient pruning techniques for the search of optimal projection vectors (space-time mappings). We only summarize the main ideas: 1) Only consider co-prime vectors, 2) only consider co-prime vectors that have the properties that at least two points in $\mathcal{I}$ are projected onto each other. This leads to a search space of co-prime vectors in a convex polytope called difference-body of points in $\mathcal{I}$. Finally, in this reduced search space, we can exploit symmetry to exclude search vectors $v = -v'$ such that typically, only few projection vector candidates v have to be investigated. In order to count the number of points in a projected index space, *Ehrhart polynomials* [5,3] may be evaluated to count the number of points (control elements) in the projected space.

Let $u = (0\ 1\ 0)^{\mathrm{T}}$ be a projection vector and $\lambda = (0\ 1\ 2)$ be a schedule vector candidate during exploration. Herewith, index points I are mapped onto processors p at time t

$$\begin{pmatrix} p \\ t \end{pmatrix} = \begin{pmatrix} 1 & 0 & 0 \\ 0 & 0 & 1 \\ 0 & 1 & 2 \end{pmatrix} I.$$

This point set can also be described by the following polytope $\mathcal{I}_{pt}$

$$\mathcal{I}_{pt} = \left\{ I = \begin{pmatrix} i \\ k \\ t \end{pmatrix} \in \mathbb{Z}^3 \ \middle| \ \begin{pmatrix} -1 & 0 & 0 \\ 0 & 1 & -1 \\ 0 & -2 & 1 \\ 1 & -1 & 0 \\ 0 & 1 & 0 \end{pmatrix} \begin{pmatrix} i \\ k \\ t \end{pmatrix} \geq \begin{pmatrix} -4 \\ -4 \\ 0 \\ 0 \\ 0 \end{pmatrix} \right\}.$$

The transformed index space is visualized in Fig. 7 (a), its shape is like a skewed pyramid. The triangular shape of the processor array is shown in Fig. 7 (b). For example, at time step $t = 0$ and $t = 1$ only five processor elements are making

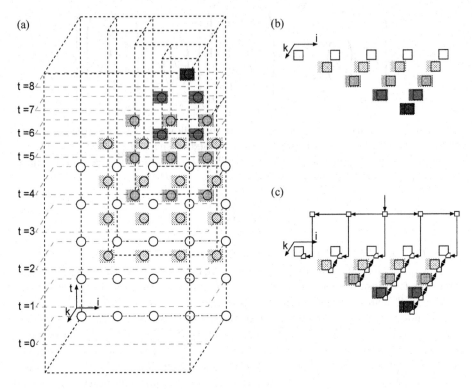

Fig. 7. In (a), the mapped index space of the LU-decomposition is shown, where $N = 5$, $u = (0\ 1\ 0)^T$, and $\lambda = (0\ 1\ 2)$. The isotemporal hyperplanes are visualized. The matching processor array is shown in (b). In (c), the control structure for the processor array is shown.

computations (marked as white points in Fig. 7), at time $t = 2$ and $t = 3$ in total nine processors are used, at time $t = 4$ twelve processors, at time $t = 5$ seven processors, and so on.

Next, an optimal hyperplane direction is determined. By solving the corresponding linear program (see Eq. (4)), the normal vector $v = (1\ 0\ 0)$ is obtained as an optimal solution vector. Using this direction all processor with $k = 0$ can be started at time 0. Therefore, a broadcast is sent to all the white processor elements in Fig. 7 (c). In Fig. 8 (a), an exemplary slice for $v = (1\ 0\ 0)$ and $i = 4$ of the mapped index space is shown. The boundary control paths are

$$L = \left(\left(\begin{pmatrix} 4 \\ 0 \\ 0 \end{pmatrix}, \begin{pmatrix} 4 \\ 0 \\ 4 \end{pmatrix} \right), \left(\begin{pmatrix} 4 \\ 0 \\ 4 \end{pmatrix}, \begin{pmatrix} 4 \\ 1 \\ 5 \end{pmatrix} \right), \left(\begin{pmatrix} 4 \\ 1 \\ 5 \end{pmatrix}, \begin{pmatrix} 4 \\ 2 \\ 6 \end{pmatrix} \right), \ldots \right.$$

$$\left. \ldots, \left(\begin{pmatrix} 4 \\ 2 \\ 6 \end{pmatrix}, \begin{pmatrix} 4 \\ 3 \\ 7 \end{pmatrix} \right), \left(\begin{pmatrix} 4 \\ 3 \\ 7 \end{pmatrix}, \begin{pmatrix} 4 \\ 4 \\ 8 \end{pmatrix} \right) \right)$$

for the left path and

$$R = \left(\left(\begin{pmatrix} 4 \\ 0 \\ 0 \end{pmatrix}, \begin{pmatrix} 4 \\ 1 \\ 2 \end{pmatrix} \right), \left(\begin{pmatrix} 4 \\ 1 \\ 2 \end{pmatrix}, \begin{pmatrix} 4 \\ 2 \\ 4 \end{pmatrix} \right), \left(\begin{pmatrix} 4 \\ 2 \\ 4 \end{pmatrix}, \begin{pmatrix} 4 \\ 3 \\ 6 \end{pmatrix} \right), \dots \right.$$

$$\left. \dots, \left(\begin{pmatrix} 4 \\ 3 \\ 6 \end{pmatrix}, \begin{pmatrix} 4 \\ 4 \\ 8 \end{pmatrix} \right) \right)$$

for the right path. The δ-delays that are necessary for controlling the boundary of the slice are computed as follows for the left path L

$$\begin{aligned}
\text{delay}(0) &= (p_{40}, p_{40}, 4 - 0), & \delta_L &= 4 \\
\text{delay}(1) &= (p_{40}, p_{41}, 5 - 4), & \delta_L &= 1 \\
\text{delay}(2) &= (p_{41}, p_{42}, 6 - 5), & \delta_L &= 1 \\
\text{delay}(3) &= (p_{42}, p_{43}, 7 - 6), & \delta_L &= 1 \\
\text{delay}(4) &= (p_{43}, p_{44}, 8 - 7), & \delta_L &= 1,
\end{aligned}$$

and for the right path R

$$\begin{aligned}
\text{delay}(0) &= (p_{40}, p_{41}, 2 - 0), & \delta_R &= 2 \\
\text{delay}(1) &= (p_{41}, p_{42}, 4 - 2), & \delta_R &= 2 \\
\text{delay}(2) &= (p_{42}, p_{43}, 6 - 4), & \delta_R &= 2 \\
\text{delay}(3) &= (p_{43}, p_{44}, 8 - 6), & \delta_R &= 2.
\end{aligned}$$

The controlled processors are shown in Fig. 8 (b), the edges between the controller elements are annotated by the delays δ_L and δ_R respectively. At time 0 the processor element p_{40} is enabled by its controller. After two time steps ($\delta_R = 2$) the next processor element p_{41} is enabled. Every second time unit the start signal is propagated two the right neighbor and the corresponding processor is enabled. The first stop signal is produced at time step 4 where processor p_{40} is disabled. Then, one processor element from p_{41} to p_{44} is turned off at each subsequent time step.

The utilization of our new control methodology for the LU-decomposition algorithm shows several advantages very well compared to the classically approaches of control generation [14, 13, 21]. An extension of a given index space to a right prism is not necessary. In our case of the LU-decomposition, only approximately half of the number of data transfers (propagations) are necessary. The energy reduction is evident.

5   Conclusion

In this paper, we have introduced a new method for controlling the operations of loop-like algorithms when mapped onto processor arrays. The idea is to reconstruct the border of an index polytope of computation by propagation of a single

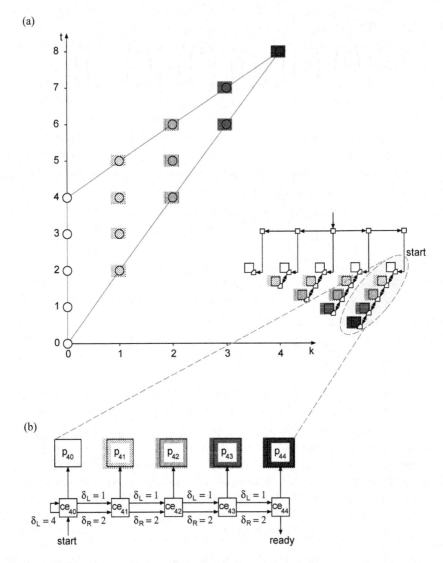

Fig. 8. In (a), a slice for $i = 4$ of the mapped index space $\mathcal{I}_{pt}$ is visualized. In (b), the corresponding controller structure of the processor array is shown. The edges between the controller elements are annotated by the δ-delays. The lower edges between the control elements propagate every second time step a start signal to its right neighbor. After the delay $\delta_L = 4$, subsequently the stop signal is sent from one control element to its right neighbor.

start and a single stop event locally to neighbor processors that identifies the execution intervals of each processor. The effort amounts to the fixed amount of two control signals. Contrary to existing approaches, our approach is much more area- and energy-conscious.

Our method can be seen complementary to existing control generation approaches that are still necessary, e.g., for replacing iteration dependent predicates of operations *inside* a given index space by predicates on locally propagated control signals.

The presented approach can easily be extended for a more general class of index spaces, so-called *linearly bounded lattices*:

$$\mathcal{I} = \{I \in \mathbb{Z}^n \mid I = M\kappa + c \ \wedge \ A\kappa \geq b\}$$

where $\kappa \in \mathbb{Z}^l$, $M \in \mathbb{Z}^{n \times l}$, $c \in \mathbb{Z}^n$, $A \in \mathbb{Z}^{m \times l}$ and $b \in \mathbb{Z}^m$. Like throughout this paper, $\{\kappa \in \mathbb{Z}^l \mid A\kappa \geq b\}$ defines an integral convex polyhedron or in case of boundedness a polytope in $\mathbb{Z}^l$. This set is affinely mapped onto iteration vectors I using an affine transformation $(I = M\kappa + c)$.

Our new distributed loop control methodology is integrated as part of the PARO design system and can be used during the process of automated synthesis of regular circuits. PARO is a design system project for modeling, transforming, optimization, and processor synthesis for the class of piecewise linear algorithms. For further information on the PARO design system project, check the following website: http://www-date.upb.de/research/paro/.

References

1. Atmel Inc. *AT6000 FPGA Configuration Guide*.
2. Marcus Bednara and Jürgen Teich. Synthesis of FPGA Implementations from Loop Algorithms. In *Proc. of the First International Conference on Engineering of Reconfigurable Systems and Algorithms (ERSA01)*, pages 1–7, Las Vegas, Nevada, June 2001.
3. Philippe Clauss and Vincent Loechner. Parametric Analysis of Polyhedral Iteration Spaces. *Journal of VLSI Signal Processing*, 19(2):179–194, July 1998.
4. Alain Darte, Leonid Khachiyan, and Yves Robert. Linear Scheduling is Nearly Optimal. *Parallel Processing Letters*, 1(2):73–81, 1991.
5. Eugène Ehrhart. *Polynômes arithmétiques et Méthode des Polyèdres en Combinatoire*, volume 35 of *International Series of Numerical Mathematics*. Birkhäuser Verlag, Basel, 1. edition, 1977.
6. Frank Hannig and Jürgen Teich. Design Space Exploration for Massively Parallel Processor Arrays. In Victor Malyshkin, editor, *Parallel Computing Technologies, 6th International Conference, PaCT 2001, Proceedings*, volume 2127 of *Lecture Notes in Computer Science (LNCS)*, pages 51–65, Novosibirsk, Russia, September 2001. Springer.
7. Richard M. Karp, Raymond E. Miller, and Shmuel Winograd. The Organization of Computations for Uniform Recurrence Equations. *Journal of the Association for Computing Machinery*, 14(3):563–590, 1967.
8. Robert H. Kuhn. Transforming Algorithms for Single-Stage and VLSI Architectures. In *Workshop on Interconnection Networks for Parallel and Distributed Processing*, pages 11–19, West Layfaette, Indiana, April 1980.
9. Sun Yuan Kung. *VLSI Array Processors*. Prentice Hall, Englewood Cliffs, New Jersey, 1987.

10. Christian Lengauer. Loop Parallelization in the Polytope Model. In Eike Best, editor, *CONCUR'93*, Lecture Notes in Computer Science 715, pages 398–416. Springer-Verlag, 1993.
11. Dan I. Moldovan. On the Design of Algorithms for VLSI Systolic Arrays. In *Proceedings of the IEEE*, volume 71, pages 113–120, January 1983.
12. Alexander Schrijver. *Theory of Linear and Integer Programming*. Whily – Interscience series in discrete mathematics. John Wiley & Sons, Chichester, New York, 1986.
13. Jürgen Teich. *A Compiler for Application-Specific Processor Arrays*. Shaker (Reihe Elektrotechnik). Zugl. Saarbrücken, Univ. Diss, ISBN 3-86111-701-0, Aachen, Germany, 1993.
14. Jürgen Teich and Lothar Thiele. Control Generation in the Design of Processor Arrays. *Int. Journal on VLSI and Signal Processing*, 3(2):77–92, 1991.
15. Jürgen Teich and Lothar Thiele. Control Generation in the Design of Processor Arrays. In Josef A. Nossek, editor, *Parallel Processing on VLSI Arrays*. Kluwer Academic Publishers, 1992.
16. Jürgen Teich and Lothar Thiele. Partitioning of Processor Arrays: A Piecewise Regular Approach. *INTEGRATION: The VLSI Journal*, 14(3):297–332, 1993.
17. Lothar Thiele. On the Design of Piecewise Regular Processor Arrays. In *Proc. IEEE Symp. on Circuits and Systems*, pages 2239–2242, Portland, 1989.
18. Lothar Thiele. Scheduling of Uniform Algorithms with Resource Constraints. *Journal of VLSI Signal Processing*, 10:295–310, 1995.
19. Michael Wolfe. *High Performance Compilers for Parallel Computing*. Addison-Wesley, Redwood City, California, 1996.
20. Xilinx Inc. `http://www.xilinx.com/partinfo/ds003-2.pdf`.
21. Jingling Xue. *The Formal Synthesis of Control Signals for Systolic Arrays*. PhD thesis, Univ. of Edinburgh, March 1992.

Iterative Compilation

P.M.W. Knijnenburg[1], T. Kisuki[1], and M.F.P. O'Boyle[2]

[1] LIACS, Leiden University, the Netherlands
{peterk,kisuki}@liacs.nl
[2] ICSA, Edinburgh University, UK
mob@dcs.ed.ac.uk

Abstract. In this paper, we give an overview of a novel approach to the problem of how to select compiler optimizations, their parameters, and the order in which to employ them. In particular, we concentrate on the problem of how to select tile sizes and unroll factors simultaneously. We approach this problem in an architecturally adaptive manner by means of iterative compilation, where we generate many versions of a program and decide upon the best by actually executing them and measuring their execution time. We evaluate several iterative strategies. We compare the levels of optimization obtained by iterative compilation to several well-known static techniques and show that we outperform each of them on a range of benchmarks across a variety of architectures. Next we discuss how to incorporate static models as a means to filter out certain combinations of transformations that are unlikely to produce good results. Finally, we show that the approach is applicable to real programs by employing the technique to three SPECfp benchmarks.

1 Introduction

The growth in the use of computing technology is matched by a continuing demand for higher performance in all areas of computing. This demand for ever greater performance has led to an exponential growth in hardware performance and architecture evolution which has placed enormous stress on compiler technology. Traditional approaches to compiler optimizations are based on static analysis and simplified internal machine models, and use a hardwired compiler strategy. Such an approach can no longer be used in a computing environment that is continually changing. This is especially true for embedded processors where, moreover, there is no need for backward compatibility and hence for each new platform many applications need to be rewritten. Furthermore, modern architectures have very complex internal organizations, like high issue widths, out-of-order execution, deep memory hierarchies, etc. Therefore, simplified machine models that only take into account a small part of an actual architecture, only provide very rough performance estimates that are too imprecise to statically select the best optimizations. What is required is an approach which evolves and adapts to architectural change without sacrificing performance and, moreover, takes into account runtime behavior of platforms and applications. Therefore, compilers must be able to navigate a transformation space and have a metric,

E.F. Deprettere et al. (Eds.): SAMOS 2001, LNCS 2268, pp. 171–187, 2002.

whether it be static analysis or profile information, to accurately determine the worth of a transformation.

In order to solve these problems, we have proposed *iterative compilation* where many variants of the source program are generated and the best one is selected by actually profiling these variants on the target hardware [13]. This framework is essentially target neutral since it consists of a driver module that navigates through the optimization space and a source to source restructurer that allows the specification of the transformations it employs. The native compiler is used as back end compiler and it is treated together with the platform as a black box. In the present paper, we use real execution time to search the space for a minimal point and by using a generic iterative compilation strategy, we can find excellent optimizations across a range of architectures, outperforming static techniques significantly. Thus, we obtain highly architecture specific optimizations in an architecture independent manner. Although such an approach is usually ruled out in terms of excessive compilation time, it is precisely the approach used by expert programmers. Hence, the iterative approach is highly attractive in situations which require high performance, such as scientific codes that are run many times like weather prediction models, or in the case of vendor supplied library routines, or for embedded systems where compilation time can be amortized across the number of products shipped.

In this paper we restrict attention to two well-known program transformations: loop tiling [9,19] and unroll-and-jam [5]. Both transformations are targeted towards cache exploitation. Unroll-and-jam, moreover, duplicates the loop body to expose more instructions to the hardware that can be executed in parallel. These two transformations, therefore, are highly interdependent and their compound result gives rise to a highly irregular optimization space [4,15]. As we require effective utilization of the memory hierarchy and internal parallelism, we need to combine both of these transformations. However, combining the best tiling transformation for locality with the best unrolling factor for ILP, however, does not necessarily give the best overall transformation as transformation application is not orthogonal in effect. The close interaction between tiling and unrolling can be seen in Figure 1, which shows that a small deviation from 'good' tile sizes and unroll factors can cause a huge increase in execution time and even a slow down with respect to the original program. Therefore, we believe that the simultaneous determination of tile sizes and unroll factors provides an excellent test case for the applicability of iterative compilation. The approach itself can be used for any given set of compiler optimizations or compiler switches. However, many optimizations are on/off and therefore an approach based on search trees is more applicable in this situation. In [22] we have shown how such trees and the present case of large search spaces can be unified. Moreover, there exists a spectrum of iterative techniques from those based purely on static analysis, to purely iterative which makes few assumptions about the program/processor. Our framework allows the integration of these approaches by using the results of different static analysis as "seed points" in the optimization space, i.e., they form part of the initial set of points with which to start the iterative evaluation.

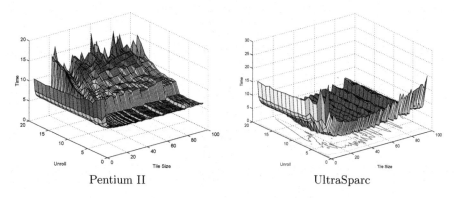

Pentium II   UltraSparc

Fig. 1. Execution Time MxM for Unrolling and Tiling

This paper is organized as follows. In section 2 the implementation of our iterative compilation system is briefly discussed. In order to assess the efficiency of our approach, we use a collection of small benchmark kernels and three target platforms in section 3. In section 4 we show that we can find good tile sizes and unroll factors by visiting only a small fraction of the entire optimization space. We also assess the quality of the optimization found by comparing it to two well-known static tile size selection algorithms and show that we outperform each of them in almost all cases. In section 5 we discuss how to incorporate static cache models in order to filter out bad candidates and thus reducing compilation time. In section 6 we show that the approach is applicable to realistic SPECfp benchmarks. Finally, we discuss related work in section 7, and a broader perspective and some concluding remarks in section 8.

2   Implementation of Iterative Compilation System

In this section we briefly discuss how the iterative compilation system is implemented. Figure 2 shows an overview of the system. For more details, consult [16]. The compilation system is centered around a global driver that reads a list of transformations that it needs to examine together with the range of their parameters. The driver keeps track of the different transformations evaluated so far and decides which transformations have to be applied next using a search algorithm to steer through the optimization space. We have implemented several search algorithms, including a genetic algorithm, simulated annealing, pyramid search, window search and random search. The global driver invokes the source to source compiler MT1 [2] and instructs it which transformation to apply. MT1 has two mechanisms to control the application of transformations: a Transformation Definition Language (TDL) and a Strategy Specification Language (SSL) [2]. For each transformation included in the list of transformations, a transformation needs to be specified in the TDL-file. The global driver constructs an SSL file that specifies the order in which to apply certain transformations and outputs

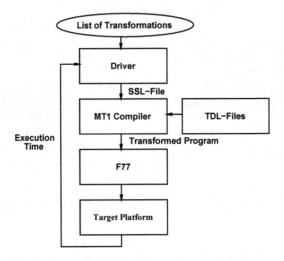

Fig. 2. The Compilation Process

it to MT1. After a predetermined number of iterations, the global driver stops searching and outputs the transformed program with the shortest execution time.

3   Benchmarks and Platforms

In this section we discuss the benchmarks and platforms used in the experiments described below. In order to assess the efficiency of iterative compilation for selecting tile sizes and unroll factors, we use many small kernel benchmarks from multimedia applications that exhibit a wide variety of memory access behavior. In this way, we are able to give a statistically relevant analysis of the results. Therefore, we chose the following benchmarks.

- Matrix-Matrix Multiplication (MxM). We use all 6 possible loop orders to generate 6 benchmarks with highly different memory access behavior. We use data input sizes of $N = 256$, $N = 300$ and $N = 301$.
- Matrix-Vector Multiplication (MxV). We use the two possible loop orders. We use data input sizes $N = 2048$, $N = 2300$ and $N = 2301$.
- Forward Discrete Cosine Transform (FDCT) which is one of the most important routines from the low-level bit stream video encoder H263. We use 6 possible loop orders and moreover the 6 variations of the second main computation loop from FDCT that consists of a multiplication of a transposed matrix. These loops are hand optimized in the reference implementation and we undid some of this optimization in order to remove a dependence that would prohibit some transformation. We use data input sizes of $N = 256$, $N = 300$ and $N = 301$ that are larger than those used in H263 but that stress the cache in our platforms.
- Finite Impulse Response filter, one of the most important DSP operations, with data sizes of $N = 8192$, $N = 8300$ and $N = 8301$.

We have conducted our experiments on four different platforms: Pentium II, Pentium III, Hewlett-Packard Precision Architecture (HP-PA 712/60) and UltraSparc I. In order to compile a transformed version of the source program we used the native Fortran77 or g77 compiler with full optimization on.

We restrict attention to tile sizes from 1 to 100 and unroll factors from 1 to 20.

4   Performance of Iterative Compilation

In this section we discuss the performance we can obtain from iterative compilation. We compare this performance with two well known static techniques. We also briefly discuss the required compilation time.

4.1   Search Algorithms

One parameter in the global driver is the search algorithm it employs to navigate the search space. We have implemented the following search algorithms.

Genetic algorithm. First, an initial population of 20 programs is randomly selected. Second, in the crossover phase, for a number of individuals a crossover point is determined in the bit representation of the tile sizes and unroll factors. Different parts of the upper half and lower half of these 'chromosomes' are concatenated. Third, in the mutation phase, bits are flipped in the chromosomes. Finally, the entire new population is evaluated based on execution time and individuals are deleted until a new population of 20 is reached.

Simulated annealing. Initially, a random point is selected and neighboring points are inspected. We move to the point with lowest execution time, or with a certain probability depending on the current temperature to a point with higher execution time. The temperature is subsequently decreased. We keep track of the best point visited so far.

Pyramid or Grid search. We define a top level grid over the search space and evaluate each point on this grid. We order the points in a priority queue. Around the best points we refine the grid.

Window search. We define windows over the search space. Initially, the window is the entire space. We take a number of samples and order them in a priority queue. Around the best points we define a smaller window.

Random search. We randomly generate parameters.

We conducted a number of experiments to establish good values for the different parameters in the algorithms [13].

4.2   Results

In this section we show how much speedup we obtain as a function of the number of iterations, where we show the best speedup found so far. Due to space limitations we only show a few typical examples. See [13] for a more complete discussion.

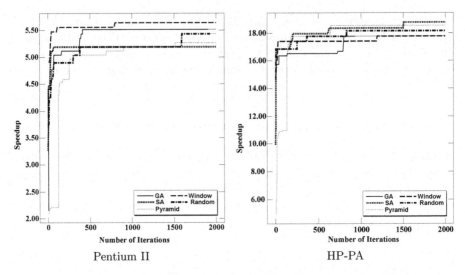

Pentium II   HP-PA

Fig. 3. Rectangular tiling. Speedup MxM – ikj version ($N = 256$)

Rectangular Tile Sizes. First, we discuss rectangular tile sizes together with unroll factors. In this case, the search space consists of $20 \times 100 \times 100 = 200,000$ points. We let the search algorithm run for 2000 iterations. The results are given in Figure 3. The x-axis denotes the number of iterations, that is, the number of times a transformed version of the program is generated, compiled and executed. The y-axis denotes the speedup of the fastest version found so far, where speedup is measured against the execution time for the original non-transformed program.

The first observation is that iterative compilation indeed yields high levels of optimization. We have shown [14] that these high levels of optimization are found across all our benchmarks and platforms for all data input sizes. In section 4.3 we give a more quantified assessment of this by comparing iterative compilation to two well-known static techniques.

The second observation is that these search algorithms do not differ much in their efficiency: Speedups found are within 5% on average of each other. We need on average between 750 and 1000 iterations to obtain the maximum speedup. However, iterative compilation reaches high levels of optimization much earlier and the last few hundred iterations are used for a small increase in the final outcome. SA and Random reach their maximum fastest. Pyramid search is slowest because initially we define a grid over the entire search space that consists of 500 points. We have shown [14] that we need only a fraction of the number of iterations for maximal speedup to reach 90% of this maximum: between 0.03% and 0.13% of the entire search space. However, the absolute number of iterations required is still high.

We conclude that iterative compilation is capable of finding good unroll factors and tile sizes across a wide variety of benchmarks, data input sizes and platforms, visiting between 0.375% and 0.5% of the search space. However, rect-

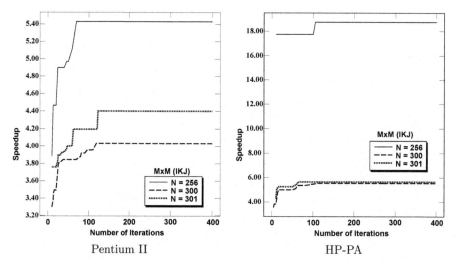

Fig. 4. Square tiling. Speedup MxM – ikj version

angular tile sizes require a search space of 200,000 points. Therefore, in the next section, we consider the possibility to search for square tiles that reduces the size of the search space to 2000 points.

Square Tile Sizes. Next, we search for square tile sizes, reducing the size of the search space by a factor 100 to 2000 points. We have implemented four search algorithms: GA, Pyramid, Random and SA using 400 iterations and found that they reached their maximum improvement in about the same number of steps [14]. Therefore, we only present the results using Pyramid search.

Comparing the speedups obtained using square tiles, as shown in Figure 4, with the speedups obtained using rectangular tiles shows that square tiling is within 5% on average from rectangular tiling [14]. Therefore, the difference between the different search algorithms for rectangular tiling is of the same order of magnitude as the difference between square and rectangular tiling. This shows that in our benchmark set square tiles can provide the same speedup as rectangular tiles do and therefore we can restrict attention to square tiles.

The next observation is that iterative compilation reaches high levels of optimization rapidly. The average number of iterations is 116.2. We have shown [13] that we improve by a factor of 8 over searching for rectangular tile sizes. We conclude that for the present benchmarks square tiles are as good as rectangular tiles, but much faster.

4.3 Comparison with Static Techniques

In this section we quantify the efficiency of iterative compilation by comparing the performance improvements to two static tile size selection algorithms. The

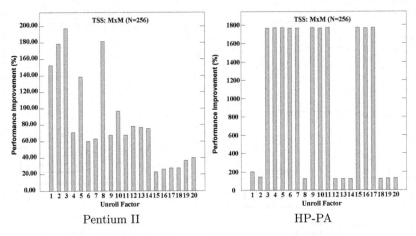

Fig. 5. Improvement over TSS for MxM – ikj version

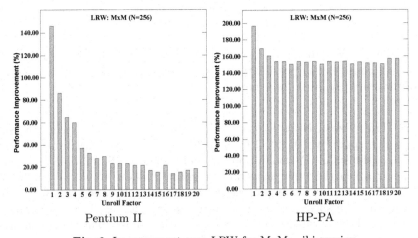

Fig. 6. Improvement over LRW for MxM – ikj version

first algorithm, TSS by Coleman and McKinley [9], considers the size of the working set in the loop body and requires that this working set is smaller than the cache size. It also takes into account an estimate of the cross interference between different arrays and tries to minimize this cross interference. We unrolled the loop a number of times and computed the tile size using TSS for the unrolled loop. The second algorithm, LRW by Lam, Rothberg and Wolf [19], does not consider the working set nor the cross interference rate. It computes a tile size based only on the size of the cache. We have used this tile size together with different unrolling factors. The results are given in Figures 5 and 6.

We immediately observe that iterative compilation outperforms these static techniques significantly, up to 1800% for MxM-IKJ on the HP-PA. This means that TSS does not give a speedup at all whereas our approach finds a speedup of 18. Note that we show that this improvement holds for each unroll factor less than or equal to 20 that the compiler might choose. In [14] it is shown that this holds for almost each benchmark, data size and platform. In the other cases only a very slight degradation of about 2% can be observed. We conclude that iterative compilation outperforms existing static techniques significantly.

4.4   Compilation Time

In this section we discuss the compilation time required for iterative compilation [13]. For 400 iterations, we need on average 14.6 minutes on Pentium II, 65.23 minutes on HP-PA, and 64.49 minutes on UltraSparc I. In case of the Pentium and UltraSparc, most time is spent in executing the transformed program. However, for HP-PA, the time required for native Fortran77 compilation is the dominant factor and the time required for the global driver can be larger than the execution time of the transformed program. Hence most reduction in time required for iterative compilation can be obtained from reducing the number of actual executions, that need both native compilation and running the program. One such approach in discussed in the next section.

4.5   Discussion of Performance

In this section we have shown that iterative compilation is capable of finding high levels of optimization. In general, we observe that high speedups are found within the first few iterations and that many more program executions are required to find the final optimal program version. Hence iterative compilation clearly shows a Law of Diminishing Returns. This is to be expected, since many search algorithms, like Simulated Annealing or Genetic Algorithms, exhibit this kind of behavior in general. Moreover, this property can be of advantage, since in a production environment it is likely that only a limited number of profiles will be employed. Next, we have have shown that for our benchmark set iterative compilation outperforms static techniques significantly: on average we improve about 30% over these techniques [13]. Furthermore, we have shown that the required compilation times are long but not inhibitively so for a limited number of profiles. Therefore, we believe that the approach is applicable in production environments where performance is crucial and compilation times can be amortized over many program runs, like is the case for many scientific codes and embedded systems. Next, we can summarize the experiments done in this section in a so-called *trade-off graph* [13] as depicted in Figure 7(a). This graph contains a number of *equi-optimization curves* indicating the percentage of benchmarks that reach a certain percentage of the maximal speedup as a function of the number of program executions. The iterative algorithm that randomly selects transformations is used for this graph and it is called the Execution-Only Algorithm (EO) and the speedup it obtains is called the Execution-Only speedup. From this graph we can deduce, for example, that after 100 executions, 48% of the benchmarks were fully optimized and thus reached 100% of the maximal speedup. Likewise, after 50 executions, 77% of the benchmarks reached at least 90% of the maximal speedup. After 20 executions, almost every benchmark reached at least 60% of this speedup. This graph can be used by a programmer to trade-off the number of profiles he can afford and the levels of optimization he would obtain. Finally, although the best tile sizes and unroll factors are dependent upon the data input size, we have shown [16,22] that in many cases the transformations found for a given data input size give good speedups for other input sizes.

5   Static Cache Models

In the previous section we have shown that iterative compilation is very effective. However, we need many profiles for this purpose and compilation time, that includes searching, program transformation, back end compilation and profiling, is extremely time consuming. In order to reduce compilation time, we propose to incorporate target specific models in the driver module, covering part of the behavior of the underlying platform, to estimate the effect of transformations [18,17]. In this way we use static cache models in order to filter out program versions that are unlikely to produce good results. We distinguish two approaches.

Execution driven. The driver searches through the optimization space and the model is used to filter out bad candidate transformations during the search. Only if the model predicts that a transformation may be better than the best one found so far, profiling of the transformed program will take place.

Model driven. The models are used to rank a collection of transformations before any profiling takes place. Only the transformations with highest ranking are profiled. The transformation that gives rise to the shortest execution time is chosen.

We use two kinds of cache model. First, as an upperbound for the present approach, we use a full level 1 cache simulator that we have developed ourselves to compute hit rates. This model is too expensive to be used in practice but we include it since it is more accurate than any other static model. We interpret results obtained for the simulator as upperbound results with which we can compare other models. Second, as a realistic case, we use a simple model proposed by Coleman and McKinley [9] that uses an approximation of the working set WS and selects the tile size giving rise to the largest working set that still fits in the cache. In order for models to be effective, they must be far less costly to evaluate than profiling the program. This obviously does not hold for the cache simulator but we include it in this study for theoretical reasons.

5.1   Search Algorithms

We have implemented five search strategies employing cache models [18,17]. Due to space limitations, we only discuss the three most relevant ones.

Execution Driven Search. We consider the following strategy.

- **EXEC-CS.** A new point next is selected and evaluated if the cache hit rate $H(\text{next})$ is within a factor α of the current best cache hit rate $H(\text{current})$. By experimentation, we found that a slack factor $\alpha = 99.9\%$ is optimal. The search algorithm will stop after N combinations are executed.

```
current = initial transformation
REPEAT
    next = next transformation
    IF H(next) ≥ α × H(current)
    THEN execute(next)
            IF exec_time(next) < exec_time(current)
            THEN current = next
```

Model Driven Search. We consider the following two strategies.

- **MOD-CS.** First, we calculate the cache hit rate of a large collection of tile sizes and unrolling factors using the cache simulator. The N combinations with the highest hit rates are executed.

```
calculate cache hit rates
rank transformations on hit rate
current = best transformation
REPEAT
    next = next best transformation
    execute(next)
    IF exec_time(next) < exec_time(current)
    THEN current = next
```

- **MOD-CM.** In this strategy, we select for each unroll factor the largest tile size such that the working set WS is within $\gamma\%$ of the cache size CS. By experimentation we found that $\gamma = 40\%$ is a good value. We select $N/20$ combinations with largest tile size for each unroll factor.

```
current = initial transformation
FOREACH Unroll Factor
    next = next largest tile size
            s.t. WS(next) ≤ γ × CS
    execute(next)
    IF exec_time(next) < exec_time(current)
    THEN current = next
```

5.2   Results

In this section we discuss the results we obtained for iterative compilation incorporating cache models. For practical purposes, it is important to restrict the number of program executions to be small. To analyze the efficiency of iterative compilation for this case, we use a *trade-off graph* [13]. The trade-off graph for

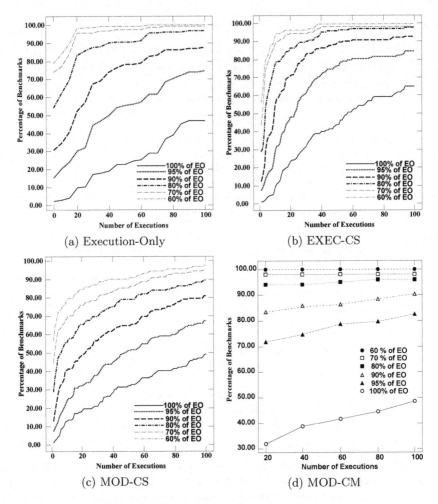

Fig. 7. Trade-off graphs

the algorithm that only uses profiles and no models and that is studied in the previous section, is depicted in Figure 7(a). We call this algorithm the Execution-Only Algorithm (EO) and it is used as the base case with which to compare the other algorithms.

Execution Driven Search. Inspecting Figures 7(a) and 7(b), we see that EXEC-CS only needs about half as many executions as the Execution-Only Algorithm and still obtains the same trade-off. For example, we can see that the levels of optimization obtained after 25 program executions is about the same as the levels of optimization obtained by EO after 50 executions, and likewise after 50 executions it is the same as EO obtains after 100 executions.

Next, using an Execution driven approach, accurate cache models improve the Execution-Only Algorithm substantially by reducing the number of executions by 50%. More accurate knowledge of the back end compiler and the target platform, and a tight feedback between source level restructurer and code generator is required. Obviously, this connection makes the implementation of an iterative compilation strategy more complex. Next, we have also shown that less accurate models, like the working set size constraint, can be almost as effective as a full cache simulator if only a limited number of up to 30 program executions is allowed. This number seems reasonable in a production compiler where large numbers of profiles would be too time consuming.

Model Driven Search. From Figure 7(c) it follows that for up to 10 executions, the strategy MOD-CS is as effective as EXEC-CS. For more executions, EXEC-CS is superior. This shows that a cache model that assumes that all memory references go through the cache is not an adequate model for real platforms. Moreover, the left-most point in the trade-off graph for MOD-CS corresponds to a strategy where we only use static model information and select the program version with highest hit rate, as is customarily done in traditional compilers. This shows that a static L1 cache simulator ignores many issues that are crucial for performance, like level 2 cache, contention for the bus between the memory hierarchy and the CPU, the execution pipeline, or the capability to exploit ILP, etc. It also follows that a strategy that only uses static knowledge obtained from a highly accurate cache model will be outperformed by iterative strategies that also use profiling information.

In the strategy MOD-CM we execute programs in batches of 20 (one for each unroll factor). Figure 7(d) shows that MOD-CM is superior to EXEC-CS for 20 executions and reaches about the same levels of optimization for 40 executions. Comparing the trade-off graphs from Figures 7(b) and 7(f), we see that after 20 executions using the MOD-CM strategy, we reach the same level of optimization as EXEC-CS does after 30 to 40 executions. Comparing Figure 7(d) to Figure 7(a), we see that these levels of optimization are reached in the Execution-Only approach after about 70 executions. MOD-CM is also superior to EXEC-CS for up to 80 executions. Only if we would allow 100 executions, these latter strategies prove to be better than MOD-CM. This shows that, although it is only a crude approximation of the exact hit rate, the working set size constraint is highly effective.

5.3   Discussion of Static Models

In this section we have shown that static cache models can reduce the number of required profiles substantially, up to 50% and for a small number of profiles even up to 70%. This shows that static models can be used to good effect in the iterative compilation framework. Comparing the Execution driven and Model driven approaches, we have shown that for up to 20 profiles the Model driven approach can be superior. In fact, 20 profiles using the MOD-CM strategy gives the same levels of optimization as the EXEC-CS strategy does after 30 to 40 profiles and as the Execution-Only Algorithm does after about 70 executions,

Table 1. Performance Improvement (%) for SPECfp benchmarks

	Pentium II	Pentium III	HP-PA	UltraSparc
Tomcatv	31.4	25.3	38.6	22.6
Swim	21.7	2.31	8.35	17.73
Mgrid	8.0	1.29	17.38	15.1

giving an improvement of MOD-CM over EO of 70%. If we would allow more pro-files, Execution driven selection is superior. Since we expect that in a production compiler simple models like this working set size constraint will be preferable to highly complex models and that such a compiler would have a small budget for profiling, this result indicates that in this situation a Model driven search procedure can be preferable.

6   Realistic Applications

Although iterative compilation is highly effective for kernels, the question re-mains how the approach fares on realistic applications. In this section we show that our approach is applicable to the SPECfp benchmarks Tomcatv, Swim, and Mgrid. We have considered several strategies for employing iterative compila-tion to these full fledged benchmarks [22]. In this paper, we only discuss the following strategy: First, we profiled the programs using the SPEC reference data to determine the routines that are most important. These routines were then optimized by our iterative approach again using the reference data. We ap-plied loop tiling, unroll-and-jam, and array padding as transformations, where padding consists of adding dummy elements to an array by extending the column dimension. Padding changes the position in the cache where elements are placed and thus cache behavior. We have shown [22] that the effect of padding is very sensitive to the pad factor employed and that good pad factors change dramat-ically over different architectures. We searched for the best parameters for each of these transformations. To determine these parameters, we first searched for a pad factor and next we simultaneously searched for tile sizes and unroll factors.

The results for this strategy are given in Table 1. We see that we obtain high levels of optimization for all benchmarks and platforms, except for Pentium III where only for Tomcatv good improvements are found. It is interesting to observe that most of these improvements are due to array padding and that the other transformations only give marginal gains over padding. This can be explained by the fact that in these applications not much locality is present that can be exploited by tiling and that the issue width of these machines is narrow so that unroll-and-jam has limited effect also. In [22] we discuss more platforms and several other strategies. We show that on average we improve 20% over state-of-the-art compilers. Moreover, we show that using the SPEC train data during the iterative compilation phase produces an optimized version of the program that also is highly optimized for the reference data, reaching almost the same improvements as when we used reference data during the optimization phase.

7 Related Work

Over the past years, many authors have considered limited search techniques for optimization purposes. In particular, for tiling and unrolling, Coleman and McKinley [9] and Lam, Rothberg and Wolf [19] employ a restricted search for tile sizes based on a simple cache model. In [6] an improved tile size selection algorithm is presented that also uses a static searching technique. Carr [5] computes several unroll factors and chooses the best in order to minimize the difference in machine and loop balance. In contrast to these approaches, the present approach uses actual execution times and moreover considers both loop tiling and unrolling at the same time.

Whaley and Dongarra [25], and Bilmes et al. [3] describe systems for generating highly optimized BLAS routines that probe the underlying hardware to find optimal transformation parameters. They show to be capable of outperforming vendor supplied, hand optimized library BLAS routines. The present approach, however, describes a full compiler.

Wolf, Maydan and Chen [26] have described a compiler that also searches for the optimal optimization by considering the entire optimization space. Han, Rivera and Tseng [11] also describe a compiler that searches for tile and pad sizes using static models. In contrast to the present approach, however, their compilers use static cost models to evaluate the different optimizations. From this paper it follows that our approach based on actual execution times delivers superior performance and can adapt to any architecture, requiring no prior modeling phase. Chow and Wu [7] apply 'fractional factorial design' to decide on a number of experiments to run for selecting a collection of compiler switches. They, however, focus on on/off switches and do not consider the choice of parameter values that might come from a large range of values. Bodin and co-workers explore in [23,12] the interplay between loop unrolling and software pipelining that can be fully integrated with the present approach since they target the code generation phase.

Over the past years, many proposals have been put forward to use profile information that are currently being employed in commercial compilers [8]. Profiles are also used to identify runtime constants that can be exploited at compile time [21]. This paper can be seen as taking profiling one step further by using many profiles for deciding between many alternatives.

Diniz and Rinard propose Dynamic Feedback where several versions of a code section are generated [10] and at runtime, the best version is selected during a sampling phase. This is repeated periodically to adapt dynamically to different execution environments. Voss and Eigenmann overlap code generation with program execution and periodically generate new variants of code sections using different compilers that run in a separate thread [24]. The most important assumption in these approaches, however, is that the execution environment can change during the run of a program. For embedded systems this is not the case and the selection of optimizations can be done at compile time. Moreover, these approaches can cause code bloat and/or require special OS support which is also unwanted for embedded systems. Several approaches generate code at runtime, by exploiting runtime constants [1] or by partial evaluation [20]. For embedded systems these approaches are less suited since they entail code generation overhead at runtime and much of their effect can be obtained at compile time.

8   Conclusion

In this paper we have discussed iterative compilation and shown that this approach can achieve high speedups, outperforming static techniques. This approach generates many transformed versions of the source program and searches for the best by compiling and executing these programs. In this way, within 50 iterations, high levels of optimization on average can be found. The obvious drawback of iterative compilation is its long compilation time. In order to reduce this compilation time, we propose to add static models in the driver. These models can be used to filter out certain program executions. These models should be accurate enough to cover a large portion of the search space or, alternatively, should be accurate for certain aspects of the search space. We have shown that in this way we can reduce the number of required profiles by 50%. Finally, we have shown that our approach is applicable to realistic codes. In the long term we envisage a compilation system where the user can trade-off levels of optimization and compilation time by tuning the complexity and accuracy of static models and the number of programs that are actually executed.

References

1. J. Auslander, M. Philipose, C. Chambers, S.J. Eggers, and B.N. Bershad. Fast, effective dynamic compilation. In *Proc. PLDI*, pages 149–159, 1996.
2. A.J.C. Bik, P.J. Brinkhaus, P.M.W. Knijnenburg, and H.A.G. Wijshoff. Transformation mechanisms in MT1. Technical Report 2000-21, LIACS, Leiden University, 2000.
3. J. Bilmes, K. Asanović, C.W. Chin, and J. Demmel. Optimizing matrix multiply using PHiPAC: A portable, high-performance, ANSI C coding methodology. In *Proc. ICS*, pages 340–347, 1997.
4. F. Bodin, T. Kisuki, P.M.W. Knijnenburg, M.F.P. O'Boyle, and E. Rohou. Iterative compilation in a non-linear optimisation space. In *Proc. Workshop on Profile and Feedback Directed Compilation*, 1998.
5. S. Carr. Combining optimization for cache and instruction level parallelism. In *Proc. PACT*, pages 238–247, 1996.
6. J. Chame and S. Moon. A tile selection algorithm for data locality and cache interference. In *Proc. ICS'99*, pages 492–499, 1999.
7. K. Chow and Y. Wu. Feedback-directed selection and characterization of compiler optimizatons. In *Proc. 2nd Workshop on Feedback Directed Optimization*, 1999.
8. R. Cohn and P.G. Lowney. Feedback directed optimization in Compaq's compilation tools for Alpha. In *Proc. 2nd Workshop on Feedback Directed Optimization*, 1999.
9. S. Coleman and K.S. McKinley. Tile size selection using cache organization and data layout. In *Proc. PLDI*, pages 279–290, 1995.

10. P. Diniz and M. Rinard. Dynamic feedback: An effective technique for adaptive computing. In *Proc. PLDI*, pages 71–84, 1997.
11. H. Han, G. Rivera, and C.-W. Tseng. Software support for improving locality in scientific codes. In *Proc. CPC2000*, pages 213–228, 2000.
12. K. Heydemann, F. Bodin, and P.M.W. Knijnenburg. Global trade-off between code size and performance for loop unrolling on VLIW architectures. Technical report, INRIA/IRISA, 2001.
13. T. Kisuki, P.M.W. Knijnenburg, and M.F.P. O'Boyle. Combined selection of tile sizes and unroll factors using iterative compilation. In *Proc. PACT*, pages 237–246, 2000.
14. T. Kisuki, P.M.W. Knijnenburg, and M.F.P. O'Boyle. Iterative compilation for tile sizes and unroll factors: Implementation, performance, search strategies. Technical Report TR2000-06, LIACS, Leiden University, 2000.
15. T. Kisuki, P.M.W. Knijnenburg, M.F.P. O'Boyle, F. Bodin, and H.A.G. Wijshoff. A feasibility study in iterative compilation. In *Proc. ISHPC'99*, volume 1615 of *Lecture Notes in Computer Science*, pages 121–132, 1999.
16. T. Kisuki, P.M.W. Knijnenburg, M.F.P. O'Boyle, and H.A.G. Wijshoff. Iterative compilation in program optimization. In *Proc. CPC2000*, pages 35–44, 2000.
17. P.M.W. Knijnenburg, T. Kisuki, and K. Gallivan. Cache models for iterative compilation. In *Proc. Eur-Par*, 2001.
18. P.M.W. Knijnenburg, T. Kisuki, K. Gallivan, and M.F.P. O'Boyle. The effect of cache models on iterative compilation for combined tiling and unrolling. In *Proc. FDDO-3*, pages 31–40, 2000.
19. M.S. Lam, E.E. Rothberg, and M.E. Wolf. The cache performance and optimizations of blocked algorithms. In *Proc. ASPLOS*, pages 63–74, 1991.
20. R. Marlet, C. Consel, and P. Boinot. Efficient incremental run-time specialization for free. In *Proc. PLDI*, pages 281–292, 1999.
21. M. Mock, M. Berryman, C. Chambers, and S.J. Eggers. Calpa: A tool for automating dynamic compilation. In *Proc. 2nd Workshop on Feedback Directed Optimization*, 1999.
22. M.F.P. O'Boyle, P.M.W. Knijnenburg, T. Kisuki, and G. Fursin. Evaluating iterative compilation in massive optimization spaces. Preprint, University of Edinburgh, 2001.
23. P. van der Mark, E. Rohou, F. Bodin, Z. Chamski, and C. Eisenbeis. Using iterative compilation for managing software pipeline – unrolling tradeoffs. In *Proc. SCOPES99*, 1999.
24. M.J. Voss and R. Eigenmann. ADAPT: Automated de-coupled adaptive program transformation. In *Proc. ICPP*, 2000.
25. R. C. Whaley and J. J. Dongarra. Automatically tuned linear algebra software. In *Proc. Alliance*, 1998.
26. M.E. Wolf, D.E. Maydan, and D.-K. Chen. Combining loop transformations considering caches and scheduling. *Int'l. J. of Parallel Programming*, 26(4):479–503, 1998.

Processor Architectures for Multimedia Applications

P. Pirsch, A. Freimann, C. Klar, and J.P. Wittenburg

Institute of Microelectronic Circuits and Systems, University of Hannover

Abstract. An overview on processor architectures for multimedia applications is presented. Emphasis is on architectural strategies to achieve the required processing power of real-time applications. Architectural approaches for exploitation of the inherent parallelization resources of signal processing schemes are first discussed. The impact of algorithm on the appropriate architectures is displayed for three representative multimedia applications. The discussed applications are block-based video coding as used in MPEG-2, multiplexing for video broadcasing based on OFDM and object oriented video coding according to MPEG-4. Characteristic processor architectures adapted to the needs of these applications are introduced. Architectural structures of the AxPe-DSP, the HiPAR-DSP and a MPEG-4 system are presented as examples. Advances in multimedia processing require processors with high flexibilty on parallel processing and dynamic adaptation capabilties. As promising architectural concepts for advanced multimedia applications reconfigurable computing, simultaneous multithreading, and associative controlling are discussed.

1 Introduction

Driven by the still increasing demand for audio-visual communication services, hardware solutions for applications ranging from Web-Browsing, digital TV or 3G and 4G wireless communication to telemedicine or interactive games, became key components of the emerging multimedia market.

Multimedia processing requires extreme demands on computing, transmission, and storage devices. In particular, video processing tasks lead to extremely high computational demands. Video requires processing of continuous data streams at high rates. Simultaneously, real time conditions have to be met to satisfy the needs of human perception. Adding audio and other data streams increases these already huge processing power, data bandwidth, and storage requirements.

Because one of the driving forces behind the commercial success of wireless communication are small mobile platforms, there are additional stringent requirements for the hardware implementation: Low power consumption, compact size and last but not least low cost. While the palm size battery powered devices as planned as multimedia terminals for the next generation mobile communication standards may consume almost some 100mW at maximum, they will have to deliver a processing power equal to or even exceeding those of most recent general purpose processors for desktop applications(usually consuming more than 20W).

Currently available standard processing devices are not able to fulfill the requirements of multimedia processing without special adaptation. Architectural enhancements

E.F. Deprettere et al. (Eds.): SAMOS 2001, LNCS 2268, pp. 188–206, 2002.

have therefore been introduced aiming to exploit the special algorithm characteristics. Employment of specialized operations or modules, increase of clock frequency, and parallel processing are the most important means suitable to increase processor performance. To fulfill the real-time demands of video communication schemes, most modern architectures employ all these measures. On the one hand, parallel processing offers a high potential to increase performance; the different approaches to exploit parallelization resources of algorithms have significant impact on processor architecture. On the other hand, measures to increase clock frequency and to employ dedicated operations or modules do not differ significantly for processors in the scope of this article. Thus, this paper will focus on parallelization resources and parallel processing.

Looking beyond the scope of current hardware implementations, the continuing development of new, more sophisticated applications results in steadily increasing demands on hardware devices. On the one hand, computational performance requirements will continue to grow, e.g. to improve video and sound quality or to introduce new functionality. On the other hand, future multimedia applications will be characterized by a growing algorithmical diversity and decreasing predictability at the computational flow. The inflexibility of recent architectures and their inability to deal with those new demands already led to consequences for the recent MPEG-4 standardizations [9]. Several proposals using object-based schemes – which are promising in terms of coding efficiency, but difficult to parallelize due to the problematic predictability of object number, size, and shape – were considered as *not implementable in real time* using today's hardware. Hence, they were not considered for the final draft.

The purpose of this paper is to provide an overview on recent state of the art approaches for programmable multimedia DSPs and to introduce promising concepts aiming at the implementation of current trends in algorithm development. Section 2 starts with a general overview of different parallelization levels and the respective architectural methodologies to exploit them. Advantages and challenges of these methodologies are outlined. In Section 3 the impact of algorithm on the processor architectures is discussed for three examples: block-based video coding (e.g., H.263 [11], MPEG-1,2 [8]), Digital Video Broadcasting, and object-based video coding (e.g., MPEG-4). These examples are representative for the range of the application field but differ significantly in their parallelization resource profiles. Examples of processor designs targeting each respective application with focus on their specific mix of architectural measures to exploit parallelism are provided. Section 4 examines the changing requirements of future multimedia applications and describes three promising architectural approaches – Simultaneous Multithreading, Reconfigurable Computing and Associative Controlling – to target the novel challenges of such applications. Finally Section 5 summarizes the paper in a brief conclusion.

2   Parallelization Resources

A prerequisite of parallel processing is the existence of sequences of instructions that can be executed independently of results of preceding instructions. Amount and distribution of such sequences are features of algorithms. Architectural measure to exploit these parallelization resources can be classified by the strategies to distribute concurrent instructions, i.e. data-level, task-level, and instruction-level parallel processing.

Fig. 1. Example for data level parallel processing: Distribution of image segments to processing elements.

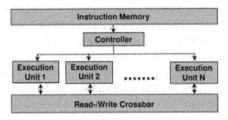

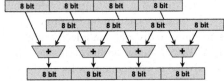

Fig. 2. Basic structure of Single Instruction Stream – Multiple Data Stream (SIMD) Architecture.

Fig. 3. Subword-parallel Arithmetic Unit (also called Split-ALU). Because the same operation is performed on all subwords, this is a special form of SIMD-architecture.

2.1   Data-Level Parallelism

Data-level parallel processing can be utilized if segments of input data can be processed independently. In this case, these segments are distributed to different processing elements (Fig. 1) of the same functionality. A typical architecture is SIMD (Fig. 2).

Data-level parallelism offers a very large parallelization resource in image processing applications, because in many algorithms (e.g., motion estimation, transforms etc.) operations on several pixels can be processed independent of each other. However, two major issues aggravate the utilization of data-level parallelism: 1.) Data has to be accessed and exchanged concurrently, which results in very high bandwidth. Architectural support for efficient access to data is achieved by more or less sophisticated memory crossbars and can be seen as one major challenge for data-level parallel processing. 2.) If the processing scheme requires conditional branches, the SIMD-processing prerequisite that all functional units execute the same instruction cannot be fulfilled. There are ways to deal with this problem (e.g., provide both instruction streams in sequence and enable/disable units accordingly), but the resulting performance is always decreased. Thus, in case of highly irregular control flow, SIMD-processing will not achieve a reasonable speed-up.

So called subword-parallel arithmetic units (Fig. 3) are a special form of SIMD-architectures, which are of significant importance to multimedia applications. The idea behind such units is that hardware implementations of arithmetic functions (especially additions and multiplications) operating on long words (e.g., 64 or 32 bit) can be sub-

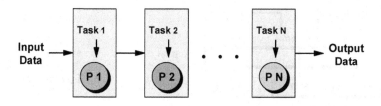

Fig. 4. Task level parallel processing by assignment of subtasks to individual processing units.

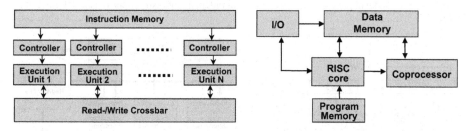

Fig. 5. Basic structure of homogeneous Multiple Instruction Stream – Multiple Data Stream (MIMD) architecture. All processing- and control units are identical.

Fig. 6. Example of heterogeneous MIMD or coprocessor architecture. These architectures benefit from a specialization of processing units.

divided to perform multiple concurrent operations at lower word width at virtually no additional hardware cost. Because luminance and chrominance samples are typically quantized to eight bit only, this is totally sufficient for many video applications. Hence, the majority of multimedia-DSPs features subword-parallel units.

2.2   Task-Level Parallelism

Task level parallel processing, also called macro pipelining, is possible if an algorithm consists of several subsequent tasks which can be processed independently of each other. In this case the tasks can be assigned to different processing elements (Fig. 4) usually working in a pipeline decoupled by memory. The size of these memories depends on the amount of data the subtasks are working on. Macro pipelining increases the latency of algorithms significantly. In case of communication applications this latency can become unacceptable. Typical architectures exploiting this level of parallelism are MIMD-processors (multiple instruction stream, multiple data stream). Such architectures may feature other identical functional units (homogeneous MIMD, Fig. 5) or differing functional units (heterogeneous MIMD or coprocessor architectures, Fig. 6). The latter are more common, especially for applications with a fixed processing power distribution to the individual subtasks. In that case, the specialization of functional units can lead to highly efficient realizations. However, the task-level parallelization resource is limited as such, because few applications feature more than 10 individual subtasks [17]. Furthermore, MIMD architectures are considered difficult to program, especially due to task synchronization and inter-task data exchange issues.

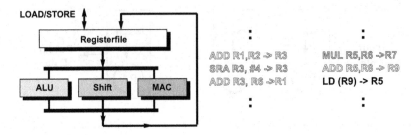

Fig. 7. Instruction level parallelism: Issuing several independent instructions to parallel functional units.

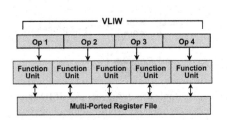

Fig. 8. Basic execution structure of Very Long Instruction Word approach. Processor employs composite instructions generated from scalar code at compile time.

Fig. 9. Superscalar architecture (with Tomasulo scheduler [21]) Architecture can detect and concurrently issue independent instructions fetched from scalar code.

2.3   Instruction-Level Parallelism

Instruction-level parallel processing utilizes the distribution of instructions to different execution units (Fig. 7). Smaller sequences of independent instructions exist in almost all sequential signal processing algorithms. For the distribution of instructions these sequences have to be detected either prior to runtime by the compiler (as for VLIW architectures, Fig. 8) or by hardware (as in superscalar architectures, Fig. 9). Considering instruction level parallelism with respect to signal processing applications – which typically feature a rather predefined and regular control flow – latencies caused by pipeline hazards at conditional branches do not impact performance. Instead, data throughput is the major aim. Under these conditions, a dynamic hardware scheduling approach like in superscalar architectures would not achieve better results than a static approach like VLIW. The small hardware costs of the simple scheduler of a VLIW architecture makes this the controlling scheme of choice for DSPs. However, in both cases a register file serves as source and destination for the data processed by the concurrently issued instructions. This register file, in combination with the data distribution crossbars, can become very cost intensive in terms of silicon area and delay.

The amount of instruction parallelism is limited by conditional branches and data dependencies. Within a basic block (i.e., a segment of unconditionally executed code between two branches) the amount of parallelism is limited to 3-5. Measures as register renaming (dynamic or static to avoid register allocation dependencies) and speculative branch prediction can extend this amount to about 5-8 [24]. However, it is important to note that it is possible to transform other parallelization resource levels to instruction level parallelism, which features the lowest granularity of all levels. This can be done for data-level parallelism employing loop unrolling or by utilization of multithreading (see Section 4) regarding task-level parallelism.

3   Impact of Algorithms on Architectures

Three parallelization resources were introduced in the previous section. This section provides three multimedia application examples which benefit from the exploitation of these parallelization resources in terms of an efficient processing. First the processing characteristic and the requirements for each example are pointed out to derive an appropriate architecture meeting these requirements. The applications shown here are:

- Block-based video coding using the MPEG-2 and H.263 standard
- Digital Video Broadcasting using the OFDM technique for generating the transmission signals
- Object-based video coding using MPEG-4 toolbox for providing multimedia services

3.1   Block-Based Video Coding

The block-based coding of video data is incorporated in several hybrid video coding schemes like ITU-H.263 [11] or MPEG-2 [8]. In these schemes, coding is performed on macroblocks which are rectangular a-priori defined segments of the video frames.

Several subtasks in the coding and decoding process are data-independent sequences of operations with pre-defined data access patterns on macroblock data. Examples of these tasks are motion estimation and compensation for the reduction of temporal redundancy and discrete cosine transform and its inverse for the reduction of spatial redundancy. As these subtasks are performed on predefined data blocks, parallel processing on macroblock-level can be used to increase the system performance.

Data-dependent and control intensive subtasks like quantization and variable length coding are also part of the coding framework. Whereas the data-independent tasks comprise a large number of operations to perform for coding one frame, the data-dependent tasks require much fewer operations but sophisticated control.

Due to this, a signal processing architecture for block-based video coding should provide adapted functional units for these two different kinds of subtasks. To keep pace with the evolving family of hybrid coding standards a programmable solution is appropriate. In the following, a processor, AxPe-DSP, is presented which aims this approach by exploiting the data-level and task-level parallelization resources.

The AxPe processor consists of a RISC core for the data-dependent coding and overall controlling tasks and a separate SIMD-coprocessor for the data-dependent and computation intensive tasks [7]. In Fig. 10 a, the block diagram of this processor is shown. The coprocessor consists of three main modules: A local memory for input data and intermediate results, an arithmetic processing unit, and a microprogrammable

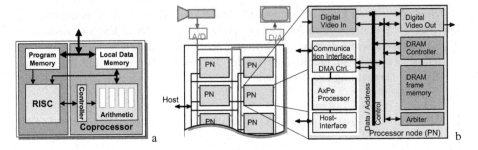

Fig. 10. a: Architecture of the video signal processor AxPe. **b**: Multiprocessor system with multiple AxPe processing nodes.

control unit. The arithmetic processing unit features a fourfold parallel ALU/multiply pipeline in combination with a shared multi-operand accumulator, and a shifter/limiter. The RISC processor contains an on-chip program memory, a register file, a 16 bit ALU, and a shift/limit/multiply pipeline. This pipeline is well suited for fast processing of quantization, inverse quantization, and variable length coding. Due to separated execution modules and memories in coprocessor and RISC processor, both modules can work in parallel. The processing power of a single AxPe is sufficient for coding or decoding 352×288 pixel images with a frame rate of up to 25 Hz.

For applications that require higher frame resolutions and frame rates than can be handled with one AxPe, multiple processors can be combined to form one multiprocessor system. Each of the processors operates in parallel on one segment of the image. If all processors use the same input and output busses for their parallel data accesses to the frame memory the bandwidth of the memory bus and the size of the local memories will be a bottleneck. To overcome these issues, each processor of the multiprocessor system is extended by adding embedded DRAM memory.

In Fig. 10 b, the architecture of the multiprocessor system consisting of several processing nodes is shown. Each processing node includes an AxPe processor with host and communication interface, an embedded DRAM with controller, video interfaces, and a bus arbiter. The video interface of each processor transfers autonomously video data between external devices and the embedded 4 Mbit DRAM. Different video and sampling formats are supported in addition to flexible frame resolutions. In parallel to the transfer of video data to and from the DRAM, the video signal processor executes video coding tasks on previously recorded images. The data exchange between processor nodes is performed by the communication interface. As an interconnection network between the processor nodes a 16 bit bus-based topology is implemented which provides a sufficient bandwidth.

A subsystem of four processor nodes is implemented on one chip. A large area integrated circuit with one to four subsystems on one die is supported. Configuration with variable number of processor nodes is possible after manufacturing. This allows to overcome manufacturing faults.

The AxPe take advantage of the SIMD controlling principle for the coprocessor part to provide parallel and fast arithmetic. The advantages of the MIMD principle is exploited by combining several AxPe processor nodes together with embedded DRAM on one die. Thus, the AxPe is a powerful processor for video coding using the MPEG-2 or H.263 standard.

3.2   Digital Video Broadcasting

Another example for multimedia applications, Digital Video Broadcasting, gained in importance during the last decade. Before the video and audio data is broadcasted it is compressed by using the ISO standard MPEG-2. The broadcast is done via satellite or cable. The terrestrial broadcasting (DVB-T) is currently investigated in several projects.

As the video stream has a high data rate, its terrestrial transmission needs therefore a high data bandwidth. In general, a single-carrier transmission will not be able to handle this high data rate. Hence, a multi-carrier transmission technique is used. The preferred technique for this purpose is the Orthogonal Frequency Division Multiplexing (OFDM) technique [19].

The principle of the OFDM technique is that the whole transmission channel is divided into a number of sub-channels. The carriers of the sub-channels are orthogonal to each other, which means that the spectra of each sub-channel are zero at the point where the other channels' spectra have their maximum.

The data stream is multiplexed and single bits or blocks of bits are assigned to the sub-channels. The generation of the transmission signal is done digitally by an inverse fast Fourier transform (IFFT). In the receiver the signal is transformed by a fast Fourier transform (FFT). Then the data can be demultiplexed to reconstruct the data stream. The achievable data rate of the transmission depends on the computational power of the DSP, so a high performance DSP should be used to obtain a high data throughput. In the case of European DVB-T the datarate is 34 Mbit/s transmitted in a 7 MHz bandwidth using 2k subcarriers of 3 kHz bandwidth each [19].

Because the Fourier transform has to be computed as fast as possible, the algorithmic principle is now analyzed in order to find an appropriate DSP architecture. The discrete Fourier transform is given by the formula

$$X[k] = \sum_{n=0}^{N} x[n] W_N^{nk} \qquad 0 \leq k \leq N \text{ and } W_N = e^{-j\frac{2\pi}{N}} \tag{1}$$

In [3], a fast processing scheme, which needs as less operations as possible, is deduced from this equation, the fast Fourier Transform (FFT). The resulting processing graph of the radix-2 FFT is given in Fig. 11. A core task in this scheme is the so called butterfly. A butterfly is represented by a cross in Fig. 11, i.e., one butterfly uses samples $x[0]$, $x[4]$ and the complex constant W_N^0 to compute the input for the next stage by the addition of $x[0]$ and $x[4]$ and the subtraction of $x[4]$ from $x[0]$ and the subsequent multiplication by W_N^0.

There are independent operations within each butterfly. Thus, the addition can be done concurrently to the subtraction or the multiplication. This property could be supported by a VLIW architecture. Another important property which has impact on the optimized architecture is the fact that the butterflies can be computed in parallel because

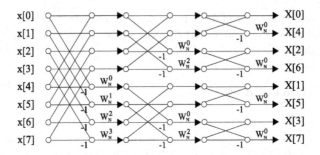

Fig. 11. FFT processing graph for a 8-point FFT. [12]

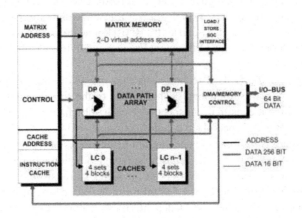

Fig. 12. The architecture of the HiPAR-DSP.

of the data independence in each stage. This property can be exploited by using a SIMD architecture.

For parallel data processing within a stage an efficient data exchange between the parallel processing units is necessary. A sophisticated memory architecture can meet this requirement. In the following, the HiPAR-DSP [12] is presented which combines such a memory architecture and the SIMD and VLIW principles.

The HiPAR-DSP is a fully programmable DSP for image and video coding. It is designed to fulfill these tasks in real-time. Due to the properties of the presented FFT and other image processing algorithms a **Hi**ghly **PAR**allel **D**igital **S**ignal **P**rocessor (HiPAR-DSP) is necessary to achieve a high processing speed. The architecture of the HiPAR-DSP is presented in Fig. 12. The scalable array of concurrently working datapaths provide an effective way to employ the high parallelization opportunities in algorithms which are often used in multimedia applications. To each datapath a private datacache is associated to provide the storage of individual data.

A central RISC controller manages the datapath array in a SIMD controlling scheme, which is very suitable for regular data parallel algorithms. The RISC controller fetches the instruction stream from the instruction cache. An instruction word is a VLIW featuring 3 operations which are transferred to the datapaths. All three operations can be processed

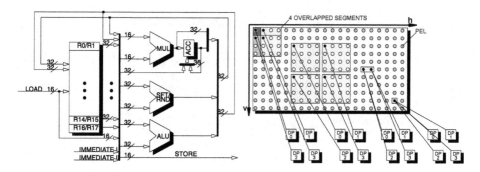

Fig. 13. The datapath of the HiPAR-DSP.

Fig. 14. Access patterns to shared *matrix* memory.

in parallel by each datapath. This leads to a high utilization of the three arithmetic units of each datapath (Fig. 13). The multiply/accumulate unit is able to handle 16 bit input data and accumulate the products up to 36 bit. The shift & round and the arithmetic logical unit (ALU) can work on 32 bit long integer values for enhanced precision requirements. Additionally some arithmetic operations can operate on subwords.

The FFT as well as many other image processing algorithms require an easy data exchange between the parallel processing units. Therefore, the HiPAR-DSP features a shared memory, called matrix memory, which enables a conflict free concurrent access from all datapaths in a single clock cycle. In addition to the data exchange the matrix memory has functions to manipulate the order of the data, like transposing the data in the matrix memory. This is often useful for two-dimensional image processing. In Fig. 14, the behavior of the matrix memory is shown. It is a two-dimensional memory with access pattern in shape of a matrix. Other access patterns like vectors or matrices with offsets between the elements of the matrix are also possible.

The high exploitation of the SIMD and the VLIW concepts in the HiPAR-DSP provides a high computational performance. A 4k point FFT is executed in 153.6 ms on the HiPAR-DSP using 16 datapaths at a clockrate of 100 MHz [12].

3.3   Object-Based Video Coding

The new generation of multimedia applications provide complex services, e.g., teleshopping, interactive TV, internet games, or mobile video communication. The integration of different types of multimedia data and services is achieved by the introduction of an object-based approach for the description and coding of multimedia content. The MPEG-4 standard [2][9][10] defines a standardized framework for these types of applications. Key aspects of MPEG-4 [6] include, among others, independent coding of objects in a picture, the ability to interactively composite these objects into a scene at the display, transmission of 3D scene descriptions; temporal and spatial scalability, and improved error resilience.

In MPEG-4, a video scene consists of one or more audio-visual objects (AVOs) from multiple sources. A visual object (VO) can consist of one or several video object

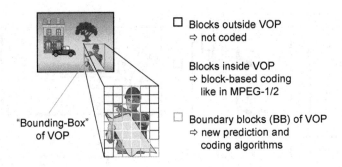

Fig. 15. Different block types in a VOP.

layers. One instance in time of a video object layer is called a video object plane (VOP). Individual VOPs delivered to an MPEG-4 decoder are allowed to have arbitrary shapes. As a consequence, the shape of an object has to be transmitted in addition to its texture.

Each VOP is coded and transmitted independently. The composition is performed in the decoder. The independent transmission and processing of each VOP allows interactive modification of the VOPs, e.g., the user can decide whether to show a particular VOP or not.

Similar to MPEG-2, MPEG-4 video object planes are divided into smaller quadratic blocks of pixels. At the object boundaries, these blocks contain visible pixels which are part of the current video object, as well as transparent pixels that lie outside the object (Fig. 15). These so-called boundary blocks (BB) require a special treatment in encoding and decoding. A block inside the object has only visible pixels and can therefore be coded like in MPEG-2 style. Blocks which lie outside the object do not need to be coded.

The MPEG-4 standard is divided into three profiles with different levels: The Simple Profile has no support for arbitrary shaped objects and therefore is similar to existing hybrid coding standards like H.263 plus the use of reversible variable length codes (VLC) for error resilience mode.

The Core Profile introduces objects with shapes. This implies new algorithms for coding, pre- and post-processing of shape texture data, and composition of video objects in the scene. For the decoding part, the BBs require a special treatment while blocks with no shape information (i.e., opaque) are treated like conventional (Simple Profile) blocks. However, the composition stage has to be performed for all blocks of a VOP. The most computation-intensive algorithms involved in shape and BB coding include context-based arithmetic encoding (CAE) and padding of texture data.

The Main Profile, finally, adds sprite decoding, which allows full perspective transforms of VOPs, thus making the composition quite demanding in terms of both, computational complexity and bandwidth requirements.

Besides the backward compatibility to MPEG-1/2, MPEG-4 includes additional and improved algorithms to support new services. To improve the coding efficiency, new algorithms are included, such as Global Motion Compensation (GMC) and Quarter-Pel Motion Compensation. Also the MPEG-4 standard contains new algorithms for the coding of the boundary blocks, e.g. Context Based Arithmetic Encoding (CAE)

Table 1. The algorithmic classes in a MPEG-4 system.

	Algorithm example	Type of parallelism	Complexity, processing requirements	Data types
Stream Processing	Parsing Composition RLD, VLD	mostly sequential	high complexity non-word aligned processing	short (<16 bit int)
Macroblock processing	DCT/IDCT Filters ME, MC	data, instruction	low complexity high data bandwidth block oriented	short (8, 16 [32 bit] int)
Presentation processing	Compositing Rendering Graphics	data	medium complexity high data bandwidth irregular access	medium (16, 32 bit, int floating point)
Sequential word aligned processing	Audio Codecs CELP HVXC	data, instruction	medium complexity irregular data access	Varying (8 -24bit int, floating point)

or Shape Adaptive DCT (Discrete Cosine Transform). All in all a large set of highly computational intensive tasks are needed for encoding and decoding of MPEG-4 data streams. The increasing diversity of the algorithm leads to less predictable computational requirements of the application. Due to this variety of different algorithms and the highly data-dependent tasks a programmable solution with extensive use of parallel processing elements is favored.

An analysis of a word-width optimized MPEG-4 software reference model as a basis for the processor partitioning showed four classes of algorithms with similar properties in terms of complexity, processing requirements, and parallelization potential (Table 1). An approach for a processor architecture to implement MPEG-4 systems is, therefore, a functional partitioning [13]. Each class of algorithm is mapped on an optimized processor. The optimization of each processor can then be done in terms of instruction set, implemented types of parallel processing, and load-store capabilities. As seen by the other examples also the VLIW and SIMD concepts can be exploited here to provide data-level parallelism.

The algorithmic partitioning of MPEG-4 type processing is directly mirrored in the architecture of the multimedia processor shown in Fig. 16. On a single chip a heterogeneous multiprocessor (MIMD) with different cores for audio processing, stream processing, presentation processing, and video processing is implemented. As an example, the following description concentrates only on the video processing section of the processor. The video processor, also called macroblock engine [1], consists of two parallel functional units or datapaths, a vector and a scalar datapath (Fig. 17). The scalar datapath operates on 32-bit data words in a 32-entry register file and provides control instructions such as jump, branch, and loop. The vector datapath is equipped with a 64-entry register file of 64-bit width. The 64-bits-wide arithmetic execution units in the vector path incorporate subword parallelism by processing either two 32-bit, four 16-bit, or eight 8-bit data entities in parallel within a 64-bit register operand. With its support for subword parallelism, the vector datapath is particularly suited to process the repetitive operations of typical macroblock algorithms at high throughput.

The macroblock engine's parallel datapaths are controlled by a dual-issue 64-bit VLIW. By default, the first slot's instruction is issued to the vector path, and the second one is issued to the scalar path, enforcing parallel execution. However, also two vector

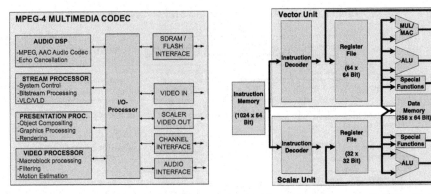

Fig. 16. Architecture of the MPEG-4 processor with its processing units dedicated to the different algorithmic classes.

Fig. 17. Macroblock engine for the video section.

or two scalar instructions can be paired within a VLIW. The flexible utilization of the VLIW minimizes the number of void instruction slots and promotes code density.

In this processor the MIMD concept is exploited by combining several optimized functional units. In the macroblock engine's datapaths the VLIW architectural approach is exploited as well.

4   Future Trends

The previous section presents three current multimedia applications and processor architectures, which exploit the parallelization resources described in Section 2 to provide optimized solutions for the particular application. For future multimedia applications, the presented architectures are not powerful enough. These application require a high efficiency in dealing with data-dependent, irregular control flow, and with multiple tasks of lower parallelization potential while being able to handle several multimedia data streams simultaneously. Therefore, new architectural approaches are required which offer a more flexible style of parallel processing and a dynamic adaptation capability. The availability of such approaches would furthermore promote the adoption of more sophisticated algorithms that deviate radically from traditional schemes and have not yet found their way into international standards (e.g., MPEG-4) due to implementation aspects.

In the following, three innovative architectural concepts [16] – reconfigurable computing, simultaneous multithreading, and associative controlling – are discussed in detail, and their potential benefits for emerging multimedia signal processing applications are pointed out.

4.1   Reconfigurable Computing

Traditionally, a designer has to decide between performance or generality when implementing applications, leading, on the one hand, to hardware realizations that are customized to specific problems and exploit parallel, spatial execution of operations or tasks (e.g., custom VLSI, ASICs, or gate-arrays). On the other hand, there are flexible software solutions (e.g., software written for available DSPs, microcontrollers, embedded or general-purpose microprocessors).

A relatively new development in integrated circuits, Field-Programmable Gate Arrays (FPGAs) with static RAM (SRAM) programming technology, offers a further option. They allow post-fabrication customization (e.g., to different multimedia standards) or an adaptation to specific algorithms at run time. In conventional programmable multimedia processors, a flexible software is executed on a fixed hardware architecture; in reconfigurable computing, the hardware is flexible as well. Therefore, the main benefit of reconfigurable architectures concerning multimedia applications is the combination of almost software flexibility with high performance. Results obtained deliver an order of magnitude or more improvement over general purpose microprocessors' performance. Hence, there is a growing interest in reconfigurable, mostly FPGA-based, processing environments and prototypes [20] in application fields like pattern recognition, image processing, and encryption.

There are many variations on FPGA designs; all of them basically consist of an array of configurable logic blocks (CLBs) of different or identical complexity, implementing the logic part, and a programmable grid of interconnections, linking the CLBs according to the circuit requirements. The functionality of an FPGA is determined by programming SRAM switches that configure the CLBs and the interconnection network. Configurations can be dynamically changed by downloading a new configuration bitstream any time needed.

On a more general level, reconfigurable units comprise a reconfigurable network and basic logic cells. They can be classified using different criteria; one is, e.g., how the reconfigurable system is coupled with its host system. Static, closely coupled systems have reconfigurable units on a processor's data path. Loosely coupled systems, on the other hand, are attached as coprocessors on a separate board.

The most important criterion, however, is the granularity of the composing modules, i.e., of the architecture's basic physical elements (see [18] for more details). In terms of implementation efficiency, it is very important that the architecture's granularity matches the granularity of the mapped application. Levels of granularity range from coarse to fine grain, i.e., from instruction level over reconfigurable arithmetic and data paths to reconfigurable logic or gates.

Fine granular architectures consist of simple logic cells. To achieve a high utilization, the interconnection between these cells often demands large and universally configurable routing resources. Although deriving the highest degree of flexibility, for complex operations a large number of basic cells and routing resources is needed. In this case, fine grained reconfigurable systems are not as efficient as coarse grained ones. Examples of fine granular architectures are typically FPGA-based systems [5].

Coarse granular architectures (Fig. 18), in contrast, consist of more complex basic cells. A single cell may contain an arithmetic module or a complete processor element including data memory, instruction memory, ALU, and controller. Because of more dedicated cells, the local routing resources have a restricted flexibility, whereas the global interconnections between different basic cells are as flexible as in the case of fine granular architectures.

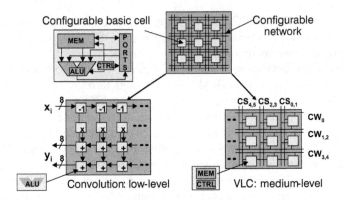

Fig. 18. Example of a coarse grained reconfigurable architecture, e.g. MATRIX [14].

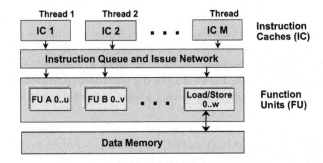

Fig. 19. Generic structure of SMT based architecture.

4.2   Simultaneous Multithreading

The idea behind multithreading is to enlarge the available amount of concurrently exe-cutable instructions by providing access to more than a single independent instruction stream. Larger or smaller independent sequences of instructions (so-called threads) can be found in almost all algorithms. Regarding multimedia processing schemes, this starts at the top level with independent tasks, is often applicable to subtasks or below, and ex-tends down to the bottom level of independent instructions as exploited by conventional VLIW or superscalar architectures. Even data level parallelism can be represented by defining several independent threads of identical instructions. Automatic (tool-driven) extraction of independent tasks or subtasks from sequential code is difficult and usu-ally inefficient. However, especially in signal processing, the programmer has a detailed knowledge of the interdependencies of tasks and subtasks. Control instructions marking independent threads can be easily inserted, and the code can be optimized to generate as many threads as possible.

Fig. 19 shows a generic SMT-controlled architecture which is based on a general-purpose processor architecture [22][23][26]. Basically, the architecture is a straightfor-ward extension of a standard superscalar architecture. A few instructions are fetched concurrently from an instruction cache and stored into an instruction queue. From the instruction queue, a dispatcher unit selects executable instructions and issues them simultaneously to functional units of the required types. In principle, there is no limitation regarding functionality and type of functional units; even complex data paths or subword parallel units are possible, enabling easy adaptation to multimedia applications. Memory access takes place via a special I/O type of functional unit connecting to cache memories. Different from the superscalar architecture is the fact that the instructions to be dispatched can originate from more than a single thread. Hence, the controller has to keep track of the status information of several threads and the interdependencies between them (e.g., synchronization). Unlike in general purpose applications, where threads are often derived from multiprogramming and thus synchronization is not essential, multimedia applications require an efficient (i.e., register based) synchronization scheme.

Even though the focus in multimedia signal processing shifts from low-level to medium- and high-level algorithms, a significant share of low-level processing remains. In other words, tasks with a major amount of data-parallel resources and predictable memory accesses and branch behavior remain in every application. Though data-parallel loops can easily be interpreted as independent threads, data-level parallelization using threads is comparably inefficient. A straightforward approach is to introduce subword parallelism in SMT architectures [15]. However, there are SMT-specific limitations regarding the efficiency of subword parallelism: SMT draws one of its major performance gains by sharing the processor's functional units by several threads. Consequently, four independent 16-bit units should show a much better utilization than a 64-bit subword parallel unit. Issuing the same instruction to multiple functional units and hence saving instruction fetch and issue resources is a reasonable extension or alternative to subword parallelism in SMT architectures.

Simultaneous multithreading is a powerful controlling concept suitable to target the challenges of future multimedia signal processing schemes. Major advantages are the possibility to exploit all possible levels of parallelization while keeping the programming model simple and utilization high even for larger numbers of functional units. The remaining low-level share of multimedia applications can be exploited for further improvement of the throughput rate. First simulation results [25] indicate that SMT is capable of achieving a high speed-up for the targeted class of algorithms featuring unbalanced workloads, undetermined branches, and random (cache-) memory accesses.

4.3 Associative Controlling

The currently dominating controlling concepts for parallel signal processors, MIMD and SIMD, each favor different kinds of parallelism. MIMD architectures can exploit data- and task-level parallelism, at the cost of additional hardware for controllers and a more complex programming model due to the asynchronous processing of the data paths. SIMD architectures are, in general, efficient for exploiting data-level parallelism with identical, predetermined operations on data segments, due to decreased hardware cost and a simpler programming model. Frequent data-dependent decisions generally do not achieve a good utilization of the parallel data paths in an SIMD controlled processor.

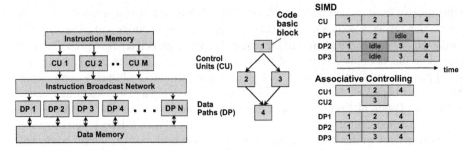

Fig. 20. Generic structure of an associative controlling architecture.

Fig. 21. Example of a control flow on an associative controlling architecture compared to the same control flow executed on a SIMD architecture.

Although increasing in algorithm complexity, multimedia algorithms still exhibit a significant amount of data-level parallelism. In order to combine advantages of both controlling schemes for such applications, a new controlling scheme for parallel architectures, referred to as *Associative Controlling* [4], has been developed. The goal of this new scheme is to provide a hardware-efficient way to control parallel resources while achieving an acceptable level of programming complexity.

For the proposed architecture, a program is considered a directed graph of code basic blocks. Each basic block contains a sequence of instructions. For associative controlling, a set of controllers fetches instructions from a shared instruction memory. These instruction streams are supplied to all data paths, which select one of the streams to execute at run time. The selection of the instruction stream to execute is performed on a basic block level. In general, the number of controllers is significantly smaller than the number of data paths but greater than one. Fig. 20 illustrates the generic structure of an architecture with M control units and N data paths that incorporates the associative controlling concept.

The advantage of associative controlling compared to SIMD controlling is an increased processing power for program segments containing data-dependent branches. As soon as a conditional branch occurs and two data paths match different conditions, an additional instruction stream is generated, and the branch can be processed in parallel (Fig. 21).

Besides the parallel execution of data-dependent branches associative controlling enables independent and parallel processing of different program segments of an application. Therefore, the resources of an associatively controlled processor can be divided into several processing clusters. Each cluster consists of a subset of the control units and data paths.

With these features, associative controlling allows an efficient execution of conditional branches, the partitioning of the processing resources at run time, and therefore the exploitation of available parallelism at task, data, and instruction level. Within each processing cluster, the array of data paths can be programmed like a SIMD architecture, preserving this well-understood programming model.

5   Conclusion

Multimedia applications use a wide variety of different signal processing algorithms. Due to the fact that these applications mostly have real-time requirements, the processing unit must provide a computational power high enough to meet the real-time requirements. In Section 2, parallelization resources were introduced which can be exploited to derive optimized processing architectures for the application, how it was shown in Section 3. For each of three examples of applications, block-based video coding, Digital Video Broadcasting, and object-based video coding, the possible parallelization resources were pointed out. An architecture of a processor which exploits these resources was shown.

Due to the increasing complexity in the algorithms for future multimedia applications, the presented state of the art architectures are not able to provide the required flexibility for the increasing irregular control flow or the changing demands at run time in these applications. Therefore, three new architectures, reconfigurable computing, simultaneous multithreading, and associative controlling, were introduced in Section 4 which are promising approaches to deal with these new requirements of future multimedia applications.

Acknowledgements

The authors wishes to acknowledge the contributions of M. Berekovic, J. Hilgenstock, H. Kloos, M. B. Kulaczewski, S. Moch, and H.-J. Stolberg.

References

1. M. Berekovic, H.-J. Stolberg, M. B. Kulaczewski and P. Pirsch, "Instruction Set Extension for MPEG-4 Video," *Journal of VLSI Signal Processing 23*, pp. 27–49, 1999.
2. L. Chiariglione, "Impact of MPEG Standards on Multimedia Industry," *Multimedia Signal Processing, Proc. of the IEEE*, Vol. 86, No. 6, pp. 1222–1227, June 1998.
3. J. W. Cooley and J. W. Tukey, "An Algorithm for the Machine Computation of Complex Fourier Series," *Mathematics of Computation*, Vol. 9, pp. 297–301, Apr. 1965.
4. W. Gehrke and K. Gaedke, "Associative Controlling of Monolithic Parallel Processor Architectures," *IEEE Transactions on Circuits and Systems for Video Technology*, vol. 5, no. 5, pp. 453–464, Oct. 1995.
5. S. A. Guccione, "List of FPGA-based Computing Machines," http://www.io.com/~guccione/HW_list.html, last updated August 21, 2000.
6. B. Haskell, P. G. Howard, Y. A. Lecun, A. Puri, J. Ostermann, M. R. Civanlar, L. Rabiner, L. Bottou and P. Haffner, "Image and Video Coding - Emerging Standards and beyond," *IEEE Trans. on Circuits and Systems for Video Technology*, Vol. 8 No. 7, pp. 878–891, Nov. 1998.
7. K. Herrmann, S. Moch, J. Hilgenstock and P. Pirsch, "Implementation of a Multiprocessor System with Distributed Embedded DRAM on a Large Area Integrated Circuit," *Proc. IEEE International Symposium on Defect and Fault Tolerance in VLSI Systems (DFT2000)*, pp. 105–113, Oct. 2000.
8. ISO/IEC 13818-2, "Generic coding of moving pictures and associated audio, (MPEG-2), Part 2: Video," Nov. 1993.
9. ISO/IEC JTC11/SC29/WG11 N2323, "Overview of the MPEG-4 Standard," July 1998.

10. ISO/IEC JTC11/SC29/WG11 W2502, "ISO/IEC 14496-2. Final Draft international standard. Part 2: Visual," Atlantic-City, Oct. 1998

11. ITU-T Recommendation Draft H.263, "Video Coding for Low Bitrate Communications," International Telecommunication Union, May 1996.

12. H. Kloos, L. Friebe, J. P. Wittenburg, W. Hinrichs, H. Lieske and P. Pirsch, "HiPAR-DSP 16, A new DSP for Onboard Real-Time SAR Systems," *Proc. of 15th Aerosense Conference on Phototonic and Quantum Technologies for Aerospace and Application III*, July 2001.

13. J. Kneip, S. Bauer, J. Volmer, B. Schmale, P. Kuhn, M. Reiÿmann, "The MPEG-4 Video Coding Standard - a VLSI point of view," *IEEE International Workshop on Signal Processing Systems SIPS98*, Boston, Oct. 1998.

14. E. Mirsky, A. DeHon, "MATRIX: A Reconfigurable Computing Architecture with Configurable Instruction Distribution and Deployable Resources," *Proceedings of the IEEE Symposium on FPGAs for Custom Computing Machines*, pp. 157–166, Apr. 1996.

15. H. Oehring, U. Sigmund, T. Ungerer, "Simultaneous Multithreading and Multimedia," *Proc. of the Workshop on Multithreaded Execution, Architecture and Compilation*, Orlando, Jan. 1999.

16. P. Pirsch, "Architectures for Multimedia Signal Processing," *Proc. IEEE Workshop on Signal Processing Systems*, Oct. 1999.

17. P. Pirsch, J. Kneip, K. Rönner, "Parallelization Resources of Image Processing Algorithms and their Mapping on a Programmable Parallel Videosignal Processor," *Proc. of the International Symposium on Circuits and Systems 1995*, pp. I-562–565, Seattle, 1995

18. B. Radunovic and V. Milutinovic, "A Survey of Reconfigurable Computing Architectures," *8th International Workshop on Field-Programmable Logic and Applications*, pp. 376–385, Tallinn, Estonia, Aug./Sept. 1998.

19. H. Rohling, R. Grünheid and D. Galda, "OFDM Air Interface for the 4th Generation of Mobile Communication Systems," *Proc. of the 6th International OFDM-Workshop*, pp. 1–28, Hamburg, Germany, Sept. 2001.

20. Russell Tessier and Wayne Burleson, "Reconfigurable Computing for Digital Signal Processing: A Survey," *Journal of VLSI Signal Processing*, vol. 28, pp. 7–28, 2001.

21. R. M. Tomasulo, "An Efficient Algorithm for Exploiting Multiple Arithmetic Units," *IBM Journal of Research and Development*, volume 11 (1), pp. 25-33, IBM, 1967

22. D. M. Tullsen, S. J. Eggers, H. M. Levy, "Simultaneous Multithreading: Maximizing On-Chip Parallelism," *Proc. of the 22nd Annual International Symposium on Computer Architecture*, June 1995.

23. D. M. Tullsen, J. L. Lo, S. J. Eggers, H. M. Levy, "Supporting Fine-Grain Synchronization on a Simultaneous Multithreaded Processor," *Technical Report #UW-CSE-98-06-02*, University of Washington, June 1998.

24. David W. Wall, "Limits of Instruction-Level Parallelism," *Fourth International Symposium o Architectural Support for Programming Languages and Operating Systems*, pp. 176-188, Apr. 1991

25. J. P. Wittenburg, P. Pirsch, G. Meyer, "A Multithreaded Architecture Approach to Parallel DSPs for High Performance Image Processing Applications," *Proc. of the IEEE Workshop on Signal Processing Systems*, Oct. 1999.

26. W. Yamamoto, M. J. Serrano, A. R. Talcott, R. C. Wood, M. Nemirovski, "Performance Estimation of Multistreamed, Superscalar Processors," *Proceedings of the 27th Annual Hawaii International Conference on System Sciences*, Honolulu, 1994.

Microcoded Reconfigurable Embedded Processors: Current Developments

Stephan Wong, Stamatis Vassiliadis, and Sorin Cotofana

Computer Engineering Laboratory,
Electrical Engineering Department,
Delft University of Technology,
Delft, The Netherlands
{Stephan,Stamatis,Sorin}@CE.ET.TUDelft.NL

Abstract. It is well-known that the main disadvantages associated with reconfigurable hardware are long reconfiguration latencies, high opcode space requirements, and complex decoder hardware. To overcome these disadvantages, we use microcode since it allows emulation of "complex" operations which are performed using a sequence of smaller and simpler operations. Microcode is used to control the reconfiguration of the reconfigurable hardware, either online or off-line, and the execution on the reconfigurable hardware. Due to the multitude of microcodes and their sizes, it is not feasible to provide on-chip storage for all microcodes. Consequently, the loading of microcode into a limited on-chip storage facility is becoming increasingly more important. In this paper, we present two methods of loading microcodes into such an on-chip storage facility.

1 Introduction

Traditionally, embedded processor design was very much similar to microcontroller design. This meant that for each targeted set of applications, an embedded processor was designed in specialized hardware (commonly referred to as Application Specific Integrated Circuits (ASICs)). In the early nineties, we were witnessing a shift in the embedded processor design approach fueled by the need for faster time-to-market. This resulted in the utilization of programmable processor cores that were augmented with specialized hardware units, which were still implemented in ASICs. This meant that time-critical tasks were implemented in specialized hardware units while other less time-critical tasks were implemented in software to be run on the programmable processor core [1]. This approach allows a programmable processor core to be re-used for different sets of applications without redesigning it. This leaves only the specialized hardware units to be (re-)designed for the targeted set of applications.

Currently, we are witnessing a new trend in embedded processor design that is again quickly reshaping the embedded processor design approach. Time-critical tasks are now being implemented in field-programmable gate array (FPGA) structures or comparative technologies [2,3,4,5] instead of ASICs. The reasons for and the benefits of such an approach include the following:

- **Increased flexibility:** The functionality of the embedded processor can be quickly changed and allows early implementation of future functionalities not specified at design time.

E.F. Deprettere et al. (Eds.): SAMOS 2001, LNCS 2268, pp. 207–223, 2002.
© Springer-Verlag Berlin Heidelberg 2002

- **Good-enough performance:** The performance of FPGAs has increased tremendously and is quickly approaching that of ASICs [6]. Furthermore, due to the mostly high-level specification of embedded processor designs (usually in VHDL), existing designs can be mapped on new FPGA structures much faster and fully exploit the performance benefits they provide.
- **Faster design times:** Faster design times are achieved by re-using intellectual property (IP) cores or by slightly modifying them. Design faults can be quickly identified and rectified without the need for additional embedded processor roll-outs.

The above mentioned benefits have even resulted in that programmable processor cores are under consideration to be implemented in the same FPGA structures, e.g., [7]. However, the utilization of such reconfigurable hardware also poses several issues that must be addressed:

- **Long reconfiguration latencies:** This is the time it takes for the reconfigurable hardware to change its functionality. When considering dynamic run-time reconfigurations, such latencies may greatly penalize the performance, because any computation must be halted until the reconfiguration has finished.
- **Limited opcode space:** The utilization of a programmable processor core that also controls the reconfigurable hardware has resulted in the fact that many instructions (usually associated with a single operation) must be introduced that initiate and control the reconfiguration and execution processes. Extending the functionality of the FPGA structure now puts much strain on the opcode space.
- **Complicated decoder hardware:** The multitude of newly introduced instructions greatly increased the complexity of the decoder hardware.

In this paper, we discuss a new approach using microcode that alleviates the mentioned problems. Microcode consists of a sequence of (simple) microinstructions that, when executed in a certain order, performs "complex" operations. This approach allows "complex" operations to be performed on much simpler hardware. In this paper, we consider the reconfiguration (either off-line or run-time) and execution processes as complex operations. The main benefits of our approach can be summarized as follows:

- **Reduced reconfiguration latencies:** The usage of microcode to control the reconfiguration process allows such code to be cached inside the embedded processor. This allows faster access times to the reconfiguration microcode and thus in turn reduces the reconfiguration latencies.
- **Reduced opcode space requirements:** As will be explained later, the usage of microcode requires only the inclusion of several instructions that point to such microcode. By executing microcode, we perform the required operation(s). Therefore, there is no need for separate instructions for each and every supported operation.
- **Reduced decoder hardware complexity:** Due to the inclusion of only a few instructions (that point to the microcode), we do not require complex (instruction) decoding hardware.

An important aspect when utilizing microcodes is how to load them into an on-chip storage facility. This paper proposes two simple microcode loading methods. The first method loads microcode in a straightforward manner by overwriting already loaded microcodes. The second method does this by taking into account which microcodes are frequently used and thus only overwriting less frequently used microcodes.

This paper is organized as follows. Section 2 discusses the concept of microcode and shows an example of how microcode can be utilized to support reconfiguration of reconfigurable hardware and the execution on such hardware. Section 3 discusses in short the MOLEN reconfigurable microcoded processor [8] which utilizes microcode to also support partial reconfigurability. In Section 4, we discuss two methods of how microcodes can be loaded into an on-chip storage facility. Finally, Section 5 concludes this paper with some closing remarks.

2   What Is Microcode?

Microcode, introduced in 1951 by Wilkes [9], constitutes one of the key computer engineering innovations. Microcode allowed the emulation of "complex" instructions by means of "simple" hardware (operations) and thus provided a prime force to the development of computer systems as we know them today. Microcode de facto partitioned computer engineering into two distinct conceptual layers, namely: architecture[1] and implementation. This is in part because emulation allowed the definition of complex instructions which might have been technologically not implementable (at the time they were defined), thus projecting an architecture to the future. That is, it allowed computer architects to determine a technology-independent functional behavior (e.g., instruction set) and conceptual structures providing the following possibilities:

- Define the computer's architecture as a programmer's interface to the hardware rather than to a specific technology dependent realization of a specific behavior.
- Allow a single architecture to be determined for a "family" of implementations giving rise to the important concept of compatibility. Simply stated, it allowed programs to be written for a specific architecture once and run at "infinitum" independent of the implementations.

Since its beginnings, as introduced by Wilkes, microcode has been a sequence of micro-operations (microprogram). Such a microprogram consists of pulses for operating the gates associated with the arithmetical and control registers. Figure 1 depicts the method of generating this sequence of pulses. First, a timing pulse initiating a micro-operation enters the decoding tree and depending on the setup register R, an output is generated. This output signal passes to matrix A which in turn generates pulses to control arithmetical and control registers, thus performing the required micro-operation. The output signal also passes to matrix B, which in its turn generates pulses to control the setup register R (with a certain delay). The next timing pulse will therefore generate the next micro-operation in the required sequence due to the changed register R.

Microcode has become a major component requiring a large development effort from mainframes to PC processors. To illustrate the magnitude and the importance

---

[1] Architecture here and in the rest of the presentation denotes the attribute of a system as seen by the programmer, i.e., the conceptual structure and functional behavior of the processor, and it is distinct from the organization of the dataflow and physical implementation of the processor [10].

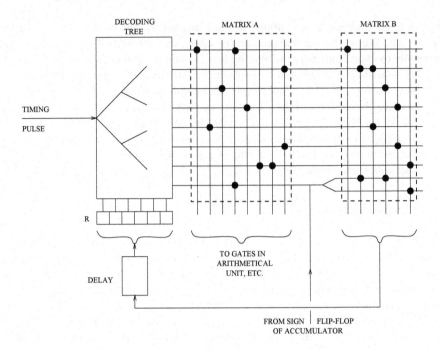

Fig. 1. Wilkes' microprogram control model [9].

Table 1. Some facts from two IBM Enterprise Servers [11].

system	# of assembler languages	# of higher languages	modules	LOC	DLOC
IBM ES/4381	3	1	1,505	480,692	791,696
IBM ES/9370	6	2	3,130	796,136	1,512,750

that microcode has played, we present some key facts of "real" machine microcode in Table 1 [10]. In this table, it can be observed that several languages have been developed/used (3, 6 assembler languages and 1, 2 higher level languages for the 4381, 9370 respectively) with a substantial amount of microcode being developed for the implementations. This is indicated by the number of modules used, the number of lines of actual microcode (LOC), and the number of lines of actual microcode together with comments (DLOC).

Over the years, the Wilkes' model has evolved into a high-level microprogrammed machine as depicted in Figure 2. In this figure, the control store contains the microinstructions (that represent one or more micro-operations) and the sequencer determines the next microinstruction to execute. The control store and the sequencer correspond to the matrices A and B respectively in the Wilkes' model. The machine's operation is as follows:

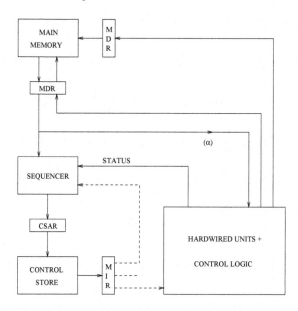

Fig. 2. A high-level microprogrammed machine.

1. The control store address register (CSAR) contains the address of the next microin-struction located in the control store. The microinstruction located at this address is then forwarded to the microinstruction register (MIR).
2. The microinstruction register (MIR) decodes the microinstruction and generates smaller micro-operation(s) accordingly that need to be performed by the hardware unit(s) and/or control logic.
3. The sequencer utilizes status information from the control logic and/or results from the hardware unit(s) to determine the next microinstruction and stores its control store address in the CSAR. It is also possible that the previous microinstruction influences the sequencer's decision regarding which microinstruction to select next.

As mentioned before, the MIR generates micro-operation(s) depending on the mi-croinstruction. In the case that only one micro-operation is generated controlling a single hardwired resource, the microinstruction is called vertical. In all other cases, the microin-struction is called horizontal. The execution of the microinstructions stops whenever the *end_op* microinstruction is encountered.

It should be noted that in microcoded engines not all instructions access the control store. As a matter of fact, only emulated instructions have to go through the microcode logic. All other instructions that have been implemented will be executed directly by the hardware (following path (α) in Figure 2). That is, a microcoded engine is as a matter of fact a hybrid of the implementation having emulated instructions and hardwired instructions[2].

---

[2] That is, contrary to some believes, from the moment it was possible to implement instructions, microcoded engines always had a hardwired core that executed RISC instructions.

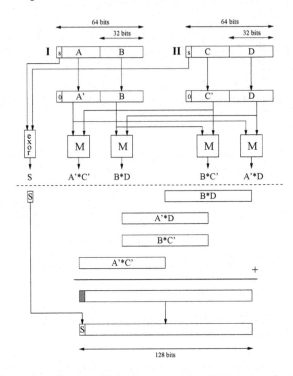

Fig. 3. Performing 64-bit multiplication using four 32-bit unsigned multipliers.

2.1 A Microcode Example

In this section, we discuss how to perform a 64-bit signed magnitude multiplication. Obviously, a single 64-bit signed multiplier can be implemented in hardware to perform the required operation. However, in this example we have elected to perform the operation using four 32-bit unsigned multipliers. This example shows that operations exhibiting common functionalities will greatly benefit from our approach. We must note that this example only serves illustration purposes and our approach is in no way limited to such "small" structures. In this example, we assume that the scheme has to be implemented in an FPGA and discuss how the reconfiguration process of the FPGA can be performed using microcode. Finally, we discuss how microcode can also be used to control the execution process on the FPGA.

A signed magnitude multiplication of two 64-bit numbers I and II can be performed using four 32-bit unsigned multipliers as follows (see Figure 3):

1. Substitute the sign bits of both numbers I and II with zeroes.
2. Perform an exor over the two sign bits. This determines the sign of the final result.
3. Perform four 32-bit unsigned multiplications on the 32-bit parts of both remaining numbers.
4. Add the intermediate results of the four multiplications.
5. Substitute the most significant bit of the result after addition with the new sign bit.

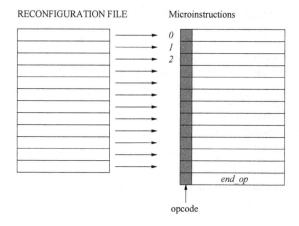

Fig. 4. A straightforward translation from reconfiguration file to reconfiguration microprogram.

The aforementioned multiplication can be placed inside an FPGA by writing a VHDL model, synthesizing it to obtain a reconfiguration file, and then loading the resulting reconfiguration file into the FPGA. In most of the traditional approaches, each reconfiguration file was associated with a reconfiguration instruction and by issuing such an instruction, a reconfiguration of the FPGA was performed. These approaches require continuous architectural extensions, i.e., adding new reconfiguration instructions, for new functions implemented on the FPGA. Consequently, it puts a lot of strain on the opcode space of any instruction set. We propose to use microcode to control the reconfiguration process and show later on that only one new instruction is needed for this purpose.

A straightforward method that translates a reconfiguration file into a reconfiguration microprogram is depicted in Figure 4. A reconfiguration file is sliced into smaller pieces of equal size that will constitute the latter part of a microinstruction. The (microinstruction) opcode identifies the microinstruction as containing reconfiguration file slices. The *end_op* microinstruction signifies the end of the reconfiguration microprogram. The reconfiguration of the FPGA can still be performed using existing hardware simply by ignoring the microinstruction opcodes. We are aware that many techniques, e.g., encoding or compression of microinstruction fields, can be applied to reduce the reconfiguration microprogram size, but they do not conceptually add anything to this discussion and are therefore left out of this discussion.

Having obtained a reconfiguration microprogram, we can mark the sections responsible for reconfiguring certain parts of the FPGA. We show a higher level representation of the reconfiguration microprogram in Table 2 since showing it at microinstruction level does not provide any insight.

Instead of introducing new instructions for each and every reconfiguration microprogram, we introduce a *single* instruction (called SET) that points to the location of the first microinstruction of the reconfiguration microprogram. By executing the microprogram starting from this location till the end_op microinstruction, the reconfiguration is performed. The SET instruction format is as follows:

Table 2. A high-level reconfiguration microprogram

setup datapaths from register file towards input register
setup the input registers
setup the substitution datapaths
setup the intermediate registers
setup datapaths towards multipliers
setup multiplier 1
setup multiplier 2
setup multiplier 3
setup multiplier 4
setup the exor
setup datapaths towards addition structure
setup the addition structure
setup the pre-result register
setup datapath from exor towards end result register
setup end result register
setup datapath from result register towards register file
end_op

Table 3. A high-level execution microprogram

load   the input values from register file
substitute the sign bits with zeroes
exor   the two sign bits
multiply   sub-fields
add   the remaining intermediate results
substitute the most significant bit with new sign bit
end_op

SET, resident/pageable, location address; *execute the reconfiguration microcode starting from 'location address'. Continue execution until the* end_op *microinstruction is encountered.*

The meaning of 'resident/pageable' and how it effects the interpretation of the 'location address' field is discussed later. Similar to using microcode to control the reconfiguration process, we can also use microcode to control the execution process of the implementation that is currently loaded into the FPGA. For example, an execution microprogram of the multiplication depicted in Figure 3 is given in Table 3. Again, we introduce a single instruction (called EXECUTE) that points to the location of the first microinstruction of the (now) execution microcode. The instruction format is as follows:

EXECUTE, resident/pageable, location address; *execute the execution microcode from 'location address'. Continue execution until the* end_op *microinstruction is encountered.*

The most obvious storage facility for all the microprograms (either reconfiguration or execution) is the main memory. However, the loading of microprograms can have a tremendous effect on the overall performance, because no computations can start before the FPGA is configured. Assuming a straightforward translation of a reconfiguration file into a reconfiguration microprogram, the following example gives a good estimate of the load latency of an average-sized reconfiguration file:

- Assume that it takes approximately 1.5 reconfiguration byte to reconfigure one gate in an FPGA, it would require 1.5 Mbytes to reconfigure 1 million gates of an average-sized Xilinx Virtex-II FPGA.
- Assume that we use a high-speed RAMBUS memory to store such a reconfiguration file and that the memory bandwidth is 3.2 GByte/s, it would require about 0.5 milliseconds to load the reconfiguration file.
- Assuming that the FPGA is tied to a 1 GHz processor, the 0.5 milliseconds of load latency translates into 500.000 processor cycles in which the processor has to wait before the reconfiguration can even start.

A load latency that corresponds to 500.000 lost processor cycles is huge and it is obvious that it must be reduced. There are two ways to reduce the load latencies. First, frequently used microprograms can be stored on-chip (*resident*) close to the FPGA with the control store (see Figure 2 and assume that the hardwired units have been replaced with FPGA units) being the most obvious location. Second, other less frequently used microprograms are stored in the main memory and can be cached (*pageable*) on-chip. Due to the close proximity of the microprograms to the FPGA, load latencies can be greatly reduced. Both methods are supported by the SET and EXECUTE instructions in which the 'resident/pageable'-field determine the interpretation of the 'location address'-field, i.e., as a control store address or as a memory address. The second method is slightly more complicated than the first one, because it encompasses the translation of memory addresses into control store addresses (CS-α). Section 4 discusses in more detail the loading (paging) of microprograms into the control store and several related issues. Before we do that, we shortly present the MOLEN reconfigurable microcoded processor that utilize microcode to support reconfigurable hardware that can also be partially reconfigured.

3 The MOLEN Reconfigurable Microcoded Processor

In the previous section, we discussed the concept of microcode and microcoded processor organizations. Furthermore, we presented an example of performing 64-bit signed magnitude multiplication using four 32-bit unsigned multipliers. In this example, we introduced the utilization of microcode in both the reconfiguration and execution processes. Recently, we have introduced the MOLEN reconfigurable microcoded processor that is utilizing microcode to incorporate architectural support for reconfigurable hardware structures such as FPGAs [8]. Its internal organization is depicted in Figure 5.

In this organization, instructions are fetched from the memory and stored in the instruction buffer (I_BUFFER). The ARBITER fetches instructions from the I_BUFFER and performs a partial decoding on the instructions in order to determine where they should be issued. Instructions that have been implemented in fixed hardware are issued to the core processing (CP) unit. The instructions entering the CP unit are further decoded and then issued to their corresponding functional units. The source data are fetched from

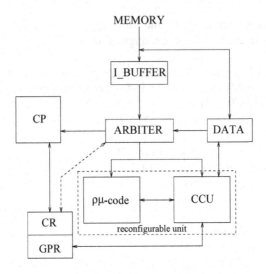

Fig. 5. The internal organization of the MOLEN processor.

the general-purpose registers (GPRs) and the results are written back to the same GPRs. Other status information are stored in the control registers (CRs).

The reconfigurable unit consists of a custom configured unit (CCU)[3] and the $\rho\mu$-code unit (shown in Figure 6 as the combination of the sequencer and the ρ-CONTROL STORE). An operation[4] executed by the reconfigurable unit is divided into two distinct process phases: **set** and **execute**. The **set** phase is responsible for reconfiguring the CCU hardware enabling the execution of the operation. Such a phase may be subdivided into two subphases, namely partial **set** (*p*-**set**) and complete **set** (*c*-**set**). The *p*-**set** phase is envisioned to cover common functions of an application or set of applications. More specifically, in the *p*-**set** phase the CCU is *partially* configured to perform these common functions. While the *p*-**set** sub-phase can be possibly performed during the loading of a program or even at chip fabrication time, the *c*-**set** sub-phase is performed during program execution. Furthermore, the *c*-**set** sub-phase only partially reconfigures remaining blocks in the CCU (not covered in the *p*-**set** sub-phase) in order to *complete* the functionality of the CCU by enabling it to perform other less frequent functions.

For the reconfiguration of the CCU, reconfiguration microcode[5] within the $\rho\mu$-code unit (either already resident or loaded from main memory) is executed to perform the actual reconfiguration. It can be noted that in case the reconfigurable logic cannot be partially set or in case the partial setting is not convenient then the *c*-**set** can be used by itself to perform the entire configuration. The **execute** phase is responsible for the actual execution of the operation on the CCU.

---

[3] Such a unit could be for example implemented by a Field-Programmable Gate Array (FPGA).

[4] An operation can be as simple as an instruction or as complex as a piece of code of a function.

[5] The reconfiguration microcode is generated by translating the needed reconfiguration file into reconfiguration microcode (see Section 2.1).

In the **execute** phase, the operation is performed by executing execution microcode within the $\rho\mu$-code unit (either already resident or loaded from main memory). By executing the execution microcode on the CCU (already configured to the needed implementation), the desired operation is performed. We must note that both the **set** and **execute** phases do not specify a certain operation that needs to be performed and then execute the corresponding reconfiguration or execution microcode. Instead, the p-**set**, c-**set**, and **execute** instructions directly point to the location where the reconfiguration or execution microcode is stored. In this way, different operations are performed by executing different reconfiguration microcodes and different execution microcodes, respectively. That is, instead of specifying new instructions for the operations (requiring instruction opcode space), we simply point to location addresses. We have shown that the location of the microcode can be either on-chip (called *resident*) or in the main memory (called *pageable*).

Summarizing, the MOLEN reconfigurable microcoded processor utilizes three new instructions to support reconfiguration of and execution on reconfigurable hardware. The combination of p-**set** and c-**set** allows even the support for partial (run-time) reconfigurations. Furthermore, by separating support for any operation into two distinct phases, the **set** and **execute** phases, allows reconfiguration latencies to be hidden when they are scheduled far apart from each other. Finally, by keeping microcode close to the CCU inside the $\rho\mu$-code unit, we can greatly reduce load latencies of microcodes. In the next section, we present two methods of how to load microcode that is stored in the main memory into the $\rho\mu$-code unit.

4 Loading of Microprograms

As mentioned before, our approach provides permanent on-chip storage for frequently used microprograms[6] and temporary on-chip storage for less frequently used microprograms that must be loaded from the main memory. In the traditional microcoded machine (see Figure 2), resident microprograms were stored inside the control store. In our approach, we utilize a modified control store, called the reconfigurable control store (ρ-CONTROL STORE), to store both frequently used and less frequently used microprograms. The ρ-CONTROL STORE is discussed in Section 4.1, which also introduces the problem of loading microprogram into the ρ-CONTROL STORE. This is followed by a discussion of two microprogram loading methods that utilize the ρ-CONTROL STORE in Sections 4.2 and 4.3.

4.1 The Reconfigurable Control Store

The reconfigurable control store (ρ-CONTROL STORE) together with an extended sequencer is depicted in Figure 6.

Both the sequencer and the ρ-CONTROL STORE operate as described in Section 2 with the following differences:

---

[6] In this section, we do not distinguish between reconfiguration microcode and execution microcode. They are conceptually the same and are referred to in this section as microprograms.

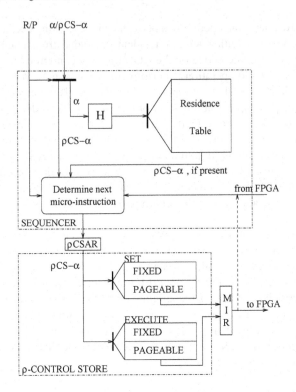

Fig. 6. Internal organization of the ρ-CONTROL STORE and the sequencer.

- The residence table contains the most recent translations of memory addresses (α) into ρ-CONTROL STORE addresses (ρCS-α). The actual translation is performed by a hashing function (H) since the memory address space is much larger than the one of the ρ-CONTROL STORE.
- The residence/pageable (R/P) bit determines the interpretation of the 'location address'-field of both the SET and EXECUTE instructions.
- The basic addressable unit inside the ρ-CONTROL STORE is a module which consists of at least one microinstruction up to several hundreds of microinstructions. Since a microprogram may consist of several modules (possibly of varying size), we assume for simplicity's sake that every block within the ρ-CONTROL STORE can store the largest known module.

Two problems might occur when loading microprograms. The first problem occurs when a microprogram exceeds the available storage space. The second problem occurs when several microprograms must be loaded, but their combined size exceeds the available storage space. The first problem can be solved by loading a smaller set of modules that constitute the larger microprogram. When considering separate modules as distinct microprograms, we can translate the first problem into the second one. The second problem can be solved by swapping out currently loaded microprograms in order to create storage space for the to be loaded microprogram. In this paper, we propose two methods to solve the two mentioned problems. The first method (called *straight*) loads the microprogram starting from a certain point in the ρ-CONTROL STORE and continues until the end is reached. All remaining (non-loaded) modules must be accessed from the main memory. The second method (called *evict*) tries to create enough storage space inside the ρ-CONTROL STORE when remaining storage space is too small for the to be loaded microprogram.

4.2   The *Straight* Loading Method

In this section, we discuss the *straight* microprogram loading method. Before discussing the method, we assume the following

- Each block in the ρ-CONTROL STORE has a $first$ bit which tells whether the block contains the first microinstruction (and thus the first module) of a microprogram or not.
- Each block in the ρ-CONTROL STORE is indexed by the memory address of the first microinstruction of the module that is loaded into the block in question.
- Jumps (conditional or direct) inside the modules only jump to the first instruction of modules.

Considering the case that we want to load microprogram A for the first time into the ρ-CONTROL STORE and the first instruction of microprogram has the memory address α, the *straight* method works as follows:

1. Determine using address α which entry in the residence table to use. Each residence table entry is associated with a ρ-CONTROL STORE block.
2. Start loading the microprogram into this block and mark the block with the $first$ bit set to one. The remaining modules of the microprogram are written into the consecutive blocks and their $first$ bits are all set to zero. This is done until the end of the storage space is reached or the *end_op* microinstruction is encountered.

The execution of the microprogram starts by determining the correct ρ-CONTROL STORE block using the residence table. The actual execution can only start if the corresponding $first$ bit of the block is set and continues until:

- a jump microinstruction is encountered;
- the *end_op* microinstruction is encountered;
- another block with the $first$ bit set is encountered;
- the end of the ρ-CONTROL STORE is encountered.

In the first scenario, the memory address of the jump microinstruction must be compared to the memory addresses (of the first microinstruction of the module) that are stored also in the ρ-CONTROL STORE. In this way, the correct ρ-CONTROL STORE block to jump to can be found and in case it is not found, than the module in question must be executed from the main memory. In the latter two situations, the remaining modules of the microprogram must be executed from the main memory since no mechanisms are present to remedy these situations. In both situations the performance is greatly penalized due to increased loading latencies. In addition, there are two scenarios during the execution of a microprogram that can increase the occurrence of the latter two situations:

- Microprograms are loaded into the ρ-CONTROL STORE that overwrites frequently used microprograms. This might result in many reloadings of the frequently used microprograms (when blocks with the $first$ bit set to one are overwritten) or in the execution of modules from the main memory (when latter parts are overwritten).
- The hashing function favors blocks at the end of the ρ-CONTROL STORE. This results in that many microprograms will not be loaded in their entirety and thus requiring the execution of non-loaded modules from the main memory.

The first scenario is difficult to avoid since the starting location of a microprogram within the ρ-CONTROL STORE is very much determined by the hashing function. In order to avoid the first scenario, further research must be performed on how to define the hashing function given a certain set of microprograms. The second scenario can be more easily avoided using the following two enhancements:

- An additional $fail$ counter (initialized at zero) is added to all the residence table entries. Every time that a microprogram has to be loaded starting from a certain block location and it fails, the $fail$ counter of the corresponding residence table entry is incremented with a constant that is greater than one. The next time the same microprogram must be loaded, the microprogram is loaded into $fail$ block locations higher than indicated by the residence table entry. In this way, the chance of a microprogram not being loaded in its entirety will decrease.
- Allow microprograms that reach the end of the ρ-CONTROL STORE to wrap around and continue loading from the first block location.

4.3   The *Evict* Loading Method

In the previous section, we have discussed the *straight* method of loading microprograms that does not take into account that some microprograms might be used more frequently than others. In this section, we propose the *evict* loading method which evicts less frequently used microprograms in order to create more storage space when loading a new microprogram. Again, the same assumptions as for the *straight* method apply here. The *evict* microprogram loading method is described as follows:

1. Determine the next possible empty block to start loading the microprogram by:
   - determining the first unused block in the ρ-CONTROL STORE.
   - if this is not possible, determine the least recently used block.
2. Load the first module into the indicated block until:
   - an *end_op* instruction is encountered in the microprogram. In this case, stop loading.
3. Consider the remainder of the microprogram as a new microprogram with the module following the lastly loaded module as the first module of the new microprogram. Continue with step 1.

While the approach remains simple, the actual implementation of the *evict* method is much more complex. This is due to the fact that the location of microprogram modules in the main memory is addressed by the memory address of the first microinstruction of such modules. Therefore, when a microprogram is split into several pieces inside the ρ-CONTROL STORE, the memory addresses of the first microinstruction within the modules must be kept. Furthermore, when executing jumps within a microprogram, additional accesses to the residence table must be performed to determine the correct ρ-CONTROL STORE block to jump to. In addition, another table next to the residence table must be introduced, which is called the occupancy table. The following describes what information must be kept inside both tables:

- OCCUPANCY TABLE: This table is indexed by ρ-CONTROL STORE addresses and contains as many entries as there are ρ-CONTROL STORE blocks. Each entry contains the following information:
    - occupancy bit: this bit indicates whether the associated ρ-CONTROL STORE block is in use or not.
    - LRU: this contains the least recently used information.
- RESIDENCE TABLE: In the *evict* loading method, no hashing function is performed anymore before the residence table. It contains as many entries as there are ρ-CONTROL STORE blocks. The residence table is mainly used to store translations of memory addresses to ρ-CONTROL STORE addresses. The following information is kept per entry:
    - α: memory address. This address indicates from which memory location the microprogram was fetched.
    - ρCS-α: ρ-CONTROL STORE address. This address indicates to which block in the ρ-CONTROL STORE the microprogram module is loaded.
    - α_{next}: next memory address. This address indicates where to jump to in case that the loaded microprogram does not contain the *end_op* instruction.

In order to further explain the *evict* loading method, we discuss an example which loads a microprogram and also executes this microprogram. The following assumptions are made:

- The microprogram has a length of 10 modules (starting with module 1). The memory addresses of the modules i are α_i.
- Module 4 contains a conditional branch to module 9.
- Module 10 contains a conditional branch to module 5.

Loading the microprogram. The loading of the microprogram is performed as follows:

1. Determine the next possible block into which we can start loading. This is assumed to be ρCS-α_1.
2. Start loading the microprogram into the ρ-CONTROL STORE in block ρCS-α_1.
3. The occupancy table must be updated to reflect the used/occupied block. Furthermore, in the residence table an entry is made which contains at least the following information:

- α_1: the memory address of the first microinstruction of the microprogram.
- ρCS-α_1: the ρ-CONTROL STORE block address.
- $\alpha_{next} = \alpha_2$: The memory address of the microinstruction which starts the remainder of the microprogram, if exist.

4. If the *end_op* microinstruction was not encountered, assume the remaining microprogram to be a new microprogram starting at α_2, which is the address of the first instruction of the next module. Perform steps 1 through 4 for the remaining modules until all 10 modules are loaded.

In essence, the residence table is used to store both the 'memory address to ρ-CONTROL STORE address'-translations and link these modules using α_{next}. It must be noted that in the case that the ρ-CONTROL STORE is smaller than the to be loaded microprogram, earlier loaded modules will be overwritten. This results in a performance penalty, since at the time that these modules are needed, they must be either executed or loaded again from the main memory.

Executing the microprogram. The execution starts by performing a search inside the residence table for the memory addres in order to determine the residence table entry containing the ρ-CONTROL STORE address. The execution starts from the location indicated by the ρ-CONTROL STORE address. The execution of the microprogram is not fully described as no specifics on the micro-program were given. However, some key points during execution (especially considering the conditional branches) are discussed:

- After executing module i, module $i + 1$ must be executed. In this case, α_{next} is used, which corresponds to the memory address of the first microinstruction of the next module, to lookup the ρ-CONTROL STORE block in which the next module is stored.
- If the conditional branch in module 4 decides to jump forward, the next module to be executed is 9. Using the residence table, we can lookup α_9 and find ρCS-α_9.
- If the conditional branch in module 10 decides to jump backwards, the next module to be executed is module 5. Using the residence table, we can lookup α_5 and find ρCS-α_5.

The *evict* loading method has one major performance limiting scenario, namely in the case that a microprogram consists of many modules. In this case, a lot of accesses to the residence table must be made to find the correct module to continue execution.

5   Conclusion

In this paper, we discussed the usage of an extension to microcode to control both the reconfiguration process of reconfigurable hardware and the execution process on such hardware. Furthermore, we suggest that only two new instructions are needed in order to support reconfigurable hardware at the architectural level. We have also presented the MOLEN reconfigurable microcoded processor that utilize an additional instruction in order to also include support for partial reconfigurations. Finally, this paper also discussed the loading of microprograms from the main memory into an on-chip storage facility (the ρ-CONTROL STORE). This is, because it is not practical to store all microprograms on-chip. Two microprogram loading methods, *straight* and *evict*, were proposed and discussed in more detail.

References

1. S. Rathnam and G. Slavenburg, "An Architectural Overview of the Programmable Multimedia Processor, TM-1," in *Proceedings of the COMPCON '96*, pp. 319–326, 1996.
2. D. Cronquist, P. Franklin, C. Fisher, M. Figueroa, and C. Ebeling, "Architecture Design of Reconfigurable Pipelined Datapaths," in *Proceedings of the 20th Anniversary Conference on Advanced Research in VLSI*, pp. 23–40, March 1999.
3. R. Razdan and M. Smith, "A High-Performance Microarchitecture with hardware-programmable Functional Units," in *Proceedings of the 27th Annual International Symposium on Microarchitecture*, pp. 172–180, November 1994.
4. R. Wittig and P. Chow, "OneChip: An FPGA Processor with Reconfigurable Logic," in *Proceedings of the IEEE Symposium on FPGAs for Custom Computing Machines*, pp. 126–135, April 1996.
5. J. Hauser and J. Wawrzynek, "Garp: A MIPS Processor with a Reconfigurable Coprocessor," in *Proceedings of the IEEE Symposium of Field-Programmable Custom Computing Machines*, pp. 24–33, April 1997.
6. "Virtex-II 1.5V FPGA Family: Detailed Functional Description ." http://www.xilinx.com/partinfo/databook.htm.
7. "Nios Embedded Processor." http://www.altera.com/products/devices/excalibur/exc-nios_index.html.
8. S. Vassiliadis, S. Wong, and S. Cotofana, "The MOLEN $\rho\mu$-Coded Processor," in *Proceedings of the 11th Internal Conference on Field-Programmable Logic and Applications (FPL2001)*, pp. 275–285, August 2001.
9. M. V. Wilkes, "The Best Way to Design an Automatic Calculating Machine," in *Report of the Manchester University Computer Inaugural Conference*, pp. 16–18, July 1951.
10. A. Padegs, B. Moore, R. Smith, and W. Buchholz, "The IBM System/370 Vector Architecture: Design Considerations," *IEEE Transactions on Computers*, vol. 37, pp. 509–520, May 1988.
11. G. Triantafyllos, S. Vassiliadis, and J. Delgado-Frias, "Software Metrics and Microcode Development: A Case Study," *Journal of Software Maintenance: Research and Practice*, vol. 8, pp. 199–224, May-June 1996.

A Reconfigurable Functional Unit for TriMedia/CPU64. A Case Study

Mihai Sima[1,2], Sorin Cotofana[1], Stamatis Vassiliadis[1],
Jos T.J. van Eijndhoven[2], and Kees Vissers[3]

[1] Delft University of Technology, Department of Electrical Engineering,
Mekelweg 4, 2628 CD Delft, The Netherlands
{M.Sima,S.D.Cotofana,S.Vassiliadis}@et.tudelft.nl
[2] Philips Research Laboratories, Department of Information and Software Technology,
Professor Holstlaan 4, 5656 AA Eindhoven, The Netherlands
jos.van.eijndhoven@philips.com
[3] TriMedia Technologies, Inc., 1840 McCarthy Boulevard, Milpitas, California 95035, USA
kees.vissers@trimedia.com

Abstract. The paper presents a case study on augmenting a TriMedia/CPU64 processor with a Reconfigurable (FPGA-based) Functional Unit (RFU). We first propose an extension of the TriMedia/CPU64 architecture, which consists of a RFU and its associated instructions. Then, we address the computation of the 8×8 IDCT on such extended TriMedia, and propose a scheme to implement an 8-point IDCT operation on the RFU. Further, we address the decoding of Variable Length Codes and describe the FPGA implementation of a Variable Length Decoder (VLD) computing facility. When mapped on an ACEX EP1K100 FPGA from Altera, our 8-point IDCT exhibits a latency of 16 and a recovery of 2 TriMedia cycles, and occupies 42% of the FPGA's logic array blocks. The proposed VLD exhibits a latency of 7 TriMedia cycles when mapped on the same FPGA, and utilizes 6 of its embedded array blocks. By using the 8-point IDCT computing facility, an 8×8 IDCT including all overheads can be computed with the throughput of 1/32 IDCT/cycle. Also, with the proposed VLD computing facility, a single DCT coefficient can be decoded in 11 cycles including all overheads. Simulation results indicate that by configuring each of the 8-point IDCT and VLD computing facilities on a different FPGA context, and by activating the contexts as needed, the augmented TriMedia can perform MPEG macroblock parsing followed up by a pel reconstruction with an improvement of 20-25% over the standard TriMedia.

1 Introduction

A common issue addressed by computer architects is the range of performance improvements that may be achieved by augmenting a general purpose processor with a reconfigurable core. The basic idea of such approach is to exploit both the general purpose processor capability to achieve medium performance for a large class of applications, and FPGA flexibility to implement application-specific computations. Thus far FPGA-augmented processors have predominantly assumed a simple general purpose core [1,2,3,4]. Considering the class of VLIW machines, two general research questions may be raised:

E.F. Deprettere et al. (Eds.): SAMOS 2001, LNCS 2268, pp. 224–241, 2002.

- What are the influences of reconfigurable arrays on the performance of *commercially available* VLIW processors?
- What are the architectural changes needed for incorporating the reconfigurable array into the processor core?

In an attempt to answer to these questions, we will present a case study on augmenting a TriMedia/CPU64 processor with a Reconfigurable (FPGA-based) Functional Unit (RFU). With such RFU, the user is given the freedom to define and use any computing facility subject to the FPGA size and TriMedia/CPU64 organization. In order to evaluate the potential performance of the augmented TriMedia/CPU64, we chose a significant chunk of MPEG decoding as benchmark. In particular, since the video data accounts for more than 80% of the whole MPEG bit stream [5], we considered the parsing of Variable-Length (VL) coded data at the macroblock layer followed by a pel reconstruction procedure as benchmark. That is, all the *data elements* corresponding to slice and higher layers are considered as being constants for our experiment.

We decided to provide hardware support for two functions of the selected benchmark: 8-point (1-D) Inverse Discrete Cosine Transform (IDCT) and Variable-Length Decoder (VLD). By developing VHDL code and mapping it with Altera tools, we evaluated the performance of these FPGA-based functions. Further, a program which is MPEG-compliant has been written in C, and then compiled, scheduled and finally simulated with TriMedia tool-chain. For a typical MPEG string with 10% intra-coded, 70% B-coded, and 20% P-coded macroblocks, we found that the augmented TriMedia/CPU64 can perform macroblock parsing followed up by a pel reconstruction with an improvement of 20-25 % over the standard TriMedia. Given the fact that TriMedia/CPU64 is a 5 issue-slot VLIW processor with 64-bit datapaths and a very rich multimedia instruction set, such an improvement within the target media processing domain indicates that the hybrid TriMedia/CPU64 + FPGA is a feasible approach.

The paper is organized as follows. For background purposes, we briefly present several issues concerning MPEG and the FPGA architecture in Section 2. Section 3 describes the architectural extension of TriMedia/CPU64. Implementation issues related to 1-D IDCT and VLD computing facilities and their corresponding instructions are discussed in Sections 4 and 5. The 8×8 IDCT and entropy decoder implementations are then described in Sections 6 and 7. The execution scenario of the chosen benchmark on both standard and extended TriMedia, and experimental results are presented in Section 8. Section 9 completes the paper with some conclusions and closing remarks.

2   Background

Data compression is the reduction of redundancy in data representation, carried out for decreasing data storage requirements and data communication costs. A typical video codec system is presented in Figure 1 [5,6]. The lossy source coder performs filtering, transformation (such as DCT, subband decomposition, or differential pulse-code modulation), quantization, etc. The output of the source coder still exhibits various kinds of statistical dependencies. The (lossless) entropy coder exploits the statistical properties of data and removes the remaining redundancy after the lossy coding.

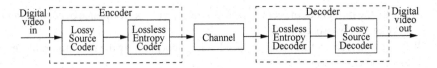

Fig. 1. The block diagram of a generic video codec – adapted from [6,5].

In MPEG, the DCT-Quantization pair is used as a lossy coding technique. The DCT algorithm processes the video data in blocks of 8×8, decomposing each block into a weighted sum of 64 spatial frequencies. At the output of DCT, the data is also organized in 8×8 blocks of coefficients, each coefficient representing the contribution of a spatial frequency for the video block being analyzed. Since the human eye cannot readily perceive high spatial frequency activity, a quantization step is carried out. The goal is to force as many DCT coefficients as possible to zero within the boundaries of the prescribed video quality. Then, a zig-zag operation transforms the matrix into a vector in which the coefficients are ordered from the lowest frequencies to the higher ones. The subsequent compression step is carried out by the entropy coder which consists of two major parts: Run-Length Coder (RLC) and Variable-Length Coder (VLC). The RLC represents consecutive zeros by their run lengths. Since not each and every zero is coded, the number of samples is reduced. The RLC output data are composite words, also referred to as *source symbols*, which describe pairs of zero-run lengths and quantized DCT coefficient values. When all the remaining coefficients in a vector are zero, they are all coded by the special symbol *end-of-block*. Variable length coding, is a mapping process between source symbols and *variable length codewords*. The VLC assigns shorter codewords to frequently occuring source symbols, and vice versa, so that the average bit rate is reduced. In order to achieve maximum compression, no specific guard bits between two consecutive symbols are generated. As a result, decoding procedure must recognize the code length as well as the symbol itself in this case.

Subsequently, we will focus on the MPEG decoding, i.e., on the inverse operation of MPEG coding. Further, we will briefly present the theoretical background of Inverse Discrete Cosine Transform (IDCT), entropy decoding, as well as some issues related to the MPEG standard.

2.1   Inverse Discrete Cosine Transform

The transformation for an N point 1-D IDCT is defined by [7]:

$$x_i = \frac{2}{N} \sum_{u=0}^{N-1} K_u X_u \cos \frac{(2i+1)u\pi}{2N}$$

where X_u are the inputs, x_i are the outputs, and $K_u = \sqrt{1/2}$ for $u = 0$, otherwise is 1. For MPEG, a 2-D IDCT processes an 8×8 matrix X [5]:

$$x_{i,j} = \frac{1}{4} \sum_{u=0}^{7} \sum_{v=0}^{7} K_u K_v X_{u,v} \cos \frac{(2i+1)u\pi}{16} \cos \frac{(2j+1)v\pi}{16}$$

One strategy to compute the 2-D IDCT is the standard row-column separation: an 1-D transform is computed for each row (horizontal IDCTs) and subsequently for each column (vertical IDCTs) of the data matrix. This strategy can be combined with different 1-D IDCT algorithms to further reduce the computational complexity. One of the most efficient 1-D IDCT algorithms has been proposed by Loeffler [8]. A slightly different version of the Loeffler algorithm in which the $\sqrt{2}$ factors are moved around has been proposed by van Eijndhoven and Sijstermans [9]. In our experiment, we will use this modified algorithm (see Figure 2).

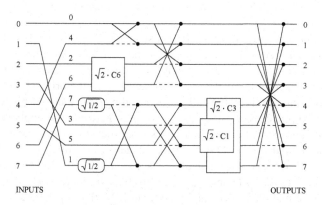

Fig. 2. The modified 'Loeffler' algorithm – from [9].

In the Figure, the round block signifies a multiplication by $C_0' = \sqrt{1/2}$. The butterfly block and the associated equations are presented in Figure 3.

$$O_0 = I_0 + I_1$$
$$O_1 = I_0 - I_1$$

Fig. 3. The butterfly – from [8].

A square block depicts a rotation which transforms a pair $[I_0, I_1]$ into $[O_0, O_1]$. The symbol of a rotator and the associated equations are presented in Figure 4. Although an implementation of such a rotator with three multiplications and three additions is possible [8], we use the direct implementation of the rotator with four multiplications and two additions, since it shortens critical path and improves numerical accuracy. Therefore, multiplications by constants C_0', C_1', S_1', C_3', S_3', C_6', and S_6' have to be carried out. For more details regarding this problem, we refer the reader to the bibliography [10].

2.2 Entropy Decoder

In MPEG, the entropy decoder consists a Variable-Length Decoder (VLD) followed by a Run-Length Decoder (RLD). The input to the VLD is the incoming encoded bit stream,

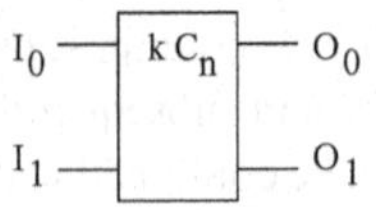

$$I_0 \longrightarrow \boxed{k\,C_n} \longrightarrow O_0 \qquad O_0 = I_0 k \cos \frac{n\pi}{16} - I_1 k \sin \frac{n\pi}{16} = C'_n I_0 - S'_n I_1$$

$$I_1 \longrightarrow \phantom{\boxed{k\,C_n}} \longrightarrow O_1 \qquad O_1 = I_0 k \sin \frac{n\pi}{16} + I_1 k \cos \frac{n\pi}{16} = S'_n I_0 + C'_n I_1$$

Fig. 4. The rotator – [8].

and the output is the decoded symbols. Since the code length of the symbol is variable, both the input and output bit rate of a VLD cannot be kept constant. Three different decoder types are possible [6]: constant input rate, constant output rate, and variable input-output rate.

The *constant-input-rate* VLD decodes a fixed number of bits and produces a variable number of symbols per cycle. An example of such decoder which decodes one bit per cycle is described in [11]. The decoder employs a binary tree search technique in which a token is propagated in a reverse tree constructed from the original codes. Although some improvements of this method allow for decoding more than one bit per cycle [12], the tree-based approaches are not suitable for high performance applications such as high-definition television, because high clock rate processing is needed.

A *constant-output-rate* VLD decodes one codeword (symbol) per cycle regardless of its length [13]. Generally speaking, a constant-output-rate VLD contains a look-up table which receives the variable-length code itself as the address. The decoded symbol (run-level pair or end-of-block) and the codeword length are generated in response to that address. Since the longest codeword excluding Escape has 17 bits, the LUT size could reach 131072 ($= 2^{17}$) words for a direct mapping of all possible codewords.

A *variable-input-output-rate* VLD is a mixture of the first two VLDs. It is implemented as a repeated table look-up, each step decoding a variable size chunk of bits. If a valid code was encountered, a run/level pair or an end-of-block is generated. If a miss is detected, a chunk size for the next look-up is generated. In this way, the short (most probable) are preferentially decoded. A variable-input-output-rate VLD exhibits an acceptable decoding throughput, while the size of the look-up table is resonable small.

The run-length decoder passes the VLC-decoded codewords through if they are not run-length codes, otherwise it outputs the specified number of zeros.

2.3   Macroblock Parsing and Pel Reconstruction

The macroblock parsing process reads the VL coded data string from which all the headers corresponding to slice and higher layers have been removed, and outputs various symbols: *decoding parameters* at the macroblock layer (*macroblock_address_increment, macroblock_type, coded_block_pattern*, and *quantizer_scale*), *motion values*, and *composite symbols* (*run/level* pairs and *end_of_block*). The decoding of the Variable-Length Codes (VLC) is performed according to a set of VLC tables defined by the MPEG standard. The motion values are used by a motion compensation process which is not considered here. However, since these values are decoded during the macroblock parsing, the overhead associated with the decoding of the motion values will be taken into consideration in the subsequent experiment.

Following the macroblock parsing, a pel reconstruction process recreates 8×8 matrices of pels. The pel reconstruction module is depicted in Figure 5. Its functionality is as follows. First, 8×8 matrices of DCT quantized coefficients are recreated by a Matrix Reconstruction module. Second, an inverse quantization (InvQ) is performed. An 8×8 quantization table, and a multiplicative quantization factor (*quantizer_scale*) are used in the InvQ process. Third, a DC prediction unit reconstructs the DC coefficient in intra-coded macroblocks. Finally, an IDCT is performed. In connection with Figure 5 and the subsequent experiment, we would like to mention that the VLC decoder and IDCT will benefit from reconfigurable hardware support.

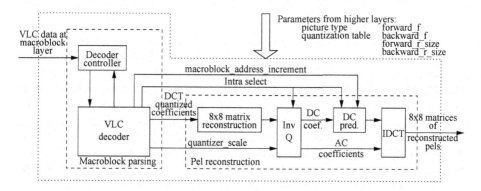

Fig. 5. Macroblock parsing and pel reconstruction module – adapted from [5].

We conclude this section with a review on the architecture of the FPGA we used as an experimental reconfigurable core.

2.4   The FPGA Architecture

Field-Programmable Gate Arrays (FPGA) [14] are devices which can be configured *in the field* by the end user. In a general view, an FPGA is composed of two constituents: *Raw Hardware* and *Configuration Memory*. The function performed by the raw hardware is defined by the information stored into the configuration memory. Generally speaking, a multiple-context FPGA [15] is an FPGA having the configuration memory replicated in order to contain several configurations for the raw hardware. That is, a multiple-context FPGA contains an on-chip cache of raw hardware configurations, which are referred to as *contexts*. Such a cache allows a context switch to occur on the order of nanoseconds [16]. However, loading a new configuration from off-chip is still limited by low off-chip bandwidth.

In the sequel, we will assume that the architecture of the raw hardware is identical with that of an ACEX 1K device from Altera [17]. Our choice could allow future single-chip integration, since both ACEX 1K FPGAs and TriMedia are manufactured in the same TSMC technological process. Briefly, an ACEX 1K device contains an array of Logic Cells, each including a 4-input Look-Up Table (LUT), a relative small number of

Embedded Array Blocks, each EAB being actually a RAM block with 8 inputs and 16 outputs, and an interconnection network. In order to have a general view, we mention that the logic capacity of the ACEX 1K family ranges from 576 logic cells and 3 EABs for EP1K10 device to 4992 logic cells and 12 EABs for EP1K100 device. The maximum operating frequency for synchronous designs mapped on an ACEX 1K FPGA is 180 MHz. More details regarding the architecture and operating modes of ACEX 1K devices, as well as data sheet parameters can be found in [17].

3 An Architectural Extension for TriMedia/CPU64

TriMedia/CPU64 is a 64-bit 5 issue-slot VLIW core [18], launching a long instruction every clock cycle. It has a uniform 64-bit wordsize through all functional units, the register file, load/store units, on-chip highway and external memory. Each of the five operations in a single instruction can (in principle) read two register arguments and write one register result. The architecture supports subword parallelism and is optimized with respect to media processing. With the exception of floating point divide and square root, all functional units have a recovery[1] of 1, while their latency[2] ranges from 1 to 4. The TriMedia/CPU64 VLIW core also supports multi-slot operations, or super-operations. Such a super-operation occupies two neighboring slots in the VLIW instruction, and maps to a double-width functional unit. This way, operations with more than 2 arguments and/or more than one result are possible.

First we propose that the TriMedia/CPU64 processor is augmented with a Reconfigurable Functional Unit (RFU) which consists mainly of a multiple-context FPGA core. A hardwired Configuration Unit which manages the reconfiguration of the raw hardware is associated to the reconfigurable functional unit, as it is depicted in Figure 6. The reconfigurable functional unit is embedded into TriMedia as any other hardwired functional unit is, i.e., it receives instructions from the instruction decoder, reads its input arguments from and writes the computed values back to the register file. In this way, only minimal modifications of the basic architecture are required.

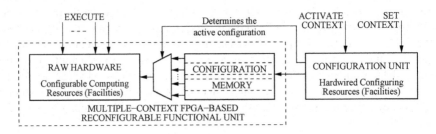

Fig. 6. The organization of the RFU and associated configuration unit.

---

[1] Minimum number of clock cycles between the issue of successive operations.
[2] Clock cycles between the issue of an operation and availability of its results.

In order to use the RFU, a kernel of new instructions is needed. This kernel constitutes the extension of the TriMedia/CPU64 instruction set architecture we propose. It
includes the following instructions: SET_CONTEXT, ACTIVATE_CONTEXT, and EXECUTE.
Loading a context information into the RFU configuration memory is performed under
the command of a SET_CONTEXT instruction. The ACTIVATE_CONTEXT instruction controls the swaping of the active configuration with one of the idle on-chip configuration.
The operations performed by the computing resources configured on the raw hardware
are launched by EXECUTE instructions. In this way, the execution of an RFU-mapped
operation requires three basic stages: set, activate, and execute [19].

The user is given a set of EXECUTE instructions encompassing different operation
patterns: single- or double-slot operations, operations with an immediate argument, etc.
It is the user responsibility to choose the appropriate EXECUTE instruction corresponding
to the pattern of the operation to be executed. At the source code level, this may be done
by setting up an *alias*, as it is described subsequently. Since the EXECUTE instructions
are executed on the RFU without checking of the active configuration, it is still the user
responsibility to perform the management of the active and idle configurations.

For the semantics of an operation performed by a computing facility, its latency,
recovery, and slot assignment are all user definable, the source code of the application
should contain information to augment the Machine Description File [20]. Assuming for
example a user-defined VLD instruction, a way to specify such information is to annotate
the source code as follows:

.alias	VLD	EXEC_3	; specifies the alias EXECUTE_3
			; (super-op with two inputs and outputs)
.latency	VLD	7	; specifies the VLD latency
.recovery	VLD	7	; specifies the VLD recovery
.slot	VLD	1+2	; specifies the slot assignment of the VLD instruction

In a similar way, the user can define as many RFU-related instructions as he/she wants.

The next section will present the sintax and semantics of the 1-D IDCT and VLD
instructions, as well as implementation issues of the corresponding computing facilities.

4   1-D IDCT Instruction and Computing Facility

Since the standard TriMedia provides a good support for transposition and matrix storage,
we expect to get little benefit if we configure the entire 2-D IDCT into FPGA. Our goal is
to balance the cost of storing the intermediate 2-D IDCT results into an FPGA-resident
transpose matrix memory against obtaining free slots into TriMedia. Consequently, only
a super-operation computing the 1-D IDCT of eight 16-bit values packed in two 64-bit
registers is considered. The sintax of such operation is:

1-D_IDCT   Rx, Ry → Rz, Rw

where the registers Rx and Ry specify the inputs, and Rz and Rw, the outputs. All registers
Rx, Ry, Rz, and Rw encompass the common format presented in Table 1.

Table 1. 1-D_IDCT – The common format of registers Rx, Ry, Rz, and Rw (vec64sh).

Field name	Acronym	Width (bit)	Position (bit)	Type (TriMedia)	Range	Description
1st value	–	16	63...48	int16	–	–
2nd value	–	16	47...32	int16	–	–
3rd value	–	16	31...16	int16	–	–
4th value	–	16	15...0	int16	–	–

Since there are no dependencies in computing the 1-D IDCT on each row (column) of the 8×8 matrix, a pipelined 1-D IDCT is desirable. A recovery of 1 of such computing resource implies that the FPGA clock frequency is equal with the TriMedia clock frequency. Nowadays, the current TriMedia clock frequency is greater than 200 MHz, while the maximum allowable clock frequency for ACEX 1K is 180 MHz. Therefore, an 1-D IDCT hypothetical implementation having a recovery of 1 is not a realistic scenario, and a recovery of 2 or more is mandatory for the time being. In the sequel, we will assume a recovery of 2 for 1-D IDCT and a 200 MHz TriMedia. This implies that the pipelined implementation of 1-D IDCT will work with 100 MHz clock frequency.

All the operations required to compute 1-D IDCT are implemented using 16-bit fixed-point arithmetic. Since an implementation of the rotator with four multiplications is preferred [10], the computation of 1-D IDCT requires 14 multiplications. As all the multiplications are to be performed in parallel, an efficient implementation of each multiplication is of crucial importance. For all multiplications, the multiplicand is a 16-bit signed integer represented in 2's complement notation, while the multiplier is a positive integer constant of 15 bits or less. As claimed in [21], these word lengths in connection with fixed-point arithmetic are sufficient to fulfill the IEEE numerical accuracy for IDCT in MPEG applications [22].

A general multiplication scheme for which both multiplicand and multiplier operands are unknown at the implementation time exhibits the largest flexibility at the expenses of higher latency and larger area. If one of the operands is known at the implementation time, the flexibility of the general scheme becomes useless, and a customized implementation of the scheme will lead to improved latency and area. A scheme which is optimized against one of the operands is referred to as *multiplication-by-constant*. Since such a scheme is more appropriate for our application, we will use it subsequently.

To implement the multiplication-by-constant scheme, we built a partial product matrix, where only the rows corresponding to a '1' in the multiplier operand are filled in. Then, reduction schemes which fit into a pipeline stage running at 100 MHz are sought. It should be emphasized that a reduction algorithm which is optimum on a certain FPGA family may not be optimum for a different family.

In connection with the partial product matrix, reduction modules which can run at 100 MHz when mapped on an ACEX 1K are presented in Figure 7. All the designs are synchronous, i.e., both inputs and outputs are registered. The estimations have been obtained by compiling VHDL source codes with Leonardo Spectrum™ from Exemplar, followed by a place and route procedure performed by MAX+PLUS II™ from Altera. The 100 MHz reduction modules are summarized below:

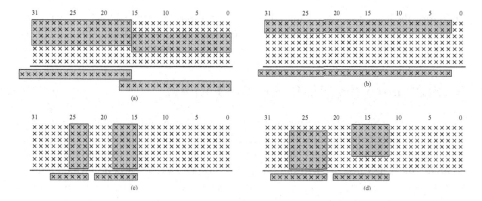

Fig. 7. 100 MHz reduction modules on ACEX 1K.

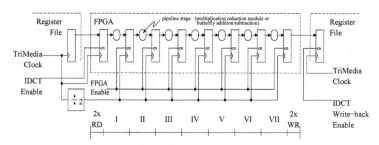

Fig. 8. The 1-D IDCT pipeline

- Horizontal reductions of three, or four 16-bit lines to one line (Fig. 7 – a).
- Horizontal reduction of only two 30-bit lines to one line (Fig. 7 – b).
- Vertical reductions of three or four 7-bit columns to one line (Fig. 7 – c).
- Vertical reductions of six 5- or 6-bit columns to one line (Fig. 7 – d).

We do not go into details about the implementations of the multipliers and we refer the reader to [10]. We still mention the latency of each multiplier: $\times C_0'$ latency $= 2$, $\times C_1'$ latency $= 3$, $\times S_1'$ latency $= 3$, $\times C_3'$ latency $= 3$, $\times S_3'$ latency $= 3$, $\times C_6'$ latency $= 3$, $\times S_6'$ latency $= 2$, where the constants C_n', and S_n' have the meaning as in Figure 4.

The sketch of the 1-D IDCT pipeline is depicted in Figure 8 (the Roman numerals specify the pipeline stages). Considering the critical path, the latency of the 1-D IDCT is composed of:

- one TriMedia cycle for reading the input operands from the register file into the input flip-flops of the 1-D IDCT computing resource;
- two FPGA cycles for computing the multiplication by constant C_0';
- one FPGA cycle for computing all additions to rotators $\sqrt{2}C_1$ and $\sqrt{2}C_3$.
- three FPGA cycles for computing the multiplication by constant C_1';
- one FPGA cycle for computing the additions in the last stage of the transform;
- one TriMedia cycle for writing back the results from the output flip-flops of the 1-D IDCT computing resource into the register file.

Therefore, the latency of the 8-point 1-D IDCT operation is $1+(2+1+3+1)\times2+1 = 16$ TriMedia cycles. We evaluated that 1-D IDCT uses 42% of the logic elements of an ACEX EP1K100 device and 257 I/O pins from a total of 333.

5   VLD Instruction and Computing Facility

As mentioned in Section 3, computing resources which can perform rather complex operations are worth to be implemented on the RFU. Also, as with all hardwired computing resources, the latency of an RFU-configured computing resource should be known at compile time. Therefore, we will subsequently consider a VLD instruction which returns a DCT symbol (*run/level* pair or *end-of-block*) per execution. That is, a constant-output-rate VLD is to be employed. With such decoder, no benefits from preferentially decoding the short (most probable) codewords can be achieved.

A super-operation pattern with two input (Rx, Ry) and two output (Rz, Rw) registers is assigned to the variable-length decoder:

$$\textbf{VLD}\ \ \textbf{Rx, Ry} \rightarrow \textbf{Rz, Rw}$$

The Rx register specifies the decoding parameters which identify the type of the symbol to be decoded: AC/DC, luminance/chrominance, intra/non-intra, MPEG-1/MPEG-2, and B14/B15 decoding table [5]. The second register, Ry, contains the first 64 bits of the VL compressed string. The decoded symbol and its code length will be stored into registers Rz and Rw, respectively. Since the VLD does not know the start of the next variable-length codeword until the current codeword is decoded, a new **VLD** operation can be launched only after the previous one has completed. Consequently, a recovery lower than the latency gives no advantages, and such implementation should not be sought. The formats of the registers Rx, Ry, Rz, Rw are shown in Tables 2, 3, 4, and 5.

Table 2. VLD-1 – The format of the first argument (parameter) register – Rx (`uint32`).

Field name	Acronym	Width (bit)	Position (bit)	Type (TriMedia)	Range	Description
Decoding parameters	dec_param	32	31...0	uint32	–	
Not used	–	27	31...5	n.a.	n.a.	
MPEG standard	mpeg_s	1	4	bit	$\{0,1\}$	= 1 for MPEG-2
Intra VLC format	i_vlc_f	1	3	bit	$\{0,1\}$	= 0 for B14 table
Intra/PB	intra_pb	1	2	bit	$\{0,1\}$	= 1 for intra macroblock
Luma/Chroma	y_c	1	1	bit	$\{0,1\}$	= 1 for luminance
DC/AC Coefficient	dc_ac	1	0	bit	$\{0,1\}$	= 1 for DC coefficient

Conceptually, a constant-output-rate VLD computes the codeword length by looking-up the 17 leading bits of the incoming stream into a table. Then, the VLD sends the code length and the leading bits to other circuitry to determine the *run* and *level* and immediately shifts the incoming stream by a number of bits equal with *code length*. When the number of the codewords is large, long VLCs exhibit common leading bits,

Table 3. VLD-1 – The format of the second argument register – Ry (uint64).

Field name	Acronym	Width (bit)	Position (bit)	Type (TriMedia)	Range	Description
MPEG string	–	64	63...0	uint64	n.a.	The first bit of the MPEG string is the most-significant bit

Table 4. VLD-1 – The format of the returned value in register Rz (vec64ub).

Field name	Acronym	Width (bit)	Position (bit)	Type (TriMedia)	Range	Description
Not used		32	63...32	*any*	n.a.	
Level	level	16	31...16	int16	–	Extracted as two uint8.
Run	run	8	15...8	uint8	–	
Code-length	code_length	8	7...0	uint8	–	

Table 5. VLD-1 – The format of the returned value in register Rw (vec64ub).

Field name	Acronym	Width (bit)	Position (bit)	Type (TriMedia)	Range	Description
Not used	–	32	63...32	*any*	n.a.	
Not used	–	8	31...24	uint8	n.a.	
Exit controls	–	8	23...16	uint8	–	
valid_decode	valid_decode	1	19	bit	$\{0,1\}$	= 1 when valid decode
error	error	1	18	bit	$\{0,1\}$	= 1 when error
EOB	EOB	1	17	bit	$\{0,1\}$	= 1 when end-of-block
exit_flag	exit_flag_1	1	16	bit	$\{0,1\}$	= 1 when exit condition
Not used	–	8	15...8	uint8	n.a.	
Exit flag	–	8	7...0	uint8	$\{0,1\}$	
exit_flag	exit	1	1	bit	$\{0,1\}$	= 1 exit condition

called *prefix*es. By exploiting these common prefixes, the size of the LUT can be reduced because the prefixes are no longer redundant in the LUT [23,24]. The basic idea is to group the VLCs by their common prefixes, and to provide a LUT for for each and every group, which can decode the codewords in the corresponding group.

Since a single EAB of an ACEX 1K device can implement a lookup table of 8 inputs, we partitioned the VLC table according to this FPGA architectural characteristic, as presented in Table 6.

In order to reduce the latency, the implementation of the VLD makes use of advanced computation. The run and level for each and every group were decoded in parallel, as the valid symbol would belong to that group. In parallel, the code length of the symbol along with some *selection signals* are determined. Then, the selection of the proper run and level pair is carried out. The sketch of the implementation is presented in Figure 9.

Table 6. The partitioning of the VLC codes of AC coefficients into groups and classes.

Name of the group	No. of symbols in the class	Class / Leading bit-sequence	Code length	Bypassed bit-sequence	Effective address length
DC Group 0	2	1	1 + s	–	n.a.
End-of-block	1	10	2	–	n.a.
AC Group 0	2	11	2 + s	–	n.a.
Escape	1	0000 01	6 + 18/(14,22)	–	n.a.
Group 1	2	011	3 + s	0	3
	4	010	4 + s		4
	4	0011	5 + s		5
	2	0010 1	5 + s		5
	8	0001	6 + s		6
	8	0000 1	7 + s		7
	16	0010 0	8 + s		8
Group 2	16	0000 001	10 + s	0000 00	5
	32	0000 0001	12 + s		7
	32	0000 0000 1	13 + s		8
Group 3	32	0000 0000 01	14 + s	0000 0000 0	6
	32	0000 0000 001	15 + s		7
	32	0000 0000 0001	16 + s		8

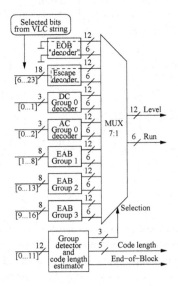

Fig. 9. The VLD implementation sketch.

Regarding the groups 1, 2, and 3, one, six, and nine leading bits are shifted out from the original VLC string, respectively. The three resulted strings are each sent to a different EAB, and three run/level pairs are generated as if the shifted leading bits would have been those mentioned in the column *Bypassed header*. By means of combinatorial circuits, the same procedure is carried out for groups 0, end-of-block, and escape.

Each of the leading bit-sequence which define the VLC class is decoded by a multiple-input gate. Once the class is detected, a multiplexer will select the proper output from the outputs of EABs, EOB detector, Escape detector, and Group 0 decoding. The code length of the decoded symbol is generated according to the detected class.

By simulation, we found that the FPGA-based VLD operation exhibits a latency of 7 TriMedia cycles. 6 EABs of an ACEX EP1K100 device are used.

6 8×8 IDCT

The functionality of the 8×8 IDCT can be implemented in both software and reconfigurable hardware. We will evaluate their performance subsequently.

8×8 IDCT implementation on standard TriMedia. In the current implementation of the 2-D IDCT on the standard TriMedia/CPU64 architecture, all computations are done with 16-bit values, and make intense use of SIMD-style operations. The 8×8 matrix is stored in sixteen 64-bit words, each containing a half row of four 16-bit elements. Therefore, four 16-bit elements can be processed in parallel by a single word-wide operation. Next to that, being a 5-issue slot VLIW processor, TriMedia/CPU64 can execute 5 such operations per clock cycle.

This strategy is used for both the horizontal and vertical IDCTs. First, eight 1-D IDCTs (two SIMD 1-D IDCTs) are computed using the modified 'Loeffler' algorithm [9]. Then, the transpose of the 8×8 matrix is performed by a transpose unit which covers a double issue slot. A TRANSPOSE super-operation can generate the upper respectively lower two words of a transposed 4×4 matrix in one cycle. Therefore, the 8×8 matrix transpose is computed in eight basic operations. Finally, eight 1-D IDCTs (two SIMD 1-D IDCTs) are computed with the results generated by the transposition as inputs. Following the described procedure, a complete 2-D IDCT including all overheads (mostly composed of load and store operations) can be performed in 56 cycles [18].

8×8 IDCT implementation on extended TriMedia. As described in Section 4, a super-operation which can compute the 1-D IDCT on eight 16-bit values represented as two 64-bit words is available in extended TriMedia. The 1-D IDCT operation has a latency of 16, a recovery of 2, and can be issued on the slot pair 1+2. To calculate the 2-D IDCT, eight 1-D IDCT are firstly computed. Then, eight TRANSPOSE super-operations are scheduled on the slot pairs 1+2 or 3+4 to transpose the 8×8 matrix. Finally, eight 1-D IDCTs complete the 2-D IDCT. Before and after each 2-D IDCT, LOAD and STORE operations fetch the input operands from main memory into register file, and store the results back into memory, respectively.

In order to keep the pipeline full, back-to-back 1-D IDCT operation is needed. That is, a new 1-D IDCT instruction has to be issued every two cycles. Since true dependencies forbid issuing the last eight 1-D IDCTs of a 2-D IDCT so that to fulfill back-to-back requirement, the 2-D IDCTs are processed in chunks of two, in an interleaved fashion. A number of $2 \times 16 = 32$ registers are needed for this interleaved processing pattern. The code was manually scheduled. We found that the computational performance of 2-D IDCT exhibited a throughput of $1/32$ IDCT/cycle and a latency of 42 cycles [10].

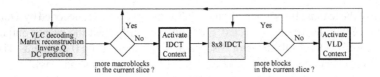

Fig. 10. The computing scenario of the macroblock parsing and pel reconstruction routine.

7 Entropy Decoder

The functionality of the entropy decoder can be implemented in both software and reconfigurable hardware. We will evaluate their performance subsequently.

Entropy decoder implementation on standard TriMedia. The implementation of the entropy decoder on standard TriMedia is a modified version of that proposed in [25]. The VLD has variable input-output rate, and is implemented as a repeated table-lookup. Each lookup decodes a chunk of bits, and determines if a valid code has been encountered. In case of a valid decode, a run-level pair is generated, or an escape or end-of-block flag is set. If a *miss* is detected, an offset into the VLC table and a chunk-size for a second-level lookup is generated. This process of signaling an incomplete decode and generating a new offset may be repeated up to three times. When a valid symbol has been encountered, it is stored into the 8×8 matrix at the location defined by the *run* value. After compiling the C code and performing the scheduling procedure, we evaluated that a table lookup takes 21 cycles. Consequently, the entropy decoding of a single DCT coefficient may take between 21 and 63 cycles. The size of all lookup tables is 10 KB.

Entropy decoder implementation on extended TriMedia. In this approach, the entropy decoder benefits on a VLD super-operation which returns a *run-level* pair or an *end-of-block*. By employing software pipelining techniques, useful computations for run-length decoding may be scheduled in the delay slots of the VLD operation. That is, the 8×8 empty matrix is successively filled in with *level* values at the positions specified by *run* values. In this way, a symbol is processed completely in one iteration. By simulation, we evaluated that a single DCT coefficient can be decoded in 11 cycles including all overheads.

8 Experimental Results

In order to determine the potential impact on performance provided by the multiple-context reconfigurable core, we will consider a benchmark consisting of a macroblock parsing followed by pel reconstruction procedure. Therefore, we operate at MPEG slice level, i.e., the *data elements* on slice and above layers are assumed to be constants. The computing scenario is presented in Figure 10. First, a variable-length decoding of a macroblock (header and DCT coefficients extraction) is performed. Then, the 8×8 matrices are recreated, and inverse quantization followed by DC coefficient prediction for intra-coded macroblocks are carried out. After all macroblocks in a slice have

```
.alias   VLD              EXEC_3  ; alias of the VLD instruction
.alias   IDCT             EXEC_3  ; alias of the IDCT instruction
         SET_CONTEXT      VLD     ; load context VLD
         SET_CONTEXT      IDCT    ; load context IDCT
...
         ACTIVATE_CONTEXT VLD     ; configure VLD resource
...
         VLD Rx, Ry → Rz, Rw      ; execute VLD
...
         ACTIVATE_CONTEXT IDCT    ; configure IDCT resource
...
         IDCT Rx, Ry → Rz, Rw     ; execute IDCT
...
```

Fig. 11. The extended TriMedia/CPU64 sample code.

been decoded, a burst of 2-D IDCTs is launched in order to reconstruct the initial pels. During computation, the 1-D IDCT and VLD computing resources are activated by an ACTIVATE_CONTEXT instruction, as needed. All the contexts of the RFU are configured at application load time, i.e., a number of SET_CONTEXT instructions are scheduled on the top of the program code. A code sample using the instructions of the architectural extension is presented in Figure 11. As it can be observed, the VLD and IDCT exhibit the same execution pattern: two inputs and two outputs.

Therefore, our experiment includes two approaches: *pure software* and *FPGA-based*. As mentioned, a DCT coefficient is decoded in 21-63 cycles, and a 2-D IDCT can be computed in 56 cycles in the pure software approach. In the FPGA-based approach, a DCT coefficient is decoded in 11 cycles, and the 2-D IDCT is carried out with the throughput of 1/32 IDCT/cycle. Based on the published work in the field of multiple-context FPGAs [16], we make a conservative assumption and consider that the context switching penality is 10 cycles.

8.1 Pel Reconstruction Performance Evaluation

A program which is MPEG-compliant has been written in C, compiled and scheduled with TriMedia development tools. The performance evaluation has been done assuming that, despite of the large lookup tables which are stored into memory, the standard TriMedia/CPU64 will never cope with a cache miss. In other words, we compare an 'ideal-cache" standard TriMedia with a multiple-context FPGA-augmented TriMedia.

We will present the results according to two scenarios: *worst-case*[3] and *average-case*. In both cases we assumed an average of 5 non-zero DCT coefficients per block. In the worst-case scenario, we assumed that all DCT coefficients produce a *hit* on the first level lookup for the pure software implementation. In the same worst-case scenario, we also assumed that the overhead introduced by parsing the macroblock headers has the largest value (for example, the quantization value is assumed to be updated every

---

[3] Considered from our point of view.

Table 7. Performance improvements of FPGA-augmented TriMedia/CPU64 over 'ideal-cache" (standard) TriMedia/CPU64 for a macroblock parsing followed by pel reconstruction application.

		Worst-case scenario	Average-case scenario
Intra-coded macroblocks	prior to IDCT	15%	25%
	after IDCT	19%	29%
P-coded macroblocks	prior to IDCT	10%	21%
(1 block / macroblock)	after IDCT	14%	25%
P-coded macroblocks	prior to IDCT	13%	24%
(3 blocks / macroblock)	after IDCT	18%	27%
B-coded macroblocks	prior to IDCT	8%	17%
(1 block / macroblock)	after IDCT	12%	20%
B-coded macroblocks	prior to IDCT	11%	22%
(3 blocks / macroblock)	after IDCT	17%	25%

macroblock). Since the worst-case scenario is statistically not relevant, we evaluated the performances in a average-case scenario. In such scenario, we assumed that two of five DCT coefficients produce a *miss* at the first lookup. Also, we weighted the overhead introduced by parsing the macroblock header with the transmiting probability of different decoding parameters of the macroblock layer. The results are presented in Table 7. The numbers indicate the improvements we get for the number of cycles.

Finally, we proceeded to a global evaluation of the performance improvement. For an MPEG string with 10% intra-coded, 70% B-coded, and 20% P-coded macroblocks, the improvement for augmented TriMedia is $20 - 25\%$ in the average-case scenario.

9   Conclusions

We have proposed an architectural extension for TriMedia/CPU64 which encompasses a multiple-context FPGA-based reconfigurable functional unit and the associated instructions. On the augmented TriMedia, we estimated a performance improvement of $20 - 25\%$ over a standard TriMedia for a macroblock parsing followed by a pel reconstruction application, at the expenses of three new instructions: SET_CONTEXT, ACTIVATE_CONTEXT, EXECUTE. As future work, we intend to consider the motion compensation and to evaluate the improvements for a complete MPEG decoder.

References

1. Razdan, R., Smith, M.D.:   A High Performance Microarchitecture with Hardware-Programmable Functional Units. In: 27th Annual Intl. Symposium on Microarchitecture – MICRO-27, San Jose, California, (1994) 172–180.
2. Wittig, R.D., Chow, P.: OneChip: An FPGA Processor With Reconfigurable Logic. In: IEEE Symposium on FPGAs for Custom Computing Machines, Napa Valley, California, (1996) 126–135.
3. Hauser, J.R., Wawrzynek, J.: Garp: A MIPS Processor with a Reconfigurable Coprocessor. In: IEEE Symposium on FPGAs for Custom Computing Machines, Napa Valley, California, (1997) 12–21.

4. Kastrup, B., Bink, A., Hoogerbrugge, J.: ConCISe: A Compiler-Driven CPLD-Based Instruction Set Accelerator. In: IEEE Symposium on FPGAs for Custom Computing Machines, Napa Valley, California, (1999) 92–100.
5. Mitchell, J.L., Pennebaker, W.B., Fogg, C.E., LeGall, D.J.: MPEG Video Compression Standard. Chapman & Hall, New York, New York (1996).
6. Sun, M.T.: Design of High-Throughput Entropy Codec. In: VLSI Implementations for Image Communications. Volume 2. Elsevier Science Publishers B.V., Amsterdam, The Netherlands (1993) 345–364.
7. Rao, K.R., Yip, P.: Discrete Cosine Transform. Algorithms, Advantages, Applications. Academic Press, San Diego, California (1990).
8. Loeffler, C., Ligtenberg, A., Moschytz, G.S.: Practical Fast 1-D DCT Algorithms with 11 Multiplications. In: Intl. Conference on Acoustics, Speech, and Signal Processing (ICASSP '89), (1989) 988–991.
9. van Eijndhoven, J., Sijstermans, F.: Data Processing Device and method of Computing the Cosine Transform of a Matrix. PCT Patent No. WO 9948025 (1999).
10. Sima, M., Cotofana, S., van Eijndhoven, J.T., Vassiliadis, S., Vissers, K.: 8 × 8 IDCT Implementation on an FPGA-augmented TriMedia. In: IEEE Symposium on FPGAs for Custom Computing Machines, Rohnert Park, California, (2001).
11. Mukherjee, A., Ranganathan, N., Bassiouni, M.: Efficient VLSI Design for Data Transformation of Tree-Based Codes. IEEE Transactions on Circuits and Systems **38** (1991) 306–314.
12. Kinouchi, S., Sawada, A.: Variable Length Code Decoder. U.S. Patent No. 6,069,575 (2000).
13. Lei, S.M., Sun, M.T.: An Entropy Coding System for Digital HDTV Applications. IEEE Transactions on Circuits and Systems for Video Technology **1** (1991) 147–155.
14. Brown, S., Rose, J.: Architecture of FPGAs and CPLDs: A Tutorial. IEEE Transactions on Design and Test of Computers **13** (1996) 42–57.
15. DeHon, A., T. Knight, J., Tau, E., Bolotski, M., Eslick, I., Chen, D., Brown, J.: Dynamically Programmable Gate Array with Multiple Context. U.S. Patent No. 5,742,180 (1998).
16. Trimberger, S., Carberry, D., Johnson, A., Wong, J.: A Time-Multiplexed FPGA. In: IEEE Symposium on FPGAs for Custom Computing Machines, Napa Valley, California, (1997) 22–28.
17. ***: ACEX 1K Programmable Logic Family. Altera Datasheet, San Jose, California (2000).
18. van Eijndhoven, J.T.J., Sijstermans, F.W., Vissers, K.A., Pol, E.J.D., Tromp, M.J.A., Struik, P., Bloks, R.H.J., van der Wolf, P., Pimentel, A.D., Vranken, H.P.E.: TriMedia CPU64 Architecture. In: Intl. Conference on Computer Design, Austin, Texas, (1999) 586–592.
19. Sima, M., Vassiliadis, S., Cotofana, S., van Eijndhoven, J.T., Vissers, K.: A Taxonomy of Custom Computing Machines. In: First PROGRESS Workshop on Embedded Systems, Utrecht, The Netherlands, (2000) 87–93.
20. Pol, E.J.D., Aarts, B.J.M., van Eijndhoven, J.T.J., Struik, P., Sijstermans, F.W., Tromp, M.J.A., van de Waerdt, J.W., van der Wolf, P.: TriMedia CPU64 Application Development Environment. In: Intl. Conference on Computer Design, Austin, Texas, (1999) 593–598.
21. van Eijndhoven, J.: 16-bit compliant software IDCT on TriMedia/CPU64. Internal Report, Philips Research Laboratories (1997).
22. ***: IEEE Standard Specifications for the Implementations of 8 × 8 Inverse Discrete Cosine Transform. IEEE Std 1180-1990 (1991).
23. Choi, S.B., Lee, M.H.: High Speed Pattern Matching for a Fast Huffman Decoder. IEEE Transactions on Consumer Electronics **41** (1995) 97–103.
24. Min, K.-Y., Chong, J.-W.: A Memory-Efficient VLC decoder Architecture for MPEG-2 Application. In: IEEE Workshop on Signal Processing Systems, Lafayette, Louisiana, (2000) 43–49.
25. Pol, E.J.D.: VLD Performance on TriMedia/CPU64. Internal Report, Philips Research Laboratories (2000).

Caches with Compositional Performance*

Henk Muller, Dan Page, James Irwin, and David May

Department of Computer Science, University of Bristol, Bristol BS8 1UB, UK
http://www.cs.bris.ac.uk/

Abstract. One of the challenges in designing systems is adopting a design method with compositional properties. *Compositional functionality* guarantees that two components that each perform a task can be integrated without affecting the semantics of either task. *Compositional performance* means that two components can be integrated so that the timing of neither components changes. In this paper we describe the hardware and software needed in order to build cache memories that have those compositional properties. This *partitioned cache* allows the system designer to design individual components of an application program in the knowledge that cache performance is fully deterministic; ie. integrating these components will not affect the performance of any component.

1 Introduction

When designing systems one of the main challenges is adopting a design approach that is compositional. Compositional design means that one can design components of a system independently and compose them without affecting functionality or performance. This applies to the design of parts of an application program, an item of hardware specified in VHDL, or some software library module.

In this paper we are going to focus on one component found in many systems: the cache memory. Functionally, a cache is mostly transparent to the programmer. From a performance viewpoint, the cache may have a significant impact. On average, introducing a cache will improve the performance, but very little can be predicted about cache performance of specific applications. Even if we know the exact performance characteristics of two software modules when executing on a specific cache, it is still very difficult to predict the performance of the combined modules.

Many solutions have been proposed to improve cache performance, including set-associative caches [1] and victim caches [2], but all work on statistical properties which are of little value when designing a real-time system. We present a solution where the cache is exposed to the compiler and has some extra hardware attached that allows data streams to be segregated where necessary. The compiler analyses the application program and automatically generates code with composable performance properties.

* This work supported by EPSRC grant GR/L78970.

E.F. Deprettere et al. (Eds.): SAMOS 2001, LNCS 2268, pp. 242–259, 2002.
© Springer-Verlag Berlin Heidelberg 2002

In Section 2 we will first elaborate on compositional properties, before quantifying conventional cache performance and its lack of composability. As a solution we suggest the use of partitioned caches as described in Sections 3 and 4. Like conventional caches they are transparent to the programmer in terms of functionality but, in addition, have compositional performance characteristics. This means that system designers can produce software components in the knowledge that the cache performance is predictable. We quantify these performance results in Sections 5 and 6.

2   Compositional Design Strategies

Composability is an issue in designing any type of system; whether it is special purpose hardware, general purpose processors, or software. This issue must be addressed by the tools and software library modules that are used for design and implementation, for example, the hardware description language used to design hardware, and the programming language used for implementing programs. Composability spans the hardware software divide in that composability of software may be restricted by the underlying hardware.

As an introduction to composability we will first discuss two programming languages in Sections 2.1 and 2.2. Compositional properties of programming languages are well studied, since a major issue in designing a programming language is to allow programmers to design, implement, and test modules independently, before integrating them in a final phase.

After that, we discuss cache memories which present some major issues in producing composable systems. A cache is functionally transparent, and improves the performance of a program on average. However, even though the performance improves on average, it is very difficult to predict what exactly happens to the performance of two components that both use the same cache. Subsequent sections present a novel caching strategy which addresses this issue.

2.1   Example 1: Haskell

Haskell [3] is a purely functional programming language, defined in the mid-1990's. Purely functional programming requires the programmer to write a function that given some input produces some output. A fundamental requirement of such a function is that it can only operate on the input passed to the function; there is no global state on which functions can operate.

As a direct consequence of this purely functional approach, the language has very strong compositional properties. Two functions that are defined can be executed in any order, including in parallel, and they will always produce the same result. Once a module has been defined to implement, for example, a hash-table, this module can be employed in any other place and will always implement a hash-table. This can be achieved in other languages, such as C, C++ and Java, but Haskell *enforces* compositional behaviour; one *cannot* implement side effects.

Haskell is strong at compositional functionality but it is not very strong at compositional performance. One example of this fact is as a result of the Haskell garbage collection system. Garbage collection is an essential part of the language but the user cannot determine at compile-time when garbage collection will take place. Even if the performance characteristics of two functions are known exactly, the performance may therefore change when they are composed, because the garbage collector may require a significant execution time in one function since the other function has produced a lot of garbage.

2.2 Example 2: Occam

Occam [4] has a different approach to guarantee composability. Side effects are an essential part of Occam, but at compile time a *disjointness* check is performed. This checks which variables are used in a module and that they are not used by any other module that executes concurrently. The disjointness check guarantees that any program that is accepted by the compiler will not contain any state modifications that are unsafe.

The Occam approach gives a degree of composability in that any concurrent activity that is accepted by the compiler will run deterministically since there are no race conditions on the global state. Of course, one can write an Occam program in which a module relies on side effects, and hence different compositions of function calls will result in different answers.

Occam has a very strong compositional performance model. The language is designed so that all memory allocation, including any stacks, is performed at compile-time. Hence, the order in which functions are executed is irrelevant to the performance. When functions are executed concurrently, the performance will rely on what the underlying hardware can achieve. Having said that, there is one element of the hardware where the performance cannot easily be predicted: the cache memory. The performance of a function will always depend on what is present in the cache, and on which other functions are being executed.

2.3 Compositional Caching

As stated earlier, composability is not strictly a property of either hardware or software. As an example, suppose that we have two modules, one producing elements and one consuming elements, which are executed a the for-loop sketched in Figure 1. Ideally the performance of this loop would be equivalent to the performance of the producer being called a 1000 times, the consumer being called a 1000 times plus the overhead of a for-loop. Unfortunately, this is not necessarily the case depending on the cache architecture of the host system.

Suppose that the system employs a direct mapped data cache. If the function produce is called 1000 times in a row, each nth iteration would cause a cache miss, where n is the line size of the cache. Similarly, the consumer would have one cache miss every n iterations.

When the two functions are integrated and called subsequently from one for-loop, the arrays y and z may map on the same line in the cache (which is very likely given that the array y is exactly a power of 2 in size), and we will end up with a cache miss on every entrance to both the producer and the consumer. One cache miss to load the line covering the y array, which will displace the line of z, which is to be reloaded when consumer is called.

```
int y[ 16384 ];
int z[ 16384 ];

int produce( int index )
{
  return y[ index ];
}

void consume( int index, int value )
{
  z[ index ] = value;
}

void main()
{
  int i;
  int x;

  for( i = 0; i < 1000; i++ )
  {
    x = produce( i );
    consume( i, x );
  }
}
```

Fig. 1. Example program with poor composability due to cache performance.

Although this may seem like a contrived example there are actually many programs where this interference occurs. Powers of two are often used as array sizes, and even within functions such as matrix multiplications, various data structures can interfere in the cache. An interesting example is a GIF decoder which uses two arrays, each sized a power of 2. Figure 2 plots the execution time of a GIF decoder. We have manually inserted some padding between those arrays; and depending on the amount of padding we can see the performance vary. On this particular machine, a Silicon Graphics infinite reality engine, the effects are relatively minor, but on other architectures we have observed performance variations of up to 30%.

Unpredictable behaviour is exacerbated when we run programs on a multi-threaded machine, modelled on the HEP [5] and *T [6] multi-threaded architectures, as is shown in Figure 3. Here we show the hit-ratios of a cache running 1, 2, 4, and 8 GIF decoders in parallel on a multi-threaded machine. One can observe that depending on the number of threads and the associativity of the caches performance deteriorates; we will come back to this in Section 6.

3 Partitioned Cache Hardware

In order to address some of the problems with designing composable cache systems we propose the use of a partitioned cache. This novel design consists of a

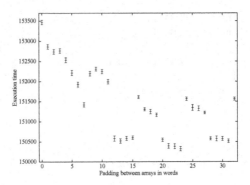

Fig. 2. Performance of a GIF decoder, along the horizontal axis we have inserted a varying amount of padding. The vertical error bars denote the standard deviation.

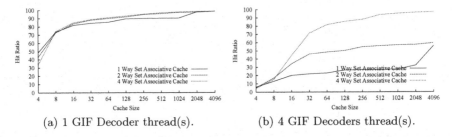

(a) 1 GIF Decoder thread(s).   (b) 4 GIF Decoders thread(s).

Fig. 3. Multi-threaded performance of multiple GIF decoder threads.

direct-mapped style cache that can be dynamically partitioned into protected regions by the use of specialised cache management instructions. By modifying the load/store mechanism and tagging each memory access with a partition identifier, each access is routed through a partition dedicated to dealing with it.

Unlike conventional caches, the partitioned cache is visible to software running on the host processor. This allows the compiler and operating system to allocate partitions of the cache to specific data objects and streams of instructions so as to control persistence and eliminate interference. This has the knock on effect of improving the predictability and determinism of the cache.

The idea of exposing the cache to the programmer has been proposed before [7], and has been worked on by Juan et. al. [8], Kirk [9] and Mueller [10]. The most obvious deficiency of all these systems is the inflexible manner in which cache partitions are allocated and the blinkered approach in using entirely hardware or software based designs. These techniques lack interaction from the one component, the compiler, that enables them to revolt against conventional, average case optimised cache design. By employing the compiler to analyse the source program and configure the cache so as to achieve the best performance possible, a partitioned cache benefits from a combined hardware/software approach. This sidesteps the problems of being tied to one paradigm in particular, and allows the cache to reap the benefits of being specialised to any given application program.

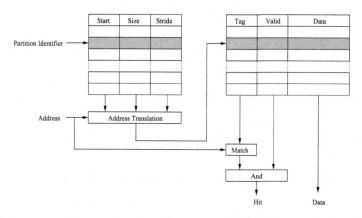

Fig. 4. A flow-diagram of a partitioned cache.

3.1 Architecture

Our partitioned cache [11] is a direct-mapped like block of cache memory which uses a *partition descriptor table* to hash incoming memory address traffic into cache line addresses. Figure 4 shows a flow-diagram of the operation of a partitioned cache. Information is extracted from the partition descriptor table by using an index, the *partition identifier*, provided with each memory access. This information is used to hash the memory address so that it maps onto a subsection, or *partition*, of the cache.

In order to maximise the density of useful data stored, the partitioned cache allows each cache line to be filled with data from non-contiguous, regularly strided memory locations. The stride, or distance between each address in a cache line, is a property of the partition owning the cache line and is used in the translation of memory accesses to map memory locations into the cache. For example, as demonstrated in Figure 5, a conventional cache with 4 words in each cache line will need 4 lines to store the addresses 0, 4, 8, 12 which could be generated by an array reference such as $a[4 * i]$, without conflict. A partitioned cache can store these accesses in one line provided the partition is configured with a stride of 4. In order for this scheme to be successful, we assume that lower levels of the memory hierarchy [12,13,14] can efficiently service such requests.

The presence of strided cache lines requires that the address translation mechanism which converts memory addresses into cache addresses is slightly more complex than usual. The purpose of the address translation mechanism, or address hashing function, is to distribute memory addresses in the cache so as to use all of the available cache space. In the context of a partitioned cache, the hash function needs to restrict the mapping so that memory addresses can only appear in the cache space owned by the target partition, and to populate the cache partition as fully as possible with incoming references.

Considering Figure 4 where p_{start}, p_{stride} and p_{size} are the start line, stride and size of a partition p, we can express our hashing function as follows:

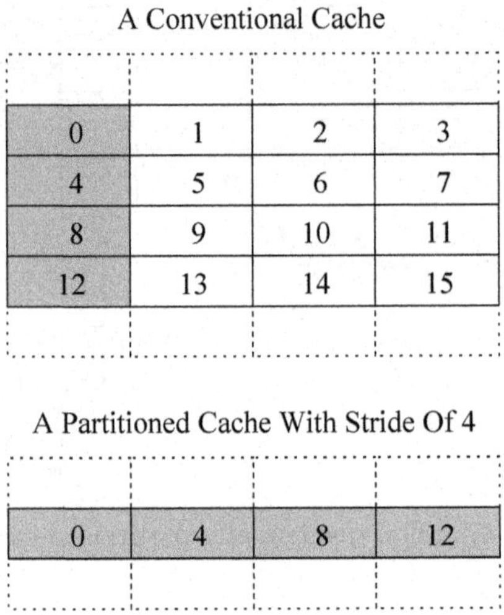

A Conventional Cache

0	1	2	3
4	5	6	7
8	9	10	11
12	13	14	15

A Partitioned Cache With Stride Of 4

0	4	8	12

Fig. 5. Strided cache lines in a partitioned cache.

$$p_{offset} = ((addr/nwords) \gg lsb(p_{stride})) \bmod p_{size}$$
$$p_{line} = p_{start} + p_{offset}$$

That is, the cache line p_{line} for an address $addr$ is given by the sum of the starting line of the partition, p_{start}, and an offset p_{offset}. The first stage in computing the offset is given by the incoming address, $addr$, divided by the number of words per cache line, $nwords$, which must be a power of two. This is shifted right by the position of the least significant 1 bit of the partitions stride, p_{stride}, and finally restrict the cache line to the available space by taking the remainder after division by the partition size, p_{size}.

To see how this scheme will distribute the data, consider a stride of twenty which has a binary representation of 10100. After dividing the incoming address by the number of words per line we shift it right by two, the least significant non-zero bit of the stride being the bit two. If we set size of the partition to eight lines and we assume a standard of four words per cache line, the first ten accesses, to addresses 0, 20, 40, 60, 80, 100, 120, 140, 160, 180, will be placed in lines $0, 1, 2, 3, 5, 6, 7, 0, 2, 3$ of the partition. This technique ensures that as long as the partition descriptor table is configured correctly, accesses to memory using different partition identifiers will always map into disjoint partitions and will utilise all cache lines in the partition. However, the scheme may not use the lines in an optimal manner, with some being used more often than others depending on the size, stride and line length of the partition.

3.2 Partition Management

Before we consider how memory is accessed though cache partitions, it is important to understand how the partition descriptor table is managed so that the

Table 1. Partitioned cache management instructions.

Instruction	Meaning
CREPAR id, size, stride	Add partition.
DELPAR id	Remove partition.
INVPAR id	Invalidate partition.
SETIPAR id	Set instruction partition.

cache can operate correctly. The management of the cache is performed dynamically, under control of the running program or operating system. This is done by using additional machine level instructions which alter the configuration of the cache. Table 1 details the extra instructions required to manage the table of partition descriptors. An alternative to this implementation may be to offer the partition descriptor table as a memory mapped block of address space so that the programmer can access it using standard load and store instructions.

In our instruction based management scheme, the *CREPAR* instruction adds an entry to the partition descriptor table, creating a new partition. The partition descriptor is configured so that the partition is tagged with an identifier of *id* and has a stride of *stride*. Furthermore, the management mechanism ensures that the partition starts on a cache line such that the partition is *size* cache lines in size. Creation of a partition which causes partitions with duplicate identifiers is considered an error.

The *DELPAR* instruction acts to delete the partition with an identifier of *id* from the partition descriptor table. In this study, the deletion of partitions under program control, thus creating truly dynamic configuration of the cache, is not discussed. Specifically, this is due to the complexity introduced by such usage which may include, for example, fragmentation of the partitionable cache space.

Partitions may be invalidated, that is their contents marked as invalid, so that the partition is effectively emptied or flushed, using an *INVPAR* instruction. Finally, the *SETIPAR* instruction is used to control the value of the partition through which instructions are loaded by the fetch/execute engine.

3.3   Partition Access

In order for accesses to memory to be routed through the correct partition in the cache, the memory access mechanism must be augmented to provide a partition identifier. The simplest way to pass the partition identifier is by using an extra operand in each instruction. This strategy requires that the instruction set be altered and may reduce code density by increasing the number of bits required to encode each instruction. Table 2 shows the modified memory access instructions where $R[n]$ denotes an access to general purpose register n, $M[add, id]$ denotes an access to memory, through the cache, at address *add* using partition *id*.

There are other techniques for passing the partition to the cache (such as stealing memory address bits, or maintaining a "current partition register"), but

Table 2. Partitioned cache access instructions.

Instruction	Meaning
$LOAD\ dst, add, id$	$R[dst] \leftarrow M[add, id]$
$LOADIDX\ dst, add, off, id$	$R[dst] \leftarrow M[add + off, id]$
$STORE\ src, add, id$	$M[add, id] \leftarrow R[src]$
$STOREIDX\ src, add, off, id$	$M[add + off, id] \leftarrow R[src]$

because our research is mainly based in the techniques for using a partitioned cache effectively and not issues of implementation, we opted for the simplest strategy. It is important to note that the partition identifiers are effectively constants and hence it should be easy to pipeline accesses to the partition descriptor table such that the performance overhead of doing so is minimal.

Finally, where an invalid or reserved partition identifier is used, the cache foregoes the standard behaviour and passes the access straight through to the next level of the memory hierarchy. This is used to achieve *cache bypass* where the cache state is unaltered by the memory access and is useful in this context for avoiding situations where a misconfigured cache may otherwise give undefined results.

4   Using A Partitioned Cache

Automation of partition management and configuration requires the application of a number of simple algorithms in suitable compiler modules. These algorithms act to disperse a complex stream of memory accesses into a number of more simple streams. We separate memory accesses to data objects into vector, scalar and stack classes. A number of partitions are allocated to each of these classes which are configured to suit the access properties of each class.

- Vector data partitions are perhaps the most interesting data access segregation to consider. Each vector within the program normally has at least one partition dedicated to it. Deciding the parameters for a partition, and how many there should be for each vector is computed from the set of references made in the application source code.
- Scalar data partitions cache accesses to ordinary, non-vector variables. The pattern of access to scalars is determined by the register spilling and loading of scalar data generated by the compiler. Normally, the compiler can remove most scalar memory accesses using traditional optimisation techniques. The accesses that remain can be routed through a single scalar partition whose size is related to the number of scalars in each of the procedures.
- The stack partition is sized to manage stack frames effectively. In a similar way to the scalar partition, we see highly localised access patterns. The algorithm takes into consideration the stack frame size of each procedure within the program, and the existence of any recursive procedure calls. The result is a stack partition large enough to contain the most recent n-levels of recursion in protected cache space.

```
void iccg()
{
  double v[ 1024 ];
  double x[ 1024 ];
  double ipnt;
  double ipntp;
  double ii;
  int i;
  int k;

  ii₀    = 1024;
  ipntp₀ = 0;
  do
  {
    ipnt₀  = ipntp₁;
    ipntp₂ = ipntp₃ + ii₁;
    ii₂    = ii₃ / 2;
    i₀     = ipntp₄ - 1;
    for( k₀ = ipnt₁ + 1; k₁ < ipntp₅; k₂ = k₃ + 2 )
    {
      i₁         = i₂ + 1;
      x₀[ i₃ ] = x₁[ k₄ ] - v₀[ k₅ ]       * x₂[ k₆ - 1 ]
                         - v₁[ k₇ + 1 ] * x₃[ k₈ + 1 ];
    }
  }
  while( ii₄ > 0 );
}
```

Fig. 6. An example implementation of an *ICCG* kernel annotated with reference numbers.

We first establish properties of the memory accesses, whereupon the compiler partitions the program over the cache. For a full description of the algorithms used see [15,16]

4.1 References

The compiler takes a source program as input which declares a number of scalar and vector variables and uses a number of statements and expressions to perform operations on those variables. Figure 6 shows a kernel from the Livermore Loop Fortran Kernels [17] suite of benchmark programs, which computes an Incomplete Cholesky Conjugate Gradient or *ICCG*. This program typifies the kinds of operations performed by an application program on declared data objects.

The first section of the program declares two vector variables, named v and x, and five scalar variables, named *ipnt*, *ipntp*, *ii*, *i* and *k*. The variables are then used in a number of *references*, which mark instances of data access to the variable, in a sequence of statements or expressions. In the example program there are two references to the variable v, four to x, two to *ipnt*, six to *ipntp*, five to *ii*, four to i and nine to k.

We can compute a set of references for all variables in the program, even if the set turns out to be empty. From this information we can determine further properties, called the *stride*, the *group* and the *window*, which are associated with variable references and will guide the partitioning process. Given that the $\mapsto$ operation is used to denote a mapping between a symbol and a set of references to that symbol, the reference sets for our *ICCG* example in Figure 6 look like:

$$v \quad \mapsto \{ v_0, v_1 \}$$
$$x \quad \mapsto \{ x_0, x_1, x_2, x_3 \}$$
$$ipnt \mapsto \{ ipnt_0, ipnt_1 \}$$
$$ipntp \mapsto \{ ipntp_0, ipntp_1, ipntp_2, ipntp_3, ipntp_4, ipntp_5 \}$$
$$ii \quad \mapsto \{ ii_0, ii_1, ii_2, ii_3, ii_4 \}$$
$$i \quad \mapsto \{ i_0, i_1, i_2, i_3 \}$$
$$k \quad \mapsto \{ k_0, k_1, k_2, k_3, k_4, k_5, k_6, k_7, k_8 \}$$

4.2   Strides

The *stride* of a reference is the distance between successive accesses to the associated variable. This comes about through the use of subscripted references to vector variables in the program. As the subscript expression changes value, usually due to iteration of a loop, successive accesses to the variable are generated that are spaced apart by a potentially constant distance. Because our partitioned cache has a facility for strided cache lines which improve the density of useful data, the detection and use of this property is desirable.

The *ICCG* kernel uses only simple, one-dimensional array subscripts of a standard form. The strides for references to v and x are calculated and marked for use in configuring the partitions allocated to them:

$$v \quad \mapsto \{ v_0[\text{stride}=2], v_1[\text{stride}=2] \}$$
$$x \quad \mapsto \{ x_0[\text{stride}=1], x_1[\text{stride}=2], x_2[\text{stride}=2], x_3[\text{stride}=2] \}$$
$$ipnt \mapsto \{ ipnt_0, ipnt_1 \}$$
$$ipntp \mapsto \{ ipntp_0, ipntp_1, ipntp_2, ipntp_3, ipntp_4, ipntp_5 \}$$
$$ii \quad \mapsto \{ ii_0, ii_1, ii_2, ii_3, ii_4 \}$$
$$i \quad \mapsto \{ i_0, i_1, i_2, i_3 \}$$
$$k \quad \mapsto \{ k_0, k_1, k_2, k_3, k_4, k_5, k_6, k_7, k_8 \}$$

4.3   Groups

The purpose of a *group* is to collect together all references to a variable that have a similar access properties and should therefore be placed in the same cache partition. One method for creating groups of references is to collect them using the stride of the reference to determine which group it should go into. Using this strategy, each item of vector data may produce a number of reference groups, each with different strides and hence different access patterns. References to scalar variables will only ever produce one group because of the lack of associated stride based access.

For example, in the *ICCG* kernel in Figure 6, both the references to v have the same stride and so will be grouped together while the references to x will produce two groups because there are two different strides:

$$v \mapsto \{\ v_0[\text{stride}=2],\ v_1[\text{stride}=2]\ \}$$
$$x' \mapsto \{\ x_0[\text{stride}=1]\ \}$$
$$x'' \mapsto \{\ x_1[\text{stride}=2],\ x_2[\text{stride}=2],\ x_3[\text{stride}=2]\ \}$$
$$ipnt \mapsto \{\ ipnt_0,\ ipnt_1\ \}$$
$$ipntp \mapsto \{\ ipntp_0,\ ipntp_1,\ ipntp_2,\ ipntp_3,\ ipntp_4,\ ipntp_5\ \}$$
$$ii \mapsto \{\ ii_0,\ ii_1,\ ii_2,\ ii_3,\ ii_4\ \}$$
$$i \mapsto \{\ i_0,\ i_1,\ i_2,\ i_3\ \}$$
$$k \mapsto \{\ k_0,\ k_1,\ k_2,\ k_3,\ k_4,\ k_5,\ k_6,\ k_7,\ k_8\ \}$$

4.4   Windows

The final useful property of a group of references is something termed the *window*. This property is a measure of the range of different data items which are accessed with the same stride and, to some extent, relates to the persistence of data within the cache. We use the window of a group of references as a heuristic to guide the sizing of partitions created for that group. The window is only useful in groups for vector variables because scalar partitions are sized to accommodate all variables rather than a subset of some larger data object.

The *ICCG* example highlights this property fairly well. Within the inner loop of the kernel, the main computational expression makes a number of references to the variable x which have produced two reference groups. The second of these groups contains the references $x[k-1]$, $x[k]$ and $x[k+1]$ because they all have the same stride, as determined by k. By examining these references, we can see that as the loop is executed a number of times the value of $x[k+1]$, for example, may be reused as the value of $x[k-1]$ as the value of k changes. To accommodate this need for data persistence, the window of the group is computed as the difference between the minimum and maximum offsets from each group of references.

This is used in the *ICCG* example to guide the sizing of cache partitions allocated to each group so that this potential persistence requirement is exploited to gain higher performance:

$$v[\text{window}=2] \mapsto \{\ v_0[\text{stride}=2],\ v_1[\text{stride}=2]\ \}$$
$$x'[\text{window}=1] \mapsto \{\ x_0[\text{stride}=1]\ \}$$
$$x''[\text{window}=3] \mapsto \{\ x_1[\text{stride}=2],\ x_2[\text{stride}=2],\ x_3[\text{stride}=2]\ \}$$
$$ipnt \mapsto \{\ ipnt_0,\ ipnt_1\ \}$$
$$ipntp \mapsto \{\ ipntp_0,\ ipntp_1,\ ipntp_2,\ ipntp_3,\ ipntp_4,\ ipntp_5\ \}$$
$$ii \mapsto \{\ ii_0,\ ii_1,\ ii_2,\ ii_3,\ ii_4\ \}$$
$$i \mapsto \{\ i_0,\ i_1,\ i_2,\ i_3\ \}$$
$$k \mapsto \{\ k_0,\ k_1,\ k_2,\ k_3,\ k_4,\ k_5,\ k_6,\ k_7,\ k_8\ \}$$

4.5   Partitioning

Once the reference analysis process is finalised, we can create a cache partition for each group of references to vector variables and mark them so that each reference accesses the variable through the correct partition. The partitions are created so that the partition stride and size are guided by the stride and window of the group from which guided their creation. In addition to partitions for vector variables, we create single partitions for all scalar variables and another for stack accesses. The scalar partition is sized so that it can house all variables that do not fit into registers.

At this stage, the source program is annotated in such a way that the back end of the compiler can correctly generate machine level instructions to implement the partitioning scheme required. However, before this is done, the total amount of cache resource used can then be reduced by reusing partitions. A simple technique, similar to register allocation, reuses partitions allocated to one data object when its use doesn't interfere with another and the configuration of the partition matches the requirements of the two variables.

5   Compositional Performance Model

In the previous section we have described how we can segregate memory accesses. Accesses to different objects are routed through different cache partitions in order to avoid interference. Various parallel activities that operate on one or more objects will also run in separate partitions, which allows us to define an extremely simple performance model. Below, we are going to define a performance metric P for a code segment s, $P(s)$. The unit of this metric can be execution time or number of cache misses depending on the prediction model used.

This section describes how the performance of an application may be calculated. We assume that we we have measurements of its constituent parts. That is, without necessarily computing the performance of the entire application by methods described in previous sections, we may accurately compose the applications performance from smaller, computationally cheaper and more accurate studies of the application.

5.1   Basic Composition

Assuming, that we can compute the performance $P(s_1)$ and $P(s_2)$ of two code fragments s_1 and s_2, then we can now trivially compute $P(s_1; s_2)$, the performance of the sequential composition of s_1 and s_2. If s_1 and s_2 share no partitions, then $P(s_1, s_2) = P(s_1) + P(s_2)$. This is valid for both time and miss performance metrics and means we can decompose large applications into more efficient components for performance prediction. If s_1 and s_2 do share partitions, then this method of calculating $P(s_1, s_2)$ can be pessimistic as the execution of s_1 may benefit the execution of s_2. In the cases where s_1 and s_2 share partitions, an accurate performance metric is made from the whole program $s_1; s_2$ and not from their constituent performance metrics. Iterated code segments can be treated similarly.

5.2   Extension by Composition

If we extend some fragment s, by the addition of a reference $v[i]$ to form s', where $v[i]$ is executed through a unique partition, we can count the extra misses incurred for $v[i]$ independently of the other references. The instruction references require a recalculation, to consider the changed program executed through the relevant instruction partition. This situation is similar to the case where $v[i]$ shares a partition with other references in the program. Prediction of the execution time for s' will require full static simulation and the classification [18] of the data reference $v[i]$ may be independent, or require the reclassification of a group of references, as before, depending on whether $v[i]$ shares a partition. The reclassification and simulation of the instruction code is also required as is a computation for the miss counting method if that is the model used.

5.3   Multi-threading

Considering two code segments s_1 and s_2 executed in parallel, denoted by $s_1|s_2$ and pre-computed performance metrics $P(s_1)$ and $P(s_2)$, a simple definition of $P(s_1|s_2)$ is $max(P(s_1), P(s_2))$. This definition has certain constraints. As in previous examples, we assume s_1 and s_2 are disjoint in their use of partitions. If this is not the case then we may either mark the shared partition references as misses or, if the combined reference sequence can be determined, accurately predict the performance. We will also ignore inter-thread communication facilities, suggesting that they do not dominate the performance of the tasks.

The parallel computation assumes that both tasks s_1 and s_2 have the same performance metrics as when they are run independently. This is true for the miss counting models but the runtime model makes further assumptions that may be included in a throughput aware model [15].

Even without extension of the utilisation metric, the model is valid and useful. It can answer, when only the cache memory hierarchy is the component under examination, the important questions about meeting computational deadlines. This model can also be used to build an optimisation scheme.

6   Results

The GIF image decoder is a small and manageable example of a simple multimedia application. It is generally run in some sort of multi-threaded environment such as the HTML rendering engine of a web browser. To represent a realistic test, we ran between one and eight decoders operating concurrently, introducing the concurrency through the use of an explicit language level construct in the benchmark program. The execution trace of a GIF decoder is data-dependent and although each GIF decoder operates on a different image, all threads have a comparable run-time. The results of the experiment are shown in Figure 7.

The results for the partitioned cache are the single point in space with the overall performance of the cache is simply composed from the performance of

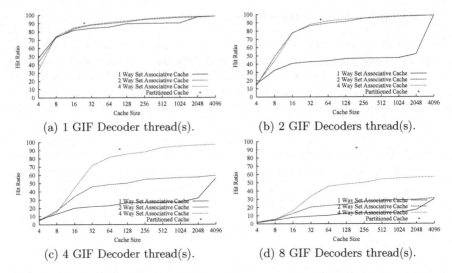

(a) 1 GIF Decoder thread(s).

(b) 2 GIF Decoders thread(s).

(c) 4 GIF Decoder thread(s).

(d) 8 GIF Decoders thread(s).

Fig. 7. Data cache performance of multiple GIF Decoder threads. The cache size is measured in lines.

the partitions. When a single GIF decoder is executed, conventional cache architectures show comparable performance profiles but, because of their lack of flexibility, scale badly and are not effective as the number of threads is increased. Data dependent application programs such as the GIF decoder would normally result in complex interference patterns between other threads in the system but by eliminating inter-thread interference with a partitioned cache, thread performance is guaranteed. In the case where there is only one thread running, the partitioned cache performs better than same sized set-associative caches due to the elimination of intra-thread or self interference. Although this benefit is largely uninteresting in multi-threaded situations, it is a potentially valuable property in high performance computer systems.

A second set of multi-threaded experiments are constructed using kernels taken from the LLFK benchmark suite. We performed two experiments, running three independent kernels in three threads, and running a parallelised kernel against a non-parallelised version. These experiments demonstrate inter and intra-thread interference between shared and non-shared data objects in a number of different threads of comparable run-time. The results are shown in Figures 8 and 9 respectively and graph the hit-ratio of a partitioned cache compared with a number of set-associative caches of a similar size.

In both experiments, as interference is introduced by running more threads either as disjoint processes of part of a parallelised algorithm, the partitioned cache can sustain high performance while the conventional caches suffer a significant drop. Although the parallelised kernel was constructed by hand, the drop in performance demonstrates the problems that can be introduced by parallelising compilers. If these compilers are not considerate of the issues involved as

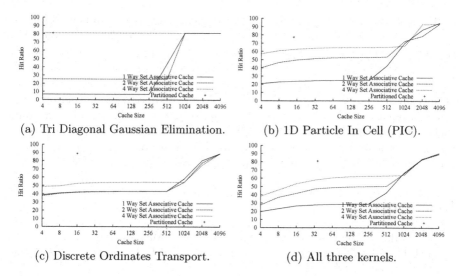

Fig. 8. Data cache performance of selected LLFK kernels both sequentially and in parallel. The cache size is measured in lines.

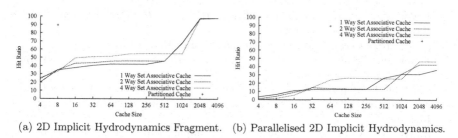

Fig. 9. Data cache performance of parallelised 2D Implicit Hydrodynamics Fragment kernel.

a result of their transformations, the good work done by finding and exploiting parallelism within a program will be undone by poor memory performance. With careful use of a partitioned cache and associated compiler technology, the gains from parallelisation of programs are protected against this kind of problem.

7   Conclusions

We have presented a cache architecture for which it is easy to predict the performance of programs running on it, because of its compositional properties. The ability to predict performance is particularly useful in real time environments, such as a set-top box. The software modules, such as the video decoder and audio decoder, can be developed and tuned independently, and the cache architecture guarantees that when integrated the performance of the two modules is a simple composition of the performance of all of the components.

Our solution partitions a direct mapped cache, each partition is used for one or more reference streams. The use of the cache is completely under control of the compiler. Because we expose the cache to the compiler, we need to modify the instruction set so that we can pass the partitioning information to the cache.

The performance of each partition can either be predicted analytically, or be measured using simulation tools. Analytical prediction of the performance of partitioned caches is far simpler than performance prediction of traditional caches because interference is controlled [15]. Whatever prediction method is chosen, compositional properties allow us to reason about the performance of the partitioned cache when the system is integrated.

References

1. A. Smith. A Comparative Study of Set Associative Memory Mapping Algorithms and Their Use for Cache and Main Memory. *IEEE Transactions on Software Engineering*, March 1978.
2. N. Jouppi. Improving Direct-Mapped Cache Performance by the Addition of a Small Fully-Associative Cache and Prefetch Buffer. In *17th International Symposium on Computer Architecture*, pp 364–373, June 1990.
3. J. Peterson and K. Hammond, editors. *Report on the Porgramming Language Haskell.* Yale University, 1996.
4. Inmos Ltd. *Occam-2 Reference Manual.* Prentice Hall, 1988.
5. J. Kowalik. *Parallel MIMD Computation: The HEP Supercomputer and its Applications.* MIT Press, 1985.
6. R. Nikhil, G. Papadopoulos, and Arvind. *T: A Multithreaded Massively Parallel Architecture. In *19th International Symposium on Computer Architecture*, pp 156–167, May 1992.
7. R. Wagner. Compiler-Controlled Cache Mapping Rules. Technical Report CS-1995-31, Duke University, December 1995.
8. T. Juan, D. Royo, and J. Navarro. Dynamic Cache Splitting. *15th International Conference of the Chilean Computational Society*, 1995.
9. D. Kirk. SMART (Strategic Memory Allocation for Real-Time) Cache Design. In *IEEE Symposium on Real-Time Systems*, pp 229–237, December 1989.
10. F. Mueller. Compiler Support for Software-Based Cache Partitioning. In *ACM SIGPLAN Workshop on Language, Compiler, and Tool Support for Real-Time Systems*, pp 137–145, June 1995.
11. D. May and H. Muller. Cache Memory. Patent Number WO045269, August 2000.
12. J. Carter, W. Hseih, L. Stoller, M. Swanson, L. Zhang, E. Brunvard, A. Davis, C. Kuo, R. Kuramkote, M. Parker, L. Schaelicke, and T. Tateyama. Impulse: Building a Smarter Memory Controller. *5th Conference on High Performance Computer Architecture*, January 1999.
13. A. Ki and A. Knowles. Secondary Cache Data Prefetching for Multiprocessors. Technical Report UMCS-97-3-1, Department of Computer Science, University of Manchester, 1997.
14. J. Fu, J. Patel, and B. Janssens. Stride Directed Prefetching in Scalar Processors. In *25th International Symposium on Microarchitecture*, pp 102–110, 1992.
15. J. Irwin. *Systems With Predictable Caching.* PhD thesis, Department of Computer Science, University of Bristol, 2001.

16. D. Page. *Effective Use of Partitioned Cache Memories.* PhD thesis, Department of Computer Science, University of Bristol, 2001.
17. F. McMahon. *The Livermore Fortran Kernels: A Computer Test Of The Numerical Performance Range.* Lawrence Livermore National Laboratory, Livermore, California, December 1986.
18. R. Arnold. Bounding Instruction Cache Performance. Master's thesis, Department of Computer Science, Florida State University, 1996.

Design of an Adaptive Architecture for Energy Efficient Wireless Image Communication*

Clark N. Taylor, Debashis Panigrahi, and Sujit Dey

Electrical and Computer Engineering Department
University of California, San Diego
La Jolla, CA 92093, USA
{cntaylor,dpani,dey}@ece.ucsd.edu

Abstract. With the projected significant growth in mobile internet and multimedia services, there is a strong demand for next-generation wireless appliances capable of image communication. However, wireless image communication faces significant bottlenecks including high energy and bandwidth consumption. Past studies have shown that the bottlenecks to wireless image communication can be overcome by developing adaptive image compression algorithms and dynamically adapting them to current channel conditions and service requirements [1,2].
In this paper, we present the design of an adaptive hardware/software architecture that enables adaptive wireless image communication. Through intelligent co-design of the proposed architecture and algorithms, we achieve an architecture which enables not only power and performance efficient implementation, but also fast and efficient run-time adaptation of image compression parameters. To achieve efficient image compression and run-time adaptation, we characterized the adaptation needs of an adaptive image compression algorithm in terms of parameters, and implemented an adaptive hardware/software architecture capable of executing JPEG image compression with different parameters. We present experimental results demonstrating that the proposed architecture enables low overhead adaptation to current wireless conditions and requirements while implementing a low cost (energy and performance) implementation of adaptive image compression algorithms.

1 Introduction

With the forthcoming introduction of 2.5G and 3G cellular telephony, together with the increasing popularity of the internet, there is a growing need for devices capable of wireless image communication. However, the transmission of images over wireless channels face significant bottlenecks such as severely limited bandwidth and energy consumption. Therefore, to effectively design systems capable of communicating image information over wireless channels, the bandwidth and energy consumption bottlenecks must be overcome.

---

* This work is supported by the UCSD Center for Wireless Communications, UC CoRe, and SRC

E.F. Deprettere et al. (Eds.): SAMOS 2001, LNCS 2268, pp. 260–273, 2002.

A characteristic of wireless communication which can be used to overcome the bandwidth and energy bottlenecks is the varying wireless channel conditions (such as changing Signal-to-Noise Ratio (SNR) over time) and diverse service requirements (such as latency) of different applications. Instead of designing a multimedia system which assumes worst-case wireless communication conditions and requirements, significant savings can be achieved by designing a system which can adapt to differing conditions and requirements.

Several previous research works have addressed adapting to current wireless conditions to conserve energy and bandwidth. In [3], the authors adapt the channel coding parameters to match current channel conditions, thereby increasing the average bandwidth available. An algorithm is proposed in [4] to modify the broadcast power of the RF power amplifier to meet quality of multimedia data requirements, thereby lowering energy consumption. In [5] a method is presented for setting both channel coding and power amplifier settings to adjust for current conditions, thereby lowering energy consumption. A methodology for adapting JPEG image compression to current wireless conditions to minimize energy and bandwidth is presented in [2]. In all of these research studies, algorithms were presented to minimize energy consumption and/or bandwidth through adaptation to current wireless and application conditions. However, none of the previous research work has addressed the architecture used for implementing an adaptive algorithm. In this paper, we present a novel hardware/software architecture which is adaptive to help conserve energy and bandwidth during wireless image communication.

Past research has presented various reconfiguration architectures at different levels of design, namely software-level, datapath-level, and logic-level, to dynamically reconfigure across different algorithms. Software level reconfigurability using general purpose or custom-fit [6] processors provide the highest amount of flexibility, but is performance limited in terms of execution time and power. Datapath level configurability, like the RAPID architecture [7], as well as logic level configurability, like FPGA based systems [8,9,10], provide better execution time and power characteristics than general purpose processors, but still cannot match the performance of an ASIC implementation for a specific application. In addition, the overhead associated with run-time reconfiguration of an FPGA based architecture (reconfiguration time and storage of configurations in memory) can be significant. Due to the need for high-performance, low power image compression which rapidly adapts to wireless communication conditions and requirements, software, datapath, and logic-level reconfigurable architectures may not be sufficient for wireless image communication.

To achieve an architecture that provides the necessary flexibility and performance for adaptive wireless image communication, we propose a hardware/software (hw/sw) adaptation methodology that considers co-design of adaptive algorithms and architectures together. In the first step, we characterize the adaptation needs of an adaptive algorithm in terms of parameters that need to be configured during the execution of the algorithm. We then develop a hw/sw architecture that provides the required adaptability by implementing portions of the algorithm in software as well as designing parameterizable hardware components. Since the software modules and hardware accelerators are designed considering the adaptation needs, the overhead of dynamic adaptation is minimal. In addition, we support efficient execution of run-time adaptation algorithms to select the appropriate parameters and configure the components accordingly. The above design methodology leads to a hardware/software adaptive architecture that provides software-like configuration overhead and ASIC-like performance. In this paper, we focus on developing such a hardware/software adaptive architecture for the adaptive image compression algorithms for wireless communication presented in [2,1].

The paper is organized as follows. In section 2, we review the process of making an algorithm adaptive through parameter identification and configuration. Section 3 describes our hardware/software adaptive architecture for wireless image communication. In section 4, we present experimental results demonstrating the efficiency of the proposed architecture in dynamically executing adaptive image compression and run-time adaptation algorithms. Section 5 concludes the paper.

2   Adaptive Image Compression

To implement an efficient hardware/software adaptive architecture for wireless image communication, it is necessary to understand the adaptive image compression and run-time adaptation algorithms being implemented. While the design of algorithms has been described earlier in [1,?], we present a brief review in this section. First, we present an overview of the JPEG image compression algorithm [11], followed by a description of the parameters used to create an adaptive image compression algorithm. We also review two run-time adaptation algorithms developed to dynamically select the proper image compression parameters.

2.1   JPEG Image Compression Algorithm

To review the creation of an adaptive image compression algorithm, we first present a brief overview of the JPEG image compression algorithm [11]. To implement JPEG image compression, the input image is divided into blocks of size 8 pixels by 8 pixels. Each of these 8x8 pixel blocks is transformed by a Discrete Cosine Transform (DCT) into its frequency domain equivalent. After the transform stage, each frequency component is quantized (divided by a certain value) to reduce the amount of information which needs to be transmitted. These quantized values are then encoded using a Huffman-encoding based technique to reduce the size of the image representation.

2.2   JPEG Image Compression Parameters

To modify the JPEG image compression algorithm to create an adaptive image compression algorithm, two parameters which can be modified at run-time were selected[1,2]. The first parameter of JPEG which can be dynamically adapted is the *quantization level*. The JPEG standard defines default quantization tables which can be scaled up or down depending on the desired quality of the final image. As the quantization level is increased, the image quality decreases, as does the amount of data to be transmitted wirelessly. The decrease in amount of data to be transmitted affects both the *communication energy* (energy consumed in the wireless transmission of the data), and the bandwidth and latency requirements of transmitting the image.

The second parameter that can be dynamically adapted is Virtual Block Size (VBS). This parameter affects the DCT portion of JPEG as first introduced in [12]. To implement VBS, the DCT still inputs the entire 8x8 block of pixels, but outputs a VBSxVBS amount of frequency information rather than an 8x8 block. For example, when the VBS is 8, all frequency information is computed. On the other hand, if the VBS is 5, all data outside the low-frequency 5x5 block is set to 0. By setting the frequency values outside the VBSxVBS block to zero, computation energy is reduced because the elements set to zero do not have to be computed or quantized, while the amount of data needed to transmit the computed image also decreases as the zero values can be encoded to result in a more compact representation.

2.3   Run-Time Adaptation Algorithms

Once an adaptive image compression algorithm has been developed, it is necessary to implement run-time adaptation algorithms which dynamically select the proper parameters for the adaptive image compression algorithm. The run-time adaptation algorithms are responsible for monitoring the current wireless and application conditions and requirements and selecting image compression parameters. The image compression parameters chosen should minimize the bandwidth and energy consumed during the compression and communication of the image.

In Fig. 1 we present a methodology for selecting the optimal parameters for the adaptive image compression algorithm at run-time while minimizing the run-time cost of executing the run-time adaptation algorithm. The methodology is divided into two sections, precomputation and run-time computation. The precomputation step generates a lookup table(s) which is used at run-time to select optimal image compression parameters (VBS and quantization level). By performing most of the computation outside of the wireless appliance (in the precomputation step), the run-time cost of adaptation to wireless and application conditions and constraints is minimized. In [1] and [2], two different algorithms were presented utilizing our parameter selection methodology to dynamically select image compression parameters that minimize energy and bandwidth consumption.

In [1], the algorithm presented (*LowOverhead*) assumes that the transmission energy/bit is constant over time. To find the optimal image compression parameters at run-time, it performs a simple lookup yielding the optimal VBS and quantization level parameters. However, assuming that the transmission energy per bit is constant may not be applicable with a changing wireless channel. In

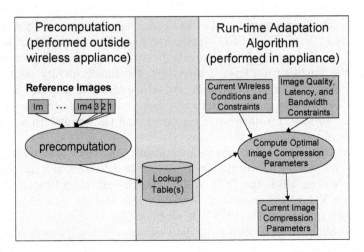

Fig. 1. Methodology for selecting optimal JPEG image compression parameters

[2], an algorithm is presented (*Variable*) for selecting optimal image compression parameters with a varying transmission energy/bit. To adjust to a varying transmission energy/bit, a different lookup table must be generated during the precomputation step. During run-time, multiple table lookups and some computation must be performed to determine the optimal image compression parameters. Therefore, the *Variable* algorithm consumes more resources than the *LowOverhead* algorithm, but can adapt to changing transmission energy conditions, making it more flexible.

With an understanding of the adaptive image compression and run-time adaptation algorithms, it is possible to design an adaptive architecture which meets the performance constraints of wireless communication while still enabling the adaptivity necessary to overcome the bandwidth and energy bottlenecks to multimedia wireless communication. In the next section, we present our hardware/software adaptive architecture allowing for algorithm-level adaptation to current wireless communication conditions and constraints.

3   Adaptive Architecture

To leverage the advantages of adapting wireless image communication to current communication conditions and requirements, we propose an adaptive architecture for wireless multimedia appliances shown in Fig. 2. Our new architecture includes some components of a traditional wireless appliance (unshaded), such as a source coder, channel coder, RF modulator, and power amplifier. It also includes two new components that we propose for adaptive image communication: the adaptive image coder and run-time adaptation algorithms, indicated by the shaded regions. The run-time adaptation algorithms are responsible for understanding the current network conditions and service requirements, and configuring the adaptive image source coder accordingly (as discussed in section 2.3). The adaptive image coder is designed to reconfigure as required to execute adaptive image compression algorithms with varying parameters over time. In the rest of this paper, we concentrate on our proposed hardware/software adaptive architecture for the adaptive image coder and run-time adaptation algorithms.

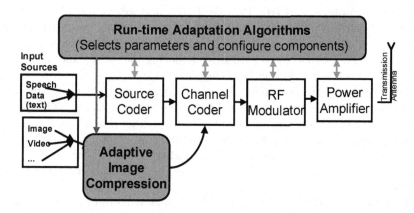

Fig. 2. Proposed adaptive architecture for multimedia wireless appliances

3.1   Hardware/Software Mapping of Algorithm Tasks

To implement an adaptive image coder which can efficiently and dynamically execute different image compression algorithms and parameters together with run-time adaptation algorithms, we developed an adaptive hardware/software (hw/sw) architecture. Traditional hw/sw co-design methodologies try to perform hw/sw mapping of tasks in order to optimize for performance and power requirements. In addition to the above objectives, we considered adaptability as an objective in mapping the tasks to a hw/sw architecture. It is well known that any software component of a system is easily configurable whereas hardware components offer less dynamic configurability. However, implementing a task in hardware results in better performance and reduced energy consumption. We discuss below how we mapped the image compression algorithm tasks to different hw/sw components to maximize performance without sacrificing flexibility.

In an image compression algorithm, the transform step is the most compute intensive portion, whereas the quantization and encoding steps are more control-intensive. Our preliminary studies on JPEG (implemented fully in software) show that the DCT transform step consumes more than 60% of the computation requirements of the JPEG algorithm. Therefore, we can obtain a significant energy and performance improvement by mapping the transform step to hardware.

Additionally, we do not have to sacrifice adaptivity through mapping the transform step to hardware. Through co-design of the adaptive image compression algorithms with the hw/sw architecture, we can know a-priori which parameters to include in the transform hardware accelerators (such as VBS in a DCT accelerator) for the adaptive algorithms. Therefore, the parameters which are used to modify the adaptive image compression algorithm at run-time can still be dynamically modified with the transform step mapped to hardware.

In addition, even though image compression algorithms may differ greatly in their encoding and quantization steps, they often have an identical transform step. For example, the SPIHT[13], AWIC[14], and JPEG2000[15] image compression algorithms all use the same transform step (DWT) even though their encoding and quantization steps vary greatly. Therefore, we can map image data transforms (DWT or DCT) to hardware, achieving the energy and performance gains desired, without a loss in flexibility.

Across different image compression algorithms, quantization is performed by multiplying the values to be quantized by pre-determined values. This operation is repeated several times within the quantization phase. Therefore, it is possible to obtain a significant performance improvement by mapping the quantization step to hardware without limiting the flexibility of the system, so long as the hardware unit is parameterizable to configure the quantization multipliers with any value.

To map the encoding of transformed and quantized data to our hardware/ soft-ware architecture, we first considered the adaptivity necessary for our image compression embedded system. Between image compression algorithms which use the same transform, the encoding step widely varies. For example, within the JPEG image compression standard, there are two possible methods for encoding information. One uses pre-defined probabilities to perform a quasi-Huffman coding method which runs much quicker, but does not achieve as good of compression. There is also a method for using true Huffman coding, requiring a pass to determine signal probabilities, which requires more computation, but yields better compression performance. Therefore, an attempt to map encoding algorithms to hardware would result in multiple hardware units. In addition, encoding is the most control-intensive portion of image compression. Therefore, the encoding step of image compression was mapped to software.

3.2   Adaptive Hardware/Software Architecture

To implement our hardware/software mapping of algorithm tasks, we developed the architecture shown in Fig. 3. Our architecture includes a general-purpose picoJava processor core [16], a hardware accelerator (DCT), an on-chip memory, and the PI-BUS[17] on-chip system bus.

To implement the software portion of the image compression algorithms, along with the run-time adaptation algorithms of our proposed mobile multimedia appliance, our architecture includes the picoJava soft core from Sun Microsystems [16]. We implement the computationally intensive tasks of adaptive image compression algorithms in parameterizable hardware units, termed as hardware accelerators, to assist in achieving high performance multimedia

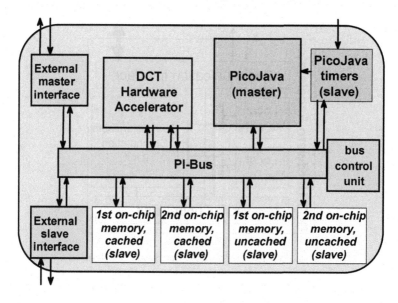

Fig. 3. Hardware/software architecture of image compression SoC

communication. The architecture of the DCT hardware accelerator is shown in Fig. 4.

The DCT hardware accelerator consists of four main sections: a parameterizable computation unit, two 64 element memories, a bus interface unit, and the DCT control unit. The architecture of the DCT hardware accelerator was designed to enable the run-time selection of image compression parameters while maximizing the performance of the accelerator. To enable the flexibility necessary for run-time parameter selection, the communication interface, control unit, and computation unit were designed to accept parameters from the picoJava processor core and execute the DCT with different Virtual Block Sizes. Therefore, by co-design of the algorithms and architecture, we were able to implement a DCT hardware accelerator which does not sacrifice the needed flexibility for wireless image communication.

On the other hand, it is imperative that our architecture be capable of meeting the real-time constraints of wireless image communication. Therefore, it is important to note that during the computation of the DCT, each pixel value is read and written to twice, quickly becoming the performance limiting factor of the DCT computation. Because memory accesses are the performance limiting factor for the DCT hardware unit, we decided to include two local 64-element memories to reduce the need for external memory accesses. The DCT hardware accelerator is designed such that while the computational unit is computing the information in one memory, the bus interface and control units are unloading and loading the other memory. Using this design for the hardware accelerator significantly boosts the performance of the JPEG image compression architecture while maintaining the flexibility necessary for adaptive image compression.

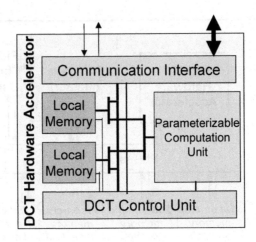

Fig. 4. Architecture of DCT hardware accelerator

We have designed the DCT hardware accelerator in VHDL code. Using Synopsys' Design Compiler to map the DCT to UMC's .18μm Cu technology [20], we found that the area of the DCT block (excluding memories) was equivalent to 66,176 NAND gates, with a critical path delay of 3.52ns, leading to a clock speed of >250 MHz. The high performance enabled by the DCT hardware accelerator design allows for ASIC-like performance during execution of the JPEG image compression algorithm.

To enable communication of the picoJava core with the DCT hardware accelerator as well as the on-chip memories, we have used the PI-Bus [17] and the associated bus control unit and master/slave interfaces. Using the PI-Bus, we are able to effectively meet all the on-chip inter-component communication needs as well as the need for external communications.

By judiciously performing hw/sw mapping with a knowledge of adaptive image compression algorithms, we have designed an architecture with good performance, while still allowing for the adaptivity necessary to reduce bandwidth and energy through adaptive image compression. In the next section, we present experimental results demonstrating the performance and flexibility of our architecture.

4   Experimental Results

In this section, we demonstrate the effectiveness of the proposed adaptive wireless image communication architecture. We demonstrate the low adaptation cost enabled by the design of our hw/sw adaptive architecture, followed by the effects of adaptation on wireless image communication. Finally, we demonstrate the performance advantage of our architecture over an embedded software architecture.

The performance (execution time) of our hardware/software architecture reported in the subsections below were obtained using a fast hw/sw co-simulation framework we developed [18]. The energy consumption results presented for hardware units were obtained using Synopsys' RTL power estimation tool. For software energy estimates, the software code is run using the RTL model of the picoJava processor core, and estimated using Synopsys' RTL power estimation tool. For all the experiments we use UMC's .18μm Cu technology [20].

4.1   Adaptation Overhead

To determine the cost of run-time adaptation in our architecture, we first present the costs of finding the correct parameters to configure the image coder with. The correct parameters are determined by the run-time adaptation algorithms discussed in section 2.3. In Table 1, we compare the execution time and energy consumed in executing the run-time adaptation algorithms with that of the JPEG image compression algorithm. The first row corresponds to the cost of executing the JPEG image compression algorithm on a 16x16 image, while the second and third row correspond to two different run-time adaptation algorithms used for determining the optimal parameters for image compression. The algorithm *LowOverhead*[1] consists of a simple lookup at run-time, but assumes a constant transmission energy per bit. The second algorithm, *Variable*[2] requires some computation in addition to multiple table lookups, but is more flexible in considering the current wireless conditions. As shown in Table 1, the energy cost of determining the adaptation parameters is at most 6μJ, which is less than 1% of the energy cost of compressing a 16x16 image (765μJ), while the execution time overhead is at most 2%. These results show that the costs of run-time adaptation are very low in our architecture, thereby enabling adaptive image compression to conserve energy and bandwidth.

Table 1. Resources required to determine optimal configuration of image compression SoC

Algorithm	Time (# cycles)	Energy (μJ)
JPEG	455981	765
LowOverhead[1]	986	0.5
Variable[2]	11,246	5.4

Once the run-time adaptation algorithms have determined the appropriate configuration for the adaptive image coder, the DCT block must be configured with the appropriate parameters. To configure the DCT block to different parameters requires 70 writes across the system bus. Assuming 4 cycles per memory write and a bus speed of 100 MHz, the configuration time is less than 30μs, with an energy consumption of less than 1 nJ. Compared with FPGA reconfiguration times which are on the order of milliseconds and millijoules, our architecture demonstrates extremely inexpensive run-time adaptation costs.

4.2   Energy and Bandwidth Savings of JPEG Image Compression Adaptation

In order to evaluate the efficiency of varying the quantization level and VBS parameters to reduce energy consumption and bandwidth requirements for wireless imageb communication, we performed several experiments using our hardware implementation of the DCT and quantization portions of the JPEG image compression algorithm. Table 2 shows the results of our experiments based on configuring the adaptive image coder between possible Virtual Block Sizes (VBS) and quantization levels for the image *Monarch*[21]. For each VBS and quantization level combination, we report PSNR (denoting quality of image), energy consumed in the transformation and quantization steps (CompE), the bandwidth required to transmit the image in number of bytes (Bandwidth), and the communication energy (CommE) consumed in transmitting those bytes using Bluetooth access technology [19]. To compute communication energy, we assume a maximum Bluetooth transmission power of 1mW, and a bandwith of 200 kbits/s. For each VBS (1-8), columns 2 through 5 present the results for a quantization level of 28, where as columns 6 through 9 correspond to a quantization level of 50.

Table 2. Effect of parameters on energy consumption

VBS	Quantization=28				Quantization=50			
	PSNR (dB)	CompE (μJ)	Bandwidth (# bytes)	CommE (μJ)	PSNR (dB)	CompE (μJ)	Bandwidth (# bytes)	CommE (μJ)
8	34.87	380	52499	2100	33.21	377	39712	1588
7	34.82	358	52358	2094	33.20	356	39669	1587
6	34.46	338	51774	2071	33.08	336	39509	1580
5	33.30	318	50167	2007	32.42	316	38461	1538
4	31.15	298	46489	1860	30.73	297	36334	1453
3	28.47	275	39042	1562	28.31	275	31301	1252
2	24.99	254	26204	1048	24.96	253	22209	888
1	20.61	235	11214	449	20.61	234	10346	414

It can be seen from Table 2 that our architecture enables tradeoffs between image quality, computation energy, bandwidth required for image transmission, and communication energy through the selection of VBS and quantization level parameters. As the VBS decreases, the computational energy decreases, as does the number of bytes to be transmitted, leading to a decrease in communication energy and bandwidth requirements. Therefore, varying the VBS in our architecture enables a tradeoff between image quality and the bandwidth required and computation and communication energy consumption. For example, for a quantization level of 28, decreasing the VBS from 8 to 4 decreases the image quality (PSNR) and Computation Energy (CompE) from 34.87dB to 31.15dB and 380μJ to 298μJ, respectively. The bandwidth required to transmit the image also decreases from 52499 to 46489 bytes, with a corresponding decrease in communication energy of 2100μJ to 1860μJ.

In addition, by varying the quantization level parameter, we observe that the computation energy does not change significantly, but the bandwidth required for image transmission, together with the communication energy change significantly with differing quantization levels. Therefore, varying the quantization level in our architecture enables a tradeoff between image quality, bandwidth required for image transmission, and communication energy. For example, with a VBS of 8, changing from a quantization level of 28 to 50 changes the image quality (PSNR) from 34.87dB to 33.21dB, while the bandwidth required for image transmission (Bandwidth) decreases from 52499 to 39712 bytes, with a corresponding decrease in communication energy (CommE) from $2100\mu J$ to $1588\mu J$.

4.3   Hardware/Software Mapping Results

In the previous two subsections, we have demonstrated the adaptivity enabled by, and the low-cost approach of varying parameters at run-time in, our adaptive hw/sw architecture. We have also demonstrated the tradeoffs between image quality, computation and communication energy, and amount of data to be transmitted enabled by adapting the image compression parameters in our hw/sw architecture. In this subsection, we also demonstrate that our hw/sw architecture has significant performance and power advantages over a pure embedded software implementation.

In Table 3, we compare our architecture with a software implementation in terms of execution time and energy consumed for the JPEG compression of an image (CutCowPI) of size 16x16 pixels. The first row corresponds to an implementation where all steps of the JPEG algorithm, namely Transform(T), Quantization(Q), and Encoding(E), are performed in software (Java) on the picoJava processor. The second row presents results for the proposed architecture, which implements Transform(T) and Quantization(Q) in hardware, and Encoding(E) in software. It can be seen that the proposed hardware/software architecture achieves a 4X timing performance improvement, and a 6X improvement in energy consumption. The improvements in execution time and energy consumption are primarily due to the parameterizable hardware implementation of the most compute-intensive portions of the algorithm. These results show that it is possible to develop a high performance, low power architecture while enabling the adaptation necessary for wireless multimedia communication.

Table 3. Comparison of our hardware/software architecture with an embedded software implementation

Software	Hardware	Performance (cycles)	Energy (mJ)
T,Q,E	–	1981287	4.520
E	T,Q	455981	0.765

5   Conclusion

One of the major challenges to the future growth of wireless image communication is the significant energy and bandwidth consumption required. One method for overcoming these bottlenecks is to use run-time adaptation of the wireless radios transmitting multimedia data. In this paper, we present an adaptive hw/sw architecture which enables run-time adaptivity through efficient execution of adaptive image compression and run-time adaptation algorithms. We have reviewed some image compression parameters which can be selected at run-time to conserve energy, and presented our methodology for performing hw/sw mapping to enable adaptivity while maintaining ASIC-like performance. We developed the adaptive hw/sw architecture through co-design of adaptive algorithms and architectures. The adaptive algorithms and architectures presented in this paper ensure minimal adaptation costs while maintaining time and power performance which is close to an ASIC implementation.

References

1. C. N. Taylor, S. Dey, and D. Panigrahi, "Energy/Latency/Image Quality Trade-offs in Enabling Mobile Multimedia Communication", in *Software Radio – Technologies and Services* (E. D. Re, ed.), pp. 55–66, Springer Verlag, 2001.
2. C. N. Taylor and S. Dey, "Adaptive Image Compression for Enabling Mobile Multimedia Communication", in *In Proceedings of IEEE International Conference on Communications*, 2001.
3. S. Kallel, S. Bakhtiyari, and R. Link, "An Adaptive Hybrid ARQ Scheme", *Wireless Personal Communications*, vol. 12, pp. 297–311, March 2000.
4. P. Cherriman and L. Hanzo, "Error-rate Based Power-controlled Multimode H.263-Assisted Video Telephony", *IEEE Transactions on Vehicular Technology*, vol. 48, pp. 1726–38, September 1999.
5. M. Goel, S. Appadwedula, N. R. Shanbhag, K. Ramchandran, and D. L. Jones, "A Low-power Multimedia Communication System for Indoor Wireless Applications", in *1999 IEEE Workshop on Signal Processing Systems. SiPS 99*, pp. 473–82, October 1999.
6. P. F. Joseph A. Fisher and G. Desoli, "Custom-Fit Processors: Letting Applications Define Architectures", in *Proceedings of the 29th IEEE/ACM International Symposium on Microarchitecture*, 1996.
7. C. Ebeling, D. C. Cronquist, and P. Franklin, "RaPiD - Reconfigurable Pipelined Datapath", in *The 6th International Workshop on Field-Programmable Logic and Applications*, 1996.
8. J. R. Hause and J. Wawrzynek, "Garp: A MIPS Processor with a Reconfigurable Coprocessor", in *The 5th Annual IEEE Symposium on Field-Programmable Custom Computing Machines*, April 1997.
9. R. D. Wittig and P. Chow, "OneChip: An FPGA Processor With Reconfigurable Logic", in *IEEE Symposium on FPGAs for Custom Computing Machines*, April 1996.
10. Y. Li, T. Callahan, E. Darnell, R. Harr, U. Kurkure, and J. Stockwood, "Hardware-Software Co-Design of Embedded Reconfigurable Architectures", in *Proceedings, 37th Design Automation Conference*, June 2000.

11. G. K. Wallace, "The JPEG still picture compression standard", in *IEEE Transactions on Consumer Electronics*, vol. 38, February 1992.

12. J. Bracamonte, M. Ansorge, and F. Pellandini, "VLSI systems for image compression. A power-consumption/image-resolution trade-off approach", in *Proceedings of the SPIE - The International Society for Optical Engineering*, vol. 2952, pp. 591–6, October 1996.

13. A. Said and W. A. Pearlman, "A New, Fast, and Efficient Image Codec Based on Set Partitioning in Hierarchical Trees", *IEEE Transactions on Circuits and Systems for Video Technology*, vol. 6, June 1996.

14. M. A. Lepley and R. D. Forkert, "AWIC: Adaptive Wavelet Image Compression", tech. rep., MITRE, September 1997.

15. C. Christopoulos, A. Skodras, and T. Ebrahimi, "The JPEG2000 Still Image Coding System: An Overview", *IEEE Transactions on Consumer Electronics*, vol. 46, pp. 1103–1127, November 2000.

16. "PicoJava MicroProcessor Core," Sun Microsystems,
    http://www.sun.com/microelectronics/picoJava.

17. PI-Bus Toolkit,
    http://www.sussex.ac.uk/engg/research/vlsi-Jan97/projects/pibus.

18. D. Panigrahi, C. N. Taylor, and S. Dey, "Interface Based Hardware/Software Validation of a System-on-Chip", in *Proceedings of 5th IEEE HLDVT Workshop*, November 2000.

19. The Official Bluetooth Info Site, http://www.bluetooth.com.

20. UMC Group, *0.18um 1P6M Logic Process Interconnect Capacitance Model (Rev. 1.2)*, July 1999.

21. Waterloo Repertoire ColorSet, http://links.uwaterloo.ca/colorset.base.html.

Design of Cam-E-leon, a Run-Time Reconfigurable Web Camera

Dirk Desmet[1], Prabhat Avasare[1], Paul Coene[1], Stijn Decneut[1],
Filip Hendrickx[1], Théodore Marescaux[1], Jean-Yves Mignolet[1], Robert Pasko[1],
Patrick Schaumont[2], and Diederik Verkest[1]

[1] IMEC, Kapeldreef 75, B-3001 Leuven, Belgium
desmetd@imec.be
http://www.imec.be
[2] UCLA Electrical Engineering Department
schaum@ee.ucla.edu
http://www.ee.ucla.edu

Abstract. This paper describes the design of a reconfigurable Internet camera, Cam-E-leon, combining reconfigurable hardware and embedded software. The software is based on the μClinux operating system. The network appliance implements a secure VPN (Virtual Private Network) with 3DES encryption and Internet camera server (including JPEG compression). The appliance's hardware can be reconfigured at run-time by the client, thus allowing to switch between several available image manipulation functions. The reconfiguration information is retrieved from a reconfiguration server on the network, thus allowing a flexible implementation of new services.

The paper describes the hardware and software architecture of the platform, the run-time reconfiguration features of the platform including the integration of the platform in the network, and the design process followed to implement the appliance starting from a high-level executable specification.

1 Introduction

Future networked appliances should be able to download services from the network and execute them locally. To support this process, the implementation of a network appliance should be flexible. This flexibility is traditionally provided through the incorporation of a programmable instruction-set processor (ISP) of which the behavior can be changed by downloading new software over the network, possibly using JAVA technology. However, computational performance of software based solutions is inadequate for many modern multi-media applications (e.g. image processing) which typically need to run on such a networked appliance. In addition, the high power dissipation of a software based solution is incompatible with the need for portability and wireless Internet connectivity. The advent of large Field-Programmable Gate Arrays (FPGA) has opened up the possibility to offer flexibility through hardware reconfiguration. The power

E.F. Deprettere et al. (Eds.): SAMOS 2001, LNCS 2268, pp. 274–290, 2002.

dissipation and computational power of an application implemented on such an FPGA lies between software based implementations and complete custom implementations (ASICs) [1]. In this paper we describe the design of a secure web camera that supports dynamic modification of its image processing capabilities by downloading of services from a configuration server in the network. The objectives of this design exercise were twofold:

- to demonstrate the concept of hardware plug-ins: user initiated run-time dynamic reconfiguration of part of the system functionality
- to evaluate the use of a software-centric approach to embedded system design where many of the system's components are based on open source software packages and hardware acceleration is introduced where needed by using a C++ based hardware/software co-design environment called OCAPI-xl [6].

The demonstration platform consists of a processor board from Axis Communications [2] running μClinux [3] and a custom designed board with 2 XILINX Virtex800 FPGAs [4]. The board is connected to an IBIS4-camera, a 1.3 megapixel CMOS image sensor developed by IMEC's spin-off FillFactory [5]. The embedded software uses a standard third-party embedded Linux platform. This software is handling the network protocol layers, as well as the (re-)configuration and control of the FPGAs. The use of Linux eases reuse of existing open-source software modules, which allows us to design the full system in a short time.

The design process starts from a full-software reference implementation, reusing a lot of open-source C and C++ based software. The design of the hardware accelerated modules, that are executed on the FPGAs, starts from this full-software reference implementation. The design is carried out using OCAPI-xl, a C++ based embedded system design environment [6]. OCAPI-xl offers the ability to describe the system in C++, using a class library that supports a system model described as a number of concurrent processes that communicate through primitives like semaphores, messages and shared variables. From this system model, a refinement process allows to translate the processes and communication into a mixed hardware-software implementation, all within a traditional C++ development environment. A final automated HDL code generation step makes the link to traditional hardware development environments to complete the FPGA implementation. In addition, OCAPI-xl supports easy integration of external interfaces and of existing software functions through a mechanism called foreign language interface. This mechanism was used here to link the hardware-models and the embedded Linux software.

In Cam-E-leon, FPGAs are used where a software implementation can not meet the performance requirements, but where flexibility is still desired. In our example this is the case for the image acquisition functionality, consisting of the camera interface (the camera is sampled at 10 MHz), the color reconstruction (de-mosaicing), user-dependent image manipulation, JPEG compression and the 3DES encryption, used in the VPN IPSEC security layer. A number of image manipulation plug-ins, selectable at run-time by the user from a web browser, demonstrate the concept of networked reconfiguration.

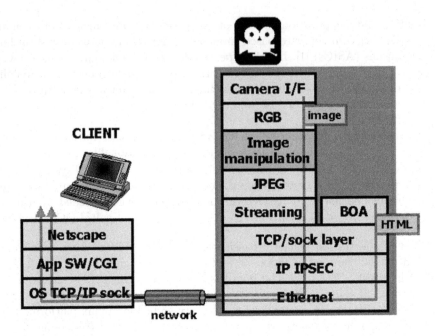

Fig. 1. Cam-E-leon system functionality. For simplicity, the functionality taking care of reconfiguration is not shown.

Specifically for the Cam-E-leon web camera, we developed the Boot-Up Reconfigurable Platforms Protocol (BRPP), a new protocol similar to BootP and DHCP, to allow the camera platform to discover and retrieve the available configurations and services on the network. At boot time the reconfigurable embedded device localizes a neighboring 'reconfiguration server', a machine that stores and serves a number of HW/SW configurations to its clients. During a second phase, the reconfigurable appliance negotiates its characteristics and required services with the reconfiguration server. The server will then respond by providing the list of available services. On request, the reconfiguration server uploads new services to the reconfigurable platform that dynamically reconfigures its FPGAs and adapts the HW/SW communication, to interface with the new application.

Section 2 provides details about the system functionality including the network protocol layer, the image capture and compression, and the security aspects. Section 3 provides details about the architecture of the implementation platform. Section 4 explains the design flow that was used to design the Cam-E-leon. Section 5 explains the run-time reconfiguration capabilities of the platform. Finally, in section 6 we summarize the main points of the paper.

2   System Functionality

Figure 1 gives an overview of the system functionality. The left-hand side of the picture shows a user terminal (client) that runs a regular browser and connects via the Internet (TCP/IP, HTTP, ...) to the Cam-E-leon appliance. Some specific application software (CGI and JAVA scripting) allows to control the remote device. The right-hand side of the picture shows the Cam-E-leon functionality. On top of the network protocol stack, we implement the web camera functionality (camera interface, RGB reconstruction, image manipulation, JPEG compression, video streaming), a web server (boa) that serves HTML pages to the client, and - not shown in the picture - some functionality to reconfigure the platform.

The physical connection is done via Ethernet. On top of that we run TCP/IP with IPSEC and VPN functionality. VPN is a technology that allows a secure connection (commonly referred to as a "tunnel") between two network devices. The security is provided through a mechanism of authentication, encryption (in our case using 3DES), and key exchange. In Cam-E-leon we use freeS/WAN [9], a public domain IPSEC library for Linux. The main performance bottleneck in the network functionality consists of the 3DES encryption. As will be explained further on, this bottleneck is removed by integrating a hardware accelerated implementation of 3DES in the system.

The image capture functionality of the system consists of the following steps: the camera interface, the RGB reconstruction (or demosaicing) and the JPEG compression. The IBIS4 CMOS camera we used in Cam-E-leon provides a picture of 1280 x 1024 x 10 bit at a sample rate of 10 MHz. The RGB reconstruction transforms this picture into a 640 x 480 pixel RGB image (3 x 8 bits), suitable for JPEG compression. The JPEG algorithm works on a YUV decimated image (in our case YUV 422) and achieves a compression ratio of a factor 30, from 900 KB/frame to 30 KB/frame. Finally, the compressed frames are streamed to the client using a modified version of Camserv [10], again a public domain software package.

In between the RGB reconstruction and the JPEG compression functionality, optional image manipulation can be performed. This part of the functionality can be downloaded over the network under control of the user. More details about this mechanism are provided in section 5.

3   System Architecture

Figure 2 shows the hardware architecture of the complete system. The system is implemented on three boards. The CMOS image sensor is mounted on a separate board together with some I/O and is clocked at 10 MHz. All the system software, including the μClinux OS, runs on an ETRAX100 processor that is mounted on a board obtained from Axis Communications running at 100 MHz. This board contains 4 MB DRAM and 16 MB Flash memory, interfaces, and the Ethernet physical interface that is used to communicate with the client. A third, custom developed, board contains the two Virtex800 FPGAs together with 2 Mbit SRAM memory each for data storage. This board can operate between 20 MHz and 50 MHz[1]. The two Virtex800 FPGAs are connected directly to each

---

[1] The Ethernet connection on this board is not used in this particular experiment. Its purpose is to allow a direct download of the hardware (re-)configuration data to the FPGAs without passing via the processor board.

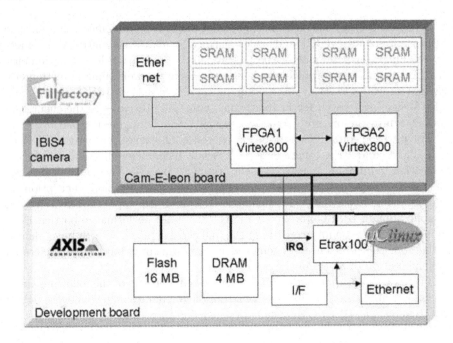

Fig. 2. Cam-E-leon system architecture.

other. Each Virtex800 FPGA further has a connection to the bus on the Axis board and a dedicated interrupt line is foreseen from each Virtex800 FPGA to the ETRAX processor.

The software image (μClinux , Camserv, IPSEC, drivers, TCP, ...) resides in the Flash memory of the Axis board. The compressed μClinux kernel including basic applications and patched with FreeS/WAN requires approximately 1 MByte (uncompressed this becomes 2.5 MB). The Flash memory further contains a file system (/mnt/flash) of about 900 KByte containing the Camserv executable, JPEG image data files, configuration files, default HTML pages, BRPP daemon, etc. Approximately 2MB of the Flash memory are used as a RAM drive to store downloaded Virtex configuration files and HTML pages. The hardware configuration files for the Cam-E-leon board are downloaded (in compressed format) over the network via the Axis board and uncompressed on the ETRAX processor before being used to reconfigure the FPGAs. In our case the configuration file for a single FPGA is approximately 50 KB when compressed with gzip. After uncompressing it becomes approximately 500 KB.

In the experiment described in this paper, one of the FPGAs contains the camera interface, RGB reconstruction, image manipulation and JPEG compression functionality. The other FPGA contains the 3DES encryption functionality. In principle all functionality could have been implemented on a single Virtex800 FPGA. The only concern was bandwidth to the memory and therefore, the

JPEG compression writes its results in the second memory attached to the second FPGA.

4   Design Flow

The design of a complex hardware-software system like the one at hand, necessitates a high-level reference model, from which every component can be refined towards its implementation description (HDL or C). For this design we start from a full software implementation of the system, making use as much as possible of Linux and open-source software. The hardware design process starts from these C/C++ implementations, and uses the OCAPI-xl design flow to gradually refine these C++ implementations to a level from which VHDL code for final implementation can be generated automatically. The design of the large JPEG encoder is explained in more detail in section 4.3. We also show how an existing VHDL module (the 3DES encryption block) can be included in the design.

4.1   All Software Reference Model

System design starts by building a full software reference model, first on a Linux PC, in a second step on the embedded processor running μClinux .

4.2   C++ for Hardware Design

C++ based design methodologies are among the latest attempts to deal with the complexity of system-on-chip (SoC) designs by introducing the object oriented programming paradigm (OOP) into the design process. The essential idea of all C++ based methodologies is to provide a set of semantic primitives required for the design of hardware (and software), complemented with the necessary simulation and code-generation engines, in a form of an extendible library of classes. The amount of semantic primitives, as well as the underlying computational model(s) can vary from one methodology to another.

The OOP paradigm is very well suited for such approach, since it allows to define and use the new primitives in the same way as the built-in data types and functions. When using a C++ based methodology, the designer must devise the system description using the predefined objects, or his own extensions. Afterwards, the description is compiled using a C++ compiler, resulting in an executable specification providing simulation and/or code generation.

OCAPI-xl can be considered a good example of a C++ based design methodology [6], specifically intended for the design of heterogeneous HW/SW systems. It features a unified approach to hardware and software code, provides parallelism at a process level, and supports communication primitives like messages or semaphores.

The basic quantum of computation is an instruction. The necessary set of arithmetic, logic, assignment, as well as looping and branching instructions is defined. To support parallel execution, OCAPI-xl provides the notion of a process

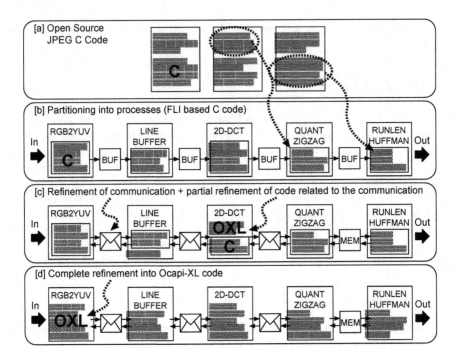

Fig. 3. JPEG Encoder Design Flow

as the basic level of parallelism and hierarchy. Communication between processes is implemented via three basic communication primitives: messages, semaphores, and shared variables. Finally, to increase flexibility, a direct interface to C++ is implemented via a so-called Foreign Language Interface (FLI). It makes possible to run any snippet of C++ code during an OCAPI-xl simulation.

Finally, the OCAPI-xl description compiles into executable code. In addition, it supports code-generation to other languages: VHDL/Verilog for hardware and C for software. The FLIs are appearing in the generated code as function calls in the C code and black-boxes with appropriate ports in the VHDL/Verilog code.

4.3   Design of a JPEG Encoder with OCAPI-xl

The design of a JPEG encoder demonstrates how a C++ based methodology allows a step-wise gradual refinement of the target application starting from a high level C code. The complete design effort can be divided into several major phases, as shown in Figure 3.

We start from an openly available JPEG encoder model included in a video conferencing software application [7]. In the first step, the parallel threads inside the encoder were identified and the corresponding C code was partitioned into OCAPI-xl processes using the FLI mechanism, as indicated in Figure 3[b]. The communication between processes was still implemented via C buffers. The following JPEG processes were identified:

- **Color convertor** transforms the color information from RGB to YUV encoding.
- **Line buffer** re-groups the camera input into 8×8 blocks.
- **2D-DCT** calculates the two-dimensional DCT.
- **Quantizer** quantizes the DCT output and simultaneously performs the zig-zag re-ordering.
- **Huffman** performs the run-length and Huffman encoding.

In the second step, the communication refinement takes place. This includes introduction of the appropriate communication primitives, i.e. messages and memory buffers instead of the C buffers, as well as writing the OCAPI-xl communication code inside of each process, as shown in Figure 3[c]. However, the core functionality is still implemented via the FLIs, so the communication scheme can be tested before coding of the behavior starts.

Finally, the C code in each FLI is gradually rewritten into OCAPI-xl code, resulting in executable specification, out of which the VHDL code can be generated. The obvious advantage of the presented methodology is the possibility to approach a design in a completely incremental way. At each stage, the complete simulation test benches from previous refinements are available and new code can be cross-checked against any of them.

Table 1 gives an overview of simulation times for different versions (image size, abstraction level) of JPEG models during the OCAPI-xl refinement.

Table 1. Simulation times for JPEG at different abstraction levels

Image size	32 x 32	256 x 256
Software reference code	1 sec	30 sec
High-level OCAPI-xl code	6 sec	289 sec
Refined OCAPI-xl code	15 sec	650 sec
Generated VHDL code	3 min	> 60 min

After synthesis of the generated VHDL code, the JPEG block occupies approximately 38 % of the Virtex800 FPGA running at 33 MHz.

4.4 Interfacing a VHDL Block in the System: The 3DES Encryption

The VPN layer is based on the Linux IPSEC implementation of freeS/WAN. The computationally most intensive part in IPSEC is the 3DES encryption. Therefore we opt for an implementation where the IPSEC layer runs mainly in software, with an hardware acceleration of the encryption function.

Rather than implementing the 3DES function ourselves, we have chosen to integrate an existing hardware implementation of this block, thus demonstrating the feasibility of IP integration. The DES hardware module was taken from [8].

In order to connect this block is our system a hardware wrapper module needs to be written. This wrapper maps the (relevant) I/O ports of the block

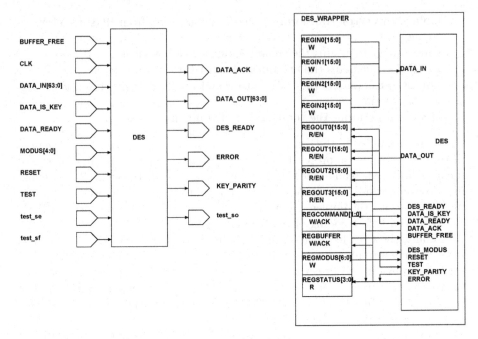

Fig. 4. DES block I/O ports and wrapper.

on the available HW/SW communication primitives: memory-mapped registers and interrupts. In this case only memory mapped registers were used. Figure 4 shows, on the left-hand side, the DES block with its I/O ports and, on the right-hand side, the interface wrapper. The interface makes use of the following types of registers:

- **W** write registers: software writes, hardware reads.
- **W/ACK** write registers with acknowledge: software writes, hardware reads and acknowledges by clearing the register. This is used to implement the command registers, by which software can trigger an action in the hardware block.
- **R** read registers: software reads, hardware writes.
- **R/EN** read registers with enable: software reads, hardware writes when enable is high.

With this interface an efficient driver can be easily written in software. Since it works fully without interrupts (polling), this driver can be easily used in the IPSEC routines, which are implemented as interrupt handlers in Linux.

When using this hardware accelerated encryption together with freeS/WAN on the processor, we can observe an important speedup. Indeed, while the elapsed time measured to transmit a 20 KB packet over the network in an all software version was 550 ms, the time with the hardware accelerated 3DES was 130 ms. This can be compared to 75 ms, when using clear text (without encryption).

5   Run-Time Reconfiguration

In the Cam-E-leon system both hardware and software modules can be reconfigured over the Internet while the camera is operating. To help with the camera's run-time reconfiguration, the boot-up reconfigurable platforms protocol (BRPP) was developed. It is a method by which a reconfigurable embedded device seeks a local reconfiguration server during boot-up to locate and dynamically retrieve hardware and software options.

The smart web-cam uses a virtual private network (VPN) link to deliver the moving images it captures. Using a web browser, a user can select from a number of image manipulation plug-ins stored on a reconfiguration server. The server uploads the new image manipulation services and dynamically reconfigures the camera's hardware and software to implement the different image manipulation function.

5.1   Boot-Up Reconfigurable Platforms Protocol

Reconfigurable platforms are meant to be deeply embedded and provide dynamically adaptable functionality. They are thus too small to store all HW/SW information. BRPP (Boot-Up Reconfigurable Platforms Protocol) has been designed to be an interface between reconfigurable platforms and remote HW/SW information.

BRPP First Phase: Service Localization. At boot time BRPP is the counterpart for reconfigurable appliances of BootP/DHCP, allowing for discovery of local reconfiguration information and optionally providing dynamic IP allocation. In this first phase the reconfigurable platform broadcasts a BRPP message on top of UDP.

The BRPP request (UDP broadcast destination port 58888) contains the following fields:

- Header Length
- Message Type (Request)
- Hardware Type (Ethernet)
- Hardware Address Length
- Max number of Hops
- Client HW Address (00:20:af:5c:c5:5e)
- Client IP Address (0.0.0.0)
- Server HW Address (00:00:00:00:00:00)
- Server IP Address (0.0.0.0)
- Reconfiguration Port (0)
- Negotiation Port (0)
- Platform Type (Cam-E-leon)
- Transaction ID
- Seconds Elapsed since Boot-Up attempt
- Checksum
- Options Length

The reconfigurable appliance announces its hardware address and platform type. On this basis a simple identification can already be performed by a BRPP server allowing it to direct the reconfigurable device to a suitable reconfiguration server. Optionally other parameters can be introduced, such as the name of a specific reconfiguration server we want to connect to. A local BRPP server answers by broadcasting a BRPP Reply.

A BRPP reply (UDP broadcast destination port 58889) consists of the following fields:

- Header Length
- Message Type (Reply)
- Hardware Type (Ethernet)
- Hardware Address Length
- Max number of Hops
- Client HW Address (00:20:af:5c:c5:5e)
- Client IP Address (146.103.4.67)
- Server HW Address (00:c0:4f:a3:4b:c3)
- Server IP Address (146.103.6.143)
- Reconfiguration Port (58888)
- Negotiation Port (58889)
- Platform Type (Cam-E-leon)
- Transaction ID
- Seconds Elapsed since Boot-Up attempt
- Checksum
- Options

The reconfiguration server may optionally provide its clients with a temporary IP address if required - i.e. if the Client IP Address field was 0.0.0.0 during BRPP request. More important, the BRPP reply contains all information about a local reconfiguration server:

1. IP address
2. Reconfiguration Port Number
3. Negotiation Port Number

This information allows the reconfigurable appliance to start negotiating with the reconfiguration server, which concludes its initiation phase. The full client-server communication for BRPP-Service Localization is illustrated in Figure 5.

BRPP Second Phase: Negotiation. Once a board has all required information to localize a reconfiguration server - whether it was previously known or discovered during the first phase of BRPP - it can start the negotiation phase (see Figure 6). The reconfigurable appliance opens a TCP connection on the negotiation port of the reconfiguration server, and sends a meta-object (ideally XML-formatted) to identify itself - platform type, user port, encryption method, ... - and asks for a particular class of services, in our case image manipulation plug-ins.

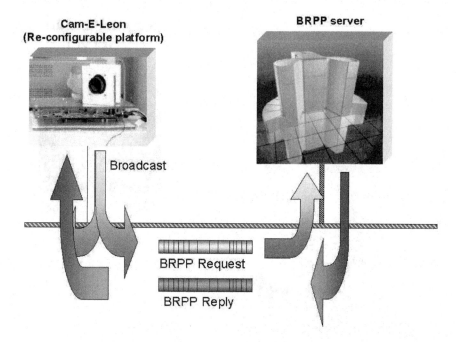

Fig. 5. BRPP Service Localization phase

The negotiation server answers with another meta-object containing the list of available services and also the user-interface to request/use these services - in our case it is a dynamically generated web-page, integrating the video streams, camera settings and the reconfiguration control part under the form of hyper-text links. The embedded platform may choose to download one of these services by default or simply wait for a client to connect and choose a particular service.

BRPP: Providing Dynamic Services to Clients. The reconfigurable appliance is now ready to provide dynamic services to clients. The end-user connecting to the Cam-E-leon, sees a web page served by the boa server of the Cam-E-leon appliance (see Figure 7) built up as a frame-set. One frame contains the stream of JPEG images. Another contains a list of available image manipulation plug-ins that can be selected by the user:

1. Standard JPEG encoder
2. Small JPEG encoder
3. "Pablo" image scrambling
4. Motion detection

The default plug-in is the standard JPEG encoder. The user can select to reconfigure the device with a small (screen) JPEG encoder which will approximately triple the frame rate. The third plug-in is an image scrambling application that will move certain regions of the captured picture to fixed locations in a Picasso

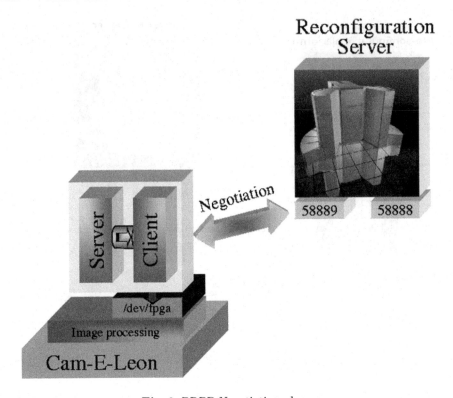

Fig. 6. BRPP Negotiation phase

painting. The fourth plug-in will direct the camera platform to transmit a still image unless some motion is detected at which point in time, life images are streamed.

The web page (Figure 7) also contains some parameters of the platform that can be modified by the user. These parameters control various settings of the camera such as exposure time, gain, ... and are not linked to the image manipulation functionality.

The image manipulation plug-ins are composed of different hardware accelerators, downloaded and instantiated at run-time on the FPGAs and of software parts mainly HTML-embedded components, such as Java-script code, transparent GIF images, etc. Reconfiguration happens when a user requests a plug-in from the services list that is not currently running on the board. The request is forwarded by the board to the reconfiguration server on the reconfiguration port (see Figure 8). The reconfiguration server replies with an object containing the bitstream for the HW part and the SW code of the specified plug-in.

The communication between reconfigurable appliance and reconfiguration board is based on the HTTP protocol. The reconfiguration server is a standard HTTP server, in our case Apache [11], running on port 58888. This allows for easy deployment on various platforms and does not require extra implementation. The

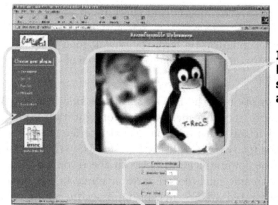

**Image served
by camera
showing
author (?)**

**List of
available
plug-ins**

**Platform pre-defined parameters
can be adapted by user on the fly**

Fig. 7. Cam-E-leon User-Interface Screen-Shot

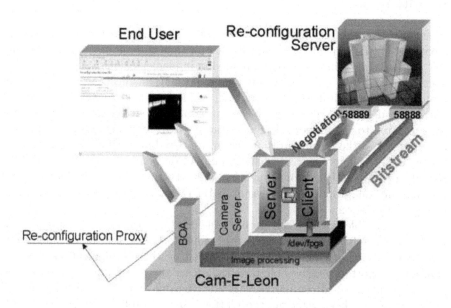

Fig. 8. BRPP Reconfiguration Chain

reconfiguration data transmitted is gzip compressed. Transmission of compressed objects doesn't only save bandwidth but also provides a simple but efficient CRC test performed by the decompression tools.

Once the reconfiguration object has been retrieved from the reconfiguration server, the board switches to a reconfiguration state to perform the following tasks:

1. Unzip the reconfiguration object and check it
2. Stop all services
3. Trigger FPGA reconfiguration with the downloaded bitstream
4. Adapt the software interface to the new components
5. Resume operation

The actual reconfiguration of the FPGA takes less than 200 ms. With a frame rate of about 5 frames/sec, this means the reconfiguration is completed within the span of about 1 frame, with minimal visual interference.

The board is then ready to provide the new service to the client that requested it, see Figure 8. The communication between the reconfigurable platform and its client - JPEG streams and reconfiguration requests - is done over a VPN using hardware accelerated 3-DES encryption. A secure communication between reconfigurable platform and reconfiguration server is not yet implemented in the demonstrator, but could easily be introduced taking advantage of the existing components such as the hardware 3DES.

Security Issues

Security in Negotiation and Service Delivery: The main focus in the development of Cam-E-leon was to demonstrate run-time reconfiguration of HW and SW plug-ins, little time was to be invested in implementation of security mechanisms. Nevertheless, secure transmission of information, authentication and non-repudiation are capital issues for reconfigurable systems. We tried as much as possible to design the middle-ware so that secure communications could be easily integrated to the framework. For instance, the reconfiguration requests from the platform to the reconfiguration server are based on HTTP. A conversion to Secure-HTTP using the existing 3DES encryption and some additional Public-Key algorithm (e.g. RSA) for authentication and symmetric key exchange, could be smoothly integrated to the design. S-HTTP natively allows for encryption method negotiation.

Reconfigurable systems, are deeply embedded and thus have to spread their hardware and software information over the network. Because the reconfigurable platform functionality can be deeply modified by the reconfiguration object it is of vital importance to be able to authenticate the reconfiguration server, ensuring the downloaded configuration is not offensive. For authentication as well as for symmetric-key exchange, the platform should probably implement some public-key algorithm such as RSA. However, key pair generation being a very computationally intensive task, might be left to another - trusted - machine and transmitted to the platform through secure means.

The integrity of the downloaded information has also to be checked, because it is of capital importance that a third party does not modify the reconfiguration information while we are downloading it. Some extra message-digestion algorithm like MD5 is thus required.

Finally, confidentiality about used services and platform type has to be guaranteed by encryption. Our experience with 3DES implemented in hardware is quite positive as it has a gain of 9x performance compared to the version running in software and also allows for a more constant information flow, reducing the jitter in the JPEG stream. Nevertheless 3DES is now an aging algorithm, one should more likely look into some newer ones as AES, ...

Security in Service Discovery: A very sensitive part of the system is the service discovery. If an embedded reconfigurable platform is to discover what services are locally provided on the local network it just booted on, it has to "trust" some of the partners in that local network. For instance, in the case of Cam-E-leon, the first phase of BRPP is a broadcast on UDP and the board expects an answer pointing to a reconfiguration server. It has to have means to distinguish whether the server it was pointed to is friendly. Naturally this could be discovered during authentication of the server just before the (BRPP) negotiation phase. Nevertheless, it may be a good idea to be able to have some "certificate" per server basis, or per service basis.

6   Conclusions

In this paper we described the design of a smart networked camera the behavior of which can be changed over the network. The camera implements video streaming functionality using motion-JPEG over a secure IPSEC/VPN network link. Both image processing functionality and encryption functionality are accelerated through FPGA hardware implementations. In addition, extra image manipulation services (plug-ins) which are available on the network can be selected by the user and dynamically downloaded on the platform where they reconfigure both hardware and software aspects. Figure 9 shows a picture of the Cam-E-leon platform.

The Cam-E-leon platform serves about 5 frames/second in normal operation (with images of 640 by 480 pixels) and uses about 6.5 Watt. Compared to a software JPEG solution, the hardware accelerated version results in a speed-up of a factor 10, improving the energy efficiency of the platform also with a factor of 10^2

References

1. A. DeHon, "The Density Advantage of Configurable Computing", *IEEE Computer*, pp. 41- 49, April 2000.
2. Axis Communications, http://www.axis.com/
3. μClinux, http://www.uclinux.org/
4. Xilinx, http://www.xilinx.com/
5. FillFactory, http://www.fillfactory.com/

---

[2] The power dissipation does not change significantly by hardware acceleration of JPEG. Software related power remains unchanged as the processor is 100 % busy with μClinux and other software anyhow. Hardware related power increases only slightly (from 3.78 Watt to 4.05 Watt) by the hardware acceleration of JPEG.

Fig. 9. The Cam-E-leon boards. The ETRAX processor board is hidden underneath the big Cam-E-leon board with the Virtex FPGAs.

6. G. Vanmeerbeeck, P. Schaumont, S. Vernalde, M. Engels, I. Bolsens, "Hardware/Software Partitioning of Embedded Systems in OCAPI-xl", *Proceedings of Ninth International Symposium on Hardware/Software Co-design (CODES-2001)*, Copenhagen, Denmark, pp. 30-35, April 2001.
7. UCB/LBNL Video Conferencing Tool (vic), http://www-nrg.ee.lbl.gov/vic/
8. http://www.ra.informatik.uni-stuttgart.de/s̃tankats/pg99.html
9. LINUX FreeS/WAN, http://www.xs4all.nl/freeswan/
10. Camserv, http://cserv.sourceforge.net/
11. Apache server, http://httpd.apache.org/

A 2D Addressing Mode for Multimedia Applications

Georgi Kuzmanov[1], Stamatis Vassiliadis[1], and Jos T.J. van Eijndhoven[2]

[1] Delft University of Technology – Electrical Engineering Dept.,
P.O. Box 5031, 2600 GA Delft, The Netherlands
{G.Kuzmanov,S.Vassiliadis}@ET.TUDelft.NL
[2] PHILIPS Research - Dept. of Information and Software Technology,
Eindhoven, The Netherlands
jos.van.eijndhoven@philips.com

Abstract. This paper discusses architectural solutions that deal with the high data throughput and the high computational power - two crucial performance requirements of MPEG standards. To increase the data throughput, we define a new data storage facility with a specific data organization and a new addressing mode. More specifically, we introduce an addressing function and refer to it as two-dimensional block addressing. Furthermore, we propose such an addressing approach, as an architectural feature and we believe it has useful properties that may position it as a basic addressing mode in future multimedia architectures. In addition, we propose an instruction set extension, utilizing the advantages of this addressing mode, as means of improving the computational power of a general-purpose super-scalar processor. To illustrate this concept, we have implemented a new instruction "ACcepted Quality" as a dedicated systolic structure. This instruction supports the corresponding function "ACQ" as defined in the Verification Model of MPEG-4. Its FPGA realization suggests 62 ns operating latency. Utilizing this result, we have made performance evaluations with a benchmark software (MPEG-4 shape encoder) using a cycle-accurate simulator. The simulation results indicate that the performance is increased by up to 10%. The introduced approach can be utilized by data encoding tools, which are based on block division of data. These tools are an essential part of many recent and up coming visual data compression standards like MPEG-4.

1 Introduction

The recent development of multimedia applications made them one of the most demanding types of workloads. Their new performance requirements already exceed the capabilities of current general-purpose architectures[1]. Therefore, the need for architectures, dedicated for the new multimedia applications, provokes the nontrivial problem to define such architectures. On the other hand, the fast development rate of the new visual data compression standards, like MPEG,

---

[1] In this paper, by architecture of any computer system, we mean the conceptual structure and functional behavior as seen by its immediate user [2]

E.F. Deprettere et al. (Eds.): SAMOS 2001, LNCS 2268, pp. 291–306, 2002.
© Springer-Verlag Berlin Heidelberg 2002

dramatically shortens the time-to-market constraints and increases the flexibility requirements. Furthermore, the enormous memory throughput and high computational power, required by the recent MPEG standards, become crucial in solving the problems with their real-time implementation.

Most of the algorithms in MPEG applications are *data intensive* and have two very important features: *data locality* and *data reusability*. These two features require a very intensive data transfer over a restricted location of data. In MPEG this transfer is non-symmetrical - memory loads are much more in number than memory stores and data are processed identically. These properties can be exploited to achieve a better performance of an MPEG architectural implementation. In addition, the support of many functionalities found in multimedia standards (e.g., MPEG-4) is optional. In such cases, it is not effective to make a hardwired architectural implementation that supports all functionalities in the standards. To keep the implementation of such a complex multimedia architecture at a reasonable cost-performance ratio, a *reconfigurable approach* can be used.

In this paper, with architectural solutions, we enable implementations that would easily meet the performance requirements of the new multimedia applications. The reported work represents parts of the research, involved into the development of a reconfigurable microcoded processor within the MOLEN project [20]. In this project, a new processor architecture is proposed that supports reconfiguration at the architectural level and achieves high flexibility in tuning a system for a specific application. The reconfiguration and execution processes are controlled by only three new instructions, allowing instructions, entire pieces of code, or their combination to execute in a reconfigurable manner. More specifically, this paper proposes the following solutions. To obtain *higher data bandwidth* we define at the *architectural level* a new addressing mode, referred to as *two-dimensional block addressing*. This addressing mode involves three architectural features:

- *Two-dimensional data storage* displayed to the immediate user of the architecture;
- *Block data type* as a basic addressable unit;
- *Two-dimensional addressing function* for random access of blocks of visual data.

To make the benefits of the defined addressing mode stronger and to *improve the computational power* of the system, we also propose an *instruction set extension*. We have implemented the new instruction "ACcepted Quality" (ACQ), which supports the identically named function in MPEG-4. This instruction utilizes the two-dimensional block addressing and is an essential part of the shape encoding process. The ACQ has been implemented as a scalable systolic structure, described in VHDL. The VHDL source has been synthesized for an FPGA chip, and netlist simulations have been run. The data, reported from the FPGA netlist simulator have been used into a cycle-accurate simulator of an out-of-order superscalar microarchitecture. Assuming Altera FPGAs and the

SimpleScalar toolset [5] for microarchitectural simulations, we reduce the calculation of the ACQ function to 62ns, allowing performance gains of the shape encoder by up to 10%.

The discussion in this paper is organized as follows. Section 2 gives some background information about data processing and organization in visual data compression standards. In Section 3 the problem with visual data alignment in conventional, linearly addressable memories is discussed. Some related work is reported in Section 4. Section 5 proposes the new addressing mode, gives a formal definition of it and suggests its possible utilization. In Section 6 a new function, utilizing the newly defined addressing, is proposed and its implementation is discussed. An evaluation of the proposed structure is performed and the results are reported in Section 7. The conclusions of this paper are included in Section 8.

2   Visual Data Presentation in MPEG

The industrial impact of the new digital technology urged the development of standards for digital video compression. All these standards aim to preserve best possible visual quality at a given bitrate range. In this paper we focus on the MPEG standards and their basic requirements. The first generation video coding standard, MPEG-1, is dedicated for data rates on the order of 1.5 Mbit/s and is intended for storing digital audio-visual information in a storage medium such as CD-ROM. MPEG-2 extends the bitrate to the range of over 10Mbit/s and is currently used as basic coding standard for digital TV broadcasting and High Definition Television (HDTV). The latest complete visual coding standard, MPEG-4 [12][13], enables data transmission at very low bit rates (64 kbit/s). The inclusion of entirely new *content-oriented* functionalities, however, makes most of the specialists refer to MPEG-4 as a new standard generation rather than the next MPEG version. While in MPEG-1,2 a whole frame of a video sequence is processed, in MPEG-4 the frame is decomposed with respect to its content and each decomposed part is processed separately.

In all MPEG standards, visual data is physically displayed as a two-dimensional plane of picture elements (pixels). The basic building block of an MPEG picture is the macroblock (MB) depicted in Figure 1. Each macroblock consists of a 16x16 array of luminance (grayscale) pixels and two 8x8-pixel chrominance (color) blocks. These three blocks actually cover the same picture area to represent its full-color and each 16x16 luminance block is processed as four 8x8-pixel blocks.

For content-based coding, MPEG-4 uses the concept of a video object plane (VOP). VOP is an arbitrarily shaped region of a frame, which usually corresponds to a semantic object in the visual scene. A sequence of VOPs in time domain is referred to as a Video Object (VO). This means that we can view a VOP as a "frame" of a VO. Each of the video objects is transmitted by a separate bitstream of arbitrary-shaped VOPs. Once the VOPs, required for a visual scene composition are available in the receiver, the corresponding frame

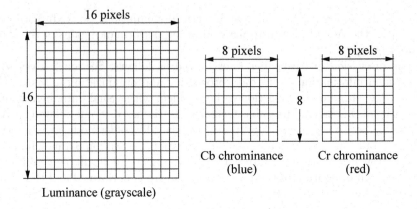

Fig. 1. The MPEG Macro Block

Fig. 2. Frame composition in MPEG-4

is reconstructed. The concept of the frame composition in MPEG-4 is sketched in Figure 2.

To distinguish an object from the background and to identify the borders of a VOP, MPEG-4 defines *shape* of an object. Shape information is provided in binary or grayscale format. The binary format represents the object shape as a pixel map, which has the same size as the bounding rectangular box of the VOP. Each pixel from this bitmap takes one of two possible values, which indicate whether a pixel belongs to the object or not. The binary shape representation of a VOP is referred to as *binary alpha plane*. This plane is partitioned into 16x16 *binary alpha blocks* and each binary alpha block is associated with the macroblock, which covers the same picture area. In the grayscale shape format, each pixel can take a range of values, which indicate its transparency. The transparency value can be used for different shape effects (e.g.,blending of two images).

3   The Addressing Problem in MPEG

Video information is represented as a scanned sequence of pixels from a two dimensional visual plane. In digital video systems, this information is usually stored into linearly addressable memories and displayed later as two-dimensional frames. In MPEG standards, this information is processed and modified between the scan and display phases. Most of data processing in these standards, however, is not performed over pixel sequences, but over certain regions (blocks of pixels) from a frame, and this arises some problems with data alignment and accessibility into systems memory. To illustrate these problems, let us take the following example. Let us assume a linearly addressable memory and a pixel plane divided into blocks with dimensions 2x2, where each pixel is represented by a byte (see Figure 3). In linear addressing spaces the basic addressable units are bytes and words. We store video information in a conventional scan-line manner and we want to access the pixel block containing pixels 1, 2, 11 and 12. This pixel block (32 bits of information) is not aligned into consecutive memory locations (see Figure 3b) and we can not access it by a single memory transfer even if we can transfer a 32-bit word per memory cycle. This may lead to delays in data processing since the processor would have to wait for the whole data delivery. For MPEG-1,2 we may tune the memory system to pack the right bytes into a word, since the scan line length is a constant, equal to the width of the frame. In MPEG-4, however, this would not be so simple. The reason is that the scan line length is equal to the width of the VOP, which in turn may take any arbitrary value.

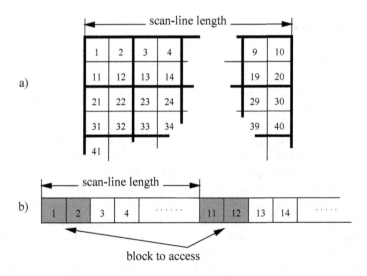

Fig. 3. Video Data Alignment into Linearly Addressable Memory: a) Pixels in a Video Frame; b) Block Access in a Scan-Line Aligned Data Memory.

The other extreme approach to access block-organized data, stored into linearly addressable memory space is to reorder data. If we store each block of pixels into consecutive bytes (Figure 4), we will be able to access the whole required information for these blocks in a single memory cycle (e.g., block with pixels 1, 2, 11 and 12). In MPEG standards, however, some of the most demanding algorithms (e.g., motion estimation) do not process only the blocks, set into the original block grid. These algorithms also require to access block data with arbitrary position in the frame. In such cases the block-oriented reordering would not help for accessing the right piece of data. For example block containing pixels 12, 13, 22 and 23 (Figure 4) can not be accessed in a single memory cycle, not even in two cycles, because its pixels are scattered through the memory.

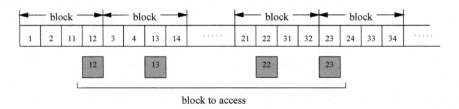

Fig. 4. Block-based Alignment of Visual Data into Linearly Addressable Memory

These two examples show that different memory organizations and addressing modes are vital for data processing speed-up of MPEG architectures and their implementations.

4   Related Work

In [14], the three common addressing paterns for vector processors are described. They are classified as *sequential, regular* and *submatrix* accesses. The submatrix access is, in essence, a two-dimensional addressing in a square vector array with firmly defined dimensions.

In [16], Park develops the ideas from [4][15][17][19] for two-dimensional data alignment into multiple memory modules. He proposes a faster buffer memory system by separating the address calculation from the address routing and solving the complex control problem of the latter. This concept for data allocation has been used in the design of graphical display systems where it is referred to as a *block subarray access*. However, it is not defined as an *architectural* issue and is not implemented within visual data compression standards.

A flexible processor, adapted to conventional motion-estimation algorithms is proposed in [6]. Some ideas for a specific data-memory organization and access are discussed and a trial-and-error data reordering is proposed for algorithm independent and optimal performance solutions. This processor is too specialized and requires additional data reordering.

An extensive exploration in memory management and organization for MPEG-4 encoders is reported in [3,18]. However the focus is in the field of low-power consumption. The proposal combines background and foreground memory in a low-power optimized hierarchy and an approach to design a processor array within the context of the derived memory organization. The power consumption is minimized by dramatically decreasing the number of background memory accesses without sacrificing speed (e.g., without changing the memory bandwidth).

Multiprocessor video processing systems with distributed embedded DRAM are discussed in [9,10]. The DRAM and local SRAM of the systems are distributed to multiple processor nodes. The integrated DRAM is primarily used as frame buffer. Loading and storing operations between local SRAM and DRAM are controlled by a DMA controller, capable of addressing rectangular image portions. A mechanism for block oriented data transfer between the processor nodes is also discussed. The memory organization is not designed for co-existence with a general-purpose processor (GPP) and is not intended for an FPGA implementation.

In [1], some instruction set extensions aiming at MPEG-4 video are proposed. New instructions are proposed for block-level processing, bitstream parsing, shape processing and padding. A VLSI MPEG-4 codec, called M-PIRE, was developed and its macroblock engine described in [8]. The same paper emphasizes on the instruction set discussion as well.

In this paper we differentiate with previous proposals in one or more of the following:

- We define the architectural aspects of a universal, reconfigurable data storage, dedicated for block-organized visual data (differentiates from [6,16]).
- The storage is compatible with any general-purpose architecture and is suitable for an implementation in a custom computing machine - a hybrid between GPP and FPGA(differentiates from [9,10]).
- The definition allows implementations with higher data throughput (differentiates from [3,18]).
- This storage should be utilized by reconfigurable accelerators, supporting important multimedia instructions. We implement the ACQ instruction for the first time (therefore not included in [1,8]).

We also differentiate from all previous proposals (including [14]) in defining the two-dimensional addressing over a two-dimensional data storage with variable dimensions.

5   The Two-Dimensional Addressing

Visual information has a two-dimensional structure, so the most natural approach for accessing it is to address a two-dimensional memory space. Since the basic unit being processed in MPEG is the pixel block, we can assume an addressing space with two dimensional logical organization, where the basic addressable units are blocks. Figure 5 depicts an abstract design model of the proposed idea.

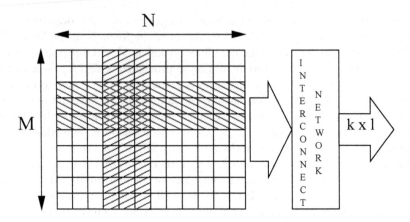

Fig. 5. An Abstract Design Model of a 2D Addressable Memory

The interconnect network is responsible for routing the right data block from the memory array to the processing units.

Definition 1 *We define the Two-Dimensional Block Addressing as the following address function:*

$$A_{k,l}^{B}(i,j) =$$

$$= \begin{vmatrix} p_{i,j} & p_{i,j+1} & \cdots & p_{i,j+k-1} \\ p_{i+1,j} & p_{i+1,j+1} & \cdots & p_{i+1,j+k-1} \\ \cdots & \cdots & \cdots & \cdots \\ p_{i+l-1,j} & p_{i+l-1,j+1} & \cdots & p_{i+l-1,j+k-1} \end{vmatrix},$$

where k, l are block dimensions;
$p_{i,j}$ represents pixel with coordinates i,j in the addressable area;
$0 \le i, k < M, 0 \le j, l < N$;
M, N are the dimensions of the 2D addressable area.

If k=l, the address function can be denoted as $A_k^B(i,j)$, so $A_{16}^B(i,j)$ denotes the 2D address i, j of a 16x16 block.

The definition includes three architectural issues:

Two-dimensional data storage displayed to the immediate user (programmer) of the architecture.

Block data type as a basic addressable data unit.

Addressing function to access blocks of visual data. The definition shows that the 2D address of a block is the same as the 2D-coordinates of its upper-leftmost pixel in the addressable area. We can also refer to the above proposed addressing scheme as a two-dimensional cutting or two-dimensional barrel shifting, performed by the access network block in Figure 5. The graphical representation of the two dimensional block addressing is depicted in Figure 6.

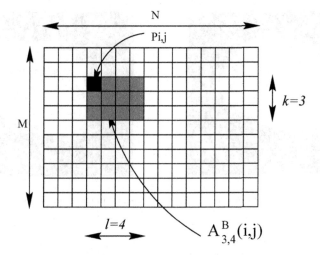

Fig. 6. 2D Block Addressing

The definition does not restrict the dimensions of the addressable area (M x N). These dimensions can take any value, depending on the application being implemented. This is very important for the implementation of MPEG-4, since each VOP has an arbitrary shape and size. Furthermore, each MPEG algorithm requires different memory amount (e.g., search area for motion estimation or a whole frame). It is important to note that we define the 2D addressing at the architectural level so it is up to the designer to propose its implementation. The memory can be implemented as an on-chip buffer with dedicated organization. The latest FPGAs of Xilinx have up to 3.5 Mb true dual-port RAM on-chip [21], allowing reconfigurable implementations of 2D addressable storages for up to 4 frames or VOPs. Read and write operations are not symmetrical in MPEG-4 where random block read is the most frequent memory access type while write operations are relatively seldom. Simpler implementations and higher speed-ups are achievable by exploiting the asymmetry between data read and write memory accesses.

6   Addressing Utilization

Besides the data throughput, the computational power of a processor can also be improved by defining instructions that utilize the proposed (block) data type and addressing mode. These instructions should support program kernels or functions that are consistent with three basic preconditions for the processed data: *block-organized visual data*, *data locality* and *data reusability*. A good candidate to utilize the proposed addressing mode that meets these three preconditions is the binary shape encoder in MPEG-4. Among the most important shape manipulations is the verification of the accepted quality of a block encoding - *the accepted quality* (ACQ) function.

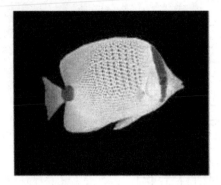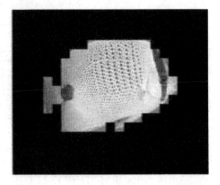

Fig. 7. Alpha threshold influence on the VOP visual quality: left - alpha_th=0; right - alpha_th=256

6.1   The Accepted Quality Function

In MPEG-4, a decision about a suitable coding mode is made for each BAB in the binary alpha map. An essential part of this process is the necessity to ascertain whether this BAB has an accepted quality under some specified lossy coding conditions. Each BAB is divided into 16 4x4 pixel blocks (PB) and this data structure is used by the criterion for an accepted quality. A dedicated function called ACQ is defined in [12]:

Definition 2 *Given the current original binary alpha block i.e. BAB and some approximation of it i.e. BAB', it is possible to define a function*

$$ACQ(BAB') = MIN(acq_0, acq_1, ..., acq_{15}),\tag{1}$$

where

$$acq_i = \begin{cases} 0 \ \ if \ SAD\_PB_i > 16 * alpha\_th \\ 1, \ otherwise. \end{cases}\tag{2}$$

and $SAD\_PB_i(BAB, BAB')$ is defined as the sum of absolute differences for PB_i, where an opaque pixel has value of 255 and a transparent pixel has value of 0. The parameter alpha_th *has values of* $\{0,16,32,64,...,256\}$.

The ACQ function shows whether the encoding (BAB') of a certain BAB gives an accepted quality result according some specified lossy coding conditions. These conditions are formally determined by the alpha threshold value. Figure 7 shows the influence of the *alpha_th* parameter on the appearance of an encoded VOP. The higher the *alpha_th* value is, the lower the acceptable quality of the encoding is. If *alpha_th=0*, then encoding will be lossless (with the highest visual quality).

We can represent SAD_PB_i as follows:

$$SAD\_PB_i = 255 \sum_{j=0}^{15} |P_{i.16+j} - P'_{i.16+j}|\tag{3}$$

where $P_{i.16+j}$ and $P'_{i.16+j}$ are the *binarized* values of the j^{-th} pixels from PB_i and PB'_i respectively and a value of *0 represents a transparent pixel* while a value of *1 - an opaque one*. According to these assumptions, we can substitute the absolute difference in (3) with a *xor* operation:

$$SAD\_PB_i = 255 \sum_{j=0}^{15} (P_{i.16+j} \oplus P'_{i.16+j})$$

$$= 255(PB_i \oplus PB'_i) = 256(PB_i \oplus PB'_i) - (PB_i \oplus PB'_i) \quad (4)$$

where $PB_i \oplus PB'_i$ denotes the bit sum of the bit-by-bit *xor* over the pixel blocks. According to Definition 2 and Equation (4):

$$acq_i = (SAD\_PB_i \leq alpha\_th * 16) =$$

$$= [256(PB_i \oplus PB'_i) \leq alpha\_th * 16 + (PB_i \oplus PB'_i)] \quad (5)$$

and

$$ACQ(BAB') = AND_{16}(acq_0, acq_1, ..., acq_{15}) \quad (6)$$

According to Definition 2, $alpha\_th * 16 = alpha\_th_5 * 256$, where $alpha\_th_5$ denotes the five MSD of $alpha\_th$. On the other hand the result of $(PB_i \oplus PB'_i)$ is a five-digit number and we can reduce the acq_i computation to the comparison of two 5-digit numbers as follows: $acq_i = [(PB_i \oplus PB'_i) \leq alpha\_th_5.\frac{256}{255}]$ and since $\frac{256}{255} \approx 1$:

$$acq_i \approx [(PB_i \oplus PB'_i) \leq alpha\_th_5] \quad (7)$$

The implementation of Equation (7) is depicted on Figure 8. We can assume the discussed structure as a basic processing element (PE) and (taking into account Equation (6)) we can build the systolic processor shown on Figure 9.

6.2   Scalability and Data Bandwidth

The proposed circuit would take two cycles for execution in a real implementation[2], and if pipelined it can produce a valid result every cycle given the data throughput requirements are met. On the other hand, the structure is scalable and can meet any memory bandwidth restrictions. For its efficiency, however, a multiple of 16 bits per cycle bandwidth is recommended, ranging between 16 and 256 bits/cyc for a single BAB. Figures 8 and 9 show the two extreme cases - a pixel block processor and a BAB processor. These two processors differ in the granularity and the throughput of the processed data. If we use the 2D addressing mode over an on-chip memory array for the ACQ engine, we can *randomly* fetch the required data amount, thus supplying the optimum data throughput.

---

[2] A cycle here is considered to be comparable to the cycle of a high speed, 2-cycle multiplier.

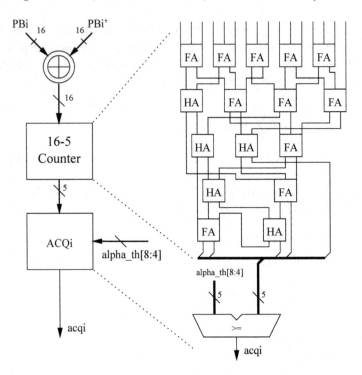

Fig. 8. Accepted quality single pixel-block processing element

Table 1. Processing speed and required data bandwidth according to the number of processing elements (for Altera FPGA)

Number of PE	Processing latency, ns	BAB/s	Data bandwidth
1	992	1 008 065	16 bit
2	496	2 016 129	32 bit
8	124	8 064 516	128 bit
16	62	16 129 032	256 bit

7   Evaluation

To evaluate the proposed structure of the ACQ function accelerator, a single processing element and an array of processing elements have been modeled in VHDL and RTL simulations have been run. The VHDL models have been synthesized for Altera FPGA. The reference software for the evaluation of the structure was Altera Max+Plus II. The simulation results indicate that each processing element performs the acq_i function within 60 ns. The evaluation of the MIN function takes about 2 ns. Table 1 suggests the processing latency and memory bandwidth, required for different number of processing elements in an

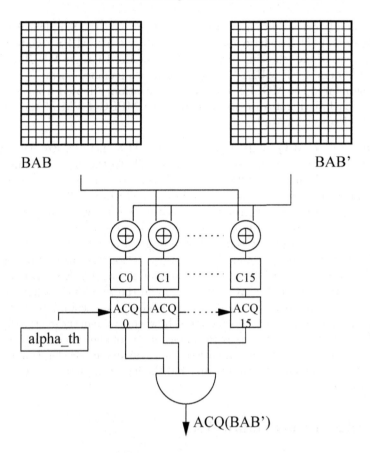

Fig. 9. The ACcepted Quality processing structure

Altera FPGA. Besides the operating latency, we use another measurement for the speed of the unit in terms of processed data units per time unit. In the proposed structure the basic data units are BABs and we achieve a speed of up to 16 129 032 BAB/s. Since there is a macroblock corresponding to any BAB and the macroblock processing speed is defined in the MPEG-4 profiles [11], we can use our results to estimate the real-time operating capabilities of the circuit. For the core and main MPEG-4 profiles, the required real-time rates are 23 860 MB/s and 97 200 MB/s (macroblocks per second) respectively. These numbers are well below our simulation results and, assuming that a macroblock manipulation involves a BAB processing as well, it is evident that the proposed ACQ engine can easily meet the real-time constrains of a dedicated MPEG-4 shape processor.

To evaluate the structure as an instruction implementation, however, we have to use the reported data into a cycle-accurate simulator of a microarchitecture. The evaluation assumptions are described bellow:

- As a simulator, we have used the *sim-outorder* from the SimpleScalar Toolset (version 2.0) [5]. The base machine has a super-scalar MIPS architecture and comprises of the following units: 4 integer ALUs, 1 integer MULT/DIV unit, 4 FP adders, 1 FP MULT/DIV-unit, and two memory ports.
- We simulated the MOLEN machine organization, adopted from [20].
- The benchmark software we used was the MPEG-4 VM of the European ACTS Project MoMuSys [7].

To utilize the ACQ instruction in the MPEG-4 encoder, we have modified its source code by including some assembly calls to the *configure* and *execute* instructions as defined in MOLEN [20]. However, we haven't modified the compiler of the SimpleScalar Toolset to model the inclusion of the new instructions. Instead, we have used the instruction annotation feature of the sim-outorder simulator. When annotating the new *configure* and *execute* instructions, we have taken into consideration the timing of the original architecture. The timings of the FPGA reconfiguration and the ACQ instruction execution have also been included into the simulation model. We simulated the MOLEN machine organization with a reconfigurable ACQ extension and the simulation results indicated up to 10% faster performance, while running the shape-encoding part of the core MPEG-4 profile. With the reported data, however, we can indirectly (by means of an instruction) estimate the performance gains of the two-dimensional block addressing. In this particular evaluation, the performance acceleration is a result both of the two-dimensional addressing and the high computational power of the ACQ instruction.

8   Conclusions and Future Work

In this paper we discussed the problem of allocating visual data in MPEG standards with respect to the efficient data access and processing. To deal with this problem, we made three new definitions for a potential MPEG architecture: a two dimensional data storage, a block data type and a new addressing function. We showed that the introduced addressing mode, referred to as two-dimensional addressing, is feasible in MPEG-4. A vector instruction ACQ utilizing the new memory access was proposed and its scalable implementation was investigated. We achieved a considerable processing speed-up, because:

- the two-dimensional addressing is more suitable and faster than conventional addressing schemes when applied over block organized visual data;
- we defined and implemented a new function that plays a key role in the investigated class of algorithms.

A combination of the new addressing mode and a set of dedicated instructions utilizing it, promises to be very beneficial for a range of MPEG algorithms. This fact addresses two directions for future research:

Memory addressing implementation. A fast and cost-effective implementation of the two-dimensional addressing will make the benefits of this mode stronger.

New instructions. Defining a complete set of dedicated instructions with respect to the two-dimensional addressing forms another research direction for an overall MPEG processing speed-up.

Acknowledgements

This research is supported by PROGRESS, the embedded systems research program of the Dutch organization for Scientific Research NWO, the Dutch Ministry of Economic Affairs, the Technology Foundation STW (project AES.5021) and PHILIPS Research Laboratories, Eindhoven, The Netherlands.

References

1. M. Berekovic, H.-J. Stolberg, M. B.Kulaczewski, P. Pirsh, H. Moler, H. Runge, J. Kneip, and B. Stabernack. Instruction set extensions for MPEG-4 video. *Journal of VLSI Signal Processing*, 23(1):27–49, October 1999.
2. G. A. Blaauw and F. P. Brooks. *Computer Architecture: Concepts and Evaluation.* Addison-Wesley, 1997.
3. E. Brockmeyer, L. Nachtergaele, F. V. Catthoor, J. Bormans, and H. J. D. Man. Low power memory storage and transfer organization for the MPEG-4 full pel motion estimation on a multimedia processor. *IEEE Transactions on Multimedia*, 1(2):202–216, June 1999.
4. P. Budnik and D. J. Kuck. The organization and use of parallel memories. *IEEE Transactions on Computers*, 20(12):1566–1569, December 1971.
5. D.C.Burger and T.M.Austin. *The simpleScalar Tool Set, Version 2.0. Technical Report CS-TR-1997-1342.* University of Wisconsin-Madison, 1997.
6. S. Dutta and W. Wolf. A flexible parallel architecture adapted to block-matching motion-estimation algorithms. *IEEE Transactions on Circuits and Systems for Video Technology*, 6(1):74–86, February 1996.
7. G.Heising and M.Wollborn. *MPEG-4 video reference software package.* ACTS AC098 mobile multimedia systems (MOMUSYS), December, 1999.
8. H.-J.Stolberg, M.Berekovic, P.Pirsch, H.Runge, H. Moller, and J.Kneip. The M-PIRE MPEG-4 codec DSP and its macroblock engine. In *IEEE International Symposium on Circuits and Systems*, volume II, pages 192–195, Geneva, Switzerland, 28-31 May 2000.
9. K. Herrmann, S. Moch, J. Hilgenstock, and P.Pirsch. Implementation of a Multiprocessor System with Distributed Embedded DRAM on a Large Area Integrated Circuit. In *IEEE International Symposium on Defect and Fault Tolerance in VLSI Systems (DFT)*, pages 105–113, October 2000.
10. J. Hilgenstock, K. Herrmann, and P.Pirsch. Memory Organization of a Single-Chip Video Signal Processing System with Embedded DRAM. In *9-th Great Lakes Symposium on VLSI*, pages 42–45, March 1999.
11. ISO/IEC JTC11/SC29/WG11 W2502. ISO/IEC 14496-2. Final Draft International Standard. Part2: Visual, Oct. 1998.
12. ISO/IEC JTC1/SC29/WG11 N3312. MPEG-4 video verification model version 16.0.
13. ISO/IEC JTC1/SC29/WG11 N4030. MPEG-4 Overview - (V.18 - Singapore Version), March 2001.

14. P. M. Kogge. *The Architecture of Pipelined Computers*. McGraw-Hill, 1981.
15. D. H. Lawrie. Access and alignment of data in an array processor. *IEEE Transactions on Computers*, C-24(12):1145–1155, December 1975.
16. J. W. Park. An efficient buffer memory system for subarray access. *IEEE Transactions on Parallel and Distributed Systems*, 12(3):316–335, March 2001.
17. J. W. Park and D. T. Harper. An efficient memory system for the SIMD construction of a gaussian pyramid. *IEEE Transactions on Parallel and Distributed Systems*, 7(8):855–860, August 1996.
18. R. Schaffer, R. Merker, and F. Catthoor. Combining background memory management and regular array co-partitioning, illustrated on a full motion estimation kernel. In *13th International Conference on VLSI Design*, pages 104–109, 3-7 January 2000.
19. D. C. van Voorhis and T. H. Morrin. Memory systems for image processing. *IEEE Transactions on Computers*, C-27(2):113–125, February 1978.
20. S. Vassiliadis, S. Wong, and S. Cotofana. The MOLEN rm-coded processor. In *11th International Conference on Field Programmable Logic and Applications (FPL)*, 2001.
21. XILINX. Virtex-II Platform FPGA Handbook, December 2000.

A Java-Enabled DSP

C. John Glossner[1,3], Michael Schulte[2], and Stamatis Vassiliadis[3]

[1] Sandbridge Technologies, Inc., / White Plains, NY, USA
glossner@sandbridgetech.com
[2] Lehigh University, / Bethlehem, PA, USA
[3] Delft University of Technology, / Delft, The Netherlands

Abstract. In this paper we explore design techniques and constraints for enabling high-speed Java-enabled wireless devices. Since Java execution may be required for 3G devices, efficient methods of executing Java bytecode are explored. We begin by setting a historical context for DSP architectures and describe salient characteristics of classical, transitional, and modern DSP architectures. We then discuss methods of executing Java bytecode - both software and hardware - and discuss the merits of each approach. We next describe the Delft-Java engine that we designed at Delft Technical University in the Netherlands. Finally, we compare this design to other techniques and comment on ways that Sandbridge Technologies is modifying organizational characteristics to achieve power-efficient Java execution.

1 Introduction

DSPs have become a ubiquitous enabler for integration of audio, video, and communications[1]. In the future world of convergence devices, efficient JAVA execution may be only one component of system performance. The DELFT-JAVA processor addresses these trends by providing facilities that enable efficient performance. Tremendous hardware and software challenges exist to realize convergence devices. First, power dissipation constraints are requiring new techniques at every stage of design - architecture, microarchitecture, software, algorithm design, logic design, circuit design, and process design. With performance requirements exploding as bandwidth demand increases, power conscious design becomes more difficult. SOC integration and low voltage process technologies will contribute to lower power system-on-a-chip (SOC) integrated circuits (ICs) but are insufficient as the only solution for streaming multimedia. Second, convergence applications are fundamentally DSP applications. In addition, these applications are becoming very complex. In wireless communications, GSM and IS-54 data rates were limited to less than 15 Kbps. Future third-generation (3G) systems may provide data rates more than 100 times the previous rates. Higher communication rates are accelerating higher processing requirements. Complexity is driving the need to program applications in high-level languages. In the past, when only small kernels were required to execute on a DSP, it was acceptable to program in assembly language. Today, resource constraints prohibit

E.F. Deprettere et al. (Eds.): SAMOS 2001, LNCS 2268, pp. 307–325, 2002.

these practices. Third, JAVA may become the dominant programming paradigm for 3G systems. NTT DoCoMo recently introduced Java-based services for its cellular subscribers and hardware solutions for efficient JAVA execution are being proposed[2]. Fourth, unlike many past developments, hardware designers will need to understand the complexities of software systems so that compilation techniques can be effective. With a large number of standards both existing and proposed for wireless communications, a programmable platform will be required for timely implementation. Fifth, embedded and DSP wireless applications have distinct requirements when compared with general purpose processors [3]. The predominant algorithmic difference is that inner loops are easily described as vectors of moderate length. A key point is that the native datatype is often a fixed-point fraction. This is in distinct contrast to general purpose processors (and most high-level languages) which operate on integer datatypes. Finally, in addition to algorithmic differences, most convergence devices will be deployed in embedded environments where real-time constraints are prevalent. Real-time behavior has a dominant influence in the design of these devices[4]. Whereas general-purpose applications can often manage with variable latency response, convergence applications, in contrast, should be able to precisely guarantee the latencies within the system.

This paper explores the design constraints in building very high performance engines that enable broadband communications. We look at existing DSPs and characterize their architectures by classical, transitional, and modern architectures. We describe the key characteristics of each generation of DSP architecture. We also look at methods of JAVA execution. We then give a brief introduction to the DELFT-JAVA engine. The DELFT-JAVA engine directly addresses efficient JAVA execution. We then present other related work. Finally, we conclude by describing how the DELFT-JAVA engine is being modified to fit ultra-low power design challenges required by 3G wireless.

2   DSP Architectures

Execution predictability in DSP systems often precludes the use of many general-purpose design techniques (e.g. speculation, branch prediction, data caches, etc.). Instead, classical DSP architectures have developed a unique set of performance enhancing techniques that are optimized for their intended market. These techniques are characterized by hardware that supports efficient filtering, such as the ability to sustain three memory accesses per cycle (one instruction, one coefficient, and one data access). Sophisticated addressing modes such as bit-reversed and modulo addressing may also be provided. Multiple address units operate in parallel with the datapath to sustain the execution of the inner kernel. Examples of classical DSPs include TI's C54x [5], Lucent's 16xx[6], and IBM's Mwave DSP[7,8].

Transitional DSP architectures have either attempted to extend existing architectures or solve a specific programming problem. The Lucent 16000 architecture extends the 1600 architecture to a dual-MAC machine while maintaining the same pipeline and programming style [6]. Likewise, TI's C55x extends the C54x to a dual-MAC machine [9]. Although these processors maintain many of the irregularities and specialized hardware of their predecessors, they provide performance gains and extend the lifetime of popular DSP families. Processors which typify transitional architectures include Infineon's Carmel DSP[10] and LSI's ZSP[11].

A special class of DSP architecture was introduced with the Media processor. Since these applications are dominated by pixel processing, an 8-bit datatype is often as important as a classical DSP's 16-bit datatype. These processors have had an influence on modern DSP architectures. Examples of media processors include IBM's Mfast [12,13,14,15], Philips' Trimedia [16], TI C80 [17], and Chromatics MPACT [18].

Another special class of processors with DSP functionality is general-purpose processors which include SIMD extensions. Examples of this include Intel's MMX[19] and PowerPC's Altivec [20]. Retrofitting DSP capability into general purpose processors has not been as successful as once envisioned. Although excellent performance can be achieved, system characteristics such as real-time constraints and power dissipation sensitivities are harder to realize on general purpose processors [21].

In classical DSP architectures, the execution pipelines were visible to the programmer and necessarily shallow to allow assembly language optimization. This programming restriction encumbered implementations with tight timing constraints for both arithmetic execution and memory access. The key characteristic that separates modern DSP architectures from classical DSP architectures is the focus on compilability. Once the decision was made to focus the DSP design on programmer productivity, other constraining decisions could be relaxed. As a result, significantly longer pipelines with multiple cycles to access memory and multiple cycles to compute arithmetic operations could be utilized. This has resulted in higher clock frequencies and higher performance DSPs.

In an attempt to exploit instruction level parallelism inherent in DSP applications, modern DSPs tend to use VLIW-like execution packets. This is partly driven by real-time requirements which require the worst-case execution time to be minimized. This is in contrast with general purpose CPUs which tend to minimize average execution times. With long pipelines and multiple instruction issue, the difficulties of attempting assembly language programming become apparent. Controlling instruction dependencies between upwards of 100 in-flight instructions is a non-trivial task for a programmer. This is exactly the area where a compiler excels. Representative examples of modern DSP architectures include Lucent/Motorola's Starcore SC140 [22], ADI's TigerSHARC[23,24], TI's C64x[25], BOPS' ManArray[26,27], and Lucent's Daytona[28].

3   Methods of Java Execution

JAVA is a C++ like programming language designed for general-purpose object-oriented programming[29]. An appeal for the usage of such a language is its "write once, run anywhere" philosophy [30]. This is accomplished by providing a JVM interpreter and runtime support for each platform[31]. In theory, any platform that supports the JAVA runtime environment will produce the same execution results independent of the platform. Due to its characteristics and possibilities, JAVA has been extensively used as a programming language of choice.

JVM translation designers have used both software and hardware methods to execute JAVA bytecode. The advantage of software execution is flexibility. The advantage of hardware execution is performance. To try to blend the benefits of both approaches hybrid techniques have also been proposed. In this section we briefly describe existing approaches. The following have been proposed thus far:

■ **Interpretation:** Current implementations of the JVM take alternative approaches to JAVA bytecode execution. One solution is interpretation. In this approach, a software program emulates the JAVA Virtual Machine. This requires software to execute multiple machine instructions for each emulated instruction. This provides cross-platform portability but poses a number of performance issues. While this approach provides for maximum flexibility, the performance achieved can be as low as 5-10% the performance of natively compiled code [32].

■ **Just-in-Time (JIT) Compilation:** For this approach translation is performed from JAVA bytecodes to native code (e.g. the machine language of the processor) just prior to executing the program. The Intel IA-32 JIT which is used in the VTune tool uses the JAVA bytecodes themselves to represent expressions rather than building an intermediate representation[33]. Using a technique called lazy code selection, native IA32 instructions are generated in a single pass with linear time complexity. They also describe lightweight implementations of several standard optimizations including common subexpression elimination, priority-based global register allocation, and array bounds check elimination. JITs have demonstrated 5-10x performance improvement over interpretation [32,34]. However, the compilation is only resident for the current program invocation. Because they utilize processor resources, the number of optimizations that can be performed prior to execution is restricted[32]. Additionally, multiple instructions are required to implement JVM instructions and there is memory overhead to load the compiler into the runtime system.

■ **Flash Compilation:** Flash compilation is a hybrid approach in that a highly optimizing JIT compiler and a JVM are integrated into a runtime environment[34,35,36]. This allows code to be loaded in an already compiled application. The compiler only optimizes loops where a performance gain is likely to be obtained. The information may come from profiled bytecode execution. Stated performance improvements of 140x interpretive approaches and 13x JIT compilers have been reported.

In the Sun HotSpot compiler[35], released in 1999, a number of optimizations are made in addition to an optimizing compiler. The memory subsystem uses direct object pointers for objects rather than handles. C and JAVA programs share the same activation stack which allows fast calling of C routines. Garbage collection is performed using an accurate, generational copy collector which speeds object allocation and collection while reducing hard to debug memory leaks. A mark-and-compact algorithm eliminates memory fragmentation and pause-less collection ensures nearly imperceptible user-visible pauses. Special support is also provided for thread synchronization. The compiler itself does on-the-fly optimizations including method inlining, dead code elimination, loop invariant hoisting, common subexpression elimination and constant propagation. More sophisticated optimizations include null-check and range-check optimizations. Because new code can be loaded dynamically, the Sun HotSpot compiler has the ability to de-optimize (e.g. reverse the inlining process) to allow modification of the natively optimized code.

In the IBM dynamic compiler[36] a small VLIW machine with a JIT com-piler hidden within the chip architecture is proposed. The first time a fragment of JAVA code is executed, the JIT compiler transparently converts the JAVA byte-codes to highly optimized RISC primitives, then parallelizes them, so multiple RISC primitives can be executed in one machine cycle. The VLIW code is saved in a portion of main memory not visible to the JAVA architecture. Subsequent executions of the same fragment do not require translation (unless cast out). They describe fast compiler algorithms for dynamic translation of JAVA byte-code to VLIW code. These algorithms parallelize across multiple paths and loop iteration boundaries. In addition, they map the JAVA stack and local variables to real registers, thereby eliminating the pushes and pops between local variables and the stack by appropriate register allocation.

■ **Off-line Compilation:** *Off-line compilers,* sometimes referred to as way-ahead-of-time compilers, translate JAVA bytecodes to machine code prior to execution. Because the scope of optimizations which can be performed in JIT compilers during JAVA execution is limited[37], an off-line compiler may devote additional time to complex optimizations. This requires that programs be dis-tributed and installed (e.g. compiled) prior to use. Since it is assumed that the compilation is performed once and maintained on a disk, additional time may be devoted to optimizations. Except for loop information, the JAVA bytecodes contain nearly the same amount of information as the source itself[34]. There-fore, an off-line compiler should be nearly as efficient as a native JAVA compiler. A restriction on off-line compilers is that all of the class files must be present (e.g. all superclasses) to perform the compilation[33].

The Toba system first translates bytecodes to C and then compiles the C program[38]. For each JAVA method, Toba works by translating it into a C function. A C local variable is created for each JAVA local variable. Indirect jumps and exceptions are handled through a giant switch statement. Exception handling is based on the runtime program counter in the JVM. Toba simulates the program counter by assigning values to a local pc variable. Hewlett Packard has a similar system[39]. Using the Toba compiler, performance improvements nearly twice a standard interpreter have been reported for FFT signal processing functions[40,41]. The Toba group found performance improvements of 2 to 10 times versus a standard interpreter[38].

■ **Native Compilation:** *Native compilers* use JAVA as a programming language and generate native code directly from the high-level source. Even though this approach is contrary to the JAVA philosophy of "write once, run anywhere" [30], it may provide a good opportunity for speed improvement since no information is lost during high-level compilation. A runtime system for linking the JAVA classes is still required and classes may potentially need to be resolved each time a method is invoked. Additionally, multiple instructions are required to implement JVM instructions. The gcj compiler is an example of a native compiler[42].

■ **Direct Execution:** The previously mentioned questions could be possibly answered using direct JAVA execution. This approach assumes hardware capabilities that execute the JVM instruction set. Our proposal also belongs to this approach. We began in 1996 to investigate the previously mentioned questions. We envisioned that hardware approaches could significantly enhance JVM execution time. At that time only Sun Microsystems proposed similar approaches to improving JAVA performance. Sun's *picoJava* implementation directly executes the JVM Instruction Set Architecture (ISA) but incorporates other facilities that improve the system level aspects of JAVA program execution[43,44,45]. The picoJava chip is a stack-based implementation with a 64 entry register-based stack cache which automatically spills and fills based on high and low-water marks. Support for garbage collection, instruction optimization, method invocation, and synchronization is provided. Because the JVM does not implement an entire machine, Sun added 115 additional extended bytecodes to the picoJava core[45]. These extended bytecode are not produced by JAVA compliant compilers. Sun partitions the bytecode into simple instructions which can be directly executed, CISC-like instructions which are implemented in microcode using 2kB ROMs, and very complicated instructions which trap. Because a register-file stack cache is used, the picoJava core has access to the top 64 entries in the stack. This allows them to fold (e.g. combine) multiple stack-based operations into one execution packet. On average, Sun found about 28% of instructions executed get folded into other instructions. Researchers at National Chiao Tung University in 1997 found that instruction folding can reduce up to 84% of all stack operations and a 4-foldable Java core could improve overall program speedup by 1.34[46,47]. Sun states that the picoJava core provides up to 5x performance improvement over JIT compilers [48].

4   The Delft-Java Engine

The DELFT-JAVA architecture has two logical views: 1) a JVM Instruction Set Architecture (ISA) and 2) a RISC-based ISA. The JVM view is stack-based with support for standard datatypes, synchronization, object-oriented method invocation, arrays, and object allocation[31]. An important property of JAVA bytecodes is that statically determinable type state enables simple on-the-fly translation of bytecodes into efficient machine code[49]. We utilize this property to dynamically translate JAVA bytecodes into DELFT-JAVA instructions.

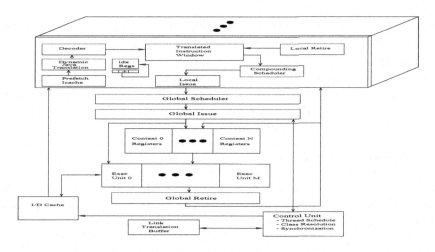

Fig. 1. Concurrent Multithreaded Organization.

Programmers who wish to take advantage of other languages which exploit the full capabilities of the DELFT-JAVA processor may do so but require a specific compiler. Some additional architectural features in the DELFT-JAVA processor which are not directly accessible from JAVA code include pointer manipulation, Multimedia SIMD instructions, unsigned datatypes, and rounding/saturation modes for DSP algorithms.

In DELFT-JAVA, nearly all instructions are executed as 32-bit fixed width instructions with an 8-bit opcode. A typical encoding useful for Java translation is add.ind.w32 idx[0], ix, iy-1, it-1. This instruction specifies a 32-bit, 2's complement integer addition. Normally, the register file is accessed with a direct reference (e.g. add rx, ry, rt). The DELFT-JAVA processor facilitates JVM translation by allowing indirect access through 3 indices into the register file that create a circular address. Figure 2 shows how the indirect access can be implemented. Using this mechanism, it is possible to provide both LIFO stack and FIFO vector operations.

An organization of the DELFT-JAVA architecture that supports multiple concurrent execution of threads and shared global execution units was presented in[50,51,52] and is shown in Figure 1. This organization provides hardware support for multiple context instruction issue and global instruction scheduling. The organization supports multiple concurrent execution of threads which share global execution units. We define a *context* as a hardware supported thread unit. Each context assumes that the processor's organization incorporates (logically) an instruction cache, a decode unit, a local instruction scheduler, a local instruction issue unit, and an instruction retire unit. A context does not include any shared resources such as a first level (L1) cache, execution units, a register file, global instruction schedulers, nor global issue units. The term *thread* is generally used to refer to the programmer's view of a thread - a possibly concurrent stream of independent executing instructions[53]. In this thesis, the term context denotes the hardware on which a thread may run. The system software may map any number of threads to a particular context.

■ **Operation:** All instructions are fetched from global shared memory and placed into a global L1 on-chip instruction cache. Each context also assumes a (logical[1]) zero level (L0) instruction cache to provide concurrent per context *instruction fetch* capacity. During normal user-level operation, all instructions are fetched as JAVA instructions. After being fetched, most JAVA instructions are *dynamically translated* into the DELFT-JAVA instruction set. Because the instructions are stored in cache memory as JAVA instructions, branching and method invocation code produced by JAVA compilers will execute properly on the DELFT-JAVA architecture. After translation, the instructions are decoded and placed in a *local instruction window*. The instruction window keeps track of issued and pending instructions. The *local instruction scheduler* is responsible for determining how instructions within the window should be scheduled. This unit takes the instructions in a RISC form and performs instruction combining and compounding. Often, in stack based architectures, a number of optimizations pertaining to stack manipulation can be efficiently combined[54,44]. The DELFT-JAVA processor may also dynamically build internal compound instructions[55]. Instructions are then sent to the *local issue unit* after they have been scheduled. The local issue unit determines if the instructions that have been locally scheduled can be issued to the global instruction scheduler. To resolve interlock dependencies, an interlock collapsing unit could be used[56].

All instructions which require access to shared resources must be forwarded to the *global instruction scheduler*. This unit schedules the aggregated instructions destined for execution units. Any number of implementation dependent scheduling policies can be utilized including priority-based, round-robin, earliest deadline, etc. The JAVA language specifies that in the absence of explicit synchronization, a JAVA implementation is free to update the main memory in any order[29]. This relaxed memory consistency model allows the scheduler to reorder the instructions from individual contexts to optimize the utilization of the shared execution units. After all instructions which request global shared resources have been scheduled, they are sent to the *global issue unit*. This unit ensures that global resources are available to begin issuing instructions. Instructions may be issued in one of two forms: single independent instructions and compound parcels. A parcel is a dynamically built compound instruction. Parcels are particularly effective in reducing the logic complexity of implementations and execute in less cycles when used in conjunction with interlock collapsing units. In a traditional processor implementation, all execution units would require bypass circuitry between each other. As the number of global execution units becomes large, it is no longer feasible to provide general bypassing between all sets of execution units. In the DELFT-JAVA processor, this requirement is removed by provided compound instructions which collapse interlocks and then scheduling the interlocked instructions within a parcel. The global issue unit has the capability of reordering the execution of individual instructions and parcels.

---

[1] logical meaning not necessarily physical.

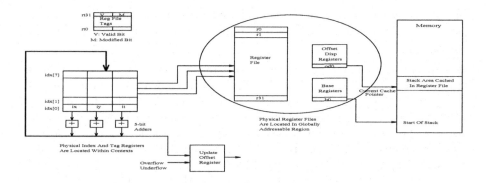

Fig. 2. Concurrent Multithreaded Registers.

If the global issue unit can find available resources, it can splice an independent instruction from an alternative context into a parcel. Since contexts are independent, this ensures that an instruction spliced into a parcel does not cause invalid results. Additionally, because each instruction contains a unique context identification, the results are forwarded to the proper context.

After global execution, all results are forwarded to the *global retire unit*. This unit removes the requirement for a general interconnection unit between all contexts and execution units. If instructions were not executed speculatively, the global retire unit writes the results to the register file after forwarding the instruction to the *local retire unit*. Otherwise, the result is maintained in the retire unit until the conditional outcome is known.

All instructions eventually return to the local retire unit in the context from which they originated. This unit is responsible for committing state to the context. Each context may retire multiple instructions per cycle.

■ **Registers:** From the perspective of a context, the register file consists of a standard 32 entry by 32-bit register array. From the perspective of the machine, this resource is managed as a global register file that is addressed by a context identifier that is appended to the instruction's register reference. An alternative organization would be to place the register files logically within a context. This organization however creates a proliferation of register file ports. Managing the register file as a global resource reduces the number of ports to the peak retire rate of the machine versus the peak retire rate of a context.

Instructions have two methods of accessing the register file: 1) direct RISC-style references and 2) indirect index access. Even though there is an indirect reference, all instructions physically execute using direct RISC-style register references. The indirect index registers are only used to translate instructions. This implies that they are not part of the register file and do not affect the execution path.

The JVM instruction set architecture is inherently stack based [31]. When executing JAVA instructions, the register file index registers create a circular buffer that is mapped to the operand stack in memory. A set of valid and modified bits are associated with each register. These bits are maintained logically within the local context. These registers automatically prefetch and spill as the stack size changes.

■ **Translation:** Indirect access to the register file plays the largest role in the translation of JAVA bytecodes. As shown in Figure 2, when executing JAVA instructions, the register file index registers create a circular buffer that is mapped to the stack in memory. A set of valid and modified bits are associated with each register. These bits are maintained logically within the local context. A JAVA instruction such as iadd goes through two intermediate phases. The first phase translates the instruction into a valid DELFT-JAVA instruction. In this case, a add.ind.w32 idx[0] it, it-1, it-1 is generated by the translation logic. If we assume that the top of the cached stack in idx[0] is currently in r5, this instruction proceeds through the decoder and is placed in the decoded instruction window as add.w32 r5, r6, r6. Functionally, this performs r5 + r6 → r6. These registers automatically prefetch and spill as the stack size changes.

■ **Execution and Context Switching:** When a thread begins execution within a context, the offset registers are written with the location of the frame, operand stack, and local variables memory locations. Additionally, the register file tags within the context are reset. When the operand stack address is written to the offset register, the context begins to generate speculative load instructions. This allows the register file to pre-fill only if there is adequate bandwidth available to the L1 cache. It also reduces cache thrashing because the L1 cache is not obligated to evict data upon a speculative load.

As instructions begin to execute, if the speculative pre-loads were successful, context execution proceeds without delay. If the pre-loads were not successful and the data is required for execution, the local context re-issues the load non-speculatively. This effectively raises the priority of the load instruction. When the data arrives at the context, a valid bit associated with that register file location is set. If the register is modified at any point during program execution, the modified bit is set. If the processor has spare resources, a speculative cache store instruction is generated. If there is spare bandwidth available, the processor stores the updated memory location and resets the modified bit. Otherwise, execution continues with a delayed write-back.

In some cases, the global thread management unit may determine that a particular software thread has resulted in a unacceptable degradation of a hardware context. In this case, the unit may make a request to the context to perform a context switch so that a new thread may be mapped to the context. Since results are only committed by the retire unit, it is possible to interrupt a context at any time. When a context becomes invalid, it signals the global instruction scheduler and issue unit to flush any remaining instructions in the queue. It then checks the modified bits of the register file to determine if any values must be written back into memory. After all state has been saved in memory, the context may signal the global thread management unit that a new thread may be mapped to the context. Even though the context is now freed to map a new thread onto it, it may still be the case that an instruction was executing at the time of the context switch request. It is the responsibility of the global retire unit to ensure that any instructions received from execution units destined for the switched context are not forwarded to the local retire unit. This is not difficult to implement when the longest instruction execution time is less than the context switch time.

■ **Control Unit:** The *control unit* is responsible for managing system resources, ensuring synchronization, cache locking, dynamically linking classes, performing I/O operations, running operating systems, loading instructions, and generally performing system functions. Since the JVM does not provide all the functionality generally required by a full operating system, many of these functions have been grouped into a special control unit. A control unit is analogous to a context except that it contains additional resources that are not necessarily required within a context. These resources could be implemented within a context but with a large number of contexts it would lead to unacceptable duplication of typically idle hardware. There are no architectural limits on the number of control units permitted in a system. The control unit is a logical independent entity so that the complexity of bussing between global system resources such as caches is significantly reduced. Some of the differences that distinguish the control unit from a context are:

First, a control unit has direct access to the *Link Translation Buffer* [51]. The LTB acts as a global repository for dynamically resolved names. During dynamic linking, the name of the class or field to be resolved is contained in the constant pool. After a process called resolution, the name contained within the constant pool can be associated with a physical location in memory. This association is placed in the Link Translation Buffer. If the control unit finds the constant pool address in the LTB and the requesting class has access permissions to the data, then the control unit very quickly returns the resolved address. There is still a potential problem that the LTB may hold data that is stale. To diminish the impact of this, the control processor regularly re-resolves addresses when it is not busy performing other tasks. A program may also completely disable the LTB or more judiciously issue `flushLTB` instructions.

Second, the global instruction scheduler has direct access to the control unit and may schedule instructions on execution units that are inherently owned by the control unit. This is to ensure that all addresses are resolved through the control unit and that all synchronization is performed by the control unit. When execution has completed, instructions are returned to the global retire unit which then returns the results to the context requesting the operation. Care is taken by the Global Retire Unit to ensure that any locks acquired for a context that have undergone a context switch are released.

Third, any unimplemented instructions trap first through the global instruction scheduler and global issue unit to the control unit. The control unit then either halts execution if it is an illegal instruction or can emulate the instruction sequence and return the instruction to the global retire unit.

Fourth, the control unit is responsible for synchronization. This is because generally it may be possible for an object to have acquired a lock but the locked object may not be fully resident in the L1 instruction cache. The easiest way to deal with this issue is to lock down all cache lines associated with object synchronization. Another alternative is to have the control unit check each address as it is brought into the cache to ensure that the address is not contained within an already locked object. If it is the context that currently owns the lock that requested the instruction, the new instructions are brought into the cache. If it is any other context requesting the instruction, the context is placed in a blocked state. This reduces thrashing within the cache and allows the thread scheduler to make better decisions about the mapping of threads to contexts.

Fifth, a thread scheduler in the control unit is responsible for mapping all of the software threads in the system to particular hardware contexts. It may update the state of threads (i.e. from active to blocked), it may preempt threads, and it may create and destroy threads. There are no restrictions on the mappings of threads to contexts. Multiple threads may be mapped to a single context or to multiple contexts.

Finally, the control unit performs all the necessary functions required in physical processors that are not required in virtual machines. These include I/O access, initialization, and system administration functions.

Enhancing Performance: Accelerating the JVM interpreter is only one aspect of JAVA performance improvement implemented in the DELFT-JAVA processor. We utilize a number of techniques including pipelining, load/store architecture, register renaming, dynamic instruction scheduling with out-of-order issue, compound instruction aggregation, collapsing units [56], branch prediction, a link translation buffer [51], and standard register files. We selectively describe some of these mechanisms.

■ **Removing Hazards:** A common problem with stack architectures is that the stack may become a bottleneck for exploiting instruction level parallelism. Since the results of operations typically pass through the top of the stack, many interlocks are generated in the translated instruction stream [57]. Register renaming allows us to remove false dependencies in the instruction stream. In addition, an interlock collapsing unit can be used to directly execute interlock dependencies[55,58,56]. After translation the instructions are placed in an instruction window.

■ **Multiple Instruction Issue:** After translation the instructions are placed in an instruction window. Once instructions are translated into a RISC-based form, superscalar techniques are used to extract instruction level parallelism from the instruction stream. Reservation stations are an effective means of determining which instructions can execute concurrently[59]. Since all thread-units operate independently, multiple instructions can be issued from each thread unit as well as multiple thread units.

■ **Bounds Checking:** The JAVA language specifies that arrays must be bounds checked[29]. Special register sets can be provided for this purpose. The microarchitecture is not required to implement them but the architecture supports the use of bounds checking.

Non-translated Instructions: Primarily, we dynamically translate arithmetic and data movement instructions. In addition to the translation process, the ar-

Table 1. Instructions with Special Support.

anewarray	invokeinterface[1]	multianewarray
arraylength	invokespecial	new
athrow	invokestatic	newarray
checkcast	invokevirtual	putfield
getfield	jsr_w[1]	putstatic
getstatic	lookupswitch[1]	tableswitch
goto_w[1]	monitorenter	wide
instanceof	monitorexit	[1](traps)

Table 2. Model Characteristics

Model	Renaming	Issue	L/S units	Latency
IS	No	inorder	∞	1
IX	No	inorder	∞	1
IR	Yes	ooo	∞	1
PS	No	inorder	∞	4
PX	No	inorder	∞	4
PR	Yes	ooo	∞	4
BR	Yes	ooo	2LV/2H	4

chitecture provides direct support for a) synchronization, b) array management, c) object management, d) method invocation, e) exception handling, and f) complex branching operations. The JAVA instructions shown in Table 1 have special support in our architecture. These instructions are dynamically translated but only the parameters which are passed on the stack are actually translated. The high-level JVM operations are translated to equivalent high-level operations in the DELFT-JAVA architecture. In addition, four instructions which are greater than the 32-bit DELFT-JAVA instruction format width trap.

5   Dynamic Translation Results

In this section we describe the results for a DSP Vector Multiply. We describe seven machine models and report on the relative performance of these models. A summary of the machine characteristics is shown in Table 2. The Ideal Stack (IS) model does not attempt to remove stack bottlenecks nor does it include pipelined execution. It assumes all instructions including memory operations complete in a single cycle. The Ideal Translated (IX) model uses the translation scheme described above. It also includes multiple inorder issue capability but no register renaming. The Ideal Translated with Register Renaming (IR) model includes out-of-order execution but with unbounded hardware resources. In addition to the ideal machines, we also calculated the performance on a more practical machine. The Pipelined Stack (PS) model assumes a pipeline latency of 4 cycles for all memory accesses to the Local Variables or Heap memory. The

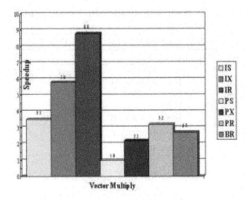

Fig. 3. Performance Results.

Pipelined Translated (PX) model and the Pipelined with Register Renaming (PR) include the same assumptions for memory latency but are equivalent to the IX and IR models in other respects. The final experiment looked at the additional constraint of bounded resource (BR) utilization. We allowed two concurrent accesses to the Local Variable and Heap memories. We maintained a four cycle latency for each memory space.

Figure 3 shows the relative performance of each of the models. We chose the Pipelined Stack as the basis for comparison since it is a potentially realizable implementation. We note that compared with a reasonable implementation, the ideal stack (IS) model is 3.5 times faster than the PS model. When we compare the IX model with the IS model, we were able to reduce the stack bottlenecks by 40%. When register renaming was also applied in the IR model, the stack bottlenecks were reduced by 60%. When bounded resources constrained the issue capacity of the BR model, the performance still was 3.2x better than the PS model. In addition, register renaming with out-of-order execution successfully enhanced performance by about 50% in comparison with the same model characteristics but with in-order execution.

Table 3 shows the summary of instructions issued, peak issue rate, and overall speedup. In the unbounded resource case, a peak issue of 6 instructions per cycle was achieved with the ideal, register-renamed, out-of-order execution model. The in-order issue peak rate was 4 instructions. When resource constraints were applied, the peak issue rate dropped to 2 and the average IPC was 0.8 even with out-of-order execution. However, the speedup achieved from the reduced stack bottlenecks was still 2.7x.

6   Related Work

Using the Tomasulo technique[59], Munsil and Wang show that an adapted algorithm on simple benchmarks could reduce stack usage[60]. Li et. al. from Tsignhua University also used a Tomasulo algorithm combined with a technique

Table 3. Machine Performance

Model	Peak Issue	IPC	Speedup
IS	1	1.0	3.5
IX	4	1.7	5.8
IR	6	2.5	8.8
PS	1	0.3	1.0
PX	4	0.6	2.2
PR	6	0.9	3.2
BR	2	0.8	2.7

called virtual registers[61]. Their JAViR processor provides concurrent access to multiple stack entries. Virtual Registers are transparent to programmers and compilers (e.g. they are not architectural registers). At runtime, the dependencies of JAVA bytecode are checked and the virtual registers present the dependencies. These are then allocated to physical registers with a reference count that records the lifetime of the result. When a result is computed it is broadcast to the reservation stations. If the reference count for the virtual register is not zero, a new physical register is allocated. Using this technique they achieved an effective IPC (instructions per cycle) of 2.89 to 4.01 with a 16 and 64 entry instruction window, respectively. The TinyJ processor from Advancel Logic Corporation also directly executes about 60% of Java bytecode[62]. Complicated bytecode are emulated with software. They have two views of the machine - a Java Virtual Machine view and a RISC-based execution engine. They transition between the two views using a DISP (JVM dispatch instruction). They provide special hardware support for a JAVA program counter and special decode registers used to accelerated the software emulated long bytecodes. They also include rudimentary DSP multiply-accumulate instructions. The ShBoom PSC1000 processor from Patriot Scientific is a stack-based machine which is semantically close to the JVM [63]. It is a 32-bit processor with a peak instruction issue of 1 per cycle. To execute JAVA, a 20kB interpreter is required. This minimal memory requirement is due to the close semantic nature of the JVM instruction set architecture and the ShBoom instruction set architecture.

7   Conclusions

In this paper we have given a historical background of DSP architecture and the design constraints that have influenced their design. We have discussed the issues and characteristics of the JAVA language and how hardware may be applied to accelerate JAVA execution. We have described the DELFT-JAVA engine that is an efficient JAVA bytecode acceleration engine without forcing undue burden on the programmer for specifying parallelism. In addition, we have compared our design to other related projects. The DELFT-JAVA engine provides for efficient JAVA execution targeted for high-performance infrastructure applications. At Sandbridge Technologies, new multithreaded organizational techniques are being explored for power-efficient high-performance JAVA execution that will allow handsets to benefit from these techniques. Some of these techniques include software-controlled performance tuning, LIW organizations (in contrast with superscalar or direct execution organizations), and alternative thread-execution models (in contrast with simultaneous multithreading). It is anticipated that these techniques may bring to the handset environment a real-time, power-efficient platform with automatic extraction of parallelism for JAVA applications.

References

1. J. Eyre and J. Bier. DSP Processors Hit the Mainstream. *IEEE Computer*, pages 51–59, August 1998.
2. Junko Yoshida. Java chip vendors set for cellular skirmish. EE Times, January 30 2001.
3. P. Lapley. *DSP Processor Fundamentals*. IEEE press, New York, 1997.
4. M. Saghir, P. Chow, and C. G. Lee. Towards Better DSP Architecture and Compilers. In *Proceedings of the International Conference on Signal Processing Applications and Technology*, pages 658–664, October 1994.
5. Texas Instruments. TMS320C54x DSP Reference Set. Volume 1: CPU and Perhipherals. Technical Report SPRU131E, Texas Instruments, June 1998.
6. Jeff Bier. DSP16xxx Targets Communictaions Apps. *Microprocessor Report*, 11(12), 1997.
7. G. Ungerboeck, D. Maiwald, H. P. Kaeser, P. R. Chevillat, and J. P. Beraud. Architecture of a Digital Signal Processor. *IBM Journal of Research and Development*, 29(2), 1985.
8. N. L. Bernbaum, B. Blaner, D. E. Carmon, J. K. D'Addio, F. E. Grieco, A. M. Jacoutot, M. A. Locker, B. Marshall, D. W. Milton, C. R. Ogilvie, P. M. Schanely, P. C. Stabler, and M. Turcotte. The IBM Mwave 3780i DSP. In *Proceedings of the 1996 International Conference on Signal Processing Applications and Technology (ICSPAT '96)*, pages 1287–1291, Boston, MA, October 1996.
9. Tom R. Halfhill. TI Cores Accelerate DSP Arms Race. *Microprocessor Report*, March 6 2000.
10. J. Eyre and J. Bier. Carmel Enables Customizable DSP. *Microprocessor Report*, 12(17), December 1998.
11. LSI Corporation. *LSI402Z Digital Signal Processor*. LSI Corporation, r20012 edition, 1999.
12. Gerald G. Pechanek, C. John Glossner, William F. Lawless, Daniel H. McCabe, Chris H. L. Moller, and Steven J. Walsh. A Machine Organization and Architecture for Highly Parallel, Scalable, Single Chip DSPs. In *Proceedings of the 1995 DSPx Technical Program Conference and Exhibition*, pages 42–50, San Jose, California, May 1995.
13. Gerald G. Pechanek, Mihilo Stojancic, Stamatis Vassiliadis, and C. John Glossner. M.F.A.S.T.: A Single Chip, Highly Parallel Image Processing Architecture. In *Proceedings IEEE International Conference on Image Processing*, volume I, pages 1375–1379, Arlington, Virginia, October 1995. IEEE Press.
14. Gerald G. Pechanek, Charles W. Kurak, C. John Glossner, Chris H. L. Moller, and Steven J. Walsh. M.F.A.S.T.: A Highly Parallel Single Chip DSP with a 2D IDCT Example. In *Proceeding of the International Conference on Signal Processing Applications and Technology*, pages 69–72, Boston, Mass., October 1995.

15. Gerald G. Pechanek, C. John Glossner, Zhiyong Li, Chris H. L. Moller, and Stamatis Vassiliadis. Tensor Product FFT's on M.*F.A.S.T.: A Highly Parallel Single Chip DSP*. In *Proceedings of DSP 95 - Digital Signal Processing and Its Applications*, Paris, France, October 1995.

16. B. Case. Philips hopes to displace DSPs with VLIW. *Microprocessor Report*, pages 12–15, December 1997.

17. C. P. Feigel. TI Introduces Four-Processor DSP Chip. *Microprocessor Report*, 8(4), March 28 1994.

18. Dave Epstein. Chromatic Raises the Multimedia Bar. *Microprocessor Report*, 9(14), October 28 1995.

19. A. Peleg and U. Weiser. MMX technology extension to the Intel architecture. *IEEE Micro*, pages 42–50, August 1996.

20. H. Nguyen and L. K. John. Exploiting SIMD Parallelism in DSP and Multimedia Algorithms Using the AltiVec Technology. In *Proceedings of the International Conference on Supercomputing*, pages 11–20, 1999.

21. J. C. Bier, A. Shoham, H. Hakkarainen, O. Wolf, G. Blalock, and Philip D. Lapsley. *DSP on General-Purpose Processors: Performance, Architecture, Pitfalls*. Berkeley Design Technology, Inc., 1997.

22. O. Wolf and J. Bier. StarCore Launches First Architecture. *Microprocessor Report*, 12(14), October 1998.

23. O. Wolf and J. Bier. TigerSHARC Sinks Teeth Into VLIW. *Microprocessor Report*, 12(16), December 1998.

24. J. Fridman and Z. Greenfield. The TigerSHARC DSP Architecture. *IEEE Micro*, 20(1):66–76, January 2000.

25. J. Turley and H. Hakkarainen. TI's New C6x Screams at 1,600 MIPS. *Microprocessor Report*, 11(2), 1997.

26. Gerald G. Pechanek, Stamatis Vassiliadis, and Nikos Pitsianis. ManArray processor interconnection network: an introduction. In *Euro-Par '99 Parallel Processing Proceedings. (Lecture notes in computer science)*, pages 761–765, Toulouse, France, August/September 1999. Springer, Berlin.

27. Gerald G. Pechanek and Stamatis Vassiliadis. The ManArray Embedded Processor Architecture. In *Proceedings of the 26-th Euromicro Conference: Informatics: inventing the future*, volume I, pages 348–355, Maastrict, The Netherlands, September 5-7 2000.

28. Bryan Ackland and Paul D'Arcy. A New Generation of DSP Architectures. In *Proceedings of the 1999 Custom Integrated Circuits Conference*, pages 531–536, 1999.

29. James Gosling, Bill Joy, and Guy Steele, editors. *The Java Language Specification*. The Java Series. Addison-Wesley, Reading, MA, USA, 1996.

30. James Gosling and Henry McGilton. The Java Language Environment: A White Paper. Technical report, Sun Microsystems, Mountain View, California, October 1995. Available from ftp.javasoft.com/docs.

31. Tim Lindholm and Frank Yellin. *The Java Virtual Machine Specification*. The Java Series. Addison-Wesley, Reading, MA, USA, 1997.

32. Cheng-Hsueh A. Hsieh, John C. Gyllenhaal, and Wen mei W. Hwu. Java Bytecode to Native Code Translation: The Caffeine Prototype and Preliminary Results. In *Proceeding of the 29th Annual Internation Symposium on Microarchitecture (MICRO-29)*, pages 90–97, Los Alamitos, CA, USA, December 2-4 1996. IEEE Computer Society Press.

33. Ali-Reza Adl-Tabatabai, Michal Cierniak, Guie-Yuan Lueh, Vishesh M. Parikh, and James M. Stichnoth. Fast, effective code generation in a just-in-time Java compiler. In *Proceeding of the ACM SIGPLAN '98 conference on Programming Language Design and Implementation (PLDI'98)*, volume 33, pages 280–290. Association for Computing Machinery, May 1998.

34. Gilles Muller, Barbara Moura, Fabrice Bellard, and Charles Consel. JIT vs. Offline Compilers: Limits and Benefits of Bytecode Compilation. Technical Report 1063, IRISA, Campus de Beaulieu, 35042 Rennes Cedex, France, December 1996. http://www.irisa.fr.

35. Sun Microsystems. The Java Hotspot Performance Engine Architecture. Sun Microsystems, 1999. http://java.sun.com/ products/ hotspot/ whitepaper.html.

36. Kemal Ebcioglu, Eric R. Altman, and Erdem Hokenek. A Java ILP Machine Based on Fast Dynamic Compilation. In *IEEE MASCOTS International Workshop on Security and Efficiency Aspects of Java*, Eilat, Israel, January 9-10 1997. IEEE Computer Society Press.

37. Michal Cierniak and Wei Li. Just-in-time optimizations for high-performance Java programs. *Concurrency: Practice and Experience*, 9(4):1063–1073, November 1997.

38. Todd A. Proebsting, Gregg Townsend, Patrick Bridges, John H. Hartman, Tim Newsham, and Scott A. Watterson. Toba: Java For Applications - A Way Ahead of Time (WAT) Compiler. In *Proceedings Third Conference on Object-Oriented Technologies and Systems (COOTS'97)*, 1997.

39. Hewlett Packard. HP Turbo Chai Release 2.0. Hewlett-Packard, May 1999. http://www.hp.com/emso/products/turbochai/TchaiPDF.pdf.

40. John Glossner, Jesse Thilo, and Stamatis Vassiliadis. Java Signal Processing: FFT's with bytecodes. In *Proceedings of the 1998 ACM Workshop on Java for High-Performance Network Computing*, Stanford University, Palo Alto, California, February 28 and March 1 1998.

41. John Glossner, Jesse Thilo, and Stamatis Vassiliadis. Java Signal Processing: FFT's with bytecodes. *Journal of Concurrency and Experience*, 10(11-13):1173–1178, 1998.

42. Cygnus. Gcj compiler, 1999.

43. Sun Microelectronics. picoJava I Microprocessor Core Architecture. Technical Report WPR-0014-01, Sun Microsystems, Mountain View, California, November 1996. Available from http://www.sun.com/ sparc/ whitepapers/ wpr-0014-01.

44. Marc Tremblay and Micahel O'Connor. picoJava: A Hardware Implementation of the Java Virtual Machine. In *Hotchips Presentation*, 1996.

45. Harlan McGHan and Mike O'Connor. PicoJava: A Direct Execution Engine For Java Bytecode. *IEEE Computer*, 31(10):22–30, October 1998.

46. L. C. Chang, L. R. Ton, M. F. Kao, and C. P. Chung. Stack operations folding in Java processors. *IEE Proceedings - Computers and Digital Techniques*, 145(5):333–343, September 1998.

47. Lee-Ren Ton, Lung-Chung Chang, Min-Fu Kao, Han-Min Tseng, Shi-Sheng Shang, Ruey-Liang Ma, Dze-Chuang Wang, and Chung-Ping Chung. Instruction Folding in Java Processor. In *1997 International Conference on Parallel and Distributed Systems*, pages 138–143, Seoul, Korea, December 12-13 1997. IEEE Computer Society Press.

48. Sun Microelectronics. Sun Microelectronic's picoJava I Posts Outstanding Performance. Technical Report WPR-0015-01, Sun Microsystems, Mountain View, California, November 1996. Available from http://www.sun.com/ sparc/ whitepapers/ wpr-0015-01.

49. James Gosling. Java Intermediate Bytecodes. In *ACM SIGPLAN Notices*, pages 111–118, New York, NY, January 1995. Association for Computing Machinery. ACM SIGPLAN Workshop on Intermediate Representations (IR95).

50. J. Glossner and S. Vassiliadis. Delft-Java Dynamic Translation. In *Proceedings of the 25th EUROMICRO conference (EUROMICRO '99)*, volume 1, Milan, Italy, September 8-10 1999.

51. John Glossner and Stamatis Vassiliadis. Delft-Java Link Translation Buffer. In *Proceedings of the 24th EUROMICRO conference*, volume 1, pages 221–228, Vasteras, Sweden, August 25-27 1998.

52. C. John Glossner and Stamatis Vassiliadis. The Delft-Java Engine: An Introduction. In *Lecture Notes In Computer Science. Third International Euro-Par Conference (Euro-Par'97 Parallel Processing)*, pages 766–770, Passau, Germany, Aug. 26 - 29 1997. Springer-Verlag.

53. Bil Lewis and Daniel J. Berg. *Threads Primer: A Guide to Multithreaded Programming*. SunSoft Press - A Prentice Hall Title, Mountain View, California, 1996.

54. Peter Wayner. Sun gambles on java chips. *Byte*, 21(11):79–85, November 1996.

55. S. Vassiliadis, B. Blaner, and R. J. Eickemeyer. SCISM: A Scalable Compound Instruction Set Machine. *IBM Journal of Research and Development*, 38(1):59–78, January 1994.

56. James Philips and Stamatis Vassiliadis. High-performance 3-1 interlock collapsing ALU's. *IEEE Transactions on Computers*, 43(3):257–268, March 1994.

57. Brian Case. Implementing the java virtual machine. *Microprocessor Report*, 10(4):12–17, March 25 1996.

58. Stamatis Vassiliadis, James Phillips, and Bart Blanar. Interlock Collapsing ALU's. *IEEE Transactions on Computers*, 42(7):825–839, July 1993.

59. R. M. Tomasulo. An Efficient Algorithm for Exploiting Multiple Arithmetic Units. *IBM Journal of Research and Development*, II:25–33, 1967.

60. Wes Munsil and Chia-Jiu Wang. Reducing Stack Usage in Java Bytecode Execution. *Computer Architecture News*, 1(7):7–11, March 1998.

61. Yamin Li, Sanli Li, Xianzhu Wang, and Wanming Chu. JAViR - Exploiting Instruction Level Parallelism for JAVA Machine by Using Virtual Register. In *The Second European IASTED International Conference on Parallel and Distributed Systems*, Vienna, Austria, July 1-3 1998.

62. Advancel Logic Corporation. TinyJ Processor Core Product Datasheet. Datasheet, July 1999.

63. Patriot Scientific Corporation. Psc1000/a microprocessor datasheet. Patriot Scientific, 1997. http://www.ptsc.com/downloads/ psc1000/specs/datasheet.pdf.

Author Index

Lecture Notes in Computer Science

For information about Vols. 1–2209
please contact your bookseller or Springer-Verlag